PLAYFAIR
CRI[illegible]

Barry M[illegible]

Front cover: Vivian Richards. Photo: Adrian Murrell/All Sport Photographic

PICK THE BEST NATWEST BANK TROPHY TEAM OF OVERSEAS PLAYERS AFTER THE FIRST THREE YEARS OF THE COMPETITION

(the term 'Overseas' means players who are not qualified to play for England)

£1250 TO BE WON

Prizes: 1st: £400 2nd: £250 3rd: £200 4th: £150
Plus twenty-five prizes of £10 each

How to enter: Pick the best NatWest Bank Trophy team from the 36 cricketers shown below who played in the competition in the first three seasons. Then write in 20 words if you would like Overseas players to continue to play in the NatWest and why.

Write the names on the entry form on the opposite page with your name and address and post to the address shown.

Your Choice
Asif Iqbal, Eldine Baptiste, Sylvester Clarke, Wayne Daniel, Winston Davis, D.S. de Silva (Sri Lanka and Shropshire), Ricardo Ellcock, Anthonie Ferreira, Joel Garner, Gordon Greenidge, Richard Hadlee, Michael Holding, Geoff Howarth, Imran Khan, Alvin Kallicharran, Kapil Dev, Peter Kirsten, Garth LeRoux, Clive Lloyd, Malcolm Marshall, Ken McEwan, Javed Miandad, Ezra Moseley (Glamorgan), Mudassar Nazar (Pakistan and Cheshire), Norbert Phillip, Neal Radford, Viv Richards, Clive Rice, Andy Roberts, Sadiq Mohammad, Sarfraz Nawaz, Franklyn Stephenson, Glenn Turner, Wasim Raja (Pakistan and Durham), John Wright, Zaheer Abbas. *Note: Ken McEwan and Javed Miandad have kept wicket during their careers.*

Rules
Judging: Each entry will be considered by a panel of cricket experts and the entry which, in the opinion of the judges, constitutes the best NatWest Trophy team will be adjudged the winner. The decision of the judges is final and binding; no correspondence will be entered into. Employees of Macdonald & Co (Publishers) Ltd and their families are not eligible to compete.
Proof of entry: All entries must be on the entry form provided. Proof of posting is not proof of entry.

ENTRY FORM

Your team in batting order, with a captain:

1

2

3

4

5

6

7

8

9

10

11

Write in no more than 20 words

Closing date: 12.00 noon Wednesday, 19 September 1984

Your name and address:

....

....

....

Post to: The Editor
Playfair Cricket Annual Competition
Queen Anne Press
Macdonald & Co (Publishers) Ltd
Maxwell House
74 Worship Street
London EC2A 2EN

Your flexible friend – a big hit wherever he goes.
NatWest Access

INDIA WORLD CHAMPIONS

By Gordon Ross

The highlight of the English summer in 1983 – for one-day enthusiasts that is – was India's victory in The Prudential World Cup against all odds and in glorious weather throughout. India, very much the outsiders, were not expected to qualify for the Semi-Finals because West Indies and Australia were in Group B with them – but they did. They were not expected to beat England in the Semi-Final – but they did. They were certainly not given a chance to beat West Indies in the Final, but for Indians everywhere there was a fairy-story ending. When India were all out for 183 on that Final day at Lord's it seemed easy for West Indies. Yet, inexplicably, they were bowled out for 140. Farokh Engineer, former Lancashire and Indian wicket-keeper, who was commenting during those final moments urged Mrs. Gandhi to declare a National day's holiday in celebration. It seemed she took his advice!

It was a high note on which for Prudential to bow out as sponsors. Their role has now been taken over by Texaco, and the other sponsorship change is that Schweppes have ended their term as sponsors of the County Championship; they have been replaced by Britannic Assurance, the Birmingham-based Insurance Company. It seemed initially that this summer's County Championship would be without a sponsor altogether, but the T.C.C.B. announced the news concerning Britannic in mid-December after the fixtures for 1984 had been released. Charles Palmer, Chairman of the Test and County Cricket Board said that Britannic's sponsorship could not have come at a more important time, with the first-class counties facing ever-increasing administrative costs. He added, 'The County Championship has a worthy history and is a legacy to us which we must always cherish. It is the most prestigious of our domestic competitions, demanding the highest technical skills and is a breeding ground for our Test players.' After England's disappointing showing in the World Cup they at least beat New Zealand 3-1 in a four-match Test series, though with the ban still in operation on players who have played in South Africa it must always be a below-strength England team. Five England players scored centuries in this series – Lamb, Gower, Tavaré,

Botham and Fowler. Bob Willis, who just seems to bowl and bowl for ever, was the leading wicket-taker.

In the domestic competitions, Essex were the three-day County Champions, pushing Middlesex, the winners in 1982, into second place. It was a golden summer for South African-born Ken McEwan who scored 2,051 runs at an average of 68.36, over 800 runs ahead of Gooch, and over 30 ahead of his batting average. The principal bowler was John Lever who needed only two more wickets for his hundred. McEwan scored eight centuries to Gooch's three, so whilst winning a Championship must always be a team effort, McEwan's batting was just the difference between winning or coming second.

The winners of the one-day competitions were Somerset the NatWest, Middlesex the Benson and Hedges (beating Essex, who beat them to the County Championship, in the Final), and Yorkshire the John Player League. The success of Yorkshire in the John Player was some compensation in the midst of all their troubles, but their history is steeped in County Championship successes and this presumably will always be their top priority.

Somerset confirmed their prowess as an outstanding one-day team when they took the 1983 NatWest to add to The Gillette Cup in 1979, and The Benson and Hedges in 1981 and 1982. It is interesting, in view of this, that Somerset have never won The County Championship; the best position they have gained is third, on five occasions: 1892, 1958, 1963, 1966 and 1981. With Botham, Richards and Garner, all match-winners in their own right, and a back-up of some very fine players, they must always be fancied.

The main points of the Test and County Cricket Board meeting in December dealing with the game's future were as follows:

(1) Move to limit counties to one overseas player from the end of 1985 narrowly rejected.
(2) West Indies to be warned that Law 42 against intimidatory bowling will be strictly enforced next summer.
(3) Counties must now bowl 117 overs in a full day's play, but slow over-rate fines are abolished.
(4) Test qualifying period for South African-born players likely to be extended.
(5) Possibility of extending the number of County Championship teams.

(6) Monte Lynch still qualified for England but faces inquiry.

The T.C.C.B. share the growing concern throughout the game and elsewhere about current regulations for players born overseas qualifying for England and its effect on the team which last season had, in Allan Lamb and Chris Smith, two South African-born players of English parentage. The board agreed to take a close look at the position possibly with a view to extending the qualification period. At present a player born abroad of English parentage must have lived in the country for four consecutive years preceding his selection.

Before the summer's Test series West Indies are to be told that, in an era when short-pitched intimidatory bowling is on the increase, the law in relation to this will be strictly enforced and umpires are to be briefed accordingly. West Indies will also be asked to agree to 96 overs a day in Tests; this has been successfully introduced in recent series, but there may be problems here in view of West Indies' battery of fast-bowlers who achieve only a slow over-rate.

The question of the possibility of more Counties in the County Championship is interesting but unlikely to materialise for a year or two yet. Applications from Northumberland and Durham as a combined team, and Shropshire, have been received. The Board confirmed that Monte Lynch, born in Georgetown, British Guiana (as it was at the time of his birth), and now a Surrey player, is still classed as qualifying for England despite his decision to tour South Africa with the unofficial West Indian side. They felt, however, that Lynch had breached the spirit and intention of the qualifying rule and they have repeated that they will ask him for an explanation on his return.

The Board also announced that in 1985 there will be six Tests against Australia, two of them at Lord's.

A point that statisticians might want explaining if they should find a puzzle in some of the overseas Test scores this winter is that it had been agreed beforehand that wides and no-balls would count against the bowler in his analysis. There is a strong body of opinion that this should always have been so. Why should they not count against the bowler – they are his fault!

So now a new cricket season begins without Gillette, Schweppes and Prudential, but the game goes on as strongly as ever because sponsors believe in it.

Pakistan v India 1982–83

FIRST TEST MATCH

PLAYED AT LAHORE, 10, 11, 12, 14, 15 DECEMBER

MATCH DRAWN

PAKISTAN

Mohsin Khan c Amarnath b Madan Lal	94	not out	101
Mudassar Nazar c Gavaskar b Kapil Dev	50	c Arun b Doshi	17
Mansoor Akhtar c Gavaskar b Kapil Dev	3	not out	14
Javed Miandad c Gavaskar b Madan Lal	17		
Zaheer Abbas b Doshi	215		
Salim Malik b Madan Lal	6		
*Imran Khan c Madan Lal b Doshi	45		
†Wasim Bari c Arun b Doshi	12		
Tahir Naqqash st Kirmani b Doshi	20		
Sarfraz Nawaz c Amarnath b Doshi	18		
Jalaluddin not out	1		
Extras (LB3, NB1)	4	(LB3)	3
Total	485	(1 wkt)	135

INDIA

*S.M. Gavaskar c Wasim b Sarfraz	83
Arun Lal c Mudassar b Imran	51
D.B. Vengsarkar c Mudassar b Imran	3
G.R. Viswanath c Wasim b Imran	1
M. Amarnath not out	109
S.M. Patil run out	68
Kapil Dev c Wasim b Sarfraz	9
R.J. Shastri lbw b Jalaluddin	7
†S.M.H. Kirmani c Wasim b Jalaluddin	10
S. Madan Lal c Salim b Sarfraz	7
D.R. Doshi b Sarfraz	0
Extras (B2, LB11, NB18)	31
Total	379

BOWLING

INDIA	*O*	*M*	*R*	*W*		*O*	*M*	*R*	*W*
Kapil Dev	39	3	149	2	—	8	2	27	0
Madan Lal	27	2	101	3	—	5	1	10	0
Amarnath	23	5	60	0	—	3	1	5	0
Doshi	32	6	90	5	—	15	2	57	1
Shastri	22	3	81	0	—	14	1	33	0
Gavaskar	—	—	—	—	—	1	1	0	0
PAKISTAN									
Imran	27	8	68	3	—	—	—	—	—
Sarfraz	31.5	11	63	4	—	—	—	—	—
Jalaluddin	34	10	93	2	—	—	—	—	—
Tahir	29	6	114	0	—	—	—	—	—
Mudassar	3	1	10	0	—	—	—	—	—

FALL OF WICKETS

	PAK *1st*	*IND* *1st*	*PAK* *2nd*
1st	85	105	55
2nd	100	111	—
3rd	126	123	—
4th	238	188	—
5th	250	294	—
6th	367	305	—
7th	438	322	—
8th	447	348	—
9th	478	375	—
10th	485	379	—

SECOND TEST MATCH

PLAYED AT KARACHI, 23, 24, 25, 27 DECEMBER

PAKISTAN WON BY AN INNINGS AND 86 RUNS

INDIA

*S.M. Gavaskar run out	8	b Imran	42
Arun Lal lbw b Sarfraz	35	lbw b Qadir	11
D.B. Vengsarkar c Mohsin b Imran	0	c Wasim b Imran	79
G.R. Viswanath c Wasim b Qadir	24	b Imran	0
M. Amarnath lbw b Imran	5	lbw b Imran	3
S.M.Patil c Javed b Qadir	4	b Imran	0
Kapil Dev c & b Sarfraz	73	b Imran	1
†S.M.H. Kirmani c Mohsin b Qadir	11	c Salim b Qadir	1
S. Madan Lal not out	3	not out	52
Maninder Singh lbw b Qadir	0	lbw b Imran	0
D.R. Doshi b Imran	0	b Imran	0
Extras (LB4, NB2)	6	(B1, LB3, W1, NB3)	8
Total	169		197

PAKISTAN

Mohsin Khan c Amarnath b Madan Lal	12
Mansoor Akhtar c Kirmani b Madan Lal	0
Salim Malik c Kirmani b Madan Lal	3
Javed Miandad b Amarnath	39
Zaheer Abbas lbw b Kapil Dev	186
Mudassar Nazar c Kirmani b Kapil Dev	119
*Imran Khan c Amarnath b Kapil Dev	33
†Wasim Bari c Arun Lal b Doshi	30
Abdul Qadir b Kapil Dev	0
Sarfraz Nawaz lbw b Kapil Dev	13
Jalaluddin not out	0
Extras (B2, LB6, W2, NB7)	17
Total	452

BOWLING

PAKISTAN	*O*	*M*	*R*	*W*		*O*	*M*	*R*	*W*
Imran	12.1	6	19	3	—	20.1	4	60	8
Jalaluddin	10	2	28	0	—	7	2	31	0
Sarfraz	16	2	49	2	—	10	2	23	0
Qadir	15	3	67	4	—	23	3	75	2
INDIA					—				
Kapil Dev	28.5	3	102	5	—	—	—	—	—
Madan Lal	23	1	129	3	—	—	—	—	—
Maninder	23	2	67	0	—	—	—	—	—
Amarnath	17	1	69	1	—	—	—	—	—
Doshi	18	1	68	1	—	—	—	—	—
					—				
					—				

FALL OF WICKETS

	IND 1st	*PAK 1st*	*IND 2nd*
1st	10	6	28
2nd	10	15	102
3rd	48	18	108
4th	55	128	112
5th	70	341	112
6th	130	397	113
7th	165	427	114
8th	168	427	197
9th	168	452	197
10th	169	452	197

THIRD TEST MATCH

PLAYED AT FAISALABAD, 3, 4, 5, 7, 8 JANUARY

PAKISTAN WON BY 10 WICKETS

INDIA

*S.M. Gavaskar c Salim b Imran	12	not out	127
Arun Lal b Sarfraz	0	c Zaheer b Sarfraz	3
D.B. Vengsarkar lbw b Imran	6	lbw b Imran	1
G.R. Viswanath b Mudassar	53	c Javed b Sarfraz	9
M. Amarnath b Mudassar	22	lbw b Imran	78
S.M. Patil c Wasim b Imran	85	b Imran	6
Kapil Dev lbw b Imran	41	c Sikander b Sarfraz	16
†S.M.H. Kirmani b Imran	66	c Wasim b Sikander	6
S. Madan Lal c Salim b Imran	54	lbw b Sarfraz	10
Maninder Singh c Mohsin b Qadir	6	lbw b Imran	2
D.R. Doshi not out	2	b Imran	4
Extras (B6, LB8, W4, NB8)	26	(B1, LB9, NB14)	24
Total	372		286

PAKISTAN

Mohsin Khan c Kirmani b Kapil Dev	4	not out	8
Mudassar Nazar c Kirmani b Kapil Dev	38	not out	2
Mansoor Akhtar c Kirmani b Kapil Dev	23		
Javed Miandad c Gavaskar b Madan Lal	126		
Zaheer Abbas c Kirmani b Madan Lal	168		
Salim Malik b Kapil Dev	107		
*Imran Khan c Madan Lal b Maninder	117		
†Wasim Bari c Kirmani b Kapil Dev	6		
Sarfraz Nawaz c Gavaskar b Kapil Dev	4		
Abdul Qadir not out	38		
Sikander Bakht b Kapil Dev	9		
Extras (LB10, NB2)	12		
Total	652	(0 wkts)	10

BOWLING

PAKISTAN	O	M	R	W		O	M	R	W
Imran	25	3	98	6	—	30.5	12	82	5
Sarfraz	23	4	95	1	—	33	11	79	4
Sikander	13	1	66	0	—	9	3	41	1
Mudassar	12	2	39	2	—	11	3	27	0
Qadir	12.3	1	48	1	—	11	1	33	0
INDIA					—				
Kapil Dev	38.4	3	220	7	—	—	—	—	—
Madan Lal	28	5	109	2	—	—	—	—	—
Doshi	29	2	130	0	—	—	—	—	—
Amarnath	16	1	68	0	—	—	—	—	—
Maninder	29	3	103	1	—	—	—	—	—
Gavaskar	2	0	10	0	—	—	—	—	—
Arun Lal	—	—	—	—	—	1.1	0	6	0
Vengsarkar	—	—	—	—	—	1	0	4	0

FALL OF WICKETS

	IND 1st	*PAK 1st*	*IND 2nd*	*2nd*
1st	6	4	27	—
2nd	17	66	28	—
3rd	22	79	48	—
4th	82	366	193	—
5th	122	367	201	—
6th	220	574	227	—
7th	235	595	236	—
8th	357	599	261	—
9th	370	612	282	—
10th	372	652	286	—

FOURTH TEST MATCH

PLAYED AT HYDERABAD, 14, 15, 16, 18, 19 JANUARY

PAKISTAN WON BY AN INNINGS AND 119 RUNS

PAKISTAN

Mohsin Khan lbw b Sandhu	24
Mudassar Nazar c Maninder b Doshi	231
Haroon Rashid b Sandhu	0
Javed Miandad not out	280
Zaheer Abbas not out	25
Salim Malik did not bat	
*Imran Khan did not bat	
†Wasim Bari did not bat	
Sarfraz Nawaz did not bat	
Abdul Qadir did not bat	
Iqbal Qasim did not bat	
Extras (B9, LB12)	21
Total (3 wkts dec)	581

INDIA

*S.M. Gavaskar c Wasim b Imran	17	c & b Iqbal	60
K. Srikkanth lbw b Sarfraz	2	c Salim b Imran	5
M. Amarnath st Wasim b Iqbal	61	c Imran b Iqbal	64
G.R. Viswanath lbw b Imran	0	lbw b Sarfraz	37
D.B. Vengsarkar c Wasim b Imran	4	not out	58
Kapil Dev b Imran	3	b Sarfraz	2
†S.M.H. Kirmani b Imran	1	lbw b Sarfraz	0
S.M. Patil c Imran b Sarfraz	2	c Imran b Qadir	9
B.S. Sandhu b Sarfraz	71	c Imran b Qadir	12
Maninder Singh not out	12	lbw b Sarfraz	4
D.R. Doshi lbw b Imran	1	b Imran	14
Extras (B1, LB7, NB7)	15	(B1, LB1, NB6)	8
Total	189		279

BOWLING

INDIA	*O*	*M*	*R*	*W*		*O*	*M*	*R*	*W*
Kapil Dev	27	2	111	0	—	—	—	—	—
Sandhu	33	7	107	2	—	—	—	—	—
Amarnath	15	0	64	0	—	—	—	—	—
Maninder	50	10	135	0	—	—	—	—	—
Doshi	41	9	143	1	—	—	—	—	—
PAKISTAN									
Imran	17.2	3	35	6	—	24.4	14	45	2
Sarfraz	19	5	56	3	—	30	4	85	4
Qadir	11	2	35	0	—	26	7	77	2
Iqbal	9	3	48	1	—	31	9	58	2
					—				
					—				

FALL OF WICKETS

	PAK 1st	*IND 1st*	*IND 2nd*
1st	60	3	8
2nd	60	44	133
3rd	511	44	134
4th	—	52	201
5th	—	61	203
6th	—	65	203
7th	—	72	223
8th	—	131	249
9th	—	184	254
10th	—	189	273

FIFTH TEST MATCH

PLAYED AT LAHORE, 23, 24, 25, 27, 28 JANUARY
(NO PLAY 27, 28)

MATCH DRAWN

PAKISTAN

Mohsin Khan c Srikkanth b Kapil Dev	7
Mudassar Nazar not out	152
Majid Khan c Kirmani b Kapil Dev	0
Javed Miandad c Viswanath b Maninder	85
Zaheer Abbas c Kirmani b Kapil Dev	13
Salim Malik b Maninder	6
*Imran Khan c Kirmani b Kapil Dev	20
†Wasim Bari c Amarnath b Kapil Dev	8
Sarfraz Nawaz c Yashpal b Kapil Dev	26
Abdul Qadir b Kapil Dev	0
Iqbal Qasim lbw b Kapil Dev	0
Extras (LB6)	6
Total	323

INDIA

*S.M. Gavaskar lbw b Imran	13
K. Srikkanth b Qadir	21
M. Amarnath c Wasim b Imran	120
Yashpal Sharma not out	63
D.B. Vengsarkar not out	1
G.R. Viswanath did not bat	
Kapil Dev did not bat	
†S.M.H. Kirmani did not bat	
B.S. Sandhau did not bat	
Maninder Singh did not bat	
T.A. Sekar did not bat	
Extras (B6, LB5, W1, NB5)	17
Total (3 wkts)	235

BOWLING

INDIA	O	M	R	W	O	M	R	W	FALL OF WICKETS	PAK 1st	IND 1st
Kapil Dev	30.5	7	85	8	—	—	—	—			
Sandhu	21	2	56	0	—	—	—	—			
Sekar	20	2	86	0	—	—	—	—	1st	22	29
Maninder	32	7	90	2	—	—	—	—	2nd	26	41
PAKISTAN									3rd	178	231
Imran	18	5	45	2	—	—	—	—	4th	191	—
Sarfraz	23.2	9	46	0	—	—	—	—	5th	202	—
Qadir	16	1	63	1	—	—	—	—	6th	244	—
Majid	1	0	4	0	—	—	—	—	7th	276	—
Mudassar	11	1	41	0	—	—	—	—	8th	323	—
Iqbal	12	3	19	0	—	—	—	—	9th	323	—
									10th	323	—

SIXTH TEST MATCH

PLAYED AT KARACHI, 30, 31 JANUARY, 1, 3, 4 FEBRUARY

MATCH DRAWN

INDIA

*S.M. Gavaskar c Wasim Bari b Tahir	5	b Imran	67
R.J. Shastri st Wasim Bari b Qadir	128	c Wasim Bari b Imran	17
M. Amarnath c Wasim Bari b Imran	19	not out	103
Yashpal Sharma c Wasim Bari b Imran	9	not out	19
D.B. Vengsarkar c & b Tahir	89		
G.R. Viswanath b Mudassar	10		
†S.M.H. Kirmani c Zaheer b Sarfraz	18		
Kapil Dev lbw b Imran	33		
B.S. Sandhu not out	32		
T.A. Sekar not out	0		
Maninder Singh did not bat			
Extras (B13, LB9, NB28)	50	(B10, W3, NB5)	18
Total (8 wkts dec)	393	(2 wkts)	224

PAKISTAN

Mohsin Khan lbw b Kapil Dev	91
Mudassar Nazar lbw b Kapil Dev	152
Javed Miandad c Kirmani b Sandhu	47
Zaheer Abbas c Amarnath b Shastri	43
Wasim Raja run out	10
*Imran Khan not out	32
†Wasim Bari c Kirmani b Sandhu	12
Sarfraz Nawaz not out	6
Salim Malik did not bat	
Abdul Qadir did not bat	
Tahir Naqqash did not bat	
Extras (B5, LB12, W1, NB9)	27
Total (6 wkts dec)	420

BOWLING

PAKISTAN	*O*	*M*	*R*	*W*		*O*	*M*	*R*	*W*
Imran	32	11	65	3	—	16	3	41	2
Sarfraz	41	10	92	1	—	14	4	45	0
Tahir	24	7	69	2	—	8	1	28	0
Qadir	13	3	86	1	—	14	2	42	0
Mudassar	15	4	30	1	—	—	—	—	—
Wasim Raja	1	0	1	0	—	5	2	12	0
Zaheer	—	—	—	—	—	8	0	24	0
Mohsin	—	—	—	—	—	1	0	3	0
Javed	—	—	—	—	—	2	0	11	0
INDIA									
Kapil Dev	33	2	137	2	—	—	—	—	—
Sandhu	28.2	4	87	2	—	—	—	—	—
Sekar	14	1	43	0	—	—	—	—	—
Maninder	16	3	49	0	—	—	—	—	—
Shastri	22	1	62	1	—	—	—	—	—
Amarnath	5	1	15	0	—	—	—	—	—

FALL OF WICKETS

	IND 1st	*PAK 1st*	*IND 2nd*
1st	47	157	43
2nd	86	269	150
3rd	109	342	—
4th	178	362	—
5th	218	371	—
6th	267	411	—
7th	316	—	—
8th	393	—	—
9th	—	—	—
10th	—	—	—

Vengsarkar (1st innings) retired hurt at 140-3 and resumed at 218-5.

New Zealand v Sri Lanka 1982–83

FIRST TEST MATCH

PLAYED AT CHRISTCHURCH, 4, 5, 6 MARCH

NEW ZEALAND WON BY AN INNINGS AND 25 RUNS

NEW ZEALAND

G.M. Turner c de Alwis b John	32
B.A. Edgar c M.D. Wettimuny b J.R. Ratnayeke	39
J.G. Wright b R.J. Ratnayake	13
*G.P. Howarth c Goonasekera b J.R. Ratnayeke	0
J.J. Crowe run out	12
J.V. Coney run out	84
R.J. Hadlee b John	12
B.L. Cairns c M.D. Wettimuny b R.J. Ratnayake	3
†W.K. Lees b de Silva	89
M.C. Snedden c sub (S.A.R. Silva) b J.R. Ratnayeke	22
E.J. Chatfield not out	10
Extras (LB14, W2, NB12)	28
Total	344

SRI LANKA

S. Wettimuny not out	63	lbw b Cairns	7
M.D. Wettimuny c Lees b Cairns	17	c Lees b Snedden	5
S. Fernando b Cairns	0	b Cairns	46
Y. Goonasekera c Lees b Cairns	4	c Turner b Cairns	8
R.S. Madugalle run out	34	c Lees b Snedden	23
*D.S. de Silva c Lees b Hadlee	7	b Chatfield	52
J.R. Ratnayeke run out	0	lbw b Cairns	7
†R.G. de Alwis c Turner b Hadlee	0	c Hadlee b Snedden	3
S. Jeganathan lbw b Cairns	6	b Chatfield	8
R.J. Ratnayake c Coney b Hadlee	1	c Howarth b Chatfield	0
V. John lbw b Hadlee	0	not out	3
Extras (B2, LB7, NB3)	12	(B2, LB5, W5, NB1)	13
Total	144		174

BOWLING

SRI LANKA	*O*	*M*	*R*	*W*		*O*	*M*	*R*	*W*
R.J. Ratnayake	31	8	125	2	—	—	—	—	—
John	12	2	45	2	—	—	—	—	—
J.R. Ratnayeke	31	9	93	3	—	—	—	—	—
de Silva	22.5	10	41	1	—	—	—	—	—
Jeganathan	5	2	12	0	—	—	—	—	—
NEW ZEALAND									
Hadlee	13.3	1	33	4	—	22	12	27	0
Snedden	10	1	30	0	—	23	6	48	3
Cairns	15	6	49	4	—	20	7	47	4
Chatfield	15	4	20	0	—	16.5	3	40	3

FALL OF WICKETS

	NZ 1st	*SL 1st*	*SL 2nd*
1st	59	49	14
2nd	93	49	26
3rd	93	55	46
4th	93	104	95
5th	137	121	108
6th	159	129	124
7th	171	133	133
8th	250	141	168
9th	292	144	170
10th	344	144	175

SECOND TEST MATCH

PLAYED AT WELLINGTON, 11, 12, 13, 14, 15 MARCH

NEW ZEALAND WON BY 6 WICKETS

SRI LANKA

S. Wettimuny c Cairns b Hadlee	8	c Coney b Hadlee	9
M.D. Wettimuny c Coney b Snedden	6	c Cairns b Snedden	0
S. Fernando c Wright b Hadlee	12	c Lees b Snedden	12
Y. Goonasekera c Lees b Cairns	13	c Lees b Chatfield	23
R.S. Madugalle run out	79	c Lees b Hadlee	13
*D.S. de Silva lbw b Chatfield	61	c Lees b Snedden	0
†S.A.R. Silva c Lees b Chatfield	8	c Crowe b Hadlee	0
J.R. Ratnayeke not out	29	b Hadlee	12
S. Jeganathan c Lees b Chatfield	5	c Lees b Chatfield	0
R.J. Ratnayake b Snedden	12	c sub b Chatfield	1
V. John c Wright b Chatfield	0	not out	8
Extras (B1, LB5, NB1)	7	(B5, LB10)	15
Total	240		93

NEW ZEALAND

G.M. Turner c Goonasekera b John	10	b J.R. Ratnayeke	29
B.A. Edgar c John b R.J. Ratnayake	10	not out	47
J.G. Wright c de Silva b R.J. Ratnayake	14		
*G.P. Howarth c S. Wettimuny b de Silva	36	c Silva b John	1
J.J. Crowe c Silva b R.J. Ratnayake	36	b R.J. Ratnayake	11
J.V. Coney c Goonasekera b John	2	c Goonasekera b de Silva	17
R.J. Hadlee c Goonasekera b John	30	not out	17
†W.K. Lees c Goonasekera b John	0		
B.L. Cairns c de Silva b John	45		
M.C. Snedden lbw b R.J. Ratnayake	5		
E.J. Chatfield not out	2		
Extras (B4, LB3, W3, NB1)	11	(LB11, NB1)	12
Total	201	(4 wkts)	134

BOWLING

NEW ZEALAND	*O*	*M*	*R*	*W*		*O*	*M*	*R*	*W*
Hadlee	25	9	47	1	—	17	5	34	4
Snedden	24	5	56	2	—	17	7	21	3
Chatfield	26.5	7	66	4	—	12	5	15	3
Cairns	20	5	53	1	—	7	2	8	0
Coney	5	2	11	0	—	—	—	—	—
SRI LANKA									
R.J. Ratnayake	24	5	81	4	—	15	0	46	1
John	25.2	9	60	5	—	8	2	38	1
J.R. Ratnayeke	14	3	36	0	—	8.1	4	20	1
de Silva	9	5	13	1	—	6	1	18	1
					—				

FALL OF WICKETS

	SL 1st	*NZ 1st*	*SL 2nd*	*NZ 2nd*
1st	14	12	0	59
2nd	14	33	12	62
3rd	34	104	12	81
4th	48	107	57	116
5th	178	141	61	—
6th	191	141	61	—
7th	194	145	78	—
8th	220	163	81	—
9th	239	169	83	—
10th	240	201	93	—

West Indies v India 1982–83

FIRST TEST MATCH

PLAYED AT KINGSTON, 23, 24, 26, 27, 28 FEBRUARY

WEST INDIES WON BY 4 WICKETS

INDIA

S.M. Gavaskar c Dujon b Marshall	20	b Holding	0
A.D. Gaekwad c Dujon b Holding	1	c Greenidge b Marshall	23
M. Amarnath c Dujon b Garner	29	c Garner b Marshall	40
D.B. Vengsarkar c Richards b Roberts	30	c Garner b Marshall	20
Yashpal Sharma c Haynes b Garner	63	c Gomes b Holding	24
R.J. Shastri c Dujon b Holding	1	not out	25
*Kapil Dev c Marshall b Roberts	5	c Dujon b Roberts	12
†S.M.H. Kirmani c Dujon b Marshall	5	c Haynes b Roberts	10
B.S. Sandhu c Garner b Roberts	68	c Garner b Roberts	0
S Venkataraghavan b Roberts	0	c Greenidge b Roberts	0
Maninder Singh not out	3	c Holding b Roberts	2
Extras (B1, LB15, NB10)	26	(B2, LB4, W1, NB11)	18
Total	251		174

WEST INDIES

C.G. Greenidge c Venkataraghavan b Shastri	70	b Kapil Dev	42
D.L. Haynes c Amarnath b Kapil Dev	25	b Kapil Dev	34
I.V.A. Richards c Venkataraghavan b Shastri	29	c Kapil Dev b Amarnath	61
H.A. Gomes c Yashpal Sharma b Shastri	4		
A.L. Logie run out	13	lbw b Kapil Dev	10
*C.H. Lloyd b Venkataraghavan	24	c Amarnath b Kapil Dev	3
†P.J. Dujon lbw b Kapil Dev	29	not out	17
M.D. Marshall c Yashpal Sharma b Kapil Dev	23	not out	0
A.M.E. Roberts c Sandhu b Shastri	17	c Kirmani b Shastri	1
M.A. Holding c Kirmani b Kapil Dev	1		
J. Garner not out	0		
Extras (B1, LB8, NB10)	19	(NB5)	5
Total	254	(6 wkts)	173

BOWLING

WEST INDIES	*O*	*M*	*R*	*W*		*O*	*M*	*R*	*W*
Holding	24	5	57	2	—	17	4	36	2
Roberts	22	4	61	4	—	24.3	9	39	5
Garner	15.4	4	41	2	—	13	6	16	0
Marshall	16	4	35	2	—	24	6	56	3
Gomes	9	0	31	0	—	7	2	9	0
Richards	1	1	0	0	—	—	—	—	—
INDIA									
Kapil Dev	25.3	6	45	4	—	13	0	73	4
Sandhu	11	4	30	0	—	3	0	22	0
Venkataraghavan	25	3	66	1	—	7	0	39	0
Maninder Singh	31	6	51	0	—	—	—	—	—
Shastri	24	8	43	4	—	—	—	—	—
Amarnath	—	—	—	—	—	2.2	0	34	0

FALL OF WICKETS

	IND 1st	*WI 1st*	*IND 2nd*	*WI 2nd*
1st	10	36	0	47
2nd	58	83	68	65
3rd	66	91	69	131
4th	98	114	112	132
5th	99	157	118	156
6th	104	186	136	161
7th	127	228	168	—
8th	234	244	168	—
9th	238	254	168	—
10th	251	254	174	—

SECOND TEST MATCH

PLAYED AT PORT OF SPAIN, 11, 12, 13, 15, 16 MARCH

MATCH DRAWN

INDIA

S.M. Gavaskar c Dujon b Holding	1	c Dujon b Garner	32
A.D. Gaekwad run out	0	c sub b Gomes	35
M. Amarnath c Lloyd b Roberts	58	lbw b Richards	117
D.B. Vengsarkar c Holding b Marshall	7	c Dujon b Roberts	45
Yashpal Sharma not out	11	b Roberts	50
R.J. Shastri c Gomes b Marshall	42	lbw b Holding	9
*Kapil Dev c Haynes b Marshall	13	not out	100
†S.M.H. Kirmani b Roberts	7	run out	30
B.S. Sandhu c Richards b Marshall	11	not out	0
S. Venkataraghavan c Richards b Roberts	1		
Maninder Singh c Dujon b Marshall	1		
Extras (B5, LB1, W3, NB14)	23	(B10, LB20, NB21)	51
Total	175	(7 wkts)	469

WEST INDIES

C.G. Greenidge b Sandhu	0
D.L. Haynes c Kirmani b Sandhu	0
I.V.A. Richards c Kirmani b Kapil Dev	1
H.A. Gomes c Gavaskar b Venkataraghavan	123
*C.H. Lloyd st Kirmani b Shastri	143
A.L. Logie c Kapil Dev b Venkataraghavan	13
†P.J. Dujon lbw b Kapil Dev	31
M.D. Marshall lbw b Shastri	14
A.M.E. Roberts b Kapil Dev	9
M.A. Holding c Vengsarkar b Maninder Singh	24
J. Garner not out	21
Extras (B4, LB7, W1, NB3)	15
Total	394

BOWLING

WEST INDIES	*O*	*M*	*R*	*W*		*O*	*M*	*R*	*W*
Holding	13	2	24	1	—	31	2	104	1
Roberts	22	5	72	3	—	25	3	100	2
Marshall	19.2	5	37	5	—	27.1	8	72	0
Garner	10	5	17	0	—	30	7	81	1
Gomes	2	1	2	0	—	19	7	45	1
Richards	—	—	—	—	—	7	4	16	1
INDIA									
Kapil Dev	31	6	91	3	—	—	—	—	—
Sandhu	19	2	69	2	—	—	—	—	—
Venkataraghavan	41	13	97	2	—	—	—	—	—
Shastri	21	2	71	2	—	—	—	—	—
Maninder Singh	26.3	7	51	1	—	—	—	—	—

FALL OF WICKETS

	IND 1st	*WI 1st*	*IND 2nd*
1st	1	0	63
2nd	5	1	132
3rd	28	1	206
4th	131	238	312
5th	146	255	325
6th	147	316	329
7th	164	324	463
8th	166	340	—
9th	171	346	—
10th	175	394	—

THIRD TEST MATCH

PLAYED AT GEORGETOWN, 31 MARCH, 2, 3, 4, 5 APRIL

MATCH DRAWN

WEST INDIES

C.G. Greenidge c Kirmani b Maninder Singh	70
D.L. Haynes c Y. Sharma b Venkataraghavan	46
I.V.A. Richards c Venkataraghavan b Sandhu	109
H.A. Gomes c Gaekwad b Kapil Dev	36
M.A. Holding run out	0
A.L. Logie c Kirmani b Sandhu	0
*C.H. Lloyd c Kirmani b Shastri	81
†P.J. Dujon c & b Venkataraghavan	47
M.D. Marshall lbw b Kapil Dev	27
A.M.E. Roberts c Gavaskar b Sandhu	36
J. Garner not out	1
Extras (B1, LB14, W1, NB1)	17
Total	470

INDIA

S.M. Gavaskar not out	147
A.D. Gaekwad c Dujon b Holding	8
M. Amarnath c Richards b Marshall	13
D.B. Vengsarkar c Richards b Garner	62
Yashpal Sharma not out	35
R.J. Shastri did not bat	
*Kapil Dev did not bat	
†S.M.H. Kirmani did not bat	
B.S. Sandhu did not bat	
Maninder Singh did not bat	
S. Venkataraghavan did not bat	
Extras (B1, LB3, NB15)	19
Total (3 wkts)	284

BOWLING

INDIA	*O*	*M*	*R*	*W*	*O*	*M*	*R*	*W*	FALL OF WICKETS		
										WI	*IND*
										1st	*1st*
Kapil Dev	30	7	68	2	—	—	—	—			
Sandhu	25.4	5	87	3	—	—	—	—			
Shastri	22	3	84	1	—	—	—	—	1st	89	24
Maninder Singh	27	3	90	1	—	—	—	—	2nd	157	68
Venkataraghavan	38	4	124	2	—	—	—	—	3rd	252	180
WEST INDIES									4th	253	—
Roberts	15	2	38	0	—	—	—	—	5th	256	—
Holding	16	1	72	1	—	—	—	—	6th	299	—
Garner	17	4	57	1	—	—	—	—	7th	387	—
Marshall	13	2	39	1	—	—	—	—	8th	417	—
Gomes	14	5	35	0	—	—	—	—	9th	460	—
Richards	4	0	24	0	—	—	—	—	10th	470	—

FOURTH TEST MATCH

PLAYED AT BRIDGETOWN, 15, 16, 17, 19, 20 APRIL

WEST INDIES WON BY 10 WICKETS

INDIA

S.M. Gavaskar c Dujon b Holding	2	c Roberts b Garner	19
A.D. Gaekwad c Marshall b Roberts	3	b Holding	55
M. Amarnath c Dujon b Marshall	91	c Dujon b Roberts	80
D.B. Vengsarkar c Marshall b Holding	15	lbw b Holding	6
Yashpal Sharma c Richards b Roberts	24	c Greenidge b Roberts	12
R.J. Shastri c Richards b Roberts	29	c Lloyd b Marshall	19
*Kapil Dev c Lloyd b Marshall	0	c Lloyd b Marshall	26
†S.M.H. Kirmani c Haynes b Roberts	11	run out	33
S. Madan Lal c Holding b Garner	6	lbw b Roberts	0
B.S. Sandhu not out	8	lbw b Roberts	4
S. Venkataraghavan c Dujon b Garner	5	not out	0
Extras (LB1, NB14)	15	(B5, LB2, NB16)	23
Total	209		277

WEST INDIES

C.G. Greenidge c Gavaskar b Madan Lal	57	not out	0
D.L. Haynes c Kapil Dev b Shastri	92	not out	0
I.V.A. Richards c Gavaskar b Venkataraghavan	80		
H.A. Gomes c sub b Venkataraghavan	6		
A.L. Logie c Amarnath b Shastri	130		
*C.H. Lloyd c sub b Venkataraghavan	50		
†P.J. Dujon c Vengsarkar b Kapil Dev	25		
M.D. Marshall c Venkataraghavan b Kapil Dev	8		
A.M.E. Roberts c Kapil Dev b Madan Lal	20		
M.A. Holding c Kirmani b Kapil Dev	2		
J. Garner not out	2		
Extras (B1, LB11, NB2)	14	(NB1)	1
Total	486	(0 wkts)	1

BOWLING

WEST INDIES	*O*	*M*	*R*	*W*		*O*	*M*	*R*	*W*	FALL OF WICKETS	*IND 1st*	*WI 1st*	*IND 2nd*	*WI 2nd*
Holding	14	4	46	2	—	21	2	75	2					
Roberts	16	4	48	4	—	19.2	3	31	4					
Marshall	13	1	56	2	—	16	1	80	2	1st	2	98	61	—
Garner	12.2	5	41	2	—	15	4	48	1	2nd	10	220	108	—
Gomes	2	1	3	0	—	8	3	20	0	3rd	39	230	109	—
INDIA										4th	91	262	132	—
Kapil Dev	32.3	7	76	3	—	—	—	—	—	5th	172	395	139	—
Sandhu	5	1	21	0	—	—	—	—	—	6th	172	454	155	—
Madan Lal	27	2	96	2	—	—	—	—	—	7th	180	458	214	—
Shastri	50	13	133	2	—	—	—	—	—	8th	196	481	276	—
Venkataraghavan	43	6	146	3	—	—	—	—	—	9th	200	483	276	—
Gaekwad	1	1	0	0	—	—	—	—	—	10th	209	486	277	—
Kirmani	—	—	—	—	—	0.0	0	0	0					

Kirmani's only delivery was a no ball.
Amarnath (2nd innings) retired hurt at 96-1 and resumed at 139-5.

FIFTH TEST MATCH

PLAYED AT ST. JOHN'S, ANTIGUA, 28, 29, 30 APRIL, 1, 2 MAY

MATCH DRAWN

INDIA

S.M. Gavaskar c Dujon b Marshall	18	c Dujon b Davis	1
A.D. Gaekwad c Richards b Roberts	3	lbw b Marshall	72
M. Amarnath c Lloyd b Davis	54	c Logie b Davis	116
D.B. Vengsarkar c Davis b Marshall	94	c Dujon b Marshall	0
Yashpal Sharma c Gomes b Roberts	3	c sub b Gomes	20
R.J. Shastri st Dujon b Gomes	102	not out	9
*Kapil Dev lbw b Holding	98	not out	0
†S.M.H. Kirmani c Greenidge b Davis	2		
S. Madan Lal not out	35		
L. Sivaramakrishnan c sub b Marshall	17		
S. Venkataraghavan b Marshal	0		
Extras (B14, LB7, W1, NB9)	31	(B8, LB11, NB10)	29
Total	457	(5 wkts dec)	247

WEST INDIES

C.G. Greenidge retired, not out	154
D.L. Haynes c Shastri b Yashpal Sharma	136
W.W. Davis b Madan Lal	14
I.V.A. Richards c Gaekwad b Madan Lal	2
H.A. Gomes lbw b Madan Lal	9
A.L. Logie hit wicket b Kapil Dev	1
†P.J. Dujon c Gaekwad b Venkataraghavan	110
*C.H. Lloyd c Yashpal Sharma b Shastri	106
M.D. Marshall b Venkataraghavan	2
A.M.E. Roberts not out	1
M.A. Holding run out	0
Extras (B6, LB5, NB4)	15
Total	550

BOWLING

WEST INDIES	*O*	*M*	*R*	*W*		*O*	*M*	*R*	*W*
Roberts	29	3	110	2	—	15	3	46	0
Holding	26	3	86	1	—	—	—	—	—
Marshall	27.5	5	87	4	—	18	7	33	2
Davis	29	1	121	2	—	23	4	54	2
Richards	11	3	13	0	—	13	1	36	0
Gomes	4	1	9	1	—	19	0	49	1
INDIA									
Kapil Dev	22	6	71	1	—	—	—	—	—
Madan Lal	35	7	105	3	—	—	—	—	—
Sivaramakrishnan	25	1	95	0	—	—	—	—	—
Shastri	46.4	5	141	1	—	—	—	—	—
Venkataraghavan	36	1	114	2	—	—	—	—	—
Gaekwad	1	0	3	0	—	—	—	—	—
Yashpal Sharma	1	0	6	1	—	—	—	—	—

FALL OF WICKETS

	IND 1st	*WI 1st*	*IND 2nd*
1st	5	296	1
2nd	28	303	201
3rd	119	323	201
4th	181	324	234
5th	337	334	245
6th	372	541	—
7th	376	547	—
8th	419	549	—
9th	457	550	—
10th	457	—	—

Greenidge retired at 301-1 in order to fly to Barbados to visit his baby daughter seriously ill in hospital. Amarnath (1st innings) retired at 98-2 and resumed at 337-5.

Sri Lanka v Australia 1982–83

TEST MATCH

PLAYED AT KANDY, 22, 23, 24, 26 APRIL
AUSTRALIA WON BY AN INNINGS AND 38 RUNS

AUSTRALIA

K.C. Wessels c Dias b de Silva	141
G.M. Wood c Ratnayake b Ranatunga	4
G.N. Yallop lbw b de Mel	98
*G.S. Chappell lbw b de Mel	66
D.W. Hookes not out	143
A.R. Border not out	47
†R.D. Woolley did not bat	
T.G. Hogan did not bat	
B. Yardley did not bat	
D.K. Lillee did not bat	
R.M. Hogg did not bat	
Extras (LB11, W1, NB3)	15
Total (4 wkts dec)	514

SRI LANKA

S. Wettimuny c Woolley b Lillee	0	b Hogan	96
E.R.N.S. Fernando c Woolley b Hogg	0	c Woolley b Lillee	3
R.L. Dias c Border b Lillee	4	b Hogan	10
*L.R.D. Mendis c Hookes b Yardley	74	c Border b Yardley	6
R.S. Madugalle c & b Yardley	9	b Yardley	0
A. Ranatunga c Lillee b Yardley	90	b Hogan	32
D.S. de Silva c Hogan b Yardley	26	c Woolley b Hogan	5
A.L.F. de Mel c Hookes b Hogan	29	c Yallop b Hogan	0
†R.G. de Alwis c Border b Yardley	3	run out	9
R.J. Ratnayake c Woolley b Border	14	run out	30
R.P.W. Guneratne not out	0	not out	0
Extras (B4, LB5, W1, NB12)	22	(B6, LB7, NB1)	14
Total	271		205

BOWLING

SRI LANKA	*O*	*M*	*R*	*W*		*O*	*M*	*R*	*W*
de Mel	23	3	113	2	—	—	—	—	—
Ratnayake	28	4	108	0	—	—	—	—	—
Ranatunga	19	2	72	1	—	—	—	—	—
de Silva	44	7	122	1	—	—	—	—	—
Guneratne	17	1	84	0	—	—	—	—	—
AUSTRALIA									
Lillee	19	3	67	2	—	11	3	40	1
Hogg	12	4	31	1	—	3	2	7	0
Chappell	1	0	2	0	—	—	—	—	—
Yardley	25	7	88	5	—	26	6	78	2
Hogan	11	1	50	1	—	25.2	6	66	5
Border	4.5	0	11	1	—	—	—	—	—

FALL OF WICKETS

	AUS 1st	*SL 1st*	*SL 2nd*
1st	43	1	17
2nd	213	5	59
3rd	290	9	120
4th	359	46	151
5th	—	142	155
6th	—	220	155
7th	—	224	162
8th	—	247	164
9th	—	270	191
10th	—	271	205

England v New Zealand 1983

FIRST CORNHILL TEST MATCH

PLAYED AT THE OVAL, 14, 15, 16, 17, 18 JULY

ENGLAND WON BY 189 RUNS

ENGLAND

G. Fowler lbw b Hadlee	1	run out	105
C.J. Tavaré run out	45	c Howarth b Bracewell	109
D.J. Gower b Hadlee	11	c Howarth b Hadlee	25
A.J. Lamb b Cairns	24	not out	102
I.T. Botham b Hadlee	15	run out	26
D.W. Randall not out	75	c Coney b Hadlee	3
V.J. Marks c Lees b Hadlee	4	c M.D. Crowe b Bracewell	2
P.H. Edmonds c & b Bracewell	12	not out	43
†R.W. Taylor lbw b Hadlee	0		
*R.G.D. Willis c J.J. Crowe b Bracewell	4		
N.G. Cowans b Hadlee	3		
Extras (B6, LB6, NB3)	15	(B8, LB23)	31
Total	209	(6 wkts dec)	446

NEW ZEALAND

J.G. Wright c Gower b Willis	0	run out	88
B.A. Edgar c Taylor b Willis	12	c Taylor b Willis	3
J.J. Crowe c Randall b Willis	0	c Lamb b Willis	9
*G.P. Howarth b Cowans	4	c Taylor b Edmonds	67
M.D. Crowe b Willis	0	c Taylor b Edmonds	33
J.V. Coney run out	44	lbw b Marks	2
R.J. Hadlee c & b Botham	84	c Taylor b Marks	11
J.G. Bracewell c & b Botham	7	c Gower b Marks	0
†W.K. Lees not out	31	run out	8
B.L. Cairns c Lamb b Botham	2	c Willis b Edmonds	32
E.J. Chatfield c Willis b Botham	0	not out	10
Extras (LB6, NB6)	12	(B3, LB1, NB3)	7
Total	196		270

BOWLING

NEW ZEALAND	O	M	R	W		O	M	R	W
Hadlee	23.4	6	53	6	—	37.2	7	99	2
Chatfield	17	3	48	0	—	35	9	85	0
Cairns	17	3	63	1	—	30	7	67	0
Bracewell	8	4	16	2	—	54	13	115	2
M.D. Crowe	5	0	14	0	—	3	0	9	0
Coney	—	—	—	—	—	27	11	39	0
Howarth	—	—	—	—	—	3	2	1	0
ENGLAND									
Willis	20	8	43	4	—	12	3	26	2
Cowans	19	3	60	1	—	11	2	41	0
Botham	16	2	62	4	—	4	0	17	0
Edmonds	2	0	19	0	—	40.1	16	101	3
Marks	—	—	—	—	—	43	20	78	3

FALL OF WICKETS

	ENG 1st	*NZ 1st*	*ENG 2nd*	*NZ 2nd*
1st	2	0	223	10
2nd	18	1	225	26
3rd	67	10	269	146
4th	104	17	322	197
5th	116	41	329	202
6th	154	125	336	210
7th	184	149	—	228
8th	191	182	—	228
9th	202	188	—	228
10th	209	196	—	270

SECOND CORNHILL TEST MATCH

PLAYED AT HEADINGLEY, 28, 29, 30 JULY, 1 AUGUST

NEW ZEALAND WON BY 5 WICKETS

ENGLAND

G. Fowler c Smith b Chatfield	9	c Smith b Chatfield	19
C.J. Tavaré c Smith b Coney	69	b Chatfield	23
D.I. Gower c Coney b Cairns	9	not out	112
A.J. Lamb c M. D. Crowe b Cairns	58	b Coney	28
I.T. Botham c Howarth b Cairns	38	c Howarth b Coney	4
D.W. Randall c Coney b Cairns	4	c Smith b Chatfield	16
P.H. Edmonds c Smith b Cairns	8	c Smith b Chatfield	0
G.R. Dilley b Cairns	0	c Smith b Chatfield	15
†R.W. Taylor not out	10	b Cairns	9
*R.G.D. Willis c J.J. Crowe b Coney	9	c Coney b Cairns	4
N.G. Cowans c Bracewell b Cairns	0	c M.D. Crowe b Cairns	10
Extras (B4, LB7)	11	(B8, LB3, W1)	12
Total	225		252

NEW ZEALAND

J.G. Wright c Willis b Cowans	93	c Randall b Willis	26
B.A. Edgar b Willis	84	c Edmonds b Willis	2
*G.P. Howarth run out	13	c Randall b Willis	20
M.D. Crowe lbw b Cowans	37	c Lamb b Willis	1
J.J. Crowe run out	0	b Willis	13
J.V. Coney c Gower b Willis	19	not out	10
R.J. Hadlee b Cowans	75	not out	6
J.G. Bracewell c Dilley b Edmonds	16		
†I.D.S. Smith c Tavaré b Willis	2		
B.L. Cairns not out	24		
E.J. Chatfield lbw b Willis	0		
Extras (B1, LB4, W1, NB8)	14	(B8, LB7, NB10)	25
Total	377	(5 wkts)	103

BOWLING

	O	M	R	W		O	M	R	W
NEW ZEALAND									
Hadlee	21	9	44	0	—	26	9	45	0
Chatfield	22	8	67	1	—	29	5	95	5
Cairns	33.2	14	74	7	—	24	2	70	3
Coney	12	3	21	2	—	8	1	30	2
Bracewell	1	0	8	0	—	—	—	—	—
ENGLAND									
Willis	23.3	6	57	4	—	14	5	35	5
Dilley	17	4	36	0	—	8	2	16	0
Botham	26	9	81	0	—	0.1	0	4	0
Cowans	28	8	88	3	—	5	0	23	0
Edmonds	45	14	101	1	—	—	—	—	—

FALL OF WICKETS

	ENG 1st	*NZ 1st*	*ENG 2nd*	*NZ 2nd*
1st	18	52	39	11
2nd	35	168	44	42
3rd	135	169	116	60
4th	175	169	126	61
5th	185	218	142	83
6th	205	304	142	—
7th	205	348	190	—
8th	209	351	217	—
9th	225	377	221	—
10th	225	377	252	—

Edgar (1st innings) retired hurt at 26-0 and resumed at 218-5.

THIRD CORNHILL TEST MATCH

PLAYED AT LORD'S, 11, 12, 13, 15 AUGUST

ENGLAND WON BY 127 RUNS

ENGLAND

C.J. Tavaré b M.D. Crowe	51	c M.D. Crowe b Hadlee	16
C.J. Smith lbw b Hadlee	0	c Coney b Hadlee	43
D.I. Gower lbw b M.D. Crowe	108	c M.D. Crowe b Gray	34
A.J. Lamb c sub b Chatfield	17	c Hadlee b Gray	4
M.W. Gatting c Wright b Hadlee	81	b Gray	15
I.T. Botham lbw b Cairns	8	c Coney b Chatfield	61
†R.W. Taylor b Hadlee	16	c & b Coney	7
N.A. Foster c Smith b Hadlee	10	c Wright b Hadlee	3
N.G.B. Cook b Chatfield	16	c Bracewell b Chatfield	5
*R.G.D. Willis c Smith b Hadlee	7	not out	2
N.G. Cowans not out	1	c Smith b Chatfield	1
Extras (B3, LB3, W2, NB3)	11	(B5, LB6, W9)	20
Total	326		211

NEW ZEALAND

J.G. Wright c Lamb b Willis	11	c Taylor b Botham	12
B.A. Edgar c Willis b Cook	70	c Lamb b Cowans	27
*G.P. Howarth b Cook	25	c Taylor b Willis	0
M.D. Crowe b Botham	46	c Foster b Cowans	12
J.V. Coney b Cook	7	c Gatting b Foster	68
E.J. Gray c Lamb b Botham	11	c Lamb b Cook	17
J.G. Bracewell c Gower b Cook	0	lbw b Willis	4
R.J. Hadlee c Botham b Cook	0	b Willis	30
B.L. Cairns c Lamb b Botham	5	b Cook	16
†I.D.S. Smith c Lamb b Botham	3	not out	17
E.J. Chatfield not out	5	c & b Cook	2
Extras (LB5, NB3)	8	(B3, LB4, NB7)	14
Total	191		219

BOWLING

NEW ZEALAND	*O*	*M*	*R*	*W*		*O*	*M*	*R*	*W*
Hadlee	40	15	93	5	—	26	7	42	3
Cairns	23	8	65	1	—	3	0	9	0
Chatfield	36.3	8	116	2	—	13.3	4	29	3
M.D. Crowe	13	1	35	2	—	—	—	—	—
Coney	8	7	6	0	—	6	4	9	1
Bracewell	—	—	—	—	—	11	4	29	0
Gray	—	—	—	—	—	30	8	73	3
ENGLAND									
Willis	13	6	28	1	—	12	5	24	3
Foster	16	5	40	0	—	12	0	35	1
Cowans	9	1	30	0	—	11	1	36	2
Botham	20.4	6	50	4	—	7	2	20	1
Cook	26	11	35	5	—	27.2	9	90	3

FALL OF WICKETS

	ENG 1st	*NZ 1st*	*ENG 2nd*	*NZ 2nd*
1st	3	18	26	15
2nd	152	49	79	17
3rd	174	147	87	57
4th	191	159	119	61
5th	218	176	147	108
6th	288	176	195	154
7th	290	176	199	158
8th	303	183	208	190
9th	318	184	210	206
10th	326	191	211	219

FOURTH CORNHILL TEST MATCH

PLAYED AT TRENT BRIDGE, 25, 26, 27, 28, 29 AUGUST

ENGLAND WON BY 165 RUNS

ENGLAND

C.J. Tavaré c Cairns b Snedden	4	c sub b Bracewell	13
C.L. Smith c Howarth b Bracewell	31	c Howarth b Snedden	4
D.I. Gower b Cairns	72	c Cairns b Bracewell	33
A.J. Lamb c Howarth b Bracewell	22	not out	137
M.W. Gatting lbw b Bracewell	14	c Lees b Cairns	11
I.T. Botham lbw b Snedden	103	c Edgar b Gray	27
D.W. Randall c Edgar b Hadlee	83	b Hadlee	13
†R.W. Taylor b Bracewell	21	b Hadlee	0
N.G.B. Cook c Lees b Snedden	4	c Lees b Cairns	26
*R.G.D. Willis not out	25	b Hadlee	16
N.G. Cowans c Bracewell b Cairns	7	b Hadlee	0
Extras (B11, LB14, NB9)	34	(B6, LB10, W1)	17
Total	420		297

NEW ZEALAND

T.J. Franklin c Smith b Botham	2	b Willis	7
B.A. Edgar c Gatting b Cook	62	c Gower b Cook	76
*G.P.Howarth c & b Cook	36	c Tavaré b Cowans	24
J.V. Coney c Gatting b Cook	20	c Taylor b Cook	68
E.J. Gray run out	7	c Gatting b Smith	3
R.J. Hadlee c Smith b Cowans	3	not out	92
†W.K. Lees lbw b Cook	1	c Lamb b Cowans	7
M.D. Crowe c & b Cook	34	c Taylor b Cowans	0
M.C. Snedden b Cowans	9	c Taylor b Cook	12
B.L. Cairns c Gower b Cowans	26	b Cook	11
J.G. Bracewell not out	1	c Taylor b Smith	28
Extras (LB5, NB1)	6	(LB2, W1, NB14)	17
Total	207		345

BOWLING

NEW ZEALAND	*O*	*M*	*R*	*W*		*O*	*M*	*R*	*W*
Hadlee	30	7	98	1	—	28	5	85	4
Snedden	28	7	69	3	—	8	1	40	1
Cairns	33.4	9	77	2	—	20	9	36	2
Bracewell	28	5	108	4	—	21	2	88	2
Coney	2	0	10	0	—	—	—	—	—
Gray	3	0	24	0	—	15	4	31	1
ENGLAND									
Botham	14	4	33	1	—	25	4	73	0
Willis	10	2	23	0	—	19	3	37	1
Cowans	21	8	74	3	—	21	2	95	3
Cook	32	14	63	5	—	50	22	87	4
Gatting	5	2	8	0	—	2	1	5	0
Smith	—	—	—	—	—	12	2	31	2

FALL OF WICKETS

	ENG 1st	*NZ 1st*	*ENG 2nd*	*NZ 2nd*
1st	5	4	5	16
2nd	94	80	58	67
3rd	136	124	61	71
4th	156	127	92	156
5th	169	131	149	161
6th	355	135	188	184
7th	356	135	188	228
8th	379	157	252	264
9th	407	201	297	290
10th	420	207	297	345

TEST MATCH AVERAGES

ENGLAND

	M	I	NO	Runs	HS	Avge	100	50	Ct	St
A.J. Lamb	4	8	2	392	137*	65.33	2	1	10	—
D.I. Gower	4	8	1	404	112*	57.71	2	1	6	—
C.J. Tavaré	4	8	0	330	109	41.25	1	2	2	—
D.W. Randall	3	6	1	194	83	38.80	—	2	3	—
I.T. Botham	4	8	0	282	103	35.25	1	1	3	—
G. Fowler	2	4	0	134	105	33.50	1	—	—	—
M.W. Gatting	2	4	0	121	81	30.25	—	1	4	—
P.H. Edmonds	2	4	1	63	43*	21.00	—	—	1	—
C.L. Smith	2	4	0	78	43	19.50	—	—	2	—
R.G.D. Willis	4	7	2	67	25*	13.40	—	—	4	—
N.G.B. Cook	2	4	0	51	26	12.75	—	—	3	—
R.W. Taylor	4	7	1	63	21	10.50	—	—	11	—
G.R. Dilley	1	2	0	15	15	7.50	—	—	1	—
N.A. Foster	1	2	0	13	10	6.50	—	—	1	—
N.G. Cowans	4	7	1	22	10	3.66	—	—	—	—
V.J. Marks	1	2	0	6	4	3.00	—	—	—	—

	Overs	Mdns	Runs	Wkts	Avge	Best	5 wI	10 wM
R.G.D. Willis	123.3	38	273	20	13.65	5-35	1	—
C.L. Smith	12	2	31	2	15.50	2-31	—	—
N.G.B. Cook	135.2	56	275	17	16.17	5-35	2	—
V.J. Marks	43	20	78	3	26.00	3-78	—	—
I.T. Botham	112.5	27	340	10	34.00	4-50	—	—
N.G. Cowans	125	25	447	12	37.25	3-74	—	—
P.H. Edmonds	87.1	30	221	4	55.25	3-101	—	—
N.A. Foster	28	5	75	1	75.00	1-35	—	—
M.W. Gatting	7	3	13	0	—	—	—	—
G.R. Dilley	25	6	52	0	—	—	—	—

NEW ZEALAND

	M	I	NO	Runs	HS	Avge	100	50	Ct	St
R.J. Hadlee	4	8	2	301	92*	50.16	—	3	1	—
B.A. Edgar	4	8	0	336	84	42.00	—	4	2	—
J.G. Wright	3	6	0	230	93	38.33	—	2	2	—
J.V. Coney	4	8	1	238	68	34.00	—	2	7	—
G.P. Howarth	4	8	0	189	67	23.62	—	1	7	—
M.D. Crowe	4	8	0	163	46	20.37	—	—	5	—
B.L. Cairns	4	7	1	116	32	19.33	—	—	2	—
W.K. Lees	2	4	1	47	31*	15.66	—	—	4	—
I.D.S. Smith	2	3	1	22	17*	11.00	—	—	10	—
M.C. Snedden	1	2	0	21	12	10.50	—	—	—	—
E.J. Gray	2	4	0	38	17	9.50	—	—	—	—
J.G. Bracewell	4	7	1	56	28	9.33	—	—	4	—
E.J. Chatfield	3	5	2	17	10*	5.66	—	—	—	—
J.J. Crowe	2	4	0	22	13	5.50	—	—	2	—
T.J. Franklin	1	2	0	9	7	4.50	—	—	—	—

The New Zealand bowling will be found on page 196.

India v Pakistan 1983-84

FIRST TEST MATCH

PLAYED AT BANGALORE, 14, 15, 17, 18, 19 SEPTEMBER

MATCH DRAWN

INDIA

S.M. Gavaskar lbw b Tahir	42	not out	103
A.D. Gaekwad b Mudassar	11	not out	66
M. Amarnath b Mudassar	4		
Yashpal Sharma c Wasim Bari b Mudassar	16		
S.M. Patil c Javed b Tahir	6		
*Kapil Dev c Mohsin b Azim	0		
R.M.H. Binny not out	83		
S. Madan Lal c Wasim Bari b Azim	74		
†S.M.H. Kirmani c Wasim Bari b Tahir	14		
S. Venkataraghavan c Salim b Tahir	5		
D.R. Doshi lbw b Tahir	0		
Extras (B1, LB8, W6, NB15)	20	(LB4, W1, NB2)	7
Total	275	(0 wkt)	176

PAKISTAN

Mohsin Khan c Kirmani b Madan Lal	17
Mudassar Nazar c Kirmani b Kapil Dev	25
Salim Malik c Amarnath b Kapil Dev	5
Javed Miandad c sub b Madan Lal	99
*Zaheer Abbas c Kapil Dev b Madal Lal	22
Wasim Raja b Doshi	39
†Wasim Bari b Kapil Dev	64
Tahir Naqqash b Kapil Dev	1
Iqbal Qasim c Gaekwad b Venkataraghavan	9
Azim Hafeez b Kapil Dev	0
Mohammad Nazir not out	0
Extras (B1, LB4, NB2)	7
Total	288

BOWLING

PAKISTAN	*O*	*M*	*R*	*W*		*O*	*M*	*R*	*W*	FALL OF WICKETS		
											IND	*PAK*
Tahir	34.5	11	76	5	—	17	2	54	0		*1st*	*1st*
Azim	39	11	102	2	—	8	2	20	0			
Mohammad	10	2	26	0	—	21	4	47	0	1st	38	32
Mudassar	23	6	44	3	—	2.1	0	19	0	2nd	42	37
Iqbal	13	7	18	0	—	12	2	29	0	3rd	72	58
Zaheer	—	—	—	—	—	1	0	3	0	4th	80	99
INDIA										5th	81	187
Kapil Dev	29	6	68	5	—	—	—	—	—	6th	85	243
Madan Lal	24	5	72	3	—	—	—	—	—	7th	240	244
Binny	18	2	42	0	—	—	—	—	—	8th	269	288
Venkataraghavan	21.1	4	49	1	—	—	—	—	—	9th	275	288
Doshi	20	5	52	1	—	—	—	—	—	10th	275	288

SECOND TEST MATCH

PLAYED AT JULLUNDUR, 24, 25, 26, 28, 29 SEPTEMBER

MATCH DRAWN

PAKISTAN

Mohsin Khan lbw b Kapil Dev	0	not out	7
Shoaib Mohammad c Kirmani b Kapil Dev	6	not out	6
Qasim Omar c Kirmani b Binny	15		
*Zaheer Abbas b Shastri	49		
Javed Miandad c Shastri b Kapil Dev	66		
Mudassar Nazar c sub (K. Srikkanth) b Shastri	24		
Wasim Raja c Kirmani b Shastri	125		
†Wasim Bari c Kirmani b Kapil Dev	0		
Tahir Naqqash b Binny	37		
Mohammad Nazir run out	2		
Azim Hafeez not out	2		
Extras (B3, LB6, W1, NB1)	11	(NB3)	3
Total	337	(0 wkts)	16

INDIA

S.M. Gavaskar b Azim	5
A.D. Gaekwad c & b Wasim Raja	201
M. Amarnath c Wasim Bari b Azim	7
Yashpal Sharma lbw b Tahir	7
S.M. Patil c Wasim Bari b Tahir	26
R.J. Shastri c Wasim Bari b Azim	26
R.M.H. Binny b Zaheer	54
*Kapil Dev lbw b Wasim Raja	4
S. Madan Lal c Wasim Bari b Wasim Raja	11
†S.M.H. Kirmani not out	8
S. Venkataraghavan b Wasim Raja	6
Extras (B2, LB4, W9, NB4)	19
Total	374

BOWLING

INDIA	*O*	*M*	*R*	*W*		*O*	*M*	*R*	*W*
Kapil Dev	32	8	80	4	—	2	0	9	0
Madan Lal	20	4	61	0	—	1	0	1	0
Binny	16	1	69	2	—	—	—	—	—
Shastri	37.2	12	63	3	—	3	2	1	0
Venkataraghavan	28	5	55	0	—	—	—	—	—
Patil	—	—	—	—	—	2	1	2	0
Gavaskar	—	—	—	—	—	1	0	3	0
PAKISTAN									
Tahir	27	3	74	2	—	—	—	—	—
Azim	23	3	65	3	—	—	—	—	—
Mudassar	28	6	80	0	—	—	—	—	—
Mohammad	52	16	76	0	—	—	—	—	—
Wasim Raja	28.5	5	50	4	—	—	—	—	—
Mohsin	5	2	9	0	—	—	—	—	—
Zaheer	6	1	14	1	—	—	—	—	—

FALL OF WICKETS

	PAK	*IND*
	1st	*1st*
1st	0	5
2nd	7	20
3rd	55	73
4th	101	137
5th	154	209
6th	169	330
7th	169	345
8th	264	353
9th	309	368
10th	337	374

THIRD TEST MATCH

PLAYED AT NAGPUR, 5, 6, 8, 9, 10 OCTOBER, MATCH DRAWN

INDIA

S.M. Gavaskar c Mudassar b Azim	50	c Mudassar b Mohammad	64
A.D. Gaekwad c Wasim Bari b Tahir	6	c Wasim Raja b Mohammad	29
D.B. Vengsarkar c Wasim Bari b Salim	21	c Mohsin b Mohammad	40
Yashpal Sharma lbw b Mohammad	13	c Wasim Bari b Azim	15
S.M. Patil c Wasim Raja b Azim	6	lbw b Wasim Raja	26
*Kapil Dev c Wasim Bari b Mudassar	32	st Wasim Bari b Wasim Raja	10
R.J. Shastri c Mudassar b Azim	52	c Mudassar b Mohammad	0
Kirti Azad c Mohsin b Azim	11	c Zaheer b Mohammad	0
S. Madan Lal c Salim b Mohammad	5	not out	32
†S.M.H. Kirmani run out	30	not out	31
R. Bhatt not out	0		
Extras (B9, LB6, W1, NB3)	19	(B7, LB7, NB1)	15
Total	245	(8 wkts dec)	262

PAKISTAN

Mohsin Khan c Kirmani b Shastri	44		
Shoaib Mohammad c Yashpal b Kapil Dev	9		
Salim Malik lbw b Kapil Dev	0	not out	0
Javed Miandad lbw b Bhatt	60		
*Zaheer Abbas c Kirmani b Kapil Dev	85		
Mudassar Nazar st Kirmani b Bhatt	78		
Wasim Raja c Yashpal b Shastri	16		
†Wasim Bari c Patil b Shastri	1		
Tahir Naqqash c Gaekwad b Shastri	6	not out	18
Mohammad Nazir not out	13		
Azim Hafeez c Patil b Shastri	4	b Kirmani	18
Extras (B1, LB1, NB4)	6	(B4, LB1, NB1)	6
Total	322	(1 wkt)	42

BOWLING

PAKISTAN	*O*	*M*	*R*	*W*		*O*	*M*	*R*	*W*
Azim	27	10	58	4	—	19	1	67	1
Tahir	19.3	3	72	1	—	23	7	55	0
Mudassar	14	2	43	1	—	—	—	—	—
Salim	3	0	7	1	—	—	—	—	—
Mohammad	22	5	50	2	—	50	19	72	5
Zaheer	—	—	—	—	—	1	1	0	0
Wasim Raja	—	—	—	—	—	10	1	46	2
Mohsin	—	—	—	—	—	3	1	7	0
Javed	—	—	—	—	—	1	0	1	0
INDIA					—				
Kapil Dev	27	8	68	3	—	1	1	0	0
Madan Lal	13	2	44	0	—	—	—	—	—
Bhatt	39	16	65	2	—	—	—	—	—
Kirti Azad	25	7	68	0	—	—	—	—	—
Shastri	30.4	7	75	5	—	—	—	—	—

FALL OF WICKETS

	IND 1st	*PAK 1st*	*IND 2nd*	*PAK 2nd*
1st	27	20	78	42
2nd	66	26	125	—
3rd	96	83	148	—
4th	103	153	172	—
5th	103	254	172	—
6th	171	287	172	—
7th	190	289	188	—
8th	205	305	207	—
9th	242	309	—	—
10th	245	322	—	—

Second Innings: Vengsarkar 2-0-15-0; Yashpal 1-0-10-0; Kirmani 2-0-9-1; Gaekwad 1-0-3-0; Gavaskar 1-1-0-0.

India v West Indies 1983–84

FIRST TEST MATCH

PLAYED AT KANPUR, 21, 22, 23, 25 OCTOBER

WEST INDIES WON BY AN INNINGS AND 83 RUNS

By mutual agreement, wides and no-balls in this series will be included in the bowler's analysis.

WEST INDIES

C.G. Greenidge c Kirmani b Amarnath	194
D.L. Haynes c Madan Lal b Kapil Dev	6
I.V.A. Richards c Kirmani b Kapil Dev	24
H.A. Gomes c Gaekwad b Shastri	21
*C.H. Lloyd c Kirmani b Bhatt	23
A.L. Logie lbw b Bhatt	0
†P.J. Dujon b Binny	81
M.D. Marshall c & b Kapil Dev	92
E.A.E. Baptiste run out	6
M.A. Holding lbw b Kapil Dev	0
W.W. Davis not out	0
Extras (B4, LB2, NB1)	7
Total	454

INDIA

S.M. Gavaskar c Dujon b Marshall	0	c Davis b Marshall	7
A.D. Gaekwad c Dujon b Marshall	4	c Richards b Marshall	5
M. Amarnath lbw b Marshall	0	b Davis	0
D.B. Vengsarkar b Marshall	14	c Davis b Marshall	65
S.M. Patil c Richards b Davis	19	b Davis	3
R.J. Shastri c Dujon b Davis	0	not out	46
†S.M.H. Kirmani b Holding	20	b Holding	14
*Kapil Dev c Gomes b Baptiste	27	c Dujon b Holding	3
R.M.H. Binny c Richards b Holding	39	c Dujon b Marshall	7
S. Madan Lal not out	63	b Holding	0
R. Bhatt b Holding	0	b Davis	6
Extras (B6, LB6, W3, NB6)	21	(B2, LB2, W1, NB3)	8
Total	207		164

BOWLING

INDIA	O	M	R	W		O	M	R	W
Kapil Dev	24.3	3	99	4	—	—	—	—	—
Madan Lal	17	5	50	0	—	—	—	—	—
Binny	17	2	74	1	—	—	—	—	—
Bhatt	34	6	86	2	—	—	—	—	—
Shastri	38	7	103	1	—	—	—	—	—
Gaekwad	1	0	6	0	—	—	—	—	—
Amarnath	7	1	30	1	—	—	—	—	—
WEST INDIES									
Marshall	15	7	19	4	—	17	7	47	4
Holding	14.4	6	37	3	—	19	2	59	3
Davis	13	2	57	2	—	16.3	3	46	3
Baptiste	11	0	58	1	—	6	1	8	0
Gomes	6	0	24	0	—	—	—	—	—

FALL OF WICKETS

	WI 1st	*IND* 1st	*IND* 2nd
1st	9	0	8
2nd	58	0	13
3rd	102	9	38
4th	157	18	43
5th	157	29	43
6th	309	49	105
7th	439	90	109
8th	449	90	135
9th	451	207	143
10th	454	207	164

SECOND TEST MATCH

PLAYED AT DELHI, 29, 30 OCTOBER, 1, 2, 3 NOVEMBER

MATCH DRAWN

INDIA

S.M. Gavaskar b Gomes	121	lbw b Holding	15
A.D. Gaekwad c Richards b Holding	8	b Daniel	32
D.B. Vengsarkar c Richards b Holding	159	b Marshall	63
Yashpal Sharma b Holding	5	lbw b Daniel	0
R.J. Shastri lbw b Davis	49	lbw b Holding	26
R.M.H. Binny lbw b Holding	52	bDaniel	32
M. Amarnath c Dujon b Daniel	1	c Davis b Marshall	0
*Kapil Dev c Lloyd b Marshall	18	c Gomes b Marshall	0
Kirti Azad lbw b Daniel	5	run out	9
S. Madan Lal c sub b Daniel	3	not out	24
†S.M.H. Kirmani not out	1	c Logie b Gomes	3
Extras (B4, LB9, W2, NB27)	42	(B5, LB10, W2, NB12)	29
Total	464		233

WEST INDIES

C.G. Greenidge lbw b Kirti Azad	33	not out	72
D.L. Haynes c Yashpal Sharma b Kapil Dev	12	b Shastri	17
W.W. Davis b Kirti Azad	19		
I.V.A. Richards lbw b Kapil Dev	67	c Gaekwad b Shastri	22
H.A. Gomes c Kirmani b Shastri	19	not out	1
*C.H. Lloyd lbw b Kapil Dev	103		
A.L. Logie c & b Kapil Dev	63		
†P.J. Dujon lbw b Kapil Dev	22		
M.D. Marshall b Kapil Dev	17		
M.A. Holding b Shastri	14		
W.W. Daniel not out	1		
Extras (B5, LB7, NB2)	14	(LB4, W1, NB3)	8
Total	384	(2 wkts)	120

BOWLING

WEST INDIES	O	M	R	W		O	M	R	W
Marshall	24	1	105	1	—	18	4	52	3
Holding	28.1	1	107	4	—	12	4	36	2
Davis	25	2	87	1	—	12	0	45	0
Daniel	21	2	86	3	—	15	3	38	3
Gomes	21	2	58	1	—	20.1	1	47	1
Richards	3	1	8	0	—	—	—	—	—
INDIA									
Kapil Dev	31	2	77	6	—	7	2	26	0
Madan Lal	15	2	59	0	—	7	0	15	0
Binny	15	3	35	0	—	3	0	16	0
Shastri	37.5	7	106	2	—	17	3	36	2
Kirti Azad	26	5	84	2	—	14	4	22	0
Gaekwad	3	1	11	0	—	1	1	0	0
Gavaskar	—	—	—	—	—	1	0	1	0

FALL OF WICKETS

	IND 1st	*WI 1st*	*IND 2nd*	*WI 2nd*
1st	28	44	20	50
2nd	206	45	63	107
3rd	221	112	73	—
4th	366	153	133	—
5th	382	173	151	—
6th	383	304	152	—
7th	422	331	153	—
8th	452	357	166	—
9th	462	370	218	—
10th	464	384	233	—

THIRD TEST MATCH

PLAYED AT AHMEDABAD, 12, 13, 14, 16 NOVEMBER

WEST INDIES WON BY 138 RUNS

WEST INDIES

C.G. Greenidge c Maninder Singh b Binny	7	b Kapil Dev	3
D.L. Haynes lbw b Binny	9	c Patil b Sandhu	1
I.V.A. Richards c Kirti Azad b Binny	8	c sub b Kapil Dev	20
H.A. Gomes c Gavaskar b Maninder Singh	38	lbw b Kapil Dev	25
*C.H. Lloyd c sub b Maninder Singh	68	c Gavaskar b Kapil Dev	33
A.L. Logie c Kirmani b Maninder Singh	0	lbw b Kapil Dev	0
†P.J. Dujon c Kapil Dev b Shastri	98	c sub b Kapil Dev	20
M.D. Marshall b Maninder Singh	10	c sub b Kapil Dev	29
W.W. Daniel run out	6	b Kapil Dev	0
M.A. Holding b Kapil Dev	16	lbw b Kapil Dev	58
W.W. Davis not out	3	not out	1
Extras (B8, LB6, NB4)	18	(LB9, NB2)	11
Total	281		201

INDIA

S.M. Gavaskar c Lloyd b Holding	90	lbw b Holding	1
A.D. Gaekwad b Holding	39	b Davis	29
N.S. Siddhu run out	15	c Dujon b Holding	4
S.M. Patil c Dujon b Marshall	22	c Daniel b Marshall	1
R.J. Shastri c Lloyd b Daniel	13	c Dujon b Holding	1
R.M.H. Binny c Haynes b Davis	5	c Greenidge b Holding	1
*Kapil Dev lbw b Daniel	31	b Davis	1
Kirti Azad b Daniel	0	b Marshall	3
†S.M.H. Kirmani c Haynes b Daniel	5	not out	24
B.S. Sandhu not out	7	lbw b Davis	1
Maninder Singh lbw b Daniel	0	lbw b Daniel	15
Extras (B7, LB4, NB3)	14	(B6, LB12, NB4)	22
Total	241		103

BOWLING

INDIA	O	M	R	W		O	M	R	W
Kapil Dev	27	5	52	1	—	30.3	6	83	9
Sandhu	14	6	33	0	—	10	1	45	1
Binny	6	0	18	3	—	—	—	—	—
Maninder Singh	34	6	85	4	—	14	1	48	0
Kirti Azad	7	0	34	0	—	4	2	7	0
Shastri	16.3	2	45	1	—	2	0	9	0
WEST INDIES									
Marshall	26	9	66	1	—	13	3	23	2
Holding	26	5	80	2	—	17	5	30	4
Daniel	11.5	0	39	5	—	6.1	2	11	1
Davis	11	3	23	1	—	11	1	21	3
Gomes	6	0	22	0	—	—	—	—	—

FALL OF WICKETS

	WI 1st	*IND 1st*	*WI 2nd*	*IND 2nd*
1st	16	127	4	1
2nd	22	148	8	7
3rd	27	174	43	8
4th	134	186	74	24
5th	134	197	75	27
6th	158	213	107	38
7th	168	214	114	39
8th	190	222	188	61
9th	230	241	188	63
10th	281	241	201	103

In each case the sub catcher was Gursharan Singh

FOURTH TEST MATCH

PLAYED AT BOMBAY, 24, 26, 27, 28, 29 NOVEMBER

MATCH DRAWN

INDIA

S.M. Gavaskar lbw b Marshall	12	c Davis b Marshall	3
A.D. Gaekwad b Holding	48	c Richards b Holding	3
D.B. Vengsarkar c Richards b Davis	100		
A. Malhotra c Dujon b Holding	32	not out	72
R.J. Shastri b Holding	77	run out	38
R.M.H. Binny lbw b Marshall	65	lbw b Davis	18
*Kapil Dev b Holding	8	c Dujon b Daniel	1
S. Madan Lal lbw b Marshall	0	not out	26
†S.M.H. Kirmani not out	43		
N.S. Yadav b Daniel	12		
Maninder Singh c Lloyd b Holding	9		
Extras (B16, LB14, W1, NB26)	57	(B1, LB6, NB5)	12
Total	463	(5 wkts dec)	173

WEST INDIES

C.G. Greenidge b Yadav	13	b Kapil Dev	4
D.L. Haynes handled the ball	55	b Maninder Singh	24
R.B. Richardson lbw b Yadav	0	b Shastri	26
I.V.A. Richards st Kirmani b Shastri	120	c Kirmani b Shastri	4
H.A. Gomes b Kapil Dev	26	not out	37
†P.J. Dujon c Kirmani b Yadav	84		
*C.H. Lloyd run out	67	not out	9
M.D. Marshall c Gavaskar b Yadav	4		
M.A. Holding c & b Yadav	2		
W.W. Daniel c Gavaskar b Shastri	0		
W.W. Davis not out	4		
Extras (B4, LB8, NB6)	18		
Total	393	(4 wkts)	104

BOWLING

WEST INDIES	O	M	R	W		O	M	R	W
Marshall	32	6	88	3	—	13	3	47	1
Holding	40.5	10	102	5	—	11	1	39	1
Davis	36	3	127	1	—	8	0	35	1
Daniel	30	3	113	1	—	14	3	45	1
Gomes	4	1	3	0	—	—	—	—	—
INDIA					—				
Kapil Dev	23	10	41	1	—	5	1	13	1
Shastri	35	8	98	2	—	13	4	32	2
Maninder Singh	27	7	71	0	—	15	7	25	1
Madan Lal	13	6	29	0	—	3	1	8	0
Binny	4	1	11	0	—	—	—	—	—
Yadav	44.1	8	131	5	—	12	5	22	0
Gaekwad	—	—	—	—	—	1	0	4	0
Gavaskar	—	—	—	—	—	1	1	0	0
Malhotra	—	—	—	—	—	1	1	0	0

FALL OF WICKETS

	IND 1st	*WI 1st*	*IND 2nd*	*WI 2nd*
1st	12	47	4	4
2nd	145	47	6	40
3rd	190	128	91	48
4th	234	205	118	68
5th	361	238	121	—
6th	372	357	—	—
7th	373	377	—	—
8th	385	383	—	—
9th	433	384	—	—
10th	463	393	—	—

P. C. A. 1984—2

FIFTH TEST MATCH

PLAYED AT CALCUTTA, 10, 11, 12, 14 DECEMBER

WEST INDIES WON BY AN INNINGS AND 46 RUNS

INDIA

S.M. Gavaskar c Dujon b Marshall	0	c Dujon b Holding	20
A.D. Gaekwad b Marshall	2	b Holding	4
D.B. Vengsarkar b Holding	23	lbw b Marshall	1
M. Amarnath c & b Marshall	0	b Holding	0
A. Malhotra c Gomes b Davis	20	c Dujon b Marshall	30
R.J. Shastri b Holding	12	b Marshall	2
R.M.H. Binny lbw b Roberts	44	c Harper b Marshall	6
*Kapil Dev b Holding	69	c Dujon b Marshall	0
†S.M.H. Kirmani b Roberts	49	b Roberts	13
N.S. Yadav c Greenidge b Roberts	10	b Marshall	4
Maninder Singh not out	0	not out	0
Extras (LB6, NB6)	12	(B1, LB5, NB4)	10
Total	241		90

WEST INDIES

C. Greenidge c Yadav b Binny	25
D.L. Haynes lbw b Kapil Dev	5
I.V.A. Richards c Kirmani b Kapil Dev	9
H.A. Gomes b Yadav	18
†P.J. Dujon c Gaekwad b Kapil Dev	0
†C.H. Lloyd not out	161
M.D. Marshall lbw b Maninder Singh	54
M.A. Holding c Shastri b Maninder Singh	17
R.A. Harper lbw b Kapil Dev	0
A.M.E. Roberts c Amarnath b Yadav	68
W.W. Davis lbw b Yadav	0
Extras (B8, LB7, W1, NB4)	20
Total	377

BOWLING

WEST INDIES	*O*	*M*	*R*	*W*		*O*	*M*	*R*	*W*	FALL OF WICKETS	*IND 1st*	*WI 1st*	*IND 2nd*
Marshall	22	7	65	3	—	15	4	37	6				
Roberts	23.4	9	56	3	—	4	1	11	1				
Davis	14	1	39	1	—	2	0	7	0	1st	0	32	14
Holding	20	4	59	3	—	9	3	29	3	2nd	9	41	29
Harper	8	2	16	0	—	—	—	—	—	3rd	13	42	29
INDIA					—					4th	41	42	33
Kapil Dev	35	5	91	4	—	—	—	—	—	5th	63	88	36
Binny	13	2	62	1	—	—	—	—	—	6th	63	175	50
Amarnath	7	1	19	0	—	—	—	—	—	7th	145	213	77
Yadav	27	1	80	3	—	—	—	—	—	8th	212	213	77
Shastri	18	2	56	0	—	—	—	—	—	9th	240	374	80
Maninder Singh	28	7	54	2	—	—	—	—	—	10th	241	377	90

SIXTH TEST MATCH

PLAYED AT MADRAS, 24, 26, 27, 28, 29 DECEMBER

MATCH DRAWN

WEST INDIES

C.G. Greenidge c Gavaskar b Shastri	34	not out	26
D.L. Haynes b Maninder Singh	23	c Vengsarkar b Shastri	24
I.V.A. Richards c Kirmani b Maninder	32		
H.A. Gomes b Yadav	28	not out	10
†P.J. Dujon c Kapil Dev b Binny	62		
*C.H. Lloyd lbw b Kapil Dev	32		
W.W. Davis c Sidhu b Binny	12		
M.D. Marshall b Kapil Dev	38		
M.A. Holding lbw b Kapil Dev	34		
A.M.E. Roberts not out	0		
R.A. Harper c & b Maninder Singh	0		
Extras (LB12, NB6)	18	(LB2, NB2)	4
Total	313	(1 wkt)	64

INDIA

A.D. Gaekwad c Harper b Marshall	0
N.S. Sidhu c Richards b Roberts	20
D.B. Vengsarkar c Harper b Marshall	0
S.M. Gavaskar not out	236
A. Malhotra c sub b Harper	9
N.S. Yadav c Dujon b Marshall	3
R.J. Shastri lbw b Davis	72
R.M.H. Binny c sub b Marshall	1
*Kapil Dev c sub b Marshall	26
†S.M.H. Kirmani not out	63
Maninder Singh did not bat	
Extras (B1, LB5, W9, NB6)	21
Total (8 wkts dec)	451

BOWLING

INDIA	*O*	*M*	*R*	*W*		*O*	*M*	*R*	*W*
Kapil Dev	15	3	44	3	—	6	2	11	0
Binny	12	1	48	2	—	2	0	14	0
Shastri	28	6	72	1	—	6	3	10	1
Yadav	28	4	96	1	—	1	0	9	0
Maninder Singh	29.3	9	41	3	—	6	2	10	0
Kirmani	—	—	—	—	—	1	0	4	0
Vengsarkar	—	—	—	—	—	1	0	4	0
WEST INDIES					—				
Marshall	26	8	72	5	—	—	—	—	—
Roberts	28	4	81	1	—	—	—	—	—
Davis	30	4	75	1	—	—	—	—	—
Holding	26	2	85	0	—	—	—	—	—
Harper	42	7	108	1	—	—	—	—	—
Gomes	8	0	24	0	—	—	—	—	—

FALL OF WICKETS

	WI 1st	*IND 1st*	*WI 2nd*
1st	47	0	38
2nd	91	0	—
3rd	100	54	—
4th	136	67	—
5th	200	92	
6th	226	262	
7th	232	269	
8th	303	308	
9th	312	—	
10th	313	—	

Australia v Pakistan 1983–84

FIRST TEST MATCH

PLAYED AT PERTH, 11, 12, 13, 14 NOVEMBER

AUSTRALIA WON BY AN INNINGS AND 9 RUNS

By mutual agreement, wides and no-balls in this series will be included in the bowler's analysis

AUSTRALIA

K.C. Wessels c Wasim Bari b Azim	12
W.B. Phillips c Tahir b Mohammad	159
G.N. Yallop b Azim	141
*K.J. Hughes b Abdul	16
A.R. Border c Wasim Raja b Azim	32
G.S. Chappell c Azim b Abdul	17
†R.W. Marsh c Wasim Bari b Azim	24
G.F. Lawson c Mohammad b Abdul	9
D.K. Lillee c Wasim Raja b Azim	0
R.M. Hogg not out	7
C.G. Rackemann did not bat	
Extras (LB9, W3, NB7)	19
Total	436

PAKISTAN

Mohsin Khan c Marsh b Hogg	8	c Border b Rackemann	24
Mudassar Nazar c Phillips b Lillee	1	c Chappell b Rackemann	27
Qasim Omar c Yallop b Rackemann	48	c Marsh b Rackemann	65
Javed Miandad c Phillips b Hogg	0	lbw b Rackemann	46
*Zaheer Abbas c Phillips b Hogg	0	c Marsh b Rackemann	30
Wasim Raja c Chappell b Rackemann	14	c Marsh b Lawson	4
†Wasim Bari c Chappell b Rackemann	0	c Marsh b Lawson	7
Tahir Naqqash not out	29	c Marsh b Rackemann	26
Abdul Qadir b Rackemann	5	run out	18
Mohammad Nazir c Chappell b Rackemann	16	c Border b Hogg	18
Azim Hafeez c Border b Lawson	1	not out	0
Extras (LB3, NB4)	7	(B4, LB7, W2, NB20)	33
Total	129		298

BOWLING

PAKISTAN	O	M	R	W		O	M	R	W
Tahir	22	6	76	0	—	—	—	—	—
Azim	27.3	5	100	5	—	—	—	—	—
Mudassar	15	1	39	0	—	—	—	—	—
Mohammad	29	5	91	1	—	—	—	—	—
Abdul	32	4	121	3	—	—	—	—	—
AUSTRALIA									
Lillee	13	3	26	1	—	29	6	56	0
Hogg	12	4	20	3	—	21.1	2	72	1
Rackemann	8	0	32	5	—	26	6	86	6
Lawson	7.2	0	48	1	—	13	1	53	2
Chappell	—	—	—	—	—	9	1	20	0

FALL OF WICKETS

	AUS	PAK	PAK
	1st	*1st*	*2nd*
1st	34	7	62
2nd	293	13	63
3rd	321	15	188
4th	369	15	197
5th	386	65	206
6th	404	68	216
7th	424	90	257
8th	424	105	267
9th	436	124	281
10th	—	129	298

SECOND TEST MATCH

PLAYED AT BRISBANE, 25, 26, 27, 28, 29 NOVEMBER

MATCH DRAWN

PAKISTAN

Mohsin Khan c Chappell b Lawson	2	b Lawson	37
Mudassar Nazar c Marsh b Lawson	24	c Wessels b Rackemann	18
Qasim Omar c Hughes b Lawson	17	not out	11
Javed Miandad c Marsh b Hogg	6	c Phillips b Rackemann	5
*Zaheer Abbas c Border b Lawson	56	not out	3
Wasim Raja c Hughes b Rackemann	27		
†Wasim Bari c Border b Rackemann	2		
Abdul Qadir b Rackemann	0		
Rashid Khan not out	13		
Mohammad Nazir c Marsh b Hogg	1		
Azim Hafeez b Lawson	2		
Extras (LB3, W1, NB2)	6	(LB6, NB2)	8
Total	156	(3 wkts)	82

AUSTRALIA

K.C. Wessels c Qasim b Azim	35
W.B. Phillips b Rashid	46
G.N. Yallop c Wasim Bari b Rashid	33
*K.J. Hughes c Mohammad b Azim	53
A.R. Border c Wasim Bari b Rashid	118
G.S. Chappell not out	150
†R.W. Marsh b Azim	1
G.F. Lawson b Abdul	49
D.K. Lillee did not bat	
R.M. Hogg did not bat	
C.G. Rackemann did not bat	
Extras (B2, LB6, W1, NB15)	24
Total (7 wkts dec)	509

BOWLING

AUSTRALIA	*O*	*M*	*R*	*W*		*O*	*M*	*R*	*W*
Lawson	17.1	1	49	5	—	10	3	24	1
Hogg	15	2	43	2	—	3	0	11	0
Rackemann	10	3	28	3	—	8	1	31	2
Lillee	8	1	33	0	—	2	0	10	0
PAKISTAN									
Azim Hafeez	37	7	152	3	—	—	—	—	—
Rashid Khan	43	10	129	3	—	—	—	—	—
Mudassar Nazar	16	2	47	0	—	—	—	—	—
Abdul Qadir	32	5	112	1	—	—	—	—	—
Moham'd Nazir	24	6	50	0	—	—	—	—	—
Wasim Raja	3	0	11	0	—	—	—	—	—
					—				

FALL OF WICKETS

	PAK 1st	*AUS 1st*	*PAK 2nd*
1st	10	56	57
2nd	39	120	59
3rd	46	124	74
4th	62	232	—
5th	124	403	—
6th	128	406	—
7th	128	509	—
8th	146	—	—
9th	147	—	—
10th	156	—	—

THIRD TEST MATCH

PLAYED AT ADELAIDE 9, 10, 11, 12, 13 DECEMBER

MATCH DRAWN

AUSTRALIA

K.C. Wessels c Zaheer b Abdul	179	c Wasim Bari b Sarfraz	2
W.B. Phillips c Wasim Bari b Azim	12	c Mudassar b Abdul	54
G.N. Yallop c Qasim b Sarfraz	68	c Javed b Abdul	14
*K.J. Hughes c Wasim Bari b Azim	30	c Mudassar b Azim	106
A.R. Border not out	117	lbw b Azim	66
G.S. Chappell c Wasim Bari b Sarfraz	6	run out	4
†R.W. Marsh c Mohsin b Sarfraz	2	retired hurt	33
T.G. Hogan run out	2	c Qasim Omar b Salim	8
G.F. Lawson c Wasim Bari b Azim	4	not out	7
D.K. Lillee c Sarfraz b Azim	25	not out	4
R.M. Hogg c Javed b Azim	5		
Extras (LB7, W4, NB4)	15	(B3, LB4, W1, NB4)	12
Total	465		310

PAKISTAN

Mohsin Khan c Phillips b Lawson	149
Mudassar Nazar c Marsh b Lillee	44
Qasim Omar c Marsh b Lillee	113
Javed Miandad lbw b Lawson	131
*Zaheer Abbas c Yallop b Hogg	46
Salim Malik c Lawson b Hogan	77
Sarfraz Nawaz c Yallop b Lillee	32
Abdul Qadir b Lillee	10
†Wasim Bari c Marsh b Lillee	0
Mohammad Nazir not out	5
Azim Hafeez c Wessels b Lillee	5
Extras (B1, LB4, NB7)	12
Total	624

BOWLING

PAKISTAN	*O*	*M*	*R*	*W*		*O*	*M*	*R*	*W*
Azim Hafeez	38.2	8	167	5	—	19	4	50	2
Sarfraz Nawaz	42	7	105	3	—	30	8	69	1
Abdul Qadir	20	1	96	1	—	47	9	132	2
Mudassar Nazar	10	2	45	0	—	—	—	—	—
Moham'd Nazir	9	0	37	0	—	27	14	39	0
Mohsin Khan	3	0	8	0	—	1	1	0	0
Javed Miandad	—	—	—	—	—	3	0	10	0
Salim Malik	—	—	—	—	—	1	0	3	1
Qasim Omar	—	—	—	—	—	1	1	0	0
AUSTRALIA									
Lawson	37	7	127	2	—	—	—	—	—
Hogg	34	3	123	1	—	—	—	—	—
Lillee	50.2	8	171	6	—	—	—	—	—
Hogan	37	8	107	1	—	—	—	—	—
Chappell	32	6	82	0	—	—	—	—	—
Border	1	0	9	0	—	—	—	—	—

FALL OF WICKETS

	AUS 1st	*PAK 1st*	*AUS 2nd*
1st	21	73	3
2nd	163	306	44
3rd	219	314	121
4th	353	371	216
5th	376	557	228
6th	378	590	293
7th	383	604	305
8th	394	612	—
9th	451	613	—
10th	465	624	—

FOURTH TEST MATCH

PLAYED AT MELBOURNE, 26, 27, 28, 29, 30 DECEMBER

MATCH DRAWN

PAKISTAN

Mohsin Khan lbw b Lillee	152	c Hughes b Lillee	3
Mudassar Nazar c Marsh b Lawson	7	lbw b Matthews	35
Qasim Omar b Maguire	23	b Lawson	9
Javed Miandad c Marsh b Maguire	27	lbw b Lillee	11
Zaheer Abbas run out	44	b Matthews	50
Salim Malik c Maguire b Lawson	35	b Lillee	14
*Imran Khan c Marsh b Lillee	83	not out	72
Sarfraz Nawaz c Hughes b Maguire	22	not out	11
Abdul Qadir c Lawson b Matthews	45	b Lawson	12
†Wasim Bari not out	6		
Azim Hafeez c Maguire b Matthews	7		
Extras (LB11, NB8)	19	(B10, LB9, W2)	21
Total	470	(7 wkts)	238

AUSTRALIA

K.C. Wessels c Wasim Bari b Azim	11
W.B. Phillips lbw b Azim	35
G.N. Yallop c Wasim Bari b Sarfraz	268
*K.J. Hughes lbw b Azim	94
A.R. Border lbw b Abdul	32
G.S. Chappell c Salim Malik b Abdul	5
†R.W. Marsh c Mudassar b Abdul	0
G.R.J. Matthews lbw b Sarfraz	75
G.F. Lawson c Mudassar b Abdul	0
J.N. Maguire c Wasim Bari b Abdul	4
D.K. Lillee not out	2
Extras (B15, LB9, NB2, W3)	29
Total	555

BOWLING

AUSTRALIA	*O*	*M*	*R*	*W*		*O*	*M*	*R*	*W*
Lawson	38	8	125	2	—	21	8	47	2
Lillee	38	11	113	2	—	29	7	71	3
Maguire	29	7	111	3	—	12	3	26	0
Matthews	28.4	7	95	2	—	21	8	48	2
Chappell	7	2	15	0	—	8	3	13	0
Border	—	—	—	—	—	5	3	9	0
Marsh	—	—	—	—	—	2	0	3	0
Wessels	—	—	—	—	—	2	1	2	0
PAKISTAN									
Sarfraz Nawaz	51	12	106	2	—	—	—	—	—
Azim Hafeez	25	8	115	3	—	—	—	—	—
Abdul Qadir	54.3	12	166	5	—	—	—	—	—
Mudassar Nazar	20	0	76	0	—	—	—	—	—
Javed Miandad	5	0	16	0	—	—	—	—	—
Zaheer Abbas	22	5	42	0	—	—	—	—	—
Salim Malik	2	1	10	0	—	—	—	—	—

FALL OF WICKETS

	PAK *1st*	*AUS* *1st*	*PAK* *2nd*
1st	13	21	3
2nd	64	70	18
3rd	112	273	37
4th	244	342	73
5th	294	354	81
6th	321	354	160
7th	349	539	213
8th	457	540	—
9th	459	553	—
10th	470	555	—

FIFTH TEST MATCH

PLAYED AT SYDNEY, 2, 3, 4, 5, 6 JANUARY

AUSTRALIA WON BY 10 WICKETS

PAKISTAN

Mohsin Khan c Border b Lillee	14	c Chappell b Lawson	1
Mudassar Nazar c Chappell b Lawson	84	b Lawson	21
Qasim Omar c Border b Lillee	15	c Marsh b Lawson	26
Abdul Qadir c Hughes b Lawson	4	c Marsh b Lillee	5
Javed Miandad c Lillee b Matthews	16	c Marsh b Lawson	60
Zaheer Abbas c Yallop b Lawson	61	c Marsh b Hogg	33
*Imran Khan c Yallop b Lawson	5	c Marsh b Hogg	10
Salim Malik c Lillee b Lawson	54	c Chappell b Lillee	7
Sarfraz Nawaz lbw b Lillee	5	c Phillips b Lillee	20
†Wasim Bari not out	7	c Phillips b Lillee	20
Azim Hafeez c Marsh b Lillee	4	not out	2
Extras (B2, LB7)	9	(LB4, NB1)	5
Total	278		210

AUSTRALIA

K.C. Wessels c Wasim Bari b Azim	3	not out	14
W.B. Phillips c Salim b Sarfraz	37	not out	19
G.N. Yallop c Wasim Bari b Mudassar	30		
G.S. Chappell lbw b Mudassar	182		
*K.J. Hughes lbw b Sarfraz	76		
A.R. Border c Wasim Bari b Mudassar	64		
G.R.J. Matthews not out	22		
†R.W. Marsh not out	15		
G.F. Lawson did not bat			
R.M. Hogg did not bat			
D.K. Lillee did not bat			
Extras (LB15, W1, NB9)	25	(NB2)	2
Total (6 wkts dec)	454	(0 wkt)	35

BOWLING

AUSTRALIA	*O*	*M*	*R*	*W*		*O*	*M*	*R*	*W*
Lillee	31.2	10	65	4	—	29.5	5	88	4
Hogg	18	1	61	0	—	14	2	53	2
Chappell	8	0	25	0	—	—	—	—	—
Lawson	25	5	59	5	—	20	7	48	4
Matthews	18	4	59	1	—	7	4	17	0
PAKISTAN					—				
Sarfraz Nawaz	53	13	132	2	—	3	1	7	0
Azim Hafeez	36	7	121	1	—	2·4	0	28	0
Mudassar Nazar	31	9	81	3	—	—	—	—	—
Abdul Qadir	34	9	105	0	—	—	—	—	—

FALL OF WICKETS

	PAK	*AUS*	*PAK*
	1st	*1st*	*2nd*
1st	18	11	5
2nd	57	66	47
3rd	67	83	56
4th	131	254	104
5th	150	407	132
6th	158	436	163
7th	254	—	163
8th	267	—	173
9th	267	—	192
10th	278	—	210

New Zealand v England 1983–84

FIRST TEST MATCH

PLAYED AT WELLINGTON, 20, 21, 22, 23, 24 JANUARY

MATCH DRAWN

NEW ZEALAND

J.G. Wright c Cook b Botham	17	c Foster b Cook	35
B.A. Edgar c Taylor b Botham	9	c Taylor b Willis	30
*G.P. Howarth c Gower b Botham	15	run out	34
M.D. Crowe b Willis	13	c Botham b Gatting	100
J.J. Crowe c Taylor b Foster	52	lbw b Botham	3
J.V. Coney c Gower b Cook	27	not out	174
R.J. Hadlee c Gatting b Botham	24	c Lamb b Foster	18
M.C. Snedden c Taylor b Willis	11	c Taylor b Foster	16
†I.D.S. Smith lbw b Botham	24	b Cook	29
B.L. Cairns c Gatting b Willis	3	c sub (Fowler) b Willis	64
E.J. Chatfield not out	4	b Cook	0
Extras (B4, LB9, NB7)	20	(B4, LB14, W2, NB14)	34
Total	219		537

ENGLAND

C.J. Tavaré b Cairns	9	not out	36
C.L. Smith c Hadlee b Cairns	27	not out	30
D.I. Gower c Hadlee b Cairns	33		
A.J. Lamb c M.D. Crowe b Cairns	13		
M.W. Gatting lbw b Cairns	19		
I.T. Botham c J.J. Crowe b Cairns	138		
D.W. Randall c M.D. Crowe b Hadlee	164		
†R.W. Taylor run out	14		
N.G.B. Cook c Smith b Cairns	7		
N.A. Foster c Howarth b Hadlee	10		
*R.G.D. Willis not out	5		
Extras (B?, LB?, NB?, W?)	24	(NB3)	3
Total	463	(0 wkt)	69

BOWLING

ENGLAND	*O*	*M*	*R*	*W*		*O*	*M*	*R*	*W*
Willis	19	7	37	3	—	37	8	102	2
Botham	27.4	8	59	5	—	36	6	137	1
Foster	24	9	60	1	—	37	12	91	2
Cook	23	11	43	1	—	66.3	26	153	3
Gatting	—	—	—	—	—	8	4	14	1
Smith	—	—	—	—	—	3	1	6	0
NEW ZEALAND									
Hadlee	31.5	6	97	2	—	—	—	—	—
Snedden	21	3	101	0	—	7	2	28	0
Cairns	45	11	143	7	—	—	—	—	—
Chatfield	28	5	68	0	—	5	0	24	0
M.D. Crowe	3	0	20	0	—	6	1	11	0
Coney	4	1	10	0	—	—	—	—	—
Edgar	—	—	—	—	—	3	1	3	0
J.J. Crowe	—	—	—	—	—	1	1	0	0

FALL OF WICKETS

	NZ 1st	*ENG 1st*	*NZ 2nd*
1st	34	41	62
2nd	39	51	79
3rd	56	84	153
4th	71	92	165
5th	114	115	279
6th	160	347	302
7th	174	372	334
8th	200	386	402
9th	208	426	520
10th	219	463	537

SECOND TEST MATCH

PLAYED AT CHRISTCHURCH, 3, 4, 5 FEBRUARY

NEW ZEALAND WON BY AN INNINGS AND 132 RUNS

NEW ZEALAND

J.G. Wright c Taylor b Cowans	25
B.A. Edgar c Randall b Pigott	1
*G.P. Howarth b Cowans	9
M.D. Crowe c Tavaré b Botham	19
J.J. Crowe lbw b Cowans	47
J.V. Coney c Botham b Pigott	41
R.J. Hadlee c Taylor b Willis	99
†I.D.S. Smith not out	32
B.L. Cairns c Taylor b Willis	2
S.L. Boock c Taylor b Willis	5
E.J. Chatfield lbw b Willis	0
Extras (B8, LB11, NB6, W2)	27
Total	307

ENGLAND

G. Fowler b Boock	4	c Howarth b Boock	10
C.J. Tavaré c J.J. Crowe b Hadlee	3	c Smith b Hadlee	6
D.I. Gower lbw b Hadlee	2	c Cairns b Hadlee	8
A.J. Lamb c Smith b Chatfield	11	c Coney b Chatfield	9
D.W. Randall c Coney b Hadlee	0	c Cairns b Hadlee	25
I.T. Botham c Chatfield b Cairns	18	c M.D. Crowe b Boock	0
M.W. Gatting not out	19	c Hadlee b Boock	0
†R.W. Taylor c J.J. Crowe b Cairns	2	run out	15
A.C.S. Pigott lbw b Cairns	4	not out	8
*R.G.D. Willis b Chatfield	6	c Howarth b Hadlee	0
N.G. Cowans c Coney b Chatfield	4	c Smith b Hadlee	7
Extras (LB5, NB4)	9	(LB2, NB3)	5
Total	82		93

BOWLING

ENGLAND	*O*	*M*	*R*	*W*		*O*	*M*	*R*	*W*
Willis	22.1	5	51	4	—	—	—	—	—
Botham	17	1	88	1	—	—	—	—	—
Pigott	17	7	75	2	—	—	—	—	—
Cowans	14	2	52	3	—	—	—	—	—
Gatting	2	0	14	0	—	—	—	—	—
NEW ZEALAND									
Hadlee	17	9	16	3	—	17.5	6	28	5
Cairns	19	5	35	3	—	9	3	21	0
Boock	6	3	12	1	—	13	3	25	3
Chatfield	8.2	3	10	3	—	11	1	14	1
					—				
					—				

FALL OF WICKETS

	NZ 1st	*ENG 1st*	*ENG 2nd*
1st	30	7	15
2nd	42	9	23
3rd	53	10	25
4th	87	10	31
5th	137	41	31
6th	203	41	33
7th	281	47	72
8th	291	58	76
9th	301	72	80
10th	307	82	93

THIRD TEST MATCH

PLAYED AT AUCKLAND, 10, 11, 12, 14, 15 FEBRUARY

MATCH DRAWN

NEW ZEALAND

J.G. Wright b Willis	130	not out	11
B.A. Edgar lbw b Willis	0	not out	0
*G.P. Howarth c Randall b Cowans	35		
M.D. Crowe c Botham b Willis	16		
J.J. Crowe b Marks	128		
J.V. Coney b Cowans	9		
R.J. Hadlee b Marks	3		
†I.D.S. Smith not out	113		
B.L. Cairns c Cowans b Foster	28		
S.L. Boock lbw b Marks	2		
E.J. Chatfield not out	6		
Extras (LB19, NB7)	26	(LB1, NB4)	5
Total (9 wkts dec)	496	(0 wkt)	16

ENGLAND

G. Fowler c Smith b Hadlee	0
C.L. Smith c Smith b Cairns	91
D.I. Gower b Boock	26
A.J. Lamb lbw b Cairns	49
D.W. Randall c Wright b Chatfield	104
†R.W. Taylor st Smith b Boock	23
I.T. Botham run out	70
V.J. Marks c Smith b Chatfield	6
N.A. Foster not out	18
*R.G.D. Willis c Smith b Hadlee	3
N.G. Cowans c Cairns b Boock	21
Extras (B7, LB13, NB8)	28
Total	439

BOWLING

ENGLAND	*O*	*M*	*R*	*W*		*O*	*M*	*R*	*W*
Willis	34	7	109	3	—	3	1	7	0
Botham	29	10	70	0	—	—	—	—	—
Cowans	36	9	98	2	—	2	1	4	0
Foster	31	8	78	1	—	—	—	—	—
Marks	40.2	9	115	3	—	—	—	—	—
NEW ZEALAND									
Hadlee	43	12	91	2	—	—	—	—	—
Cairns	40	20	52	2	—	—	—	—	—
Boock	61.3	28	103	3	—	—	—	—	—
Chatfield	45	21	72	2	—	—	—	—	—
M. Crowe	17	5	62	0	—	—	—	—	—
Coney	13	8	13	0	—	—	—	—	—
Howarth	7	1	18	0	—	—	—	—	—

FALL OF WICKETS

	NZ	*ENG*
	1st	*1st*
1st	3	1
2nd	74	48
3rd	111	143
4th	265	234
5th	293	284
6th	302	371
7th	385	387
8th	451	391
9th	461	396
10th	—	439

THE PRUDENTIAL WORLD CUP

GROUP A

9 June

England v New Zealand at The Oval

England 322-6 in 60 overs (Lamb 102)
New Zealand 216 in 59 overs (Crowe 97)
Result: England won by 106 runs
Man of the Match: A.J. Lamb

Pakistan v Sri Lanka at Swansea

Pakistan 338-5 in 60 overs (Mohsin Khan 82, Zaheer Abbas 82, Javed Miandad 72, Imran Khan 56*)
Sri Lanka 288-9 in 60 overs (Kuruppu 72, de Alwis 59*)
Result: Pakistan won by 50 runs
Man of the Match: Mohsin Khan

11 June

England v Sri Lanka at Taunton

England 333-9 in 60 overs (Gower 130, Lamb 53)
Sri Lanka 286 in 58 overs (de Alwis 58*, Mendis 56, Marks 5-39)
Result: England won by 47 runs
Man of the Match: D.I. Gower

11 & 12 June

New Zealand v Pakistan at Birmingham

New Zealand 238-9 in 60 overs
Pakistan 186 in 55.2 overs
Result: New Zealand won by 52 runs
Man of the Match: Abdul Qadir

13 June

England v Pakistan at Lord's

Pakistan 193-8 in 60 overs (Zaheer Abbas 83*)
England 199-2 in 50.4 overs (Fowler 78*)
Result: England won by 8 wickets
Man of the Match: Zaheer Abbas

New Zealand v Sri Lanka at Bristol

Sri Lanka 206 in 56.1 overs (Madugalle 60, Hadlee 5-25)
New Zealand 209-5 in 39.2 overs (Howarth 76, Turner 50)
Result: New Zealand won by 5 wickets
Man of the Match: R.J. Hadlee

15 June

England v New Zealand at Birmingham

England 234 in 55.2 overs (Gower 92*, Fowler 63)
New Zealand 238-8 in 59.5 overs (Coney 66*, Howarth 60)
Result: New Zealand won by 2 wickets
Man of the Match: J.V. Coney

16 June

Pakistan v Sri Lanka at Leeds

Pakistan 235-7 in 60 overs (Imran Khan 102*, Mahboob 77, de Mel 5-39)
Sri Lanka 224 in 58.3 overs (Wettimuny 50, Qadir 5-44)
Result: Pakistan won by 11 runs
Man of the Match: Abdul Qadir

18 June

England v Pakistan at Manchester

Pakistan 232-8 in 60 overs (Miandad 67)
England 233-3 in 57.2 overs (Fowler 69, Tavaré 58)
Result: England won by 7 wickets
Man of the Match: G. Fowler

Sri Lanka v New Zealand at Derby

New Zealand 181 in 58.2 overs (de Mel 5-32)
Sri Lanka 184-7 in 52.5 overs (Dias 64*, Kuruppu 62)
Result: Sri Lanka won by 3 wickets
Man of the Match: A.L.F. de Mel

20 June

England v Sri Lanka at Leeds

Sri Lanka 136 in 50.4 overs
England 137-1 in 24.1 overs (Fowler 81*)
Result: England won by 9 wickets
Man of the Match: R.G.D. Willis

Pakistan v New Zealand at Nottingham

Pakistan 261-3 in 60 overs (Zaheer Abbas 103*, Imran Khan 79*)
New Zealand 250 in 59.1 overs (Coney 51)
Result: Pakistan won by 11 runs
Man of the Match: Imran Khan

GROUP B

9 June

Zimbabwe v Australia at Nottingham

Zimbabwe 239-6 in 60 overs (Fletcher 69*)
Australia 226-7 in 60 overs (Wessels 76, Marsh 50*)
Result: Zimbabwe won by 13 runs
Man of the Match: D.A.G. Fletcher

9 & 10 June

India v West Indies at Manchester

India 262-8 in 60 overs (Sharma 89)
West Indies 228 in 54.1 overs
Result: India won by 34 runs
Man of the Match: Y. Sharma

11 June

India v Zimbabwe at Leicester

India 157-5 in 37 overs (Patil 50)
Zimbabwe 155 in 51 overs
Result: India won by 5 wickets
Man of the Match: Madan Lal

11 & 12 June

West Indies v Australia at Leeds

West Indies 252-9 in 60 overs (Gomes 78)
Australia 151 in 30.3 overs (Davis 7-51)
Result: West Indies won by 101 runs
Man of the Match: W.W. Davis

13 June

Australia v India at Nottingham

Australia 320-9 in 60 overs (T.M. Chappell 110, Yallop 66*, Hughes 52)
India 158 in 37.5 overs (MacLeay 6-39)
Result: Australia won by 162 runs
Man of the Match: T.M. Chappell

West Indies v Zimbabwe at Worcester

Zimbabwe 217-7 in 60 overs (Fletcher 71*, Houghton 54)
West Indies 218-2 in 48.3 overs (Greenidge 105*, Gomes 75*)
Result: West Indies won by 8 wickets
Man of the Match: C.G. Greenidge

15 June

West Indies v India at The Oval

West Indies 282-9 in 60 overs (Richards 119)
India 216 in 55 overs (Amarnath 80)
Result: West Indies won by 66 runs
Man of the Match: I.V.A. Richards

16 June

Australia v Zimbabwe at Southampton

Australia 272-7 in 60 overs (Wood 73)
Zimbabwe 240 in 59.5 overs (Houghton 84)
Result: Australia won by 32 runs
Man of the Match: D.L. Houghton

18 June

West Indies v Australia at Lord's

Australia 273-6 in 60 overs (Hughes 69, Hookes 56, Yallop 52)
West Indies 276-3 in 57.5 overs (Richards 95*, Greenidge 90)
Result: West Indies won by 7 wickets
Man of the Match: I.V.A. Richards

India v Zimbabwe at Tunbridge Wells

India 266-8 in 60 overs (Kapil Dev 175*)
Zimbabwe 235 in 57 overs (Curran 73)
Result: India won by 31 runs
Man of the Match: Kapil Dev

20 June

India v Australia at Chelmsford

India 247 in 55.5 overs
Australia 129 in 38.2 overs
Result: India won by 118 runs
Man of the Match: R.M.H. Binny

West Indies v Zimbabwe at Birmingham

Zimbabwe 171 in 60 overs (Curran 62)
West Indies 172-0 in 45.1 overs (Haynes 88*, Bacchus 80*)
Result: West Indies won by 10 wickets
Man of the Match: S.F.A.F. Bacchus

Group A

	P	*W*	*L*	*Pts*
England	6	5	1	20
Pakistan	6	3	3	12
New Zealand	6	3	3	12
Sri Lanka	6	1	5	4

Pakistan qualified for semi-finals on faster scoring rate

Group B

	P	*W*	*L*	*Pts*
West Indies	6	5	1	20
India	6	4	2	16
Australia	6	2	4	8
Zimbabwe	6	1	5	4

SEMI-FINALS

22 June

India v England at Manchester

England 213 in 60 overs (Kapil Dev 3-35)
India 217-4 in 55.4 overs (Sharma 61, Patil 51*)
Result: India won by 6 wickets
Man of the Match: M. Amarnath

West Indies v Pakistan at The Oval

Pakistan 184-8 in 60 overs (Moshin Khan 70, Marshall 3-28)
West Indies 186-2 in 48.4 overs (Richards 80*, Gomes 50*)
Result: West Indies won by 8 wickets
Man of the Match: I.V.A. Richards

PRUDENTIAL WORLD CUP FINAL

PLAYED AT LORD'S, 25 JUNE

INDIA WON BY 24 RUNS

INDIA

S.M. Gavaskar	cDujon b Roberts	2
K. Srikkanth	lbw b Marshall	38
M. Amarnath	b Holding	26
Yashpal Sharma	c sub (A.L. Logie) b Gomes	11
S.M. Patil	c Gomes b Garner	27
*Kapil Dev	c Holding b Gomes	15
Kirti Azad	c Garner b Roberts	0
R.M.H. Binny	c Garner b Roberts	2
S. Madan Lal	b Marshall	17
†S.M.H. Kirmani	b Holding	14
B.S. Sandhu	not out	11
Extras (B5, LB5, W9, NB1)		20
Total (54.5 overs)		183

WEST INDIES

C.G. Greenidge	b Sandhu	1
D.L. Haynes	c Binny b Madan Lal	13
I.V.A. Richards	c Kapil Dev b Madan Lal	33
*C.H. Lloyd	c Kapil Dev b Binny	8
H.A. Gomes	c Gavaskar b Madan Lal	5
S.F.A.F. Bacchus	c Kirmani b Sandhu	8
†P.J. Dujon	b Amarnath	25
M.D. Marshall	c Gavaskar b Amarnath	18
A.M.E. Roberts	lbw b Kapil Dev	4
J. Garner	not out	5
M.A. Holding	lbw b Amarnath	6
Extras (LB4, W10)		14
Total (52 overs)		140

Man of the Match: M. Amarnath

BOWLING

W INDIES	*O*	*M*	*R*	*W*
Roberts	10	3	32	3
Garner	12	4	24	1
Marshall	11	1	24	2
Holding	9.4	2	26	2
Gomes	11	1	49	2
Richards	1	0	8	0
INDIA				
Kapil Dev	11	4	21	1
Sandhu	9	1	32	2
Madan Lal	12	2	31	3
Binny	10	1	23	1
Amarnath	7	0	12	3
Kirti Azad	3	0	7	0

FALL OF WICKETS

	IND	*WI*
1st	2	5
2nd	59	50
3rd	90	57
4th	92	66
5th	110	66
6th	111	76
7th	130	119
8th	153	124
9th	161	126
10th	183	140

ENGLAND v WEST INDIES
1928 TO 1980-81

SERIES BY SERIES

Season		Visiting Captain	P	E W	WI W	D
1928	In England	R.K. Nunes (WI)	3	3	0	0
1929-30	In West Indies	F.S.G. Calthorpe (E)	4	1	1	2
1933	In England	G.C. Grant (WI)	3	2	0	1
1934-35	In West Indies	R.E.S. Wyatt (E)	4	1	2	1
1939	In England	R.S. Grant (WI)	3	1	0	2
1947-48	In West Indies	G.O. Allen (E)	4	0	2	2
1950	In England	J.D.C. Goddard (WI)	4	1	3	0
1953-54	In West Indies	L. Hutton (E)	5	2	2	1
1957	In England	J.D.C. Goddard (WI)	5	3	0	1
1959-60	In West Indies	P.B.H. May (E)	5	1	0	4
1963	In England	F.M.M. Worrell (WI)	5	1	3	1
1966	In England	G.S. Sobers (WI)	5	1	3	1
1967-68	In West Indies	M.C. Cowdrey (E)	5	1	0	4
1969	In England	G.S. Sobers (WI)	3	2	0	1
1973	In England	R.B. Kanhai (WI)	3	0	2	1
1973-74	In West Indies	M.H. Denness (E)	5	1	1	3
1976	In England	C.H. Lloyd (WI)	5	0	3	2
1980	In England	C.H. Lloyd (WI)	5	0	1	4
1980-81	In West Indies	I.T. Botham (E)	4	0	2	2
		At Lord's	11	4	2	5
		At Manchester	9	3	3	3
		At The Oval	10	4	4	2
		At Nottingham	5	0	3	2
		At Birmingham	3	1	0	2
		At Leeds	6	2	3	1
		At Bridgetown	8	1	2	5
		At Port of Spain	11	4	3	4
		At Georgetown	7	1	2	4
		At Kingston	9	1	3	5
		At St. John's	1	0	0	1
		In England	44	14	15	15
		In West Indies	36	7	10	19
		Total	80	21	25	34

HIGHEST INNINGS TOTALS

England			West Indies		
849	Kingston	1929-30	687-8d	The Oval	1976
619-6d	Nottingham	1957	681-8d	Port of Spain	1953-54
583-4d	Birmingham	1957	652-8d	Lord's	1973
568	Port of Spain	1967-68	596-8d	Bridgetown	1973-74
537	Port of Spain	1953-54	583-9d	Kingston	1973-74
527	The Oval	1966	563-8d	Bridgetown	1959-60
			558	Nottingham	1950

LOWEST INNINGS TOTALS

England			West Indies		
71	Manchester	1976	86	The Oval	1957
103	Kingston	1934-35	89	The Oval	1957
103	The Oval	1950	91	Birmingham	1963
107	Port of Spain	1934-35	97	Lord's	1933
111	Georgetown	1947-48	100	The Oval	1933
122	Bridgetown	1980-81	102	Bridgetown	1934-35

HIGHEST INDIVIDUAL INNINGS FOR ENGLAND

325	A. Sandham	at Kingston	1929-30
285*	P.B.H. May	at Birmingham	1957
262*	D.L. Amiss	at Kingston	1973-74
258	T.W. Graveney	at Nottingham	1957
205*	E.H. Hendren	at Port of Spain	1929-30
205	L. Hutton	at Kingston	1953-54
203	D.L. Amiss	at The Oval	1976
202*	L. Hutton	at The Oval	1950

A total of 77 centuries have been scored for England

HIGHEST INDIVIDUAL INNINGS FOR WEST INDIES

302	L.G. Rowe	at Bridgetown	1973–74
291	I.V.A. Richards	at The Oval	1976
270*	G.A. Headley	at Kingston	1934-35
261	F.M.M. Worrell	at Nottingham	1950
232	I.V.A. Richards	at Nottingham	1976
226	G.S. Sobers	at Bridgetown	1959-60
223	G.A. Headley	at Kingston	1929-30
220	C.L. Walcott	at Bridgetown	1953-54
209*	B.F. Butcher	at Nottingham	1966
209	C.A. Roach	at Georgetown	1929-30
206	E.D. Weekes	at Port of Spain	1953-54

A total of 80 centuries have been scored for West Indies

A CENTURY IN EACH INNINGS OF A MATCH
FOR ENGLAND

Nil

FOR WEST INDIES

G.A. Headley	114 & 112	at Georgetown	1929-30
G.A. Headley	106 & 107	at Lord's	1939
C.G. Greenidge	134 & 101	at Manchester	1976

A CENTURY ON DEBUT IN SERIES
FOR ENGLAND

122	E. Tyldesley	at Lord's	1928
152	A. Sandham	at Bridgetown	1929-30
107	A.H. Bakewell	at The Oval	1933
196	L. Hutton	at Lord's	1939
120	D.C.S. Compton	at Lord's	1939
140	S.C. Griffith	at Port of Spain	1947-48
114	C. Washbrook	at Lord's	1950
116	W. Watson	at Kingston	1953-54
154	M.C. Cowdrey	at Birmingham	1957
128	K.F. Barrington	at Bridgetown	1959-60
136*	E.R. Dexter	at Bridgetown	1959-60
100	R. Subba Row	at Georgetown	1959-60
101*	J.M. Parks	at Port of Spain	1959-60
112	J.T. Murray	at The Oval	1966
107	J.H. Hampshire	at Lord's	1969
106*	F.C. Hayes	at The Oval	1973
106	D.S. Steele	at Nottingham	1976

FOR WEST INDIES

176	G.A. Headley	at Bridgetown	1929-30
112	A.G. Ganteaume	at Port of Spain	1947-48
161	O.G. Smith	at Birmingham	1957
118	C.H. Lloyd	at Port of Spain	1967-68
232	I.V.A Richards	at Nottingham	1976

RECORD WICKET PARTNERSHIPS FOR ENGLAND

1st	212	C. Washbrook & R.T. Simpson at Nottingham	1950
2nd	266	P.E. Richardson & T.W. Graveney at Nottingham	1957
3rd	264	L. Hutton & W.R. Hammond at The Oval	1939
4th	411	P.B.H. May & M.C. Cowdrey at Birmingham	1957
5th	130*	C. Milburn & T.W. Graveney at Lord's	1966
6th	163	A.W. Greig & A.P.E. Knott at Bridgetown	1973-74
7th	197	M.J.K. Smith & J.M. Parks at Port of Spain	1959-60
8th	217	T.W. Graveney & J.T. Murray at The Oval	1966
9th	109	G.A.R. Lock & P.I. Pocock at Georgetown	1967-68
10th	128	K. Higgs & J.A. Snow at The Oval	1966

RECORD WICKET PARTNERSHIPS FOR WEST INDIES

1st	206	R.C. Fredericks & L.A. Rowe at Kingston	1973-74
2nd	249	L.G. Rowe & A.L. Kallicharran at Bridgetown	1973-74
3rd	338	E.D. Weekes & F.M.M. Worrell at Port of Spain	1953-54
4th	399	G.S. Sobers & F.M.M. Worrell at Bridgetown	1959-60
5th	265	S.M. Nurse & G.S. Sobers at Leeds	1966
6th	274*	G.S. Sobers & D.A.J. Holford at Lord's	1966
7th	155*†	G.S. Sobers & B.D. Julien at Lord's	1973
8th	99	C.A. McWatt & J.K. Holt at Georgetown	1953-54
9th	63*	G.S. Sobers & W.W. Hall at Port of Spain	1967-68
10th	67*	M.A. Holding & C.E.H. Croft at St. John's	1980-81

† 231 runs were added for this wicket in two separate partnerships: G.S. Sobers retired ill and was replaced by K.D. Boyce when 155 had been added.

HIGHEST RUN AGGREGATE IN A TEST RUBBER

England in England	489 (Av. 97.80)	P.B.H. May	1957
England in West Indies	693 (Av. 115.50)	E.H. Hendren	1929-30
West Indies in England	829 (Av. 118.42)	I.V.A. Richards	1976
West Indies in West Indies	709 (Av. 101.28)	G.S. Sobers	1959-60

BEST INNINGS BOWLING FIGURES

England in England	7-44	T.E. Bailey at Lord's	1957
England in England	7-44	F.S. Trueman at Birmingham	1963
England in West Indies	8-86	A.W. Greig at Port of Spain	1973-74
West Indies in England	8-92	M.A. Holding at The Oval	1976
West Indies in West Indies	7-69	W.W. Hall at Kingston	1959-60

TEN WICKETS OR MORE IN A MATCH FOR ENGLAND

13-156	A.W. Greig at Port of Spain	1973-74
12-119	F.S. Trueman at Birmingham	1963
11-48	G.A.R. Lock at The Oval	1957
11-96	C.S. Marriott at The Oval	1933
11-98	T.E. Bailey at Lord's	1957
11-149	W. Voce at Port of Spain	1929-30
11-152	F.S. Trueman at Lord's	1963
10-93	A.P. Freeman at Manchester	1928
10-142	J.A. Snow at Georgetown	1967-68
10-195	G.T.S. Stevens at Bridgetown	1929-30

TEN WICKETS OR MORE IN A MATCH FOR WEST INDIES

14-149	M.A. Holding at The Oval	1976
11-147	K.D. Boyce at The Oval	1973
11-152	S. Ramadhin at Lord's	1950
11-157	L.R. Gibbs at Manchester	1963
11-204	A.L. Valentine at Manchester	1950
11-229	W. Ferguson at Port of Spain	1947-48
10-96	H.H. Johnson at Kingston	1947-48
10-106	L.R. Gibbs at Manchester	1966
10-123	A.M.E. Roberts at Lord's	1976
10-160	A.L. Valentine at The Oval	1950

HIGHEST WICKET AGGREGATE IN A TEST RUBBER

England in England	34 (Av. 17.47)	F.S. Trueman	1963
England in West Indies	27 (Av. 18.66)	J.A. Snow	1967-68
West Indies in England	33 (Av. 20.42)	A.L. Valentine	1950
West Indies in West Indies	24 (Av. 18.95)	C.E.H. Croft	1980-81

HIGHEST MATCH AGGREGATE	1815-34 wkts at Kingston	1929-30
LOWEST MATCH AGGREGATE	309-29 wkts at Bridgetown	1934-35

SOMERSET TAKE THE THIRD NATWEST TROPHY

Somerset, who have been making a habit recently of winning one-day competitions – The Gillette in 1979 and The Benson & Hedges in 1981 and 1982 – added the NatWest to their trophies by beating Kent in the Final by 24 runs. But even the memory of this great day will probably be eclipsed by the Somerset players when they think of the Semi-Final against Middlesex on the same ground, Lord's.

Somerset, in reply to the 223 scored by Middlesex, were 52 for 5, and hope was fading away fast. It happened that Somerset had in their side just about the only man who could have turned this disaster into triumph – Ian Botham. He scored 96, and when the last over began and the scores were level, Botham knew that provided Somerset did not lose another wicket, then Somerset would have won on less wickets lost. So he played out a maiden over with great self-discipline. It transpired that even if Botham had got out trying to reach his hundred, Somerset would still have won because the result would then have been determined on the faster scoring rate after 30 overs.

Unique Final

The Final was unique in that it was the first 60 over Final to be contested over 50 overs; the rules provided for this to happen if at least thirty minutes was lost at the start of play. This turned out to be a bonus for the spectators, because on a day short of the usual early September sunshine, the light would have prevented a finish being achieved over 60 overs. This would have been a great disappointment for all concerned. As it was, it was a fine game of cricket with the advantage swaying to and fro. It first looked as if Viv Richards might score too many runs for Kent to match. This did not happen, and Chris Tavaré looked to be well in control for Kent until Vic Marks moved in with three vital wickets. Having scored an invaluable 29 runs he was Bob Willis's choice as Man of the Match. Of course he thoroughly deserved it, but Graham Dilley ran him very close by bowling much better than he had done for a long time.

1983 RESULTS

FIRST ROUND – 29 JUNE

Berkshire v Yorkshire at Reading

Berkshire 128-9 in 60 overs (Stevenson 12-2-27-5)
Yorkshire 131-3 in 50.4 overs
Result: Yorkshire won by 7 wickets
Man of the Match: G.B. Stevenson
Adjudicator: P.B.H. May

Cambridgeshire v Middlesex at Wisbech

Cambridgeshire 172 in 58.4 overs (Gadsby 63)
Middlesex 174-2 in 51 overs (Tomlins 80, Slack 60)
Result: Middlesex won by 8 wickets
Man of the Match: N.T. Gadsby
Adjudicators: T.E. Bailey and W. Watson

Dorset v Essex at Bournemouth

Dorset 111 in 59.4 overs
Essex 117-3 in 43.2 overs (McEwan 73*)
Result: Essex won by 7 wickets
Man of the Match: K.S. McEwan
Adjudicator: T.W. Graveney

Durham v Lancashire at Chester-le-Street

Lancashire 211-8 in 60 overs (Hughes 71, Abrahams 51*, Davis 12-4-32-7)
Durham 105 in 46.3 overs (Simmons 12-4-25-4)
Result: Lancashire won by 106 runs
Man of the Match: S.P. Davis
Adjudicator: J.H. Wardle

Gloucestershire v Scotland at Bristol

Gloucestershire 297-8 in 60 overs (Stovold 82, Bainbridge 75, Morton 12-1-47-4)
Scotland 209-6 in 60 overs (Racionzer 61)
Result: Gloucestershire won by 88 runs
Man of the Match: P. Bainbridge
Adjudicator: A.V. Bedser

Hertfordshire v Hampshire at Hitchin

Hertfordshire 159-6 in 60 overs (Collyer 58*, Smith 36)
Hampshire 163-1 in 48.2 overs (Greenidge 55, Smith 66)
Result: Hampshire won by 9 wickets
Man of the Match: F.E. Collyer
Adjudicator: D.C.S. Compton

Ireland v Sussex at Dublin

Sussex 265-7 in 60 overs
Ireland 141 in 52.3 overs (Masood 69)
Result: Sussex won by 124 runs
Man of the Match: M.A. Masood
Adjudicator: T.G. Evans

Kent v Cheshire at Canterbury
Kent 237-8 in 60 overs (Tavaré 99, Cowdrey 52)
Cheshire 101 in 57.5 overs (Ellison 12-3-19-4)
Result: Kent won by 136 runs
Man of the Match: C.J. Tavaré
Adjudicator: Sir Leonard Hutton

Leicestershire v Devon at Leicester
Leicestershire 253-6 in 60 overs (Tolchard 71*)
Devon 121 in 47.1 overs
Result: Leicestershire won by 132 runs
Man of the Match: R.W. Tolchard
Adjudicator: F.S. Trueman

Lincolnshire v Surrey at Sleaford
Surrey 297-6 in 60 overs (Richards 105*, Payne 56*)
Lincolnshire 168 in 59.5 overs (Brooks 51, Payne 12-0-36-5)
Result: Surrey won by 129 runs
Man of the Match: C.J. Richards
Adjudicator: R.T. Simpson

Norfolk v Glamorgan at Norwich
Glamorgan 202-9 in 60 overs
Norfolk 177 in 56.5 overs (Ontong 9-1-49-4)
Result: Glamorgan won by 25 runs
Man of the Match: R.C. Ontong
Adjudicator: D. Kenyon

Shropshire v Somerset at Wellington
Somerset 246 in 60 overs (Richards 74, Perry 11-2-39-4)
Shropshire 159 in 55.2 overs
Result: Somerset won by 87 runs
Man of the Match: B. Perry
Adjudicator: R. Tattersall *Match completed 30 June*

Suffolk v Derbyshire at Bury St. Edmonds
Derbyshire 167-4 in 56 overs (Hill 52)
Suffolk 164-8 in 60 overs (Clements 59)
Result: Derbyshire won by 6 wickets
Man of the Match: A. Hill
Adjudicator: F.R. Brown *Match completed 30 June*

Warwickshire v Oxfordshire at Edgbaston
Warwickshire 274-7 in 60 overs (Smith 60, Kallicharran 70, Amiss 54)
Oxfordshire 256 in 58 overs (Nurton 58, Fowler 119, Willis 11-0-25-4, Gifford 11-0-47-4)
Result: Warwickshire won by 18 runs
Man of the Match: P.A. Fowler
Adjudicator: J.B. Statham

Wiltshire v Northamptonshire at Swindon
Northamptonshire 285-6 in 60 overs (Larkins 65, Lamb 75)
Wiltshire 120 in 45 overs
Result: Northamptonshire won by 165 runs
Man of the Match: A.J. Lamb
Adjudicator: W.J. Edrich

Worcestershire v Nottinghamshire at Worcester
Nottinghamshire 169 in 60 overs (Patel 12-7-9-0)
Worcestershire 167 in 60 overs
Result: Nottinghamshire won by 2 runs
Man of the Match: D.B. D'Oliveira
Adjudicators: J.C. Laker and G.A.R. Lock

SECOND ROUND – 20 JULY

Yorkshire v Northamptonshire at Headingley
Northamptonshire 211-7 in 60 overs (Lamb 76)
Yorkshire 165 in 55.2 overs (Athey 54, Griffiths 10-4-33-5)
Result: Northamptonshire won by 46 runs
Man of the Match: B.J. Griffiths
Adjudicator: J.A. Jameson

Essex v Kent at Chelmsford
Kent 274-8 in 60 overs (Cowdrey 122*)
Essex 270-9 in 60 overs (Gooch 122, Hardie 61, Ellison 12-3-54-4)
Result: Kent won by 4 runs
Man of the Match: C.S. Cowdrey
Adjudicators: J.M. Parks and G.A.R. Lock

Lancashire v Somerset at Old Trafford
Lancashire 163-6 in 60 overs
Somerset 164-2 in 52.5 overs (Popplewell 68*)
Result: Somerset won by 8 wickets
Man of the Match: N.F.M. Popplewell
Adjudicator: P.J. Sharpe

Sussex v Nottinghamshire at Hove
Sussex 227-7 in 60 overs (Imran Khan 114*)
Nottinghamshire 151-8 in 60 overs
Result: Sussex won by 76 runs
Man of the Match: Imran Khan
Adjudicator: R.E. Marshall

Leicestershire v Gloucestershire at Leicester
Leicestershire 302-5 in 60 overs (Gower 138*, Davison 68)
Gloucestershire 306-6 in 59.3 overs (Zaheer Abbas 158)
Result: Gloucestershire won by 4 wickets
Man of the Match: Zaheer Abbas
Adjudicator: B.L. D'Oliveira

Surrey v Warwickshire at The Oval
Surrey 138 in 48.1 overs
Warwickshire 143-1 in 42.5 overs (Lloyd 55*)
Result: Warwickshire won by 9 wickets
Man of the Match: T.A. Lloyd
Adjudicator: F.J. Titmus

Glamorgan v Hampshire at Swansea
Hampshire 294-5 in 60 overs (Greenidge 108, Jesty 84)
Glamorgan 138 in 41.5 overs (Cowley 8.5-4-21-4)
Result: Hampshire won by 156 runs
Man of the Match: T.E. Jesty
Adjudicator: C.A. Milton

Derbyshire v Middlesex at Derby
Middlesex 240-8 in 60 overs (Barlow 62)
Derbyshire 210 in 58.2 overs (Barnett 88, Williams 9-1-36-4)
Result: Middlesex won by 30 runs
Man of the Match: K.J. Barnett
Adjudicator: C. Washbrook

QUARTER-FINALS – 3 AUGUST

Gloucestershire v Hampshire at Bristol
Gloucestershire 252-8 in 60 overs (Romaines 82)
Hampshire 256-4 in 58.2 overs (Smith 101*, Nicholas 51)
Result: Hampshire won by 6 wickets
Man of the Match: C.L. Smith
Adjudicator: F.M. Engineer

Kent v Warwickshire at Canterbury
Kent 251-8 in 60 overs (Cowdrey 56)
Warwickshire 146 in 51.5 overs (Jarvis 5-2-19-4)
Result: Kent won by 105 runs
Man of the Match: K.B.S. Jarvis
Adjudicator: J.M. Parks

Northamptonshire v Middlesex at Northampton
Northamptonshire 198-9 in 60 overs
Middlesex 199-3 in 53.4 overs (Barlow 77, Radley 63)
Result: Middlesex won by 7 wickets
Man of the Match:G.D. Barlow
Adjudicator: B.L. D'Oliveira

Sussex v Somerset at Hove
Sussex 65 in 40.4 overs (Garner 11-7-8-4, Botham 9.4-4-20-4, Gard 5 catches)
Somerset 69-3 in 23.5 overs
Result: Somerset won by 7 wickets
Man of the Match: T. Gard
Adjudicator: C.A. Milton

SEMI-FINALS – 17 AUGUST

Middlesex v Somerset at Lord's
Middlesex 222-9 in 60 overs (Tomlins 58, Slack 57)
Somerset 222-8 in 60 overs (Botham 96*, Popplewell 46)
Result: Somerset won by losing fewer wickets
Man of the Match: I.T. Botham
Adjudicator: B.L. D'Oliveira

Kent v Hampshire at Canterbury
Kent 173 in 59.2 overs (Tavaré 64, Marshall 12-6-15-4, Tremlett 12-1-38-4)
Hampshire 102 in 39.4 overs (Baptiste 12-5-20-5, Cowdrey 12-3-36-4)
Result: Kent won by 71 runs
Man of the Match: E.A. Baptiste
Adjudicator: C.A. Milton

NATWEST BANK TROPHY FINAL

PLAYED AT LORD'S, 3 SEPTEMBER

SOMERSET WON BY 24 RUNS

SOMERSET

P.W. Denning	lbw b Dilley	1
P.M. Roebuck	b Dilley	11
P.A. Slocombe	c Johnson b Baptiste	20
I.V.A. Richards	c Knott b Dilley	51
*I.T. Botham	c Johnson b Cowdrey	9
N.F.M. Popplewell	c Cowdrey b Dilley	35
J.W. Lloyds	lbw b Jarvis	10
V.J. Marks	c Benson b Cowdrey	29
J. Garner	run out	4
C.H. Dredge	not out	3
†T. Gard	did not bat	
Extras (B1, W2, NB17)		20
Total (50 overs) (9 wkts)		193

KENT

M.R. Benson	c Lloyds b Garner	0
G.W. Johnson	b Marks	27
*C.J. Tavaré	c Roebuck b Marks	39
D.G. Aslett	st Gard b Richards	14
C.S. Cowdrey	st Gard b Marks	0
E.A. Baptiste	b Botham	16
†A.P.E. Knott	c Roebuck b Dredge	17
R.M. Ellison	b Garner	21
G.R. Dilley	b Botham	19
D.L. Underwood	not out	5
K.B.S. Jarvis	c Botham b Dredge	3
Extras (B6, LB1, NB1)		8
Total (47.1 overs)		169

Man of the Match: V.J. Marks
Adjudicator: R.G.D. Willis

BOWLING

KENT	*O*	*M*	*R*	*W*
Dilley	10	1	29	4
Ellison	10	1	35	0
Jarvis	10	0	43	1
Baptiste	10	1	37	1
Cowdrey	10	2	29	2
SOMERSET				
Garner	9	2	15	2
Botham	10	0	29	2
Dredge	8.1	0	50	2
Popplewell	1	0	9	0
Marks	10	0	30	3
Richards	9	1	28	1

FALL OF WICKETS

	SM	*K*
1st	10	0
2nd	20	60
3rd	89	73
4th	95	73
5th	112	88
6th	146	112
7th	176	126
8th	190	160
9th	193	162
10th	—	169

NATWEST BANK TROPHY
PRINCIPAL RECORDS 1981–83

Highest Innings Total: 306-8 off 60 overs, Essex v Hertfordshire (Hitchin) 1981.
306-6 off 59.3 overs, Gloucestershire v Leicestershire (Leicester) 1983.
Highest Innings Total by a Minor County: 256 off 58 overs, Oxfordshire v Warwickshire (Birmingham) 1983.
Highest Innings Total by a side batting second: 306-6 off 59.3 overs, Gloucestershire v Leicestershire (Leicester) 1983.
Highest Innings Total by a side batting first and losing: 302-5 off 60 overs, Leicestershire v Gloucestershire (Leicester) 1983.
Lowest Innings Total: 65 off 40.4 overs, Sussex v Somerset (Hove) 1983.
Lowest Innings Total by a First-Class County: 65 off 40.4 overs, Sussex v Somerset (Hove) 1983.
Biggest Victory: 191 runs: Essex beat Hertfordshire (Hitchin) 1981.
There have been five victories by 9 wickets.
Highest Individual Innings: 158 Zaheer Abbas, Gloucestershire v Leicestershire (Leicester) 1983.
Highest Individual Innings by a Minor County Player: 119 P.A. Fowler, Oxfordshire v Warwickshire (Birmingham) 1983.
Centuries: 20 centuries have been scored in the competition.

Record Wicket Partnerships

1st	184	G.A. Gooch & B.R. Hardie, Essex v Hertfordshire (Hitchin)	1981
2nd	149	G.D. Barlow & C.T. Radley, Middlesex v Northamptonshire (Northampton)	1983
3rd	153	A.I. Kallicharran & D.L. Amiss, Warwickshire v Somerset (Taunton)	1982
4th	139	D.S. Steele & G. Miller, Derbyshire v Suffolk (Bury St. Edmunds)	1981
5th	166	M.A. Lynch & G.R.J. Roope, Surrey v Durham (Oval)	1982
6th	104	I.T. Botham & N.F.M. Popplewell, Somerset v Middlesex (Lord's)	1983
7th	160*	C.J. Richards & I.R. Payne, Surrey v Lincolnshire (Sleaford)	1983
8th	54	C.S. Cowdrey & R.M. Ellison, Kent v Essex (Chelmsford)	1983
9th	62	Asif Din & G.C. Small, Warwickshire v Surrey (Lord's)	1982
10th	81	S. Turner & R.E. East, Essex v Yorkshire (Leeds)	1982

Best Bowling: 7-32 S.P. Davis, Durham v Lancashire (Chester-le-Street) 1983.
Hat-Tricks: Nil
Most Wicket-Keeping Dismissals: 6 (5 ct 1st) R.W. Taylor, Derbyshire v Essex (Derby) 1981.

GILLETTE CUP WINNERS

1963 Sussex	1969 Yorkshire	1975 Lancashire
1964 Sussex	1970 Lancashire	1976 Northamptonshire
1965 Yorkshire	1971 Lancashire	1977 Middlesex
1966 Warwickshire	1972 Lancashire	1978 Sussex
1967 Kent	1973 Gloucestershire	1979 Somerset
1968 Warwickshire	1974 Kent	1980 Middlesex

NATWEST BANK TROPHY WINNERS

1981 Derbyshire	1982 Surrey	1983 Somerset

NATWEST BANK TROPHY
PRINCIPAL RECORDS 1963-1983

(including those in the former Gillette Cup)

Highest innings total: 371-4 off 60 overs, Hampshire v Glamorgan (Southampton) 1975.

Highest innings total by a Minor County: 256 off 58 overs, Oxfordshire v Warwickshire (Birmingham) 1983.

Highest innings total by a side batting second: 306-6 off 59.3 overs, Gloucestershire v Leicestershire (Leicester) 1983.

Highest innings total by a side batting first and losing: 302-5 off 60 overs, Leicestershire v Gloucestershire (Leicester) 1983.

Lowest innings total: 41 off 20 overs, Cambridgeshire v Buckinghamshire (Cambridge) 1972; 41 off 19.4 overs, Middlesex v Essex (Westcliff) 1972; 41 off 36.1 overs, Shropshire v Essex (Wellington) 1974.

Lowest innings total by a side batting first and winning: 98 off 56.2 overs, Worcestershire v Durham (Chester-le-Street) 1968.

Highest individual innings: 177 C.G. Greenidge, Hampshire v Glamorgan (Southampton) 1975.

Highest individual innings by a Minor County player: 132 G. Robinson, Lincolnshire v Northumberland (Jesmond) 1971.

Centuries: 93 were scored in the Gillette Cup. 20 have been scored in the NatWest Bank Trophy.

Record Wicket Partnerships

1st	227	R.E. Marshall & B.L. Reed, Hampshire v Bedfordshire (Goldington)	1968
2nd	223	M.J. Smith & C.T. Radley, Middlesex v Hampshire (Lord's)	1977
3rd	160	B. Wood & F.C. Hayes, Lancashire v Warwickshire (Birmingham)	1976
4th	234*	D. Lloyd & C.H. Lloyd, Lancashire v Gloucestershire (Manchester)	1978
5th	166	M.A. Lynch & G.R.J. Roope, Surrey v Durham (Oval)	1982
6th	105	G.S. Sobers & R.A. White, Nottinghamshire v Worcestershire (Worcester)	1974
7th	160*	C.J. Richards & I.R. Payne, Surrey v Lincolnshire (Sleaford)	1983
8th	69	S.J. Rouse & D.J. Brown, Warwickshire v Middlesex (Lord's)	1977
9th	87	M.A. Nash & A.E. Cordle, Glamorgan v Lincolnshire (Swansea)	1974
10th	81	S. Turner & R.E. East, Essex v Yorkshire (Leeds)	1982

Hat-tricks:	J.D.F. Larter, Northamptonshire v Sussex (Northampton)	1963
	D.A.D. Sydenham, Surrey v Cheshire (Hoylake)	1964
	R.N.S. Hobbs, Essex v Middlesex (Lord's)	1968
	N.M. McVicker, Warwickshire v Lincolnshire (Birmingham)	1971

Seven wickets in an innings: 7-15 A.L. Dixon, Kent v Surrey (The Oval) in 1968; 7-30 P.J. Sainsbury, Hampshire v Norfolk (Southampton) in 1965; 7-32 S.P. Davis, Durham v Lancashire (Chester-le-Street) in 1983; 7-33 R.D. Jackman, Surrey v Yorkshire (Harrogate) in 1970.

Most 'Man of the Match' awards: 7 C.H. Lloyd (Lancashire); 6 B.L. D'Oliveira (Worcestershire) and B. Wood (Lancashire); 5 M.C. Cowdrey (Kent), A.W. Greig (Sussex) and R.D.V. Knight (Gloucestershire and Surrey).

WINNERS OF THE 1983 PICK-A-TEAM COMPETITION

First Prize: £300 J. Hart, 17 Shirley Avenue, Shirley, Southampton, Hampshire SO1 5NF.
Second Prize: £200 Andrew Quaif, 79 Torrington Road, Ruislip Manor, Middlesex HA4 0AS.
Third Prize: £150 M. Egerton, 54 Pirie Close, Shirley, Southampton SO1 2QA.
Fourth Prize: £100 Andrew Davies, 5 Closure Place, Peterchurch, Herefordshire.

25 Runners-up: £10 each
Richard Vernon Appleyard, 38 Buckingham Road, Shoreham-by-Sea, West Sussex BN4 5UB; Tom Stacey, Rays Hill, The Mill House, Hawbridge, Nr Chesham, Bucks. HP5 2UJ; Jeremy Hudson, 108 Great Tattenhams, Epsom, Surrey; George Ozols, 26 Kestrel Drive, Sandal, Wakefield WF2 6SB; John Sheather, 188 Elms Vale Road, Dover, Kent CT1 79P; Paul Roberts, 264 Wendover, Aylesbury Estate, London SE17 2UU; A.W. Smith, Hill House, Cambridge Road, Hitchin, Herts.; I.J. Benbow, 119 St John's Avenue, Kidderminster, Worcestershire DY11 6AX; Gordon J. Brown, 9 The Haystacks, Priory Road, High Wycombe, Bucks HP13 6PY; Glen Collinge, 54 Wavertree Road, Nr Blackley, Manchester M9 3LJ; C.G. Edwards, 14 Goodwood Court, Southbourne, Emsworth, Hampshire; J.P. Cockerill, 44 St Nicholas Drive, Wybers Wood, Grimsby, South Humberside DN37 9QB; Tom Naylor, 20 Mixenden Close, Mixenden, Halifax HX2 8RA; James Ozminskys, 2 Little Grove, Rugby, Warwickshire CV22 5NL; Imtiaz Zafar, 34 Hare Street, Rochdale, Lancs OL11 1JP; Christopher Lockwood, 14 Elm Avenue, Goole, North Humberside DN14 6TF; Mike Chant, 49 Plaistow Avenue, Hodge Hill, Birmingham B36 8HQ; Nigel Selley, Tregonger, St Clether, Launceston, Cornwall; Bernard Wentworth, 1 The Ridgeway, Rebington, Wirral, Merseyside; Paul Cooke, 143 Nottingham Road, Mansfield, Notts NE18 4AE; Rod Clarke, 73 High Ash Avenue, Alwoodley, Leeds LS17 8RX; William Fiennes, Broughton Castle, Banbury, Oxon OX15 5EB; Terry Lutteral, 8 Oakleigh Close, Hopwood, Heywood, Lancs OL10 2NJ; David J. Smith, 7 St Michael's Close, Thetford, Norfolk IP24 3EG; Martin Tidy, 18 Stour Lodge, Fulwood, Preston, Lancs PR2 3EY.

The winning team will be found on page 256.

A CLIFF-HANGING BENSON & HEDGES FINAL

The record books will show that Middlesex won the Benson & Hedges Final in 1983, and you cannot take any credit from a side that wins a cup, but it would be a little nearer the mark to suggest that Essex threw it away. Middlesex kept pegging away when all hope seemed lost, and under this pressure Essex caved in to the utter dismay of their many followers. Middlesex 74 for 4 and all out 196; Essex 127 for 1, and sailing home. Their last wicket fell, with night advancing at Lord's, at 192 – five runs short of the target. Worse still they were 185 for 5, needing only 8 runs to win and 5 wickets to fall – and fall they did, like ninepins. Middlesex had practically one man alone to thank for ultimate victory. Clive Radley had scored 89 of the Middlesex total of 196, and without him, Essex would surely, even with a few hiccups, have won with comparative ease.

Talking Point

Middlesex had been involved in a talking point of the season when rain virtually blotted out their Quarter-Final game at Bristol – Gloucestershire 12 for 0 in four overs – and the match was decided by the toss of a coin. What a way to go out of a cup which means a great deal to Counties financially these days. It was not the first time this summer that Middlesex had figured in a no-result game. Not a ball was bowled in their game against Combined Universities; having been expected to beat Gloucestershire, victory over the Combined Universities was even more certain, so having to divide the spoils in the zonal table would have worked to Middlesex's disadvantage. Middlesex also suffered an abandoned match against Glamorgan at Uxbridge – another game they would have been expected to win. Only four Counties did not suffer a no-result game, so severe was the weather in May.

One of the surprises was Somerset's failure to qualify for the Quarter-Finals; having won their first match convincingly against Sussex they were beaten by Essex and Hampshire, although having to score only 139 to win against Hampshire. Kent beat Hampshire at Canterbury in a Quarter-Final game, a success they were to repeat later in the season in the NatWest.

P. C. A. 1984—3

1983 RESULTS

7 MAY

Hampshire v Essex at Southampton
Essex 260-6 in 55 overs
Hampshire 147 in 48.3 overs
Result: Essex won by 113 runs
Gold Award: K.W.R. Fletcher

Northamptonshire v Gloucestershire at Northampton
Northamptonshire 191 in 54.4 overs
Gloucestershire 192-8 in 55 overs
Result: Gloucestershire won by 2 wickets
Gold Award: P. Willey

Worcestershire v Leicestershire at Worcester
Leicestershire 198 in 52.2 overs
Worcestershire 81 in 34.4 overs
Result: Leicestershire won by 117 runs
Gold Award: J.F. Steele

7 & 9 MAY

Somerset v Sussex at Taunton
Somerset 251-7 in 55 overs
Sussex 192 in 51.2 overs
Result: Somerset won by 59 runs
Gold Award: I.V.A. Richards

Surrey v Middlesex at The Oval
Middlesex 273-6 in 55 overs
Surrey 63-2 in 20 overs
Result: Middlesex won on faster scoring rate
Gold Award: R.O. Butcher

Combined Universities v Kent at Cambridge
Kent 276-9 in 55 overs
Combined Universities 212 in 54.4 overs
Result: Kent won by 64 runs
Gold Award: N.R. Taylor

Abandoned matches:
Derbyshire v Yorkshire at Chesterfield
Lancashire v Warwickshire at Manchester
Lancashire 127-6 in 41.4 overs

14 MAY

Essex v Somerset at Chelmsford
Essex 225-8 in 55 overs
Somerset 172 in 46.3 overs
Result: Essex won by 53 runs
Gold Award: G.A. Gooch

Kent v Middlesex at Canterbury
Kent 190-7 in 55 overs
Middlesex 191-5 in 51.4 overs
Result: Middlesex won by 5 wickets
Gold Award: C.T. Radley

Sussex v Minor Counties at Hove
Minor Counties 183-4 in 55 overs
Sussex 184-5 in 48.3 overs
Result: Sussex won by 5 wickets
Gold Award: D. Bailey

Combined Universities v Glamorgan at Cambridge
Glamorgan 225 in 55 overs
Combined Universities 59 in 34 overs
Result: Glamorgan won by 166 runs
Gold Award: Javed Miandad

14 & 16 MAY

Warwickshire v Derbyshire at Birmingham
Warwickshire 287-5 in 55 overs
Derbyshire 226 in 61 overs
Result: Warwickshire won by 61 runs
Gold Award: R.G.D. Willis

15 MAY

Scotland v Worcestershire at Aberdeen
Scotland 105 in 52 overs
Worcestershire 106-5 in 45.5 overs
Result: Worcestershire won by 5 wickets
Gold Award: M.J. Weston

16 MAY

Gloucestershire v Leicestershire at Gloucester
Gloucestershire 59-1 in 27.2 overs
Match abandoned
Result: Void

Yorkshire v Nottinghamshire at Leeds
Nottinghamshire 195-8 in 55 overs
Yorkshire 170 in 51 overs
Result: Nottinghamshire won by 25 runs
Gold Award: C.E.B. Rice

17 MAY

Leicestershire v Northamptonshire at Leicester
Leicestershire 171-7 in 55 overs
Northamptonshire 174-2 in 44 overs
Result: Northamptonshire won by 8 wickets
Gold Award: A.J. Lamb

Nottinghamshire v Derbyshire at Nottingham
Nottinghamshire 226-8 in 55 overs
Derbyshire 175-9 in 55 overs
Result: Nottinghamshire won by 51 runs
Gold Award: R.J. Hadlee

Scotland v Gloucestershire at Glasgow
Scotland 90 in 54.3 overs
Gloucestershire 91-7 in 44.5 overs
Result: Gloucestershire won by 3 wickets
Gold Award: R.C. Russell

Minor Counties v Essex at Slough
Minor Counties 140-9 in 55 overs
Essex 141-1 in 41.1 overs
Result: Essex won by 9 wickets
Gold Award: K.W.R. Fletcher

17 & 18 MAY

Kent v Surrey at Canterbury
Kent 150 in 54.4 overs
Surrey 122 in 47.3 overs
Result: Kent won by 28 runs
Gold Award: G.R. Dilley

Somerset v Hampshire at Taunton
Somerset 116 in 44.1 overs
Hampshire 138 in 52.5 overs
Result: Hampshire won by 22 runs
Gold Award: C.G. Greenidge

Yorkshire v Lancashire at Leeds
Lancashire 222-6 in 55 overs
Yorkshire 87-5 in 35.4 overs
Result: Lancashire won on faster scoring rate
Gold Award: J. O'Shaughnessy

Abandoned match:
Middlesex v Glamorgan at Uxbridge

19 & 20 MAY

Essex v Sussex at Chelmsford
Sussex 208-8 in 55 overs
Essex 173 in 50.3 overs
Result: Sussex won by 35 runs
Gold Award: I.J. Gould

Hampshire v Minor Counties at Bournemouth
Minor Counties 168-9 in 55 overs
Hampshire 169-4 in 47.5 overs
Result: Hampshire won by 6 wickets
Gold Award: T.E. Jesty

Abandoned matches:
Derbyshire v Lancashire at Derby
Lancashire 68-4 in 31 overs
Glamorgan v Surrey at Cardiff
Surrey 142-5 in 44.4 overs
Leicestershire v Scotland at Leicester
Middlesex v Combined Universities at Lord's
Nottinghamshire v Warwickshire at Nottingham
Worcestershire v Northamptonshire at Worcester
Worcestershire 43-5 in 21.4 overs

21 & 23 MAY

Glamorgan v Kent at Swansea
Glamorgan 148-8 in 39 overs
Kent 149-2 in 32.5 overs
Result: Kent won by 8 wickets
Gold Award: C.J. Tavaré

Lancashire v Nottinghamshire at Manchester
Nottinghamshire 154-8 in 45 overs
Lancashire 157-3 in 40.5 overs
Result: Lancashire won by 7 wickets
Gold Award: G. Fowler

Surrey v Combined Universities at The Oval
Combined Universities 155-8 in 55 overs
Surrey 156-3 in 49.2 overs
Result: Surrey won by 7 wickets
Gold Award: S.T. Clarke

23 MAY

Gloucestershire v Worcestershire at Bristol
Worcestershire 197-6 in 37 overs
Gloucestershire 198-3 in 36.2 overs
Result: Gloucestershire won by 7 wickets
Gold Award: Zaheer Abbas

Northamptonshire v Scotland at Northampton
Scotland 135 in 54.3 overs
Northamptonshire 141-3 in 36.1 overs
Result: Northamptonshire won by 7 wickets
Gold Award: G. Cook

Sussex v Hampshire at Hove
Sussex 171 in 53 overs
Hampshire 174-7 in 53.5 overs
Result: Hampshire won by 3 wickets
Gold Award: C.L. Smith

Warwickshire v Yorkshire at Birmingham
Yorkshire 224.5 in 45 overs
Warwickshire 225-5 in 42.1 overs
Result: Warwickshire won by 5 wickets
Gold Award: C.W.J. Athey

Abandoned match:
Minor Counties v Somerset at Slough

QUARTER-FINALS – 1, 2 & 3 JUNE

Essex v Warwickshire at Chelmsford
Essex 231-8 in 55 overs
Warwickshire 168 in 50.3 overs
Result: Essex won by 63 runs
Gold Award: D.R. Pringle

Gloucestershire v Middlesex at Bristol
Gloucestershire 12-0 in 4 overs
Result: Middlesex won on the toss of a coin

Kent v Hampshire at Canterbury
Kent 198-9 in 55 overs
Hampshire 193-9 in 55 overs
Result: Kent won by 5 runs
Gold Award: R.M. Ellison

Lancashire v Northamptonshire at Manchester
Lancashire 290-5 in 55 overs
Northamptonshire 183 in 47.1 overs
Result: Lancashire won by 107 runs
Gold Award: G. Fowler

SEMI-FINALS – 6 JULY

Middlesex v Lancashire at Lord's
Lancashire 90 in 31.5 overs
Middlesex 91-4 in 30.2 overs
Result: Middlesex won by 6 wickets
Gold Award: N.G. Cowans

Kent v Essex at Canterbury
Kent 128 in 51 overs
Essex 130-1 in 46 overs
Result: Essex won by 9 wickets
Gold Award: S. Turner

ZONAL POINTS TABLE

Group A	*P*	*W*	*L*	*NR*	*Pts*
Gloucestershire	4	3	0	1	7
Northamptonshire	4	2	1	1	5
Leicestershire	4	1	1	2	4
Worcestershire	4	1	2	1	3
Scotland	4	0	3	1	1
Group B					
Lancashire	4	2	0	2	6
Warwickshire	4	2	0	2	6
Nottinghamshire	4	2	1	1	5
Derbyshire	4	0	2	2	2
Yorkshire	4	0	3	1	1

Group C	*P*	*W*	*L*	*NP*	*Pts*
Essex	4	3	1	0	6
Hampshire	4	3	1	0	6
Sussex	4	2	2	0	4
Somerset	4	1	2	1	3
Minor Counties	4	0	3	1	1
Group D					
Kent	4	3	1	0	6
Middlesex	4	2	0	2	6
Glamorgan	4	1	1	2	4
Surrey	4	1	2	1	3
Combined Universities	4	0	3	1	1

THE BENSON & HEDGES CUP FINAL

PLAYED AT LORD'S, 23 JULY
MIDDLESEX WON BY 4 RUNS

MIDDLESEX

G.D. Barlow	b Foster	14
W.N. Slack	c Gooch b Foster	1
C.T. Radley	not out	89
*M.W. Gatting	run out	22
K.P. Tomlins	lbw b Gooch	0
J.E. Emburey	c D.E. East b Lever	17
†P.R. Downton	c Fletcher b Foster	10
P.H. Edmonds	b Pringle	9
N.F. Williams	c & b Pringle	13
W.W. Daniel	not out	2
N.G. Cowans	did not bat	
Extras (B3, LB9, W4, NB3)		19
Total (55 overs) (8 wkts)		196

ESSEX

G.A. Gooch	c Downton b Williams	46
B.R. Hardie	c Downton b Cowans	49
K.S. McEwan	c Cowans b Edmonds	34
*K.W.R. Fletcher	c Radley b Edmonds	3
K.R. Pont	hit wicket b Williams	7
D.R. Pringle	lbw b Daniel	16
S. Turner	c sub (J.D. Carr) b Cowans	9
†D.E. East	c Gatting b Cowans	5
R.E. East	run out	0
N.A. Foster	b Cowans	0
J.K. Lever	not out	0
Extras (LB12, W3, NB8)		23
Total (54.1 overs)		192

Gold Award: C.T. Radley.

BOWLING

ESSEX	*O*	*M*	*R*	*W*
Lever	11	1	52	1
Foster	11	2	26	3
Pringle	11	0	54	2
Turner	11	1	24	0
Gooch	11	2	21	1
MIDDLESEX				
Daniel	11	2	34	1
Cowans	10.1	0	39	4
Williams	11	0	45	2
Emburey	11	3	17	0
Edmonds	11	3	34	2

FALL OF WICKETS

	MX	*EX*
1st	10	79
2nd	25	127
3rd	74	135
4th	74	151
5th	123	156
6th	141	185
7th	171	187
8th	191	191
9th	—	192
10th	—	192

BENSON & HEDGES CUP
PRINCIPAL RECORDS

Highest innings total: 350-3 off 55 overs, Essex v Combined Universities (Chelmsford) 1979.
Highest innings total by a side batting second: 291-5 off 53.5 overs, Warwickshire v Lancashire (Manchester) 1981.
Highest innings total by a side batting first and losing: 288-9 off 55 overs, Lancashire v Warwickshire (Manchester) 1981.
Lowest completed innings total: 56 off 26.2 overs, Leicestershire v Minor Counties (Wellington) 1982.
Highest individual innings: 198* G.A. Gooch, Essex v Sussex (Hove) 1982.

Record Wicket Partnerships

1st	241	S.M. Gavaskar & B.C. Rose, Somerset v Kent (Canterbury)	1980
2nd	285*	C.G. Greenidge & D.R. Turner, Hampshire v Minor Counties (South) (Amersham)	1973
3rd	268*	G.A. Gooch & K.W.R. Fletcher, Essex v Sussex (Hove)	1982
4th	184*	D. Lloyd & B.W. Reidy, Lancashire v Derbyshire (Chesterfield)	1980
5th	134	M. Maslin & D.N.F. Slade, Minor Counties (East) v Nottinghamshire (Nottingham)	1976
6th	114	M.J. Khan & G.P. Ellis, Glamorgan v Gloucestershire (Bristol)	1975
7th	149*	J.D. Love & C.M. Old, Yorkshire v Scotland (Bradford)	1981
8th	109	R.E. East & N. Smith, Essex v Northamptonshire (Chelmsford)	1977
9th	81	J.N. Shepherd & D.L. Underwood, Kent v Middlesex (Lord's)	1975
10th	80*	D.L. Bairstow & M. Johnson, Yorkshire v Derbyshire (Derby)	1981

Hat-tricks: G.D. McKenzie, Leicestershire v Worcestershire (Worcester) 1972. K. Higgs, Leicestershire v Surrey (Lord's) 1974. A.A. Jones, Middlesex v Essex (Lord's) 1977. M.J. Procter, Gloucestershire v Hampshire (Southampton) 1977. W. Larkins, Northamptonshire v Combined Universities (Northampton) 1980. E.A. Moseley, Glamorgan v Kent (Cardiff) 1981.
Seven wickets in an innings: 7-12 W.W. Daniel, Middlesex v Minor Counties (East) (Ipswich) 1978, 7-22 J.R. Thomson, Middlesex v Hampshire (Lord's) 1981, 7-32 R.G.D. Willis, Warwickshire v Yorkshire (Birmingham) 1981.
Most 'Gold' awards: 11 B. Wood (10 for Lancashire, 1 for Derbyshire), 9 J.H. Edrich (Surrey), G.A. Gooch (Essex).

BENSON & HEDGES CUP WINNERS

1972 Leicestershire	1978 Kent
1973 Kent	1979 Essex
1974 Surrey	1980 Northamptonshire
1975 Leicestershire	1981 Somerset
1976 Kent	1982 Somerset
1977 Gloucestershire	1983 Middlesex

YORKSHIRE WIN THE JOHN PLAYER

There can be few competitions in any sport anywhere in the world where each side's fortunes vary so much from season to season. For example, Warwickshire, who finished seventeenth in 1982 had been third the previous season. Now they continue in seventeenth place. This year's winners, Yorkshire, were sixteenth in 1982. Middlesex, who were second in 1982, were ninth this time. Nottingham, fifth in 1982 were sixteenth this time. The two principal factors behind this are probably that luck plays a greater part in a 40-over game than in any of the other competitions, and secondly, so does the weather. In a summer of inclement weather at the beginning and at the end of the season, no less than twenty-six games did not achieve a result. Since the points of the leading four Counties were 46, 46, 42, 40, and Yorkshire, the winners (level on points but having won the greater number of away games) were involved in 3 no-result games, Somerset, who were second, 3, Kent who were third, 5, and Sussex, who were fourth, 2, it becomes clear how different things might have been but for rain. It can be said that this is true of all cricket, but in a short game on Sunday afternoons, the effect is more considerable. In addition, of course, a number of games which did finish, did so on mathematical calculations after rain and not on merit.

JOHN PLAYER LEAGUE FINAL TABLE

	P	*W*	*L*	*NR*	*TIE*	*Pts*
Yorkshire (16)	16	10	3	3	0	46
Somerset (9)	16	10	3	3	0	46
Kent (4)	16	8	3	5	0	42
Sussex (1)	16	9	5	2	0	40
Hampshire (5)	16	9	6	1	0	38
Derbyshire (12)	16	7	5	4	0	36
Essex (5)	16	7	5	4	0	36
Lancashire (10)	16	5	5	5	1	32
Middlesex (2)	16	7	7	2	0	32
Glamorgan (10)	16	6	8	2	0	28
Leicestershire (3)	16	4	7	5	0	26
Surrey (12)	16	4	7	5	0	26
Worcestershire (15)	16	4	7	2	3	26
Gloucestershire (14)	16	4	8	4	0	24
Northamptonshire (8)	16	5	10	1	0	22
Nottinghamshire (5)	16	4	9	2	1	22
Warwickshire (17)	16	4	9	2	1	22

1982 positions in brackets.

JOHN PLAYER LEAGUE
PRINCIPAL RECORDS

Highest innings total: 310 for 5 off 40 overs, Essex v Glamorgan (Southend) 1983
Lowest completed innings total: 23 off 19.4 overs, Middlesex v Yorks (Leeds) 1974
Highest individual innings: 176 G.A. Gooch, Essex v Glamorgan (Southend) 1983
Record Wicket Partnerships

1st	224	J.A. Ormrod and D.N. Patel, Worcs v Hants (Southampton)	1982
2nd	273	G.A. Gooch & K.S. McEwan, Essex v Notts (Nottingham)	1983
3rd	215	W. Larkins & R.G. Williams, Northants v Worcs (Luton)	1982
4th	175*	M.J.K. Smith & D.L. Amiss, Warwicks v Yorks (Birmingham)	1970
5th	179	I.T. Botham & I.V.A. Richards, Somerset v Hants (Taunton)	1981
6th	121	C.P. Wilkins & A.J. Borrington, Derby v Warwicks (Chesterfield)	1972
7th	101	S.J. Windaybank & D.A. Graveney, Glos v Notts (Nottingham)	1981
8th	95*	D. Breakwell & K.F. Jennings, Somerset v Notts (Nottingham)	1976
9th	88	S.N. Hartley & A Ramage, Yorks v Middlesex (Lord's)	1982
10th	57	D.A. Graveney & J.B. Mortimore, Glos v Lancs (Tewkesbury)	1973

Four wickets in four balls: A. Ward, Derby v Sussex (Derby) 1970.
Hat-tricks (excluding above): R. Palmer, Somerset v Glos (Bristol) 1970. K.D. Boyce, Essex v Somerset (Westcliff) 1971. G.D. McKenzie, Leics v Essex (Leicester) 1972. R.G.D. Willis, Warwicks v Yorks (Birmingham) 1973. W. Blenkiron, Warwicks v Derby (Buxton) 1974. A. Buss, Sussex v Worcs (Hastings) 1974. J.M. Rice, Hants v Northants (Southampton) 1975. M.A. Nash, Glamorgan v Worcs (Worcester) 1975. A. Hodgson, Northants v Sussex (Northampton) 1976. A.E. Cordle, Glamorgan v Hants (Portsmouth) 1979. C.J. Tunnicliffe, Derby v Worcs (Derby) 1979. M.D. Marshall, Hants v Surrey (Southampton) 1981. I.V.A. Richards, Somerset v Essex (Chelmsford) 1982, P.W. Jarvis, Yorks v Derby (Derby) 1982, R.M. Ellison, Kent v Hants (Canterbury) 1983.
Eight wickets in an innings: 8-26 K.D. Boyce, Essex v Lancs (Manchester) 1971.

JOHN PLAYER LEAGUE CHAMPIONS

1969 Lancashire
1970 Lancashire
1971 Worcestershire
1972 Kent
1973 Kent
1974 Leicester
1975 Hampshire
1976 Kent
1977 Leicestershire
1978 Hampshire
1979 Somerset
1980 Warwickshire
1981 Essex
1982 Sussex
1983 Yorkshire

ESSEX ARE THE COUNTY CHAMPIONS

Essex became County Champions for the second time – they had first won in 1979 – when they nosed out Middlesex into second place, a matter of sixteen points behind. They thus moved up from seventh, their final place in 1982, to oust Middlesex who were County Champions in 1982. Essex owed a great deal to the superlative batting of Ken McEwan, the only player to top 2,000 runs in County Championship cricket, at an average of 68.36, and with a highest score of 189 not out. Graham Gooch came next with 1,227 runs and an average of 36.08. However, it was not simply batting that carried Essex through. John Lever took 98 wickets at an average of 16.80, and Norbert Phillip 68 at 19.67. David East, behind the stumps, had a splendid season with 65 victims, and won the Gordon's Gin Wicket-Keeper of the Year award for 1983. No less than sixteen centuries were scored by Essex players in the Championship, half of them by McEwan. Gooch, incidentally, held 33 catches. Although scoring nearly one thousand less runs, Mike Gatting of Middlesex had a batting average, like McEwan's, in the 'sixties. He was well supported by Graham Barlow and Roland Butcher, before Butcher sustained a nasty injury. John Emburey headed their bowling with 96 wickets at 17.46. Edmonds, another spinner, was second with 72 wickets at 20.70. Cowans, although an England bowler, took as few as 18 County Championship wickets for Middlesex. But the all-round challenge was not strong enough to retain the title Middlesex had won the year before.

Hampshire showed their consistency by finishing in third place exactly as they had done in 1982, and they had no less than three batsmen with averages above sixty: Robin Smith – though he played in only 5 matches – Gordon Greenidge and Chris Smith who was chosen for England during the summer. With three more players with averages in the 'forties Hampshire had powerful batting in depth. Malcolm Marshall topped the bowling with 80 wickets at 16.58. With another bowler of his calibre then Hampshire could well improve from third to first in the very near future.

The most notable improvement on the previous season was

that made by Warwickshire – seventeenth in 1982; fifth in 1983. The Warwickshire evergreens, Alvin Kallicharran and Dennis Amiss, had wonderful seasons, Kallicharran scoring 1,637 runs at an average of 54.56, and Amiss 1,571 at 43.63. Perhaps the most evergreen of them all, Norman Gifford, recruited from Worcestershire, had the most golden season of them all – 99 wickets – what a shame he couldn't have taken just one more. Chris Old, also imported from another County, took 61, though he got himself into hot water after a newspaper article.

It was a particularly disappointing season for one or two Counties, Nottinghamshire in particular, who slid down the table from fourth in 1982 to fourteenth, and Yorkshire from tenth to seventeenth. The idea of Yorkshire at the bottom of the table is hard to swallow, especially for the supporters of this famous County with its great traditions of success. Somerset and Sussex, too, had disappointing seasons, falling from sixth to tenth and from eighth to eleventh respectively. Hampshire were the only County to finish in the same position as in the previous season.

SCHWEPPES COUNTY CHAMPIONSHIP FINAL TABLE

					Bonus Points		
	P	*W*	*L*	*D*	*Bt*	*Bw*	*Pts*
1—Essex (7)	24	11	5	8	69	79	324
2—Middlesex (1)	24	11	4	9	60	72	308
3—Hampshire (3)	24	10	2	12	62	71	289
4—Leicestershire (2)	24	9	3	12	52	81	277
5—Warwickshire (17)	24	10	3	11	52	64	276
6—Northamptonshire (9)	24	7	4	13	63	77	252
7—Kent (13)	24	7	4	13	68	70	250
8—Surrey (5)	24	7	4	13	65	70	247
9—Derbyshire (11)	24	7	5	12	46	65	219
10—Somerset (6)	24	3	7	14	57	75	180
11—Sussex (8)	24	3	10	11	50	72	170
12—Gloucestershire (15)	24	3	8	13	56	61	165
13—Lancashire (12)	24	3	4	17	56	61	165
14—Nottinghamshire (4)	24	3	10	11	39	62	149
15—Glamorgan (16)	24	2	10	12	45	64	141
16—Worcestershire (14)	24	2	11	11	43	54	129
17—Yorkshire (10)	24	1	5	18	45	64	125

1982 positions in brackets.
Hampshire and Derbyshire totals include 12 pts for wins in one innings match.

COUNTY CHAMPIONS

The earliest winners of the title were decided usually by the least matches lost. In 1888 an unofficial points table was introduced and in 1890 the Championship was constituted officially. Since 1977 it has been sponsored by Schweppes.

1864	Surrey
1865	Nottinghamshire
1866	Middlesex
1867	Yorkshire
1868	Nottinghamshire
1869	Nottinghamshire
	Yorkshire
1870	Yorkshire
1871	Nottinghamshire
1872	Nottinghamshire
1873	Gloucestershire
	Nottinghamshire
1874	Gloucestershire
1875	Nottinghamshire
1876	Gloucestershire
1877	Gloucestershire
1878	Undecided
1879	Nottinghamshire
	Lancashire
1880	Nottinghamshire
1881	Lancashire
1882	Nottinghamshire
	Lancashire
1883	Nottinghamshire
1884	Nottinghamshire
1885	Nottinghamshire
1886	Nottinghamshire
1887	Surrey
1888	Surrey
1889	Surrey
	Lancashire
	Nottinghamshire
1890	Surrey
1891	Surrey
1892	Surrey
1893	Yorkshire
1894	Surrey
1895	Surrey
1896	Yorkshire
1897	Lancashire
1898	Yorkshire
1899	Surrey
1900	Yorkshire
1901	Yorkshire
1902	Yorkshire
1903	Middlesex
1904	Lancashire
1905	Yorkshire
1906	Kent
1907	Nottinghamshire
1908	Yorkshire
1909	Kent
1910	Kent
1911	Warwickshire
1912	Yorkshire
1913	Kent
1914	Surrey
1919	Yorkshire
1920	Middlesex
1921	Middlesex
1922	Yorkshire
1923	Yorkshire
1924	Yorkshire
1925	Yorkshire
1926	Lancashire
1927	Lancashire
1928	Lancashire
1929	Nottinghamshire
1930	Lancashire
1931	Yorkshire
1932	Yorkshire
1933	Yorkshire
1934	Lancashire
1935	Yorkshire
1936	Derbyshire
1937	Yorkshire
1938	Yorkshire
1939	Yorkshire
1946	Yorkshire
1947	Middlesex
1948	Glamorgan
1949	Middlesex
	Yorkshire
1950	Lancashire
	Surrey
1951	Warwickshire
1952	Surrey
1953	Surrey
1954	Surrey
1955	Surrey
1956	Surrey
1957	Surrey
1958	Surrey
1959	Yorkshire
1960	Yorkshire
1961	Hampshire
1962	Yorkshire
1963	Yorkshire
1964	Worcestershire
1965	Worcestershire
1966	Yorkshire
1967	Yorkshire
1968	Yorkshire
1969	Glamorgan
1970	Kent
1971	Surrey
1972	Warwickshire
1973	Hampshire
1974	Worcestershire
1975	Leicestershire
1976	Middlesex
1977	Kent
	Middlesex
1978	Kent
1979	Essex
1980	Middlesex
1981	Nottinghamshire
1982	Middlesex
1983	Essex

THE COUNTIES AND THEIR PLAYERS

Compiled by Barry McCaully

with the assistance of **Brian Croudy** (averages and first-class records), **Brian Heald** (Test cricket), **Vic Isaacs** and **Nigel McCaully** (limited-overs cricket).

Abbreviations

B	Born
RHB	Right-hand bat
LHB	Left-hand bat
RF	Right-arm fast
RFM	Right-arm fast medium
RM	Right-arm medium
LF	Left-arm fast
LFM	Left-arm fast medium
LM	Left-arm medium
OB	Off-break
LB	Leg-break
LBG	Leg-break and googly
SLA	Slow left-arm orthodox
SLC	Slow left-arm 'chinaman'
WK	Wicket-keeper
*	Not out or unfinished stand
HS	Highest score
HSUK	Highest score in this country
HSTC	Highest score in Test cricket if different from above
HSC	Highest score for County if different from highest first-class score
HSNW	Highest score NatWest Trophy
HSGC/NW	Highest score in Gillette Cup if higher than NatWest Trophy
HSJPL	Highest score John Player League
HSBH	Highest score Benson & Hedges Cup
BB	Best bowling figures
BBUK	Best bowling figures in this country
BBTC	Best bowling figures in Test cricket if different from above
BBC	Best bowling figures for County if different from above
BBNW	Best bowling figures NatWest Trophy
BBGC/NW	Best bowling figures in Gillette Cup if better than NatWest Trophy
BBJPL	Best bowling figures John Player League
BBBH	Best bowling figures Benson & Hedges Cup

When a player is known by a name other than his first name, the name in question has been underlined.

All Test appearances are complete to 1st September 1983.

'Debut' denotes 'first-class debut' and 'Cap' means '1st XI county cap'.

Wisden 1981 indicates that a player was selected as one of *Wisden*'s Five Cricketers of the Year for the year indicated.

Best Young Cricketer of the Year indicates that a player was so elected by the Cricket Writers Club in the year indicated.

All overseas tours on which a player played first-class cricket are listed.

Qualification for best performances: HS: 10. BB: 3 wkts.

Particulars of players who played in 1983 but have been omitted from the County sections because they are not expected to play in 1984 may be found in the Valete section on page 164.

DERBYSHIRE

Formation of present club: 1870.
Colours: Chocolate, amber and pale blue.
Badge: Rose and crown.
County Champions: 1936.
Nat West Trophy Winners: 1981.
Gillette Cup Finalists: 1969.
Best final position in John Player League: 3rd in 1970.
Benson & Hedges Cup Finalists: 1978.
Nat West Trophy Man of the Match Awards: 6.
Gillette Man of the Match Awards: 15.
Benson & Hedges Gold Awards: 30.

Secretary: R. Pearman, County Cricket Ground, Nottingham Road, Derby DE2 6DA.
Captain: K.J. Barnett

Iain Stuart ANDERSON B Derby 24/4/1960. RHB, OB. Debut 1978. 1233 runs (av. 37.36) in 1983. HS: 112 v Kent (Chesterfield) 1983. HSNW: 47 v Suffolk (Bury St. Edmunds) 1983. HSJPL: 54 v Somerset (Heanor) 1983. HSBH: 32 v Notts (Nottingham) 1983. BB: 4-35 v Australians (Derby) 1981.

Kim John BARNETT B Stoke-on-Trent 17/7/1960. RHB, LB. Debut 1979. Cap 1982. Captain 1984. Played for Boland 1982–83. Tour: D.H. Robins Under-23 in New Zealand 1979-80. NatWest Man of the Match Awards: 2. HS: 121 v Surrey (Oval) 1983. HSNW: 88 v Middlesex (Derby) 1983. HSJPL: 111 v Lancs (Derby) 1982. HSBH: 34 v Notts (Nottingham) 1980. BB: 4-76 v Warwicks (Birmingham) 1980. BBJPL: 3-39 v Yorks (Chesterfield) 1979.

Roger John FINNEY B Darley Dale 2/8/1960. RHB, LM. Debut 1982. HS: 71 v Essex (Derby) 1983. HSNW: 14* v Suffolk (Bury St Edmunds) 1983. HSJPL: 46* v Worcs (Derby) 1983: BB: 5-58 v Warwicks (Birmingham) 1983. BBJPL: 3-27 v Hants (Derby) 1983.

William Peter FOWLER B St. Helen's Lancs. RHB, SLA. Debut and played for Northern Districts 1979–80 and 1980–81. Played for Auckland 1981–82. Debut for Derby in 1982. HS: 91 v Yorks (Chesterfield) 1983: HSJPL: 37 v Worcs (Derby) 1983.

John Harry HAMPSHIRE B Thurnscoe, Yorks 10/2/1941. Son of J. Hampshire (Yorks 1937). RHB, LB. Played for Yorks 1961-81. Cap 1963. Captain 1979-80. Debut for Derby and cap 1982. Played for Tasmania in 1967-68, 1968-69, 1977-78 and 1978-79. Benefit (£28,425) in 1976. Tests: 8 between 1969 and 1975. Scored 107 on debut v West Indies (Lord's). Tours: Cavaliers in West Indies 1964-65; Commonwealth in Pakistan 1967-68; MCC in Ceylon 1969-70; MCC in Australia and New Zealand 1970-71, D.H. Robins in South Africa 1972-73, and West Indies 1974-75, Leics XI in Zimbabwe 1980-81. 1,000 runs (15); 1,596 (av. 53.20) in 1978 best. Gillette Man of the Match: 4. Benson & Hedges Gold Awards: 3. HS: 183* Yorks v Sussex (Hove) 1971. HSTC: 107 v West Indies (Lord's) 1969. HSGC/NW: 110 Yorks v Durham (Middlesbrough) 1978. HSJPL: 119 Yorks v Leics (Hull) 1971. HSBH: 85 Yorks v Warwicks (Leeds) 1980. BB: 7-52 Yorks v Glamorgan (Cardiff) 1963.

DERBYSHIRE

Alan HILL B Buxworth 29/6/1950. RHB, OB. Debut 1972. Cap 1976. Played for Orange Free State in 1976-77. Gillette Man of the Match: 1. Benson & Hedges Gold Award: 1. 1,000 runs (3): 1311 (av. 37.45) in 1983 best. HS: 160* v Warwicks (Coventry) 1976. HSGC/NW: 72 v Middlesex (Derby) 1978. HSJPL: 120 v Northants (Buxton) 1976. HSBH: 102* v Warwicks (Ilkeston) 1978. BB: 3-5 Orange Free State v Northern Transvaal (Pretoria) 1976-77.

Michael Anthony HOLDING B Kingston, Jamaica 16/2/1954. RHB, RF. Debut for Jamaica in 1972-73. *Wisden* 1976. Played for Lancs 1981. Debut for Derby 1983. Tests: 36 for West Indies between 1975-76 and 1982-83. Tours: West Indies to Australia 1975-76, 1981-82, England 1976 and 1980, Australia and New Zealand 1979-80, Pakistan 1980-81. International team to Pakistan 1981-82. HS: 67 International XI v Pakistan (Hyderabad) 1981-82. HSUK: 63 v Glamorgan (Swansea) 1983. HSTC: 58* West Indians v England (St. John's) 1980-81. HSNW: 12* v Northants (Northampton) 1981. BB: 8-92 (14-149 match) West Indies v England (Oval) 1976. BBC: 6-74 v Glos (Manchester) 1981. BBNW: 3-35 v Hants (Southampton) 1981.

Bernard Joseph Michael MAHER B Hillingdon, Middlesex 11/2/1958. RHB, WK. Debut 1981. HS: 52 v Somerset (Derby) 1983. HSJPL: 13* v Yorks (Bradford) 1983.

Geoffrey MILLER B Chesterfield 8/9/1952. RHB, OB. Debut 1973. Best Young Cricketer 1976. Cap 1976. Captain 1979-81. Tests: 32 between 1976 and 1982-83. Tours: India, Sri Lanka and Australia 1976-77, Pakistan and New Zealand 1977-78, Australia 1978-79 and 1979-80, West Indies 1980-81, Australia 1982-83. Benson & Hedges Gold Awards: 4. HS: 98* v Pakistan (Lahore) 1977-78. HSUK: 98 v India (Manchester) 1982. HSC: 95 v Lancs (Manchester) 1978. HSGC/NW: 59* v Worcs (Worcester) 1978. HSJPL: 84 v Somerset (Chesterfield) 1980. HSBH: 88* v Minor Counties (Derby) 1982. BB: 8-70 v Leics (Cleveland) 1982. BBTC: 5-44 v Australia (Sydney) 1978-79. BBNW: 3-28 v Suffolk (Bury St. Edmunds) 1983. BBJPL: 4-22 v Yorks (Huddersfield) 1978. BBBH: 3-23 v Surrey (Derby) 1979.

John Edward MORRIS B Crewe, Cheshire 1/4/1964. RHB, RM. Debut 1982. HS: 58 v Yorks (Sheffield) 1983. HSJPL: 61 v Middlesex (Chesterfield) 1983.

Ole Henrek MORTENSEN B Vejle Jutland Denmark 29/1/1958. RHB, RFM. Debut 1983. HS: 14* v Yorks (Chesterfield) 1983. BB: 6-27 v Yorks (Sheffield) 1983. BBNW: 3-16 v Suffolk (Bury St. Edmunds) 1983. BBJPL: 3-30 v Middlesex (Chesterfield) 1983.

Paul Geoffrey NEWMAN B Leicester 10/1/1959. RHB, RFM. Debut 1980. HS: 39* v Glamorgan (Derby) 1982. HSJPL: 19* v Yorks (Derby) 1982. BB: 5-51 v Essex (Derby) 1981. BBJPL 4-21 v Hants (Derby) 1983. BBBH: 4-48 v Worcs (Worcester) 1982.

Robert William TAYLOR B Stoke-on-Trent 17/7/1941. RHB, WK, RM. Debut 1960 for Minor Counties v South Africans. Debut for Derby 1961. Cap 1962. Captain 1975-76. Testimonial (£6,672) 1973 and 1981. Wisden 1976, MBE 1981. Tests: 51 between 1970-71 and 1982-83 Tours: Ceylon and Far East 1969-70, Australia and New Zealand 1970-71, Rest of the World in Australia 1971-72, West Indies 1973-74, Australia and New Zealand 1974-75, International Wanderers in South Africa 1975-76, Pakistan and New Zealand 1977-78, Australia 1978-79, Australia and India 1979-80, India and Sri Lanka 1981-82, Australia 1982-83.

Dismissed 7 batsmen in an innings (equals Test record) and 10 batsmen in match (all caught) for Test record v India (Bombay) 1979-80. Dismissed 10 batsmen in a match (all ct) v Hants (Chesterfield) 1963 and 7 in an innings (all ct) v Glamorgan (Derby) 1966. Broke world record for dismissals by a wicket-keeper in 1982-83. Gillette Man of the Match: 1. Benson & Hedges Gold Award: 1. HS: 100 v Yorks (Sheffield) 1981. HSTC: 97 v Australia (Adelaide) 1978-79. HSGC/NW: 53* v Middlesex (Lord's) 1975. HSJPL: 43* v Glos (Burton-on-Trent) 1969. HSBH: 31* v Hants (Southampton) 1976.

Colin John TUNNICLIFFE B Derby 11/8/1951. RHB, LFM. Debut 1973. Cap 1977. Hat-trick in JPL v Worcs (Derby) 1979. HS: 91 v Hants (Portsmouth) 1983. HSNW: 14* v Northants (Lord's) 1981. HSJPL: 51* v Northants (Milton Keynes) 1982. HSBH: 28 v Warwicks (Birmingham) 1979. BB: 7-36 v Essex (Chelmsford) 1980. BBNW: 5-50 v Worcs (Worcester) 1981. BBJPL: 5-24 v Northants (Derby) 1981. BBBH: 5-24 v Yorks (Derby) 1981.

John Geoffrey WRIGHT B Darfield, New Zealand 5/7/1954. LHB, RM. Debut for Northern Districts 1975-76. Debut for Derby and Cap 1977. Tests: 25 for New Zealand between 1977-78 and 1983. Tours: New Zealand to England 1978 and 1983; Australia 1980-81; D.H. Robins in Sri Lanka 1977-78. 1,000 runs (5): 1,830 (av. 55.45) in 1982 best. Benson & Hedges Gold Awards: 3. HS: 190 v Yorks (Derby) 1982. HSTC: 141 New Zealand v Australia (Christchurch) 1981-82. HSGC/NW: 87* v Sussex (Hove) 1977. HSJPL: 108 v Warwicks (Coventry) 1983. HSBH: 102 v Worcs (Chesterfield 1977.

N.B. The following players whose particulars appeared in the 1983 Annual have been omitted: M.J. Deakin, P.N. Kirsten, S. Oldham, A. Watts and B. Wood.

DERBYSHIRE

County Averages

Schweppes County Championship: Played 24, won 7, drawn 12, lost 5.

BATTING AND FIELDING

Cap		*M*	*I*	*NO*	*RUNS*	*HS*	*Avge*	*100*	*50*	*Ct*	*St*
1982	K.J. Barnett	24	40	3	1423	121	38.45	3	9	13	—
1976	A. Hill	24	40	5	1311	137*	37.45	4	6	3	—
—	I.S. Anderson	21	37	4	1233	112	37.36	1	9	23	—
1977	J.G. Wright	4	3	0	107	60	35.66	—	1	—	—
1976	G. Miller	21	30	7	699	84	30.39	—	4	13	—
1982	J.H. Hampshire	14	19	2	485	84	28.52	—	3	5	—
—	W.P. Fowler	17	26	2	591	91	24.62	—	5	8	—
—	M.A. Holding	6	5	1	90	63	22.50	—	1	2	—
—	J.E. Morris	10	20	1	361	58	19.00	—	1	4	—
1977	C.J. Tunnicliffe	17	25	0	461	91	18.44	—	2	3	—
1962	R.W. Taylor	16	21	6	267	41*	17.80	—	—	37	2
—	R.J. Finney	20	35	2	578	71	17.51	—	3	4	—
—	B.J.M. Maher	8	12	2	150	52	15.00	—	1	13	3
1980	S. Oldham	15	17	4	177	39	13.61	—	—	3	—
—	D.G. Moir	17	21	3	224	53	12.44	—	1	14	—
—	O.H. Mortensen	18	23	15	76	14*	9.50	—	—	5	—
—	P.G. Newman	7	5	0	14	12	2.80	—	—	3	—

Played in three matches: B. Wood 18, 4.
Played in two matches: A. Watts 6, 33*.

BOWLING

	Type	*O*	*M*	*R*	*W*	*Avge*	*Best*	*5 wI*	*10 wM*
M.A. Holding	**RF**	169	41	451	21	21.47	5-48	3	—
O.H. Mortensen	**RFM**	518.3	108	1605	66	24.31	6-27	3	1
R.J. Finney	**LM**	281.5	43	970	30	32.33	5-58	1	—
D.G. Moir	**SLA**	462.5	121	1385	40	34.62	5-44	2	—
G. Miller	**OB**	492.5	132	1278	37	34.54	5-71	2	—
C.J. Tunnicliffe	**LFM**	428.4	94	1372	39	35.17	4-30	—	—
S. Oldham	**RFM**	387.2	85	1120	31	36.12	4-56	—	—
P.G. Newman	**RFM**	88.5	20	321	7	45.85	3-0	—	—

Also bowled: I.S. Anderson 28-4-146-1; K.J. Barnett 3-0-13-0; W.P. Fowler 60-13-214-2; J.H. Hampshire 2-0-4-0; A. Hill 6.2-3-15-0; J.E. Morris 2-2-0-0; A. Watts 22-4-87-1; B. Wood 20-4-74-0.

County Records

First-class cricket

Highest innings totals:	For	645 v Hants (Derby)	1898
	Agst	662 by Yorks (Chesterfield)	1898
Lowest innings totals:	For	16 v Notts (Nottingham)	1879
	Agst	23 by Hants (Burton-on-Trent)	1958
Highest individual innings:	For	274 G. Davidson v Lancs (Manchester)	1896
	Agst	343* P.A. Perrin for Essex (Chesterfield)	1904
Best bowling in an innings:	For	10-40 W. Bestwick v Glamorgan (Cardiff)	1921
	Agst	10-47 T.F. Smailes for Yorks (Sheffield)	1939
Best bowling in a match:	For	16-84 C. Gladwin v Worcs (Stourbridge)	1952
	Agst	16-101 G. Giffen for Australians (Derby)	1886
Most runs in a season:		2165 (av. 48.11) D.B. Carr	1959
runs in a career:		20516 (av. 31.41) D. Smith	1927-1952
100s in a season:		8 by P.N. Kirsten	1982
100s in a career:		30 by D. Smith	1927-1952
wickets in a season:		168 (av. 19.55) T.B. Mitchell	1935
wickets in a career:		1670 (av. 17.11) H.L. Jackson	1947-1963

RECORD WICKET STANDS

1st	322	H. Storer & J. Bowden v Essex (Derby)	1929
2nd	349	C.S. Elliot & J.D. Eggar v Notts (Nottingham)	1947
3rd	291	P.N. Kirsten & D.S. Steele v Somerset (Taunton)	1981
4th	328	P. Vaulkhard & D. Smith v Notts (Nottingham)	1946
5th	203	C.P. Wilkins & I.R. Buxton v Lancs (Manchester)	1971
6th	212	G.M. Lee & T.S. Worthington v Essex (Chesterfield)	1932
7th	241*	G.H. Pope & A.E.G. Rhodes v Hants (Portsmouth)	1948
8th	182	A.H.M. Jackson & W. Carter v Leics (Leicester)	1922
9th	283	A.R. Warren & J. Chapman v Warwicks (Blackwell)	1910
10th	93	J. Humphries & J. Horsley v Lancs (Derby)	1914

One-day cricket

Highest innings totals:	NatWest Trophy	270-6 v Suffolk (Bury St. Edmund's)	1981
	John Player League	260-6v Glos (Derby)	1972
	Benson & Hedges Cup	284-6 v Worcs (Worcester)	1982
Lowest innings totals:	Gillette Cup/NatWest Trophy	79 v Surrey (Oval)	1967
	John Player League	70 v Surrey (Derby)	1972
	Benson & Hedges Cup	102 v Yorks (Bradford)	1975
Highest individual innings:	NatWest Trophy	110* P.N. Kirsten v Hants (Southampton)	1982
	John Player League	120 A. Hill v Northants (Buxton)	1976
	Benson & Hedges Cup	111* P.J. Sharpe v Glamorgan (Chesterfield)	1976
Best bowling figures:	Gillette Cup/NatWest Trophy	6-18 T.J.P. Eyre v Sussex (Chesterfield)	1969
	John Player League	6-7 M. Hendrick v Notts (Nottingham)	1972
	Benson & Hedges Cup	6-33 E.J. Barlow v Glos (Bristol)	1978

ESSEX

Formation of present club: 1876.
Colours: Blue, Gold and red.
Badge: Three seaxes with word 'Essex' underneath.
County Champions: 1979 and 1983.
Gillette Cup semi-finalists: 1978.
NatWest Trophy semi-finalists: 1981.
John Player League Champions: 1981.
Benson & Hedges Cup winners: 1979.
Benson & Hedges Cup Finalists: 1980 and 1983.
Gillette Man of Match Awards: 14.
NatWest Trophy Man of the Match Awards: 5.
Benson & Hedges Gold Awards: 37.

Secretary: P.J. Edwards, The County Ground, New Writtle Street, Chelmsford CM2 0PG.
Captain: K.W.R. Fletcher.
Prospects of Play Telephone No: Chelmsford matches only. Chelmsford (0245)87921.

David Laurence ACFIELD (Brentwood School and Cambridge) B Chelmsford 24/7/1947. RHB, OB. Debut for Cambridge U and Essex 1966. Blue 1967-68. Cap 1970. Benefit 1981. Best season's bowling: 76 wkst (av. 22.61) in 1981. HS: 42 Cambridge U v Leics (Leicester) 1967. HSC: 38 v Notts (Chelmsford) 1973. BB: 8-55 v Kent (Canterbury) 1981. BBJPL: 5-14 v Northants (Northampton) 1970. Fencing Blue, Olympic International and British Champion (sabre).

David Edward EAST B Clapton 27/7/1959. No relation to R.E. East. RHB, WK. Debut 1981. Cap 1982. NW Man of the Match: 1. HS: 91 v Sussex (Hove) 1983. HSNW: 18 v Derby (Derby) 1981. HSBH: 30 v Hants (Chelmsford) 1982. HSJPL: 43 v Derby (Derby) 1982.

Raymond Eric EAST B Manningtree 20/6/1947. RHB, SLA. Debut 1965. Cap 1967. Played for Overseas XI v Board President's XI (Calcutta) 1980-81. Benefit 1978 (£29,000). Tour: D.H. Robins to South Africa 1973-74. Hat-trick: The Rest v MCC Tour XI (Hove) 1973. BH Gold Awards: 3. HS: 113 v Hants (Chelmsford) 1976. HSGC/NW: 38* v Glos (Chelmsford) 1973. HSJPL: 25* v Glamorgan (Colchester) 1976. HSBH: 54 v Northants (Chelmsford) 1977. BB: 8-30 v Notts (Ilford) 1977. BBGC/NW: 4-28 v Herts (Hitchin) 1976. BBJPL: 6-18 v Yorks (Hull) 1969. BBBH: 5-33 v Kent (Chelmsford) 1975.

Keith William Robert FLETCHER B Worcester 20/5/1944. RHB, LB. Debut 1962. Cap 1963. County Captain 1974. Benefit 1973 (£13,000). *Wisden* 1973. Testimonial: 1982. Tests: 59 between 1968 and 1981-82. Captain in 7 and played in 4 matches v Rest of the World in 1970. Tours: Cavaliers to West Indies 1964-65, MCC Under-25 to Pakistan 1966-67, International XI to India, Pakistan and Ceylon 1967-68, Ceylon and Pakistan 1968-69, Ceylon 1969-70, Australia and New Zealand 1970-71, India, Pakistan and Sri Lanka 1972-73, West Indies 1973-74, Australia and New Zealand 1974-75, India, Sri Lanka and Australia 1976-77, India and Sri Lanka 1981-82 (captain). 1,000 runs (19) – 1,890 (av. 41.08) in 1968 best. Century in each innings (111 and 102*) v Notts (Nottingham) 1976. GC Man of the Match: 1. NW Man of the Match: 1. BH Gold Awards: 7. HS: 228* v Sussex (Hastings) 1968.

HSTC: 216 v New Zealand (Auckland) 1974-75. HSNW: 97 v Kent (Chelmsford) 1982. HSJPL: 99* v Notts (Ilford) 1974. HSBH: 101* v Sussex (Hove) 1982. BB: 5-41 v Middlesex (Colchester) 1979.

Neil Adam FOSTER B Colchester 6/5/1962. RHB, RFM. Debut 1980. Cap 1983. Test: 1 in 1983. HS: 40* v Warwicks (Nuneaton) 1983. HSTC: 10 v New Zealand (Lord's) 1983. HSJPL: 10 v Middlesex (Lord's) 1982. BB: 6-46 v Sussex (Ilford) 1983. BBNW: 3-19 v Dorset (Bournemouth) 1983. BBBH: 3-26 v Middlesex (Lord's) 1983.

Christopher GLADWIN B East Ham 10/5/1962. LHB, RM. Debut 1981. HS: 89 v New Zealanders (Chelmsford) 1983. HSJPL: 36 v Northants (Wellingborough) 1983.

Andrew Kenneth GOLDING B Colchester 5/10/1963. RHB, SLA. One match v New Zealanders 1983.

Graham Alan GOOCH B Leytonstone 23/7/1953. RHB, RM. Debut 1973. Cap 1975. *Wisden* 1979. Played for Western Province 1982-83. Tests: 42 between 1975 and 1981-82. Banned for 3 years for going on SAB tour. Tours: Australia 1978-79, Australia and India 1979-80, West Indies 1980-81, India and Sri Lanka 1981-82, SAB in South Africa 1981-82. Shared county record 2nd wicket partnership (321) with K.S. McEwan v Northants (Ilford) 1978. 1,000 runs (7) – 1,632 (av. 44.10) in 1982 best. Scored 1,363 (av. 54.60) in 1981-82. NW Man of the Match: 1. BH Gold Awards: 9. HS: 205 v Cambridge U (Cambridge) 1980. HSTC: 153 v West Indies (Kingston) 1980-81. HSNW: 122 v Kent (Chelmsford) 1983. HSJPL: 176 v Glamorgan (Southend) 1983. HSBH: 198* v Sussex (Hove) 1982 (Competition Record). BB: 7-14 v Worcs (Ilford) 1982. BBJPL: 3-14 v Derby (Derby) 1978. BBBH: 3-24 v Sussex (Hove) 1982.

Brian Ross HARDIE B Stenhousemuir 14/1/1950. RHB, RM. Debut for Scotland 1970, for Essex 1973. Cap 1974. Benefit 1983. 1,000 runs (8) – 1,522 (av. 43.48) in 1975 best. HS: 162 v Warwicks (Birmingham) 1975. HSGC/NW: 83 v Staffs (Stone) 1976. HSJPL: 108* v Yorks (Chelmsford) 1981. HSBH: 58* v Kent (Canterbury) 1983.

Mervyn Gregory HUGHES B Euroa, Victoria, Australia 23/11/1961. RHB, RFM. Debut for Victoria 1981-82. Played one match for county v New Zealanders 1983. HS: 17 Victoria v New South Wales (St Kilda) 1981-82. HSUK: 10 v New Zealanders (Chelmsford) 1983. BB: 4-69 Victoria v Queensland (Geelong) 1981-82. BBUK: 4-71 v New Zealanders (Chelmsford) 1983.

Robert James LEIPER (Chigwell School) B Woodford Green 30/8/1961. Son of J.M. Leiper (Essex 1950). LHB, RM. Debut 1981, did not play in 1983. HS: 49 v Australians (Chelmsford).

John Kenneth LEVER B Stepney 24/2/1949. RHB, LFM. Debut 1967. Cap 1970. *Wisden* 1978. Benefit: 1980 (£66,110). Played for Natal 1981-82. Tests: 20 between 1976-77 and 1981-82. Banned for 3 years for going on SAB tour. Tours: D.H. Robins to South Africa 1972-73 and 1973-74, India, Sri Lanka and Australia 1976-77, D.H. Robins in Sri Lanka 1977-78, Pakistan and New Zealand 1977-78, Australia 1978-79, Australia and India 1978-79, India and Sri Lanka 1981-82, SAB in South Africa 1981-82. Played for Overseas XI v Board President's XI (Calcutta) 1980-81. 100 wkts (3) – 106 in 1978, 1979 and 1983. GC Man of the Match: 3. NW Man of the

Match: 1. BH Gold Awards: 1. HS: 91 v Glamorgan (Cardiff) 1970. HSTC: 53 v India (Delhi) 1976-77. HSNW: 10* v Sussex (Hove) 1981. HSJPL: 23 v Worcs (Worcester) 1974. HSBH: 12* v Warwicks (Birmingham) 1975. BB: 8-49 v Warwicks (Birmingham) 1979 and v Yorks (Leeds) 1981. BBTC: 7-46 v India (Delhi) 1976-77 on debut. BBGC/NW: 5-8 v Middlesex (Westcliff) 1972. BBJPL: 5-13 v Glamorgan (Ebbw Vale) 1975. BBBH: 5-16 v Middlesex (Chelmsford) 1976.

Alan William LILLEY B Ilford 8/5/1959. RHB, WK. Debut 1978 scoring 100* in second innings. BH Gold Award: 1. HS: 100* v Notts (Nottingham) 1978. HSNW: 40 v Glos (Bristol) 1981. HSJPL: 60 v Northants (Chelmsford) 1980. HSBH: 119 v Combined Universities (Chelmsford) 1979.

Kenneth Scott McEWAN B Bedford, Cap Province, South Africa 16/7/1952. RHB, OB, WK. Played for Easter Province 1972-73 to 1977-78 and 1981-82, for T.N. Pearce's XI v West Indians (Scarborough) 1973, for Western Australia 1979-80 and 1980-81 and for Western Province 1982-83. Debut for country and cap 1974. *Wisden* 1977. Shares 2nd wicket country partnership record with G.A. Gooch. 1,000 runs (10) 2,176 (av. 64.00) in 1983 best. Scored 4 consecutive hundreds including two in match (102 and 116) v Warwicks (Birmingham) 1977. GC Man of the Match: 1. NW Man of the Match: 1. BH Gold Awards: 5. HS: 218 v Sussex (Chelmsford) 1977. HSGC/NW: 119 v Leics (Leicester) 1980. HSJPL: 162* v Notts (Nottingham) 1983. HSBH: 133 v Notts (Chelmsford) 1978. Benefit 1984.

Norbert PHILLIP B Bioche, Dominica 12/6/1948. RHB, RFM. Debut for Windward Islands 1969-70 and has also played for Combined Islands. Debut for county and cap 1978. Tests: 9 for West Indies between 1977-78 and 1978-79. Tour: West Indies in India and Sri Lanka 1978-79. HS: 134 v Glos (Gloucester) 1978. HSTC: 47 West Indies v India (Calcutta) 1978-79, HSGC/NW: 45 v Surrey (Chelmsford) 1980. HSJPL: 95 v Glos (Colchester) 1983. HSBH: 33* v Surrey (Oval) 1982. BB: 7-33 Windward Is v Leeward Is (Roseau) 1981. BBUK: 6-33 v Pakistanis (Chelmsford) 1978. BBTC: 4-48 West Indies v India (Madras) 1978-79. BBNW: 4-26 v Kent (Chelmsford) 1982. BBJPL: 6-13 v Lancs (Manchester) 1982. BBBH: 4-19 v Hants (Chelmsford) 1982.

Keith Rupert PONT B Wanstead 16/1/1953. RHB, RM. Debut 1970. Cap 1976. BH Gold Awards: 2. HS: 125* v Glamorgan (Southend) 1983. HSGC/NW: 39 v Somerset (Taunton) 1978. HSJPL: 55* v Warwicks (Birmingham) 1981. HSBH: 60* v Notts (Ilford) 1976. BB: 5-17 v Glamorgan (Cardiff) 1982. BBJPL: 4-22 v Warwicks (Birmingham) 1981. BBBH: 4-60 v Northants (Lord's) 1980.

Paul John PRICHARD B Billericay 7/1/1965. RHB. Played one JPL match in 1982. Has not played first-class cricket.

Derek Raymond PRINGLE (Felsted School and Cambridge) B Nairobi, Kenya 18/9/1958. 6ft 4½in tall. RHB, RM. Debut 1978. Cap 1982. Blue 1979-80-81. University captain 1982 but did not play in University match. BH Gold Awards: 1. Tour: Australia 1982-83. Tests: 7 in 1982 and 1982-83. HS: 127* Cambridge U v Worcs (Cambridge) 1981. HSC: 54 v Warwicks (Colchester) 1982. HSTC: 47* v Australia (Perth) 1982-83. HSNW: 19 v Kent (Chelmsford) 1983. HSJPL: 52* v Glamorgan (Southend) 1983. HSBH: 58 Combined Universities v Essex (Chelmsford) 1979. BB: 7-32 v Middlesex (Chelmsford) 1983. BBNW: 3-12 v Glos (Bristol) 1981. BBJPL: 3-11 v Worcs (Ilford) 1982. BBBH: 3-14 v Warwicks (Chelmsford) 1983.

Stuart TURNER B Chester 18/7/1943. RHB, RFM. Debut 1965. Cap 1970. Hat-trick v Surrey (Oval) 1981. Played for Natal 1976-77 and 1977-78. Benefit 1979 (£37,288). Tour: D.H. Robins to South Africa 1974-75. BH Gold Awards: 3. HS: 121 v Somerset (Taunton) 1970. HSNW: 50* v Yorks (Leeds) 1982. HSJPL: 87 v Worcs (Chelmsford) 1975. HSBH: 55* v Hants (Chelmsford) 1982. BB: 6-26 v Northants (Northampton) 1977. BBNW: 4-23 v Kent (Chelmsford) 1982, BBJPL: 5-35 v Hants (Chelmsford) 1978. BBBH: 4-19 v Combined Universities (Chelmsford) 1981.

County Averages

Schweppes County Championship: Played 24, won 11, drawn 8, lost 5.
All first-class matches: Played 26, won 11, drawn 9, lost 6.

BATTING AND FIELDING

Cap		*M*	*I*	*NO*	*RUNS*	*HS*	*Avge*	*100*	*50*	*Ct*	*St*
1974	K.S. McEwan	26	39	5	2176	189*	64.00	8	8	19	—
1975	G.A. Gooch	26	38	1	1481	174	40.02	4	7	35	—
1976	K.R. Pont	21	27	4	802	125*	34.86	2	4	3	—
1982	D.R. Pringle	17	21	4	586	102*	34.47	1	2	12	—
—	C. Gladwin	9	14	0	470	89	33.57	—	2	4	—
1963	K.W.R. Fletcher	25	36	3	1077	151*	32.63	2	5	15	—
1974	B.R. Hardie	25	37	2	1042	129	29.77	1	6	30	—
1982	D.E. East	26	32	4	635	91	22.67	—	3	63	5
1983	N.A. Foster	12	14	4	219	40*	21.90	—	—	5	—
1967	R.E. East	21	27	5	420	80*	19.09	—	1	9	—
1978	N. Phillip	19	26	0	413	80	15.88	—	1	8	—
1970	J.K. Lever	18	17	3	211	44	15.07	—	—	7	—
1970	S. Turner	15	19	2	177	30	10.41	—	—	7	—
1970	D.L. Acfield	22	22	13	74	16	8.22	—	—	7	—

Played in two matches: A.W. Lilley 2, 61, 7, 0 (3ct).
Played in one match: A.K. Golding 2, 6*; M.G. Hughes 10, 0.

BOWLING

	Type	*O*	*M*	*R*	*W*	*Avge*	*Best*	*5 wI*	*10 wM*
J.K. Lever	LFM	569	137	1726	106	16.28	7-55	8	3
N. Phillip	RFM	477.2	88	1409	69	20.42	6-4	5	—
N.A. Foster	RM	389	73	1141	51	22.37	6-46	1	—
D.R. Pringle	RM	288.4	54	928	41	22.63	7-32	2	—
S. Turner	RM	282.1	76	624	27	23.11	5-30	1	—
D.L. Acfield	OB	497.1	143	1222	43	28.41	7-100	2	1
R.E. East	SLA	338	96	889	25	35.56	5-45	1	—
K.R. Pont	RM	74	17	211	5	42.20	3-51	—	—
G.A. Gooch	RM	212	46	572	11	52.00	3-40	—	—

Also bowled: K.W.R. Fletcher 8.3-0-57-0; C. Gladwin 3-0-11-0; A.K. Golding 28-3-97-2; M.G. Hughes 31.2-2-162-6; K.S. McEwan 7-0-28-1.

County Records

First-Class Cricket

Highest innings totals:	For	692 v Somerset (Taunton)	1895
	Agst	803-4 by Kent (Brentwood)	1934
Lowest innings totals	For	30 v Yorkshire (Leyton)	1901
	Agst	14 by Surrey (Chelmsford)	1983
Highest individual innings	For	343* P.A. Perrin v Derby (Chesterfield)	1904
	Agst	332 W.H. Ashdown for Kent (Brentwood)	1934
Best bowling in an innings	For	10-32 H. Pickett v Leics (Leyton)	1895
	Agst	10-40 E.G. Dennett for Glos (Bristol)	1906
Best bowling in a match	For	17-119 W. Mead v Hants (Southampton)	1895
	Agst	17-56 C.W.L. Parker for Glos (Gloucester)	1925
Most runs in a season:		2,308 (av. 56.29) J. O'Connor	1934
runs in a career		29,162 (av. 36.18) P.A. Perrin	1896-1928
100s in a season:		9 by J. O'Connor and D.J. Insole	1934 & 1955
100s in a career:		71 by J. O'Connor	1921-1939
wickets in a season:		172 (av. 27.13) T.P.B. Smith	1947
wickets in a career		1610 (av. 26.68) T.P.B. Smith	1929-1951

RECORD WICKET STANDS

1st	270	A.V. Avery & T.C. Dodds v Surrey (Oval)	1946
2nd	321	G.A. Gooch & K.S. McEwan v Northants (Ilford)	1978
3rd	343	P.A. Gibb & R. Horsfall v Kent (Blackheath)	1951
4th	298	A.V. Avery & R. Horsfall v Worcs (Clacton)	1948
5th	287	C.T. Ashton & J. O'Connor v Surrey (Brentwood)	1934
6th	206	J.W.H.T. Douglas & J. O'Connor v Glos (Cheltenham)	1923
		B.R. Knight & R.A.G. Luckin v Middlesex (Brentwood)	1962
7th	261	J.W.H.T. Douglas & J. Freeman v Lancs (Leyton)	1914
8th	263	D.R. Wilcox & R.M. Taylor v Warwicks (Southend)	1946
9th	251	J.W.H.T. Douglas & S.N. Hare v Derby (Leyton)	1921
10th	218	F.H. Vigar & T.P.B. Smith v Derby (Chesterfield)	1947

One-day cricket

Highest innings totals:	Gillette Cup/NatWest Trophy	316-6 v Staffs (Stone)	1976
	John Player League	310-5 v Glamorgan (Southend)	1983
	Benson & Hedges Cup	350-3 v Combined Universities (Chelmsford)	1979
Lowest innings totals:	Gillette Cup/NatWest Trophy	100 v Derby (Brentwood)	1965
	John Player League	69 v Derby (Chesterfield)	1974
	Benson & Hedges Cup	123 v Kent (Canterbury)	1973
Highest individual innings:	Gillette Cup/NatWest Trophy	176 v Glamorgan (Southend)	1983
	John Player League	122 v Kent (Chelmsford)	1983
	Benson & Hedges Cup	198* G.A. Gooch v Sussex (Hove)	1982
Best bowling figures:	Gillette Cup/NatWest Trophy	5-8 J.K. Lever v Middlesex (Westcliff)	1972
	John Player League	8-26 K.D. Boyce v Lancs (Manchester)	1971
	Benson & Hedges Cup	5-16 J.K. Lever v Middlesex (Chelmsford)	1976

GLAMORGAN

Formation of present club: 1888.
Colours: Blue and gold.
Badge: Gold daffodil.
County Champions (2): 1948 and 1969.
Gillette Cup finalists: 1977.
NatWest Trophy Second Round (2): 1981 and 1983.
Best final position in John Player League: 8th in 1977.
Benson & Hedges Cup quarter-finalists (5): 1972, 1973, 1977, 1978 and 1979.
Gillette Man of the Match Awards: 13.
NatWest Man of the Match Awards: 1.
Benson & Hedges Gold Awards: 24.

Secretary: P.G. Carling, 6 High Street, Cardiff CF1 2PW.
Coach: A. Jones, M.B.E.
Captain: M.W.W. Selvey.
Prospects of Play Telephone Nos: Cardiff (0222) 29956 or 387367
Swansea (0792) 466321.

Stephen Royston BARWICK B Neath 6/9/1960. RHB, RM. Debut 1981. HS: 24 v Oxford U (Swansea) 1982. HSJPL: 12* v Sussex (Hastings) 1982. BB: 8-42 v Worcs (Worcester) 1983. BBNW: 4-14 v Hants (Bournemouth) 1981. BBJPL: 3-39 v Sussex (Ebbw Vale) 1981. BBBH: 3-28 v Somerset (Swansea) 1982.

Terry DAVIES B St. Albans, Herts 25/10/1960. RHB, WK. Debut 1979. HS: 69* v Kent (Cardiff) 1983. HSJPL: 46* v Kent (Cardiff) 1983. HSBH: 10 v Somerset (Swansea) 1982.

Winston Walter DAVIS B St Vincent 18/9/1958. RHB, RFM. Played for Windward Islands and Combined Islands 1979-80 to 1982-83. Tour: Young West Indies to Zimbabwe 1981-82. Debut for county 1982. Tests: 1 for West Indies in 1982-83. HS: 60 Windward Islands v Leeward Islands (Antigua) 1979-80. HSUK: 39* v Essex (Southend) 1983. HSTC: 14 West Indies v India (St. John's) 1982-83. BB: 7-101 v Notts (Swansea) 1982. BBNW: 3-26 v Norfolk (Norwich) 1983. BBJPL: 4-24 v Derby (Derby) 1982.

John DERRICK B Cwmaman 15/1/1963. RHB, RM. Debut 1983. HS: 24* v Warwicks (Cardiff) 1983. HSJPL: 18* v Northants (Northampton) 1983.

David Arthur FRANCIS B Clydach 29/11/1953. RHB, OB. Debut 1973. Cap 1982. 1,000 runs (1) – 1,076 (av. 38.42) in 1982. HS: 142* v Kent (Canterbury) 1982. HSGC/NW: 62* v Worcs (Worcester) 1977. HSJPL: 101* v Warwicks (Birmingham) 1980. HSBH: 59 v Warwicks (Birmingham) 1977.

Stephen Peter HENDERSON (Downside, Durham U and Cambridge U) B Oxford 24/9/1958. LHB, RM. Debut for Worcs 1977. Blue 1982-83. Debut for Glamorgan 1983. HS: 209* CU v Middx (Cambridge) 1982. HSC: 135* v Warwicks (Birmingham) 1983.

Geoffrey Clark HOLMES B Newcastle-upon-Tyne 16/9/1958. RHB, RM. Debut 1978. HS: 100* v Glos (Bristol) 1979. HSNW: 11 v Hants (Bournemouth) 1981.

HSJPL: 43* v Hants (Portsmouth) 1979. HSBH: 30 v Glos (Bristol) 1980. BB: 5-86 v Surrey (Oval) 1980. BBJPL: 3-17 v Notts (Swansea) 1980.

John Anthony HOPKINS B Maesteg 16/6/1953. RHB, WK. Younger brother of J.D. Hopkins (Glamorgan and Middlesex). Debut 1970. Cap 1977. Played for Eastern Province 1981-82. 1,000 runs (6) 1,371 (av. 33.43) 1978 best. GC Man of Match: BH Gold Awards: 4. HS: 230 v Worcs (Worcester) 1977. HSGC/NW: 63 v Leics (Swansea) 1977. HSJPL: 130* v Somerset (Bath) 1983. HSBH: 103* v Minor Counties (Swansea) 1980.

JAVED MIANDAD KHAN B Karachi 12/6/1957. RHB, LBG. Debut 1973-74 for Karachi Whites aged 16 years 5 months. Has played for various Karachi, Sind and Habib Bank teams in Pakistan. Played for Sussex 1976-79. Cap 1977. Debut for Glamorgan and cap 1980. *Wisden* 1981. Tests: 52 for Pakistan between 1976-77 and 1982-83, captain in 10 matches. Tours: Pakistan in Sri Lanka 1975-76, Australia and West Indies 1976-77, England 1978, New Zealand and Australia 1978-79, India 1979-80, Australia 1981-82 (captain), England 1982, Australia 1982-83. 1,000 runs (4) 2,083 (av. 69.43) in 1981 best including 8 centuries (both records). Also scored 1,000 runs in an overseas season 7 times. Scored 163 for Pakistan v New Zealand (Lahore) on Test debut. Century in each innings three times. GC Man of the Match: 1. BH Gold Awards: 2. HS: 311 Karachi Whites v National Bank (Karachi) 1974-75. HSUK: 200* v Somerset (Taunton) 1981 and v Essex (Colchester) 1981. HSTC: 280* Pakistan v India (Hyderabad) 1982-83. HSGC/NW: 75 Sussex v Lancs (Hove) 1978. HSJPL: 107* v Leics (Leicester) 1981. HSBH: 95 v Combined Universities (Cambridge) 1983. BB: 7-39 Habib Bank v IDBP (Lahore) 1980-81. BBUK: 4-10 Sussex v Northants (Northampton) 1977. BBTC: 3-74 Pakistan v New Zealand (Hyderabad) 1976-77.

Alan Lewis JONES B Alltwen 1/6/1957. No relation to A. and E.W. Jones. LHB. Debut 1973 aged 16 years 99 days. Cap 1983. 1,000 runs (av. 31.39) in 1983. HS: 99 v Somerset (Swansea) 1983. HSNW: 36 v Hants (Swansea) 1983. HSJPL: 82 v Warwicks (Birmingham) 1982. HSBH: 36 v Worcs (Cardiff) 1979.

Eifion Wyn JONES B Swansea 25/6/1942. Brother of A. Jones. RHB, WK. Debut 1961. Cap 1967. Benefit 1975 (£17,000). Tour: Glamorgan in West Indies 1969-70. BH Gold Award: 1. HS: 146* v Sussex (Hove) 1968. HSGC/NW: 67* v Herts (Swansea) 1969. HSJPL: 48 v Hants (Cardiff) 1971. HSBH: 39* v Minor Counties (West) (Amersham) 1977.

Barry John LLOYD B Neath 6/9/1953. RHB, OB. Debut 1972. Cap 1982. HS: 48 v Sussex (Cardiff) 1982. HSNW: 12 v Warwicks (Cardiff) 1982. HSJPL: 32 v Northants (Northampton) 1983. HSBH: 28* v Somerset (Swansea) 1982. BB: 8-70 v Lancs (Cardiff) 1981. BBJPL: 3-22 v Derby (Derby) 1980. BBBH: 4-26 v Combined Universities (Cardiff) 1982.

Hugh MORRIS (Blundell's School) B Cardiff 5/10/1963. LHB. Debut 1981. HS: 63 v Derby (Derby) 1982. HSJPL: 37 v Somerset (Bath) 1983.

Ezra Alphonse MOSELEY B Christ Church, Barbados 5/1/1958. RHB, RFM. Debut 1980 taking 6-102 v Essex (Swansea) in debut match. Cap 1981. Hat-trick in Benson & Hedges Cup v Kent (Cardiff) 1981. Did not play in 1983. BH Gold Awards: 1. HS: 70* v Kent (Canterbury) 1980. HSJPL: 20 v Worcs (Abergavenny) 1981. BB: 6-23 v Australians (Swansea) 1981. BBJPL: 4-22 v Leics (Leicester) 1981. BBBH: 4-8 v Kent (Cardiff) 1981. Did not play in 1982.

Rodney Craig ONTONG B Johannesburg, South Africa 9/9/1955. RHB, RFM. Played for Border 1972-73 to 1975-76. Transvaal 1976-77 and 1977-78, Northern Transvaal 1978-79 to 1981-82, Boland 1982-83. Debut for county 1975. Cap 1979. 1,000 runs (3) – 1,310 (av. 38.52) in 1983 best. Shared 10th wkt county partnership record (140*) with R.N.S. Hobbs v Hants (Swansea) 1981. NW Man of the Match: 1. BH Gold Awards: 1. HS: 152* v Glos (Swansea) 1982. HSGC/NW: 64 v Somerset (Cardiff) 1978. HSJPL: 100 v Northants (Abergavenny) 1982. HSBH: 50* v Glos (Swansea) 1979. BB: 7-60 Border v Northern Transvaal (Pretoria) 1975-76. BBUK: 6-62 v Sri Lankans (Cardiff) 1981. BBNW: 4-49 v Norfolk (Norwich) 1983. BBJPL: 4-31 v Middlesex (Lord's) 1979. BBBH: 4-28 v Worcs (Cardiff) 1979.

Christopher James Castell ROWE (King's School, Canterbury) B Hong Kong 27/11/1951. RHB, OB. Played for Kent 1974 to 1981. Cap 1977. Joined Glamorgan 1982. Cap 1983. 1,000 runs (2) – 1,071 (av. 32.45) in 1982 best. HS: 147* Kent v Sussex (Canterbury) 1979. HSC: 105 v Somerset (Taunton) 1982. HSNW: 19 v Norfolk (Norwich) 1983. HSJPL: 81 Kent v Somerset (Canterbury) 1980. HSBH: 54 v Somerset (Swansea) 1982. BB: 6-46 Kent v Derby (Dover) 1976. BBC: 4-29 v Notts (Ebbw Vale) 1983. BBJPL: 5-32 Kent v Worcs (Worcester) 1976.

Michael Walter William SELVEY B Chiswick 25/4/1948. RHB, RFM. Played for Surrey 1968 and 1971, Cambridge U (Blue) 1971, Middlesex 1972-82. Cap 1973. Transferred to Glamorgan as captain 1983. Cap 1983. Played for Orange Free State 1973-74. Tours: India, Sri Lanka and Australia 1976-77, Middlesex in Zimbabwe 1980-81, International XI in Pakistan 1981-82. 101 wkts (av. 19.09) in 1978. BH Gold Award: 1. HS: 67 Middlesex v Zimbabwe (Bulawayo) 1980-81. HSUK: 63 v Essex (Cardiff) 1983. HSGC/NW: 14 Middlesex v Derby (Derby) 1978. HSJPL: 38* Middlesex v Essex (Chelmsford) 1979. HSBH: 27* Middlesex v Surrey (Lord's) 1973. BB: 7-20 Middlesex v Glos (Gloucester) 1976. BBC: 6-47 v Oxford U (Oxford) 1983. BBGC/NW: 3-32 Middlesex v Somerset (Lord's) 1977. BBJPL: 5-18 Middlesex v Glamorgan (Cardiff) 1975. BBBH: 5-39 Middlesex v Glos (Lord's) 1972.

John Frederick STEELE B Stafford 23/7/1946. Younger brother of D.S. Steele of Northants. RHB, SLA. Debut 1970 for Leics. Was 12th man for England v Rest of World (Lord's) a month after making debut. Cap 1971. Joined Glamorgan for 1984. Played for Natal in 1973-74, 1975-76 and 1977-78. Benefit 1983 (£33,470). Tour: D.H. Robins to South Africa 1974-75. 1,000 runs (6) – 1,347 runs (av. 31.32) in 1972 best. Shared in 1st wkt partnership record for Leics, 390 with B. Dudleston v Derby (Leicester) 1979. Gillette Man of the Match: 3, for Leics. BH Gold Awards: 4 for Leics. HS: 195 Leics v Derby (Leicester) 1971. HSGC/NW: 108* Leics v Staffs (Longton) 1975. HSJPL: 92 Leics v Essex (Leicester) 1973. HSBH: 91, Leics v Somerset (Leicester) 1974. BB: 7-29 Natal B v Griqualand West (Umzinto) 1973-74 and 7-29 Leics v Glos (Leicester) 1980. BBGC/NW: 5-19 Leics v Essex (Southend) 1977. BBJPL: 5-22 Leics v Glamorgan (Leicester) 1979. BBBH: 5-11 Leics v Worcs (Worcester) 1983.

John Gregory THOMAS B Trebannws 12/8/1960. RHB, RM. Debut 1979. HS: 84 v Surrey (Guildford) 1982. HSNW: 24 v Hants (Swansea) 1983. HSJPL: 37 v Notts (Nottingham) 1983. BB: 5-61 v Derby (Derby) 1982. BBJPL: 5-18 v Yorks (Cardiff) 1983.

Mohammad YOUNIS AHMED (Moslem HS, Lahore) B Jullunder, Pakistan 20/10/1947. LHB, LM/SLA. Younger brother of Saeed Ahmed, Pakistan Test cricketer. Debut 1961-62 for Pakistan Inter Board Schools XI v South Zone at age of 14 years 4 months. Debut for Surrey 1965. Cap 1969. Played for South Australia in 1972-73 Sheffield Shield competition. Tours: Cavaliers to Jamaica 1969-70,

GLAMORGAN

Commonwealth to Pakistan 1970-71, D.H. Robins to South Africa 1973-74 and 1974-75, International Wanderers to South Africa 1974-75 and 1975-76. Debut for Worcs and cap 1979. Joined Glamorgan for 1984. Tests: 2 for Pakistan v New Zealand 1969-70. 1,000 runs (11) – 1,760 runs (av. 47.56) in 1969 best. Shared in 4th wkt partnership record for Worcs, 281 with J.A. Ormrod v Notts (Nottingham) 1979. BH Gold Awards: 3 (1 for Surrey). HS: 221* Worcs v Notts (Nottingham) 1979. HSTC: 62 Pakistan v New Zealand (Karachi) 1969-70. HSGC/NW: 87 Surrey v Middlesex (Oval) 1970. HSJPL: 113 Surrey v Warwicks (Birmingham) 1976 and 113 Worcs v Yorks (Worcester) 1979. HSBH: 115 Worcs v Yorks (Worcester) 1980. BB: 4-10 Surrey v Cambridge U (Cambridge) 1975. BBJPL: 3-26 v Surrey (Oval) 1979. BBBH: 4-37 Worcs v Northants (Northampton) 1980.

N.B. The following players whose particulars appeared in the 1983 Annual have been omitted: S.A.B. Daniels, A. Jones, M.J. Llewellyn and M.A. Nash.

County Averages

Schweppes County Championship: Played 24, won 2, drawn 12, lost 10.
All first-class matches: Played 26, won 2, drawn 14, lost 10.

BATTING AND FIELDING

Cap		*M*	*I*	*NO*	*RUNS*	*HS*	*Avge*	*100*	*50*	*Ct*	*St*
1979	R.C. Ontong	26	43	9	1310	112	38.52	3	7	14	—
1983	A.L. Jones	23	40	7	1036	99	31.39	—	8	15	—
1962	Alan Jones	22	37	2	1059	105	30.25	1	5	7	—
—	S.P. Henderson	10	16	2	411	135*	29.35	1	1	6	—
—	G.C. Holmes	3	6	2	116	46	29.00	—	—	1	—
1977	J.A. Hopkins	25	43	2	1123	116	27.39	2	3	16	—
—	D.A. Francis	23	39	5	903	89*	26.55	—	4	6	—
—	J. Derrick	5	5	3	52	24*	26.00	—	—	3	—
—	T. Davies	11	15	4	260	69*	23.63	—	2	18	2
1983	C.J.C. Rowe	22	33	2	721	82	23.25	—	3	8	—
—	H. Morris	8	14	3	228	34	20.72	—	—	7	—
1967	E.W. Jones	15	18	5	256	39	19.69	—	—	24	1
1980	Javed Miandad	5	6	0	114	89	19.00	—	1	5	—
—	A.H. Wilkins	14	15	3	185	54	15.41	—	1	3	—
—	W.W. Davis	15	18	9	135	39*	15.00	—	—	4	—
1982	B.J. Lloyd	14	12	2	135	38	13.50	—	—	4	—
—	J.G. Thomas	9	9	1	96	23	12.00	—	—	1	—
1983	M.W.W. Selvey	24	24	3	250	63	11.90	—	1	5	—
—	S.R. Barwick	7	7	4	31	22*	10.33	—	—	1	—
1969	M.A. Nash	5	2	1	29	27*	29.00	—	—	3	—

BOWLING

	Type	*O*	*M*	*R*	*W*	*Avge*	*Best*	*5 wI*	*10 wM*
W.W. Davis	**RFM**	452.4	110	1389	52	26.71	7-70	3	—
J.G. Thomas	**RM**	144.5	34	529	19	27.84	5-78	2	—
M.W.W. Selvey	**RFM**	629.4	138	2003	62	32.30	6-47	3	—
R.C. Ontong	**RM**	644	131	2053	56	36.66	6-64	3	—
C.J.C. Rowe	**OB**	473.4	91	1572	38	41.36	4-29	—	—
B.J. Lloyd	**OB**	288.5	47	876	21	41.71	4-93	—	—
S.R. Barwick	**RM**	129.3	21	532	11	48.36	8-42	1	—
A.H. Wilkins	**LM**	205	24	820	12	68.33	2-25	—	—

Also bowled: J. Derrick 8-1-31-0; D.A. Francis 4-0-25-0; S.P. Henderson 8-0-65-2; J.A. Hopkins 4-0-23-0; Javed Miandad 2-0-11-0; A.L. Jones 3-0-25-0; H. Morris 3.5-0-23-0; M.A. Nash 91-29-250-4.

County Records GLAMORGAN

First-class cricket

Highest innings totals:	For	587-8d v Derby (Cardiff)	1951
	Agst	653-6d by Glos (Bristol)	1928
Lowest innings totals:	For	22 v Lancs (Liverpool)	1924
	Agst	33 by Leics (Ebbw Vale)	1965
Highest individual innings:	For	287* D.E. Davies v Glos (Newport)	1939
	Agst	302* W.R. Hammond for Glos (Bristol)	1934
		302 W.R. Hammond for Glos (Newport)	1939
Best bowling in an innings	For	10-51 J. Mercer v Worcs (Worcester)	1936
	Agst	10-18 G. Geary for Leics (Pontypridd)	1929
Best bowling in a match:	For	17-212 J.C. Clay v Worcs (Swansea)	1937
	Agst	16-96 G. Geary for Leics (Pontypridd)	1929
Most runs in a season:		2,083 (av. 69.43) Javed Miandad	1981
runs in a career:		32,997 (av. 32.99) A. Jones	1957-1982
100s in a season:		8 by Javed Miandad	1981
100s in a career:		52 by A. Jones	1957-1983
wickets in a season:		176 (av. 17.34) J.C. Clay	1937
wickets in a career:		2,174 (av. 20.95) D.J. Shepherd	1950-1972

RECORD WICKET STANDS

1st	330	A. Jones & R.C. Fredericks v Northants (Swansea)	1972
2nd	238	A. Jones & A.R. Lewis v Sussex (Hastings)	1962
3rd	313	D.E. Davies & W.E. Jones v Essex (Brentwood)	1948
4th	263	G. Lavis & C. Smart v Worcs (Cardiff)	1934
5th	264	M. Robinson & S.W. Montgomery v Hants (Bournemouth)	1949
6th	230	W.E. Jones & B.L. Muncer v Worcs (Worcester)	1953
7th	195*	W. Wooller & W.E. Jones v Lancs (Liverpool)	1947
8th	202	D. Davies & J.J. Hills v Sussex (Eastbourne)	1928
9th	203*	J.J. Hills & J.C. Clay v Worcs (Swansea)	1929
10th	143	T. Davies & S.A.B. Daniels v Glos (Swansea)	1982

One-day cricket

Highest innings totals:	Gillette Cup/ NatWest Trophy	283-3 v Warwicks (Birmingham)	1976
	John Player League	266-6 v Northants (Wellingborough)	1975
	Benson & Hedges Cup	245-7 v Hants (Swansea)	1982
Lowest innings totals:	Gillette Cup/ NatWest Trophy	76 v Northants (Northampton)	1968
	John Player League	42 v Derby (Swansea)	1979
	Benson & Hedges Cup	68 v Lancs (Manchester)	1973
Highest individual innings:	Gillette Cup/ NatWest Trophy	124* A. Jones v Warwicks (Birmingham)	1976
	John Player League	130* J.A. Hopkins v Somerset	1983
	Benson & Hedges Cup	103* M.A. Nash v Hants (Swansea)	1976
		103* J.A. Hopkins v Minor Counties (Swansea)	1980
Best bowling figures:	Gillette Cup/ NatWest Trophy	5-21 P.M. Walker v Cornwall (Truro)	1970
	John Player League	6-29 M.A. Nash v Worcs (Worcester)	1975
	Benson & Hedges Cup	5-17 A.H. Wilkins v Worcs (Worcester)	1978

GLOUCESTERSHIRE

Formation of present club: 1871.
Colours: Blue, gold, brown, silver, green and red.
Badge: Coat of Arms of the City and County of Bristol.
County Champions (3): 1874, 1876 and 1877.
Joint Champions: 1873.
Gillette Cup Winners: 1973.
Nat West Trophy Quarter-finals (2): 1982 and 1983
Best position in John Player League: 6th in 1969, 1973 and 1977.
Benson & Hedges Cup Winners: 1977.
Gillette Man of the Match Awards: 17.
Natwest Man of the Match Awards: 8
Benson & Hedges Gold Awards: 25.

Secretary: D.G. Collier, County Ground, Nevil Road, Bristol BS7 9EJ.
Captain: D.A. Graveney.
Prospects of Play Telephone Nos: Bristol (0272) 48461
Prospects of Play Telephone Nos: Cheltenham (0242) 22000
Gloucester (0452) 24621

Charles William Jeffrey ATHEY B Middlesbrough 27/9/1957. RHB, RM. Debut for Yorks 1976. Cap 1980. Joined Glos for 1984. Tests: 3 in 1980 and †1980-81. Tours: West Indies 1980-81, D.H. Robins' Under-23 to New Zealand 1979-80. 1,000 runs (2) – 1,339 (av. 43.19) in 1982 best. GC Man of the Match: 2 (for Yorks). BH Gold Awards: 3. HS: 134 Yorks v Derby (Derby) 1982. HSGC/NW: 115 Yorks v Kent (Leeds) 1980. HSJPL: 118 Yorks v Leics (Leicester) 1978. HSBH: 94* Yorks v Warwicks (Leeds) 1983. BB: 3-38 Yorks v Surrey (Oval) 1978. BBJPL: 5-35 Yorks v Derby (Chesterfield) 1981. BBBH: 3-32 Yorks v Middlesex (Lord's) 1979.

Philip BAINBRIDGE B Stoke-on-Trent, Staffordshire 16/4/1958. RHB, RM. Debut 1977. Cap 1981. 1,000 runs (3) 1,217 (av. 29.68) in 1983 best. HS: 146 v New Zealanders (Bristol) 1983. HSNW: 75 v Scotland (Bristol) 1983. HSJPL: 55 v Essex (Colchester) 1983. HSBH: 80 v Somerset (Taunton) 1982. BB: 6-59 v Glamorgan (Swansea) 1982. BBNW: 3-49 v Scotland (Bristol) 1983. BBJPL: 4-27 v Middlesex (Cheltenham) 1982. BBBH: 3-21 v Notts (Gloucester) 1981.

Andrew James BRASSINGTON B Bagnall, Staffordshire 9/8/1954. RHB WK. Debut 1974. Cap 1978. Did not play in 1983. HS: 35 v Sussex (Hastings) 1982. HSGC/NW: 20 v Hants (Bristol) 1979. HSJPL: 14* v Northants (Bristol) 1982.

John Henry CHILDS B Plymouth, Devon 15/8/1951. LHB, SLA. Debut 1975. Cap 1977. BH Gold Award: 1. HS: 34* v Notts (Cheltenham) 1982. HSNW: 14* v Hants (Bristol) 1983. HSJPL: 16* v Notts (Nottingham) 1981. HSBH: 10 v Somerset (Bristol) 1979. BB: 9-56 v Somerset (Bristol) 1981. BBJPL: 4-15 v Northants (Northampton) 1976. BBBH: 3-36 v Glamorgan (Bristol) 1982.

Edward James CUNNINGHAM B Oxford 16/5/1962. LHB. Debut 1982. HS: 29* v Worcs (Bristol) 1983. HSJPL: 22 v Surrey (Oval) 1982.

Richard James DOUGHTY B Bridlington, Yorkshire 17/11/1960. RHB, RM. Debut 1981. HS: 32* v Worcs (Bristol) 1983. HSJPL: 50* v Kent (Bristol) 1983. BB: 6-43 v Glamorgan (Bristol) 1982. BBJPL: 3-34 v Somerset (Bristol) 1982.

David Anthony GRAVENEY (Millfield School) B Bristol 2/1/1953. Son of J.K. Graveney (Glos 1947-64). RHB, SLA. Debut 1972. Cap 1976. Captain 1981. HS: 119 v Oxford University (Oxford) 1980. HSGC/NW: 44 v Surrey (Bristol) 1973. HSJPL: 49 v Notts (Nottingham) 1981. HSBH: 49* v Somerset (Taunton) 1982. BB: 8-85 v Notts (Cheltenham) 1974. BBNW: 5-11 v Ireland (Dublin) 1981. BBJPL: 4-22 v Hants (Lydney) 1974. BBBH: 3-13 v Scotland (Glasgow) 1983.

David Valentine LAWRENCE B Gloucester 28/1/1964. RHB, RFM. Debut 1981. BB: 3-62 v Kent (Bristol) 1983. BBJPL: 4-41 v Somerset (Bath) 1983.

Paul William ROMAINES B Bishop Auckland, Co. Durham 25/12/1955. RHB. Played for Northants 1975-76. Debut for Glos 1982. Cap 1983. HS: 186 v Warwicks (Nuneaton) 1982. HSNW: 82 v Hants (Bristol) 1983. HSJPL: 80* v Hants (Bournemouth) 1983.

Robert Charles (Jack) RUSSELL B Stroud 15/8/1963. LHB, WK. Debut 1981. HS: 64* v Worcs (Bristol) 1983. HSNW: 14* v Leics (Leicester) 1983. HSBH: 36* v Scotland (Glasgow) 1983.

Gary Edward SAINBURY B Wanstead 17/1/1958. RHB, LM. Played for Essex 1979 and 1980. Joined Glos 1983. HS: 13 v Glamorgan (Cheltenham) 1983. BB: 6-66 v Worcs (Worcester) 1983. BBBH: 4-28 v Northants (Northampton) 1983.

John Neil SHEPHERD B St Andrew, Barbados 9/11/1943. RHB, RM. Debut 1964-65 for Barbados v Cavaliers and played for Barbados in 1967-68, 1968-69 and 1970-71. Debut for Kent 1966. Cap 1967. Played for Rhodesia 1975-76. *Wisden* 1978. Benefit 1979 (£58,537). Debut for Glos 1982. Tests: 5 for West Indies in 1969 and 1970-71. Tours: West Indies to England 1969, D.H. Robins to South Africa 1973-74 and 1974-75, International Wanderers to South Africa 1974-75. 1,000 runs (2): 1157 (av. 29.66) in 1968 best. GC Man of the Match: 1 (for Kent). BH Gold Awards: 3 (2 for Kent). HS: 170 Kent v Northants (Folkestone) 1968. HSC: 168 v Warwicks (Birmingham) 1983. HSTC: 32 West Indies v England (Lord's) 1969. HSGC/NW: 101 Kent v Middlesex (Canterbury) 1977. HSJPL: 94 Kent v Hants (Southampton) 1978. HSBH: 96 Kent v Middlesex (Lord's) 1975. BB: 8-40 West Indies v Glos (Bristol) 1969. BBC: 7-50 v Warwicks (Birmingham) 1983. BBTC: 5-104 West Indies v England (Manchester) 1969. BBGC/NW: 4-23 Kent v Essex (Leyton) 1977. BBJPL: 6-52 v Kent (Bristol) 1983. BBBH: 4-25 Kent v Derby (Lord's) 1978. Cap 1983.

Andrew Willis STOVOLD B Bristol 19/3/1953. RHB, WK. Debut 1973. Cap 1976. Played for Orange Free State in 1974-75 and 1975-76. 1,000 runs (5) 1671 (av. 42.84) in 1983 best. NW Man of the Match: 2. BH Gold Awards: 6. HS: 212* v Northants (Northampton) 1982. NSNW: 82 v Scotland (Bristol) 1983. HSJPL: 98* v Kent (Cheltenham) 1977. HSBH: 123 v Combined Universities (Oxford) 1982.

Christopher Richard TREMBATH B London 27/9/1961. RHB, RM. Debut 1982. Did not play in 1983. BB: 5-91 v Oxford U (Oxford) 1982.

GLOUCESTERSHIRE

Anthony John WRIGHT B Stevenage, Hertfordshire 27/6/1962. RHB, RM. Debut 1982. HS: 65 v Warwicks (Nuneaton) and v Somerset (Bristol) 1982. HSNW: 14 v Middlesex (Bristol) 1982. HSJPL: 52 v Essex (Cheltenham) 1982.

Syed ZAHEER ABBAS B Sailkot, Pakistan 24/7/1947. RHB, OB. Wears glasses. Debut for Karachi Whites 1965-66 and has also played for Pakistan International Airways. *Wisden* 1971. Debut for Glos 1972. Cap 1975. Tests: 49 for Pakistan between 1969-70 and 1982 and 5 matches for Rest of the World v Australia 1971-72. Tours: Pakistan to England 1971, 1974 and 1982, Australia and New Zealand 1972-73, Sri Lanka 1975-76, Australia and West Indies 1976-77, New Zealand and Australia 1978-79, India 1979-80, Australia 1981-82, Rest of the World to Australia 1971-72. 1,000 runs (11) – 2,554 (av. 75.11) in 1976 best. Scored 1,597 runs (av. 84.05) in Pakistan in 1973-74 and 1,000 runs overseas 6 times in all. 4 centuries in consecutive innings in 1970-71. Centuries in each innings of a match on 8 occasions (world record and including world record of a double century and century 4 times). Scored 100th century in 1982-83. Benefit 1983. GC Man of the Match: 4. NW Man of the Match: 1. BH Gold Awards: 1. HS: 274 Paistan v England (Birmingham) 1971. HSC: 230* v Kent (Canterbury) 1976. HSNW: 158 v Leics (Leicester) 1983. HSJPL: 129* v Middlesex (Lord's) 1981. HSBH: 98 v Surrey (Oval) 1975. BB: 5-15 Dawood Club v Railways (Lahore) 1975-76. BBUK: 3-32 v Warwicks (Gloucester) 1981.

NB. The following players whose particulars appeared in the 1983 Annual have been omitted: B.C. Broad, A.J. Hignell, Sadiq Mohammad, D.P. Simpkins and F.D. Stephenson.

County Averages

Schweppes County Championship: Played 24, won 3, drawn 12, lost 8, abandoned 1.
All first-class matches: Played 25, won 3, drawn 13, lost 8, abandoned 1

BATTING AND FIELDING

Cap		*M*	*I*	*NO*	*RUNS*	*HS*	*Avge*	*100*	*50*	*Ct*	*St*
1975	Zaheer Abbas	12	19	0	867	116	45.63	3	4	3	—
1976	A.W. Stovold	23	42	3	1671	181	42.84	4	8	16	—
1981	B.C. Broad	16	27	2	1061	145	42.44	3	3	6	—
1983	J.N. Shepherd	23	34	6	1025	168	36.60	2	6	16	—
1983	P.W. Romaines	23	41	4	1286	135	34.75	3	4	9	—
1977	A.J. Hignell	20	37	6	1044	109*	33.67	2	6	6	—
1981	P. Bainbridge	24	43	2	1217	146	29.68	1	6	14	—
—	R.J. Doughty	7	11	6	135	32*	27.00	—	—	—	—
—	A.J. Wright	10	17	2	380	56*	25.33	—	2	5	—
—	R.C. Russell	24	32	9	507	64*	22.04	—	3	46	17
1976	D.A. Graveney	22	28	8	427	94	21.35	—	2	15	—
—	E.J. Cunningham	4	6	1	83	29*	16.60	—	—	4	—
1977	J.H. Childs	20	18	2	82	19	5.12	—	—	5	—
—	G.E. Sainsbury	23	23	8	70	13	4.66	—	—	—	—
—	D.V. Lawrence	8	9	4	22	9	4.40	—	—	1	—

Played in two matches: B. Dudleston 35*, 11, 12.
Played in one match: F.D. Stephenson 21, (2ct); S.R. Tracy 0.

BOWLING

	Type	*O*	*M*	*R*	*W*	*Avge*	*Best*	*5 wI*	*10 wM*
F.D. Stephenson	RF	52.4	13	140	11	12.72	5-56	1	—
J.N. Shepherd	RM	776.1	209	2047	67	30.55	7-50	3	—
D.A. Graveney	SLA	512.1	156	1198	37	32.37	6-88	2	—
G.E. Sainsbury	LM	625.4	150	1937	58	33.39	6-66	3	—
J.H. Childs	SLA	664.5	200	1761	48	36.68	6-81	2	—
P. Bainbridge	RM	416.4	106	1199	30	39.96	4-67	—	—
E.J. Cunningham	OB	49	10	181	4	45.25	2-55	—	—
R.J. Doughty	RM	89.5	11	351	6	58.50	2-43	—	—
D.V. Lawrence	RFM	157	21	613	7	87.57	3-62	—	—

Also bowled: B. Dudleston 27.5-4-164-4; A.J. Hignell 7-1-46-0; S.R. Tracy 21-5-55-2; A.J. Wright 1-0-3-0; Zaheer Abbas 26-7-79-0.

County Records

First-class cricket

Highest innings	For	653-6d v Glamorgan (Bristol)	1928
totals:	Agst	774-7d by Australians (Bristol)	1948
Lowest innings	For	17 v Australians (Cheltenham)	1896
totals:	Agst	12 by Northants (Gloucester)	1907

GLOUCESTERSHIRE

Highest individual innings:	For	318* W.G. Grace v Yorks (Cheltenham)	1876
	Agst	296 A.O. Jones for Notts (Nottingham)	1903
Best bowling in an innings:	For	10-40 E.G. Dennett v Essex (Bristol)	1906
	Agst	10-66 A.A. Mailey for Aust (Cheltenham)	1921
		and K. Smales for Notts (Stroud)	1956
Best bowling in a match:	For	17-56 C.W.L. Parker v Essex (Gloucester)	1925
	Agst	15-87 A.J. Conway for Worcs (Moreton-in-Marsh)	1914
Most runs in a season:		2,860 (av. 69.75) W.R. Hammond	1933
runs in a career:		33,664 (av. 57.05) W.R. Hammond	1920-1951
100s in a season:		13 by W.R. Hammond	1938
100s in a career:		113 by W.R. Hammond	1920-1951
wickets in a season:		222 (av. 16.80 & 16.37) T.W.J. Goddard	1937 & 1947
wickets in a career:		3,170 (av. 19.44) C.W.L. Parker	1903-1935

RECORD WICKET STANDS

1st	395	D.M. Young & R.B. Nicholls v Oxford U (Oxford)	1962
2nd	256	C.T.M. Pugh & T.W. Graveney v Derby (Chesterfield)	1960
3rd	336	W.R. Hammond & B.H. Lyon v Leics (Leicester)	1933
4th	321	W.R. Hammond & W.L. Neale v Leics (Gloucester)	1937
5th	261	W.G. Grace & W.O. Moberley v Yorks (Cheltenham)	1876
6th	320	G.L. Jessop & J.H. Board v Sussex (Hove)	1903
7th	248	W.G. Grace & E.L. Thomas v Sussex (Hove)	1896
8th	239	W.R. Hammond & A.E. Wilson v Lancs (Bristol)	1938
9th	193	W.G. Grace & S.A.P. Kitcat v Sussex (Bristol)	1896
10th	131	W.R. Gouldsworthy & J.G. Bessant v Somerset (Bristol)	1923

One-day cricket

Highest innings totals:	Gillette Cup/NatWest Trophy	327-7 v Berkshire (Reading)	1966
	John Player League	272-4 v Middlesex (Lord's)	1983
	Benson & Hedges Cup	300-4 v Combined Universities (Oxford)	1982
Lowest innings totals:	NatWest Trophy	85 v Essex (Bristol)	1981
	John Player League	49 v Middlesex (Bristol)	1978
	Benson & Hedges Cup	62 v Hants (Bristol)	1975
Highest individual innings:	Gillette Cup/NatWest Trophy	158 Zaheer Abbas v Leics (Leicester)	1983
	John Player League	131 Sadiq Mohammad v Somerset (Imperial Ground, Bristol)	1975
	Benson & Hedges Cup	154* M.J. Procter v Somerset (Taunton)	1972
Best bowling figures:	NatWest Trophy	5-11 D.A. Graveney v Ireland (Dublin)	1981
	John Player League	6-52 v Kent (Bristol)	1983
	Benson & Hedges Cup	6-13 M.J. Procter v Hants (Southampton)	1977

HAMPSHIRE

Formation of present club: 1863.
Colours: Blue, gold and white.
Badge: Tudor rose and crown.
County Champions (2): 1961 and 1973.
Gillette Cup Semi-Finalists (2): 1966 and 1976.
NatWest Trophy Semi-Finalists: 1983.
John Player League Champions (2): 1975 and 1978.
Benson & Hedges Cup Semi-Finalists (2): 1975 and 1977.
Fenner Trophy Winners (3): 1975, 1976 and 1977.
Gillette Man of the Match Awards: 25.
NatWest Man of the Match Awards: 4.
Benson & Hedges Gold Awards: 28.

Secretary: A.K. James, County Cricket Ground, Northlands Road, Southampton SO9 2TY.
Captain: N.E.J. Pocock.

Nigel Geoffrey COWLEY B Shaftesbury (Dorset) 1/3/1953. RHB, OB. Debut 1974. Cap 1978. HS: 109* v Somerset (Taunton) 1977. HSGC/NW: 63* v Glos (Bristol) 1979. HSJPL: 74 v Warwicks (Birmingham) 1981. HSBH: 59 v Glos (Southampton) 1977. BB: 6-48 v Leics (Southampton) 1982. BBGC/NW: 4-20 v Middlesex (Lord's) 1979. BBJPL: 4-42 v Surrey (Portsmouth) 1983. BBBH: 3-39 v Sussex (Bournemouth) 1982.

Kevin St John Dennis EMERY B Swindon, Wiltshire 28/11/1960. RHB, RFM. Debut 1982. HS: 18* v Derby (Derby) 1982. BB: 6-51 v Glamorgan (Portsmouth) 1982. BBJPL: 4-21 v Leics (Leicester) 1982. BBBH: 5-24 v Essex (Chelmsford) 1982.

Christopher Frederick Evelyn GOLDIE (St Paul's School and Cambridge) B Johannesburg, South Africa 2/11/1960. RHB, WK. Debut 1981 for Cambridge U. Blue 1981-82. Debut for county 1983. HS: 77 Cambridge U v Oxford U (Lord's) 1981.

Cuthbert Gordon GREENIDGE B St Peter, Barbados 1/5/1951. RHB, RM. Debut 1970. Cap 1972. Played for Barbados 1972-73 to 1982-83. *Wisden* 1976. Tests: 41 for West Indies between 1974-75 and 1982-83. Tours: West Indies to India, Sri Lanka and Pakistan 1974-75, Australia 1975-76 and 1981-82, England 1976 and 1980, Australia and New Zealand 1979-80, Pakistan 1980-81. 1,000 runs (12) – 1,952 runs (av. 55.77) in 1976 best. Scored two centuries in match (134 and 101) West Indies v England (Manchester) 1976 and (136 and 120) v Kent (Bournemouth) 1978. Benefit 1983. Gillette Man of the Match: 3. NW Man of the Match: 1. BH Gold Awards: 5. HS: 273* D.H. Robins' XI v Pakistanis (Eastbourne) 1974. HSC: 259 v Sussex (Southampton) 1975. HSTC: 154* West Indies v India (St. John's) 1982-83. HSGC/NW: 177 v Glamorgan (Southampton) 1975 – record for GC competition. HSJPL: 163* v Warwicks (Birmingham) 1979. HSBH: 173* v Minor Counties (South) (Amersham) 1973 and shared in partnership of 285* for second wicket with D.R. Turner – the record partnership for all one-day competition. BB: 5-49 v Surrey (Southampton) 1971.

HAMPSHIRE

Trevor Edward JESTY B Gosport 2/6/1948. RHB, RM. Debut 1966. Cap 1971. Played for Border in 1973-74 and Griqualand West in 1974-75, 1975-76 and 1980-81. Played for Canterbury in 1979-80. Benefit in 1982. Tour: Australia and New Zealand 1982-83. International XI in Jamaica 1982-83. 1,000 runs (6) – 1,645 (av. 58.75) in 1982 best. Gillette Man of the Match: 3. NW Man of the Match: 2. BH Gold Awards: 7. HS: 187 v Derby (Derby) 1983. HSGC/NW: 118 v Derby (Derby) 1980. HSJPL: 166* v Surrey (Portsmouth) 1983. HSBH: 105 v Glamorgan (Swansea) 1977. BB: 7-75 v Worcs (Southampton) 1976. BBGC/NW: 6-46 v Glos (Bristol) 1979. BBJPL: 6-20 v Glamorgan (Cardiff) 1976. BBBH: 4-28 v Somerset (Taunton) 1974. Wisden 1982.

Steven John MALONE (King's School, Ely) B Chelmsford 19/10/1953. RHB, RM. Debut for Essex 1975 playing in one match v Cambridge U (Cambridge). Reappeared in corresponding match in 1978. Did not play in 1979 and made debut for Hants in 1980. HS: 23 v Kent (Bournemouth) 1981. HSBH: 16 v Essex (Southampton) 1983. BB: 7-55 v Oxford U (Oxford) 1982. BBNW: 5-34 v Cheshire (Southampton) 1981. BBJPL: 4-39 v Yorks (Basingstoke) 1980. BBBH: 4-25 v Minor Counties (Bournemouth) 1983.

Malcolm Denzil MARSHALL B St Michael, Barbados 18/4/1958. RHB, RF. Played for Barbados 1977-78 to 1982-83. Debut for county 1979. Cap 1981. Tests: 12 between 1978-79 and 1980-81. Tours: West Indies to India and Sri Lanka 1978-79, Australia and New Zealand 1979-80, England 1980, Pakistan 1980-81, Zimbabwe 1981-82, Australia 1981-82. Hat-trick in John Player League v Surrey (Southampton) 1981. 134 wkts (av. 15.73) in 1982. HS: 116* v Lancs (Southampton) 1982. HSTC: 45 West Indies v England (Oval) 1980. HSGC/NW: 21* v Middlesex (Lord's) 1979. HSJPL: 46 v Leics (Leicester) 1982. HSBH: 21 v Kent (Canterbury) 1982. BB: 8-71 v Worcs (Southampton) 1982. BBTC: 5-37 West Indies v India (Port of Spain) 1982-83. BBNW: 4-15 v Kent (Canterbury) 1983. BBJPL: 5-13 v Glamorgan (Portsmouth) 1979. BBBH: 4-26 v Kent (Canterbury) 1983. Wisden 1982.

Rajesh Jaman MARU B Nairobi, Kenya 28/10/1962. RHB, SLA. Debut for Middlesex 1980. Has joined Hants for 1984. Tour: Middlesex to Zimbabwe 1980-81. HS: 25 Middlesex v Zimbabwe (Bulawayo) 1980-81. HSUK: 18 Middlesex v Glamorgan (Swansea) 1982. BB: 4-30 Middlesex v Oxford U (Oxford) 1982.

Mark Charles Jefford NICHOLAS (Bradfield College) B London 29/9/1957. RHB, RM. Debut 1978. Cap 1982. 1,000 runs (2): 1418 (av. 37.31) in 1983 best. HS: 206* v Oxford U (Oxford) 1982. HSNW: 51 v Glos (Bristol) 1983. HSJPL: 76 v Lancs (Portsmouth) 1982. HSBH: 44 v Essex (Chelmsford) 1982. BB: 5-45 v Worcs (Southampton) 1983. BBJPL: 3-30 v Kent (Canterbury) 1983. BBBH: 3-29 v Surrey (Oval) 1980.

Robert James PARKS (Eastbourne GS) B Cuckfield, Sussex 15/6/1959. Son of J.M. Parks and grandson of J.H. Parks. RHB, WK. Debut 1980. Cap 1982. Dismissed 10 batsmen (all ct.) in match v Derby (Portsmouth) 1981. HS: 64* v Essex (Chelmsford) 1980. HSNW: 19* v Glamorgan (Cardiff) 1981. HSJPL: 36* v Leics (Leicester) 1982. HSBH: 11 v Middlesex (Lord's) 1981.

Nicholas Edward Julian POCOCK (Shrewsbury School) B Maracaibo, Venezuela 15/12/1951. RHB, LM. Debut 1976. Appointed county captain in 1980. Cap 1980. HS: 164 v Lancs (Southampton) 1982. HSGC/NW: 73* v Derby (Derby) 1980. HSJPL: 53* v Northants (Northampton) 1978. HSBH: 43* v Minor Counties (Bournemouth) 1983.

Christopher Lyall (Kippy) SMITH (Northlands HS, Durkan) B Durban, South Africa 15/10/1958. Older brother of R.A. Smith. RHB, OB. Played for Natal B 1977-78 to 1982-83. Debut for Glamorgan 1979. One match v Sri Lankans (Swansea). Debut for Hants 1980. Cap 1981. Tests: 2 in 1983. 1,000 runs (2): 1,923 (av. 53.41) in 1983 best. NW Man of the Match: 1. BH Gold Awards: 1. HS: 193 v Derby (Derby) 1983. HSTC: 43 v New Zealand (Lord's) 1983. HSNW: 101* v Glos (Bristol) 1983. HSJPL: 71 v Worcs (Worcester) 1983. HSBH: 63* v Sussex (Hove) 1983. BB: 3-35 v Glamorgan (Southampton) 1983.

Robin Arnold SMITH B Durban, South Africa 13/9/1963. Younger brother of C.L. Smith. RHB, LB. Played for Natal 1980-81 to 1982-83. Debut for Hants 1982. HS: 104* v Sussex (Basingstoke) 1983. HSJPL: 22* v Leics (Basingstoke) 1983.

Keith STEVENSON B Derby 6/10/1950. RHB, RFM. Played for Derby 1974 to 1977. Debut for Hants 1978. Cap 1979. HS: 33 Derby v Northants (Chesterfield) 1974. HSC: 31 v Derby (Portsmouth) 1981. HSGC/NW: 14 Derby v Surrey (Ilkeston) 1976. HSJPL: 11* v Somerset (Taunton) 1981. BB: 7-22 v Oxford U (Oxford) 1979. BBGC/NW: 4-21 Derby v Surrey (Ilkeston) 1976. BBJPL: 3-22 v Essex (Chelmsford) 1980. BBBH: 4-18 v Middlesex (Lord's) 1981.

Vivian Paul TERRY (Millfield School) B Osnabruck, West Germany 14/1/1959. RHB, RM. Debut 1978. Cap 1983. 1,096 runs (av. 40.59) in 1983. HS: 115 v Sussex (Eastbourne) 1983. HSNW: 21 v Glos (Bristol) 1983. HSJPL: 100* v Leics (Basingstoke) 1983: HSBH: 72 v Kent (Canterbury) 1983.

Timothy Maurice TREMLETT B Wellington, Somerset 26/7/1956. Son of M.E. Tremlett, former Somerset player. RHB, RM. Debut 1976. Cap 1983. HS: 88 v Lancs (Manchester) 1981. HSNW: 11 v Kent (Canterbury) 1983. HSJPL: 28 v Glos (Cheltenham) 1980. HSBH: 29 v Surrey (Bournemouth) 1981. BB: 6-82 v Derby (Portsmouth). BBNW: 4-38 v Kent (Canterbury) 1983. BBJPL: 4-22 v Lancs (Manchester) 1981. BBBH: 3-21 v Combined Universities (Cambridge) 1978.

David Roy TURNER B Chippenham, Wilts 5/2/1949. LHB, RM. Debut 1966. Cap 1970. Played for Western Province in 1977-78. Benefit in 1981. Tour: D.H. Robins to South Africa 1972-73. 1,000 runs (6) – 1,269 runs (av. 36.25) in 1976 best. Gillette Man of the Match: 1. BH Gold Awards: 4. HS: 181* v Surrey (Oval) 1969. HSGC/NW: 86 v Northants (Southampton) 1976. HSJPL: 109 v Surrey (Oval) 1980. HSBH: 123* v Minor Counties (South) (Amersham) 1973.

NB. The following players whose particulars appeared in the 1983 Annual have been omitted: C.C. Curzon and J.W. Southern.

County Averages

Schweppes County Championships: Played 24, won 10, drawn 12, lost 2.
All first-class matches: Played 26, won 11, drawn 12, lost 3.

BATTING AND FIELDING

Cap		*M*	*I*	*NO*	*RUNS*	*HS*	*Avge*	*100*	*50*	*Ct*	*St*
1972	C.G. Greenidge	15	27	5	1438	154	65.36	4	9	21	—
1981	C.L. Smith	21	35	3	1845	193	57.65	6	8	17	—
—	R.A. Smith	7	12	3	434	104*	48.22	3	—	1	—
1981	M.D. Marshall	16	16	4	563	112	46.91	2	2	6	—
1971	T.E. Jesty	20	30	5	1072	187	42.88	1	5	12	—
1970	D.R. Turner	12	17	3	598	122*	42.71	1	3	3	—
1983	V.P. Terry	20	33	6	1096	115	40.59	3	4	15	—
1982	M.C.J. Nicholas	26	43	5	1418	158	37.31	3	6	26	—
1980	N.E.J. Pocock	26	35	8	755	60*	27.96	—	6	30	—
1978	N.G. Cowley	23	27	9	351	29	19.50	—	—	7	—
1983	T.M. Tremlett	24	19	5	263	59	18.78	—	1	18	—
1978	J.W. Southern	15	13	5	146	45*	18.25	—	—	8	—
1982	R.J. Parks	25	15	2	180	52	13.84	—	1	51	9
1979	K. Stevenson	7	9	3	77	25	12.83	—	—	2	—
—	S.J. Malone	22	16	6	47	12	4.70	—	—	4	—

Played in six matches: K.S.D. Emery 8.
Played in one match: C.F.E. Goldie 6,0* (2ct, 1st).

BOWLING

	Type	*O*	*M*	*R*	*W*	*Avge*	*Best*	*5 wI*	*10 wM*
M.D. Marshall	**RF**	532.5	143	1327	80	16.58	7-29	5	1
T.M. Tremlett	**RM**	600.2	198	1346	63	21.36	6-82	1	—
N.G. Cowley	**OB**	440.3	147	1053	41	25.68	4-10	—	—
M.C.J. Nicholas	**RM**	274.2	74	774	27	28.66	5-45	1	—
K. Stevenson	**RFM**	187.5	39	656	21	31.23	5-81	1	—
C.L. Smith	**OB**	155	42	516	15	34.40	3-35	—	—
J.W. Southern	**SLA**	369.5	115	966	27	35.77	5-60	2	—
S.J. Malone	**RM**	547.1	123	1797	48	37.43	4-39	—	—
T.E. Jesty	**RM**	256.5	70	804	21	38.28	3-48	—	—

Also bowled: K.S.D. Emery 94-28-262-5; N.E.J. Pocock 29-3-138-1; R.A. Smith 2-0-19-0.

County Records

First-class cricket

Highest innings totals:	For	672-7d v Somerset (Taunton)	1899
	Agst	742 by Surrey (Oval)	1909
Lowest innings totals:	For	15 v Warwicks (Birmingham)	1922
	Agst	23 by Yorks (Middlesbrough)	1965
Highest individual innings:	For	316 R.H. Moore v Warwicks (Bournemouth)	1937
	Agst	302* P. Holmes for Yorks (Portsmouth)	1920

Best bowling in an innings:	For	9-25 R.M.H. Cottam v Lancs (Manchester)	1965
	Agst	9-21 L.B. Richmond for Notts (Nottingham)	1922
Best bowling in a match:	For	16-88 J.A. Newman v Somerset (Weston-super-Mare)	1927
	Agst	17-119 W. Mead for Essex (Southampton)	1895
Most runs in a season:		2,854 (av. 79.27) C.P. Mead	1928
runs in a career:		48,892 (av. 48.84) C.P. Mead	1905-1936
100s in a season:		12 by C.P. Mead	1928
100s in a career:		138 by C.P. Mead	1905-1936
wickets in a season:		190 (av. 15.61) A.S. Kennedy	1922
wickets in a career:		2,669 (av. 18.22) D. Shackleton	1948-1969

RECORD WICKET STANDS

1st	249	R.E. Marshall & J.R. Gray v Middlesex (Portsmouth)	1960
2nd	321	G. Brown & E.I.M. Barrett v Glos (Southampton)	1920
3rd	344	C.P. Mead & G. Brown v Yorks (Portsmouth)	1927
4th	263	R.E. Marshall & D.A. Livingstone v Middlesex (Lord's)	1970
5th	235	G. Hill & D.F. Walker v Sussex (Portsmouth)	1937
6th	411	R.M. Poore & E.G. Wynyard v Somerset (Taunton)	1899
7th	325	G. Brown & C.H. Abercrombie v Essex (Leyton)	1913
8th	178	C.P. Mead & C.P. Brutton v Worcs (Bournemouth)	1925
9th	230	D.A. Livingstone & A.T. Castell v Surrey (Southampton)	1962
10th	192	A. Bowell & W.H. Livsey v Worcs (Bournemouth)	1921

NB. A partnership of 334 for the first wicket by B.A. Richards, C.G. Greenidge and D.R. Turner occurred against Kent at Southampton in 1973. Richards retired hurt after 241 runs had been scored.

One-day cricket

Highest innings totals:	Gillette Cup/ NatWest Trophy	371-4 v Glamorgan (Southampton)	1975
	John Player League	292-1 v Surrey (Portsmouth)	1983
	Benson & Hedges Cup	321-1 v Minor Counties (South) (Amersham)	1973
Lowest innings totals:	Gillette Cup/ NatWest Trophy	98 v Lancs (Manchester)	1975
	John Player League	43 v Essex (Basingstoke)	1972
	Benson & Hedges Cup	94 v Glamorgan (Swansea)	1973
Highest individual innings:	Gillette Cup/ NatWest Trophy	177 C.G. Greenidge v Glamorgan (Southampton)	1975
	John Player League	166* T.E. Jesty v Surrey (Portsmouth)	1983
	Benson & Hedges Cup	173* C.G. Greenidge v Minor Counties (South) (Amersham)	1973
Best bowling figures:	Gillette Cup/ NatWest Trophy	7-30 P.J. Sainsbury v Norfolk (Southampton)	1965
	John Player League	6-20 T.E. Jesty v Glamorgan (Cardiff)	1975
	Benson & Hedges Cup	5-24 R.S. Herman v Glos (Bristol)	1975
		5-24 K.S.D. Emery v Essex (Chelmsford)	1982

KENT

Formation of present club: 1859, re-organised 1870.
Colours: Maroon and white.
Badge: White horse.
County Champions (6): 1906, 1909, 1910, 1913, 1970 and 1978.
Joint Champions: 1977.
Gillette Cup Winners (2): 1967 and 1974.
Gillette Cup Finalists: 1971.
NatWest Trophy Finalists: 1983.
John Player League Champions (3): 1972, 1973 and 1976.
Benson & Hedges Cup Winners (3): 1973, 1976 and 1978.
Benson & Hedges Cup Finalists: 1977.
Fenner Trophy Winners (2): 1971 and 1973.
Gillette Man of the Match Awards: 23.
NatWest Trophy Man of the Match Awards: 5
Benson & Hedges Gold Awards: 36.

Secretary: D. Dalby, St. Lawrence Ground, Canterbury CT1 3NZ.
Cricket Manager: B.W. Luckhurst.
Captain: C.J. Tavaré.
Prospects of Play Telephone No: Canterbury matches only, Canterbury (0227) 57323.

Derek George ASLETT B Dover 12/2/1958. RHB, LB. Debut 1981 scoring 146* in first innings. Scored 168 & 119 v Derby (Chesterfield) 1983. Cap 1983. 1,437 runs (av. 43.54) in 1983. HS: 168 v Derby (Chesterfield) 1983. HSNW: 42 v Hants (Canterbury) 1983. HSJPL: 100 v Somerset (Taunton) 1983. HSBH: 19 v Sussex (Hove) 1982. BB: 4-119 v Sussex (Hove) 1982.

Eldine Ashworth Elderfield BAPTISTE B St. John's, Antigua 12/3/1960. RHB, RFM. Debut 1981. Cap 1983. Played for Leeward Islands 1981-82 and 1982-83. NW Man of the Match: 1. HS: 136* v Yorks (Sheffield) 1983. HSNW: 22 v Warwicks (Canterbury) 1983. HSJPL: 47 v Essex (Chelmsford) 1983. HSJPL: 22 v Glos (Cheltenham) 1981. BB: 5-37 v Lancs (Maidstone) 1981. BBNW: 5-20 v Hants (Canterbury) 1983. BBJPL: 4-29 v Worcs (Canterbury) 1983.

Mark Richard BENSON (Sutton Valence School) B Shoreham, Sussex 6/7/1958. LHB, OB. Debut 1980. Cap 1981. 1,000 runs (3) – 1,515 (av. 44.55) in 1983 best. HS: 152* v Warwicks (Birmingham) 1983. HSNW: 57 v Yorks (Canterbury) 1981. HSJPL: 97 v Surrey (Oval) 1982. HSBH: 65 v Surrey (Canterbury) 1982.

Christopher Stuart COWDREY (Tonbridge School) B Farnborough, Kent, 20/10/1957. Eldest son of M.C. Cowdrey. RHB, RM. Played for 2nd XI at age of 15. Debut 1977. Cap 1979. 1,364 runs (av. 56.83) in 1983. Tours: D.H. Robins to Sri Lanka 1977-78 and New Zealand 1979-80. BH Gold Awards: 2. NW Man of the Match: 1. HS: 123 v Leics (Folkestone) 1983. HSNW: 122* v Essex (Chelmsford) 1983. HSJPL: 95 v Worcs (Canterbury) 1983. HSBH: 114 v Sussex (Canterbury) 1977. BB: 3-17 v Hants (Bournemouth) 1980. BBNW: 4-36 v Hants (Canterbury) 1983.

Graham Roy DILLEY B Dartford 18/5/1959. LHB, RFM. Debut 1977. Cap 1980. Best Young Cricketer of the Year in 1980. Tests: 17 between 1979-80 and 1983. Tours: Australia and India 1979-80, West Indies 1980-81, India and Sri Lanka 1981-82. BH Gold Award: 1. HS: 81 v Northants (Northampton) 1979. HSTC: 56 v Australia (Leeds) 1981. HSNW: 19 v Somerset (Lord's) 1983. HSJPL: 33 v Northants (Northampton) 1982. HSBH: 37* v Hants (Kent) 1983. BB: 6-66 v Middlesex (Lord's) 1979. BBTC: 4-24 v Australia (Nottingham) 1981. BBNW: 4-29 v Somerset (Lord's) 1983. BBJPL: 4-20 v Glos (Canterbury) 1980. BBBH: 4-14 v Combined Universities (Canterbury) 1981.

Richard Mark ELLISON (Tonbridge School) B Ashford (Kent) 21/9/1959. LHB, RM. Debut 1981. Cap 1983. BH Gold Award: 1. Hat-trick in JPL v Hants (Canterbury) 1983. HS: 63 v Derby (Chesterfield) 1983. HSNW: 21 v Somerset (Lord's) 1983. HSJPL: 24 v Sussex (Maidstone) 1982. HSBH: 28 v Hants (Canterbury) 1983. BB: 5-73 v Lancs (Maidstone) 1983. BBNW: 4-19 v Cheshire (Canterbury) 1983. BBJPL: 4-25 v Hants (Canterbury) 1983. BBBH: 3-22 v Hants (Canterbury) 1983.

Simon Graham HINKS B Northfleet 12/10/1960. LHB, LM, WK. Debut 1982. HS: 87 v Glamorgan (Cardiff) 1983.

Kevin Bertram Sidney JARVIS B Dartford 23/4/1953. RHB, RFM. Debut 1975. Cap 1977. NW Man of the Match: 1. Tours: D.H. Robins to Sri Lanka 1977-78, International XI to Jamaica 1982-83. BH Gold Awards: 1. HS: 14* International XI v West Indies XI (Kingston) 1982-83. HSUK: 12* v Cambridge U (Canterbury) 1977. BB: 8-97 v Worcs (Worcester) 1978. BBNW: 4-19 v Warwicks (Canterbury) 1983. BBJPL: 4-27 v Surrey (Maidstone) 1977. BBBH: 4-34 v Worcs (Lord's) 1976.

Graham William JOHNSON B Beckenham 8/11/1946. RHB, OB. Debut 1965. Cap 1970. Played for Transvaal 1981-82. 1,000 runs (3) – 1,438 runs (av. 31.26) in 1973 and 1,438 runs (av. 35.95) in 1975 best. Gillette Man of the Match Awards: 1. BH Gold Awards: 3. HS: 168 v Surrey (Oval) 1976. HSGC/NW: 120* v Bucks (Canterbury) 1974. HSJPL: 89 v Sussex (Hove) 1976. HSBH: 85* v Minor Counties (South) (Canterbury) 1975. BB: 7-76 v Northants (Canterbury) 1983. BBJPL: 5-26 v Surrey (Oval) 1974. Benefit 1983.

Alan Philip Eric KNOTT B Belvedere 9/4/1946. RHB, WK. OB. Debut 1964. Cap 1965. Best Young Cricketer of the Year in 1965. *Wisden* 1969. Played for Tasmania 1969-70. Benefit (£27,037) in 1976. Tests: 95 between 1967 and 1981. Played in 5 matches against Rest of World in 1970. Tours: Cavaliers to West Indies 1964-65, Pakistan 1966-67, West Indies 1967-68 and 1973-74, Ceylon and Pakistan 1968-69, Australia and New Zealand 1970-71, 1974-75, India, Sri Lanka and Pakistan 1972-73, India, Sri Lanka and Australia 1976-77, SAB to South Africa 1981-82. Banned for 3 years from Test cricket. 1,000 runs (2) – 1,209 runs (av. 41.68) in 1971 best. Scored two centuries in match (127* and 118*) v Surrey (Maidstone) 1972. Gillette Man of the Match Awards: 2. BH Gold Awards: 1. HS: 156 MCC v South Zone (Bangalore) 1972-73. HSUK: 144 v Sussex (Canterbury) 1976. HSTC: 135 v Australia (Nottingham) 1977. HSGC/NW: 46 v Notts (Nottingham) 1975. HSJPL: 60 v Hants (Canterbury) 1969. HSBH: 65 v Combined Universities (Oxford) 1976. Dismissed 84 batsmen (74 ct 10 st) in 1965. 81 batsmen (73 ct 7 st) in 1966, and 98 batsmen (90 ct 8 st) in 1967. Dismissed 7 batsmen (7 ct) on debut in Test cricket v Pakistan (Nottingham) 1967.

Steven MARSH B Westminster 27/1/1961. RHB, WK. Debut 1982. HS: 10* v Warwicks (Dartford) 1982.

Kevin David MASTERS B Chatham 19/5/1961. LHB, RFM. Debut 1983.

Christopher PENN B Dover 19/6/1963. LHB, RFM. Debut 1982. HS: 30 v Somerset (Taunton) 1982. HSJPL: 40 v Sussex (Maidstone) 1982. BBJPL: 3-35 v Yorks (Canterbury) 1982. BBBH: 4-34 v Surrey (Canterbury) 1982.

Laurie POTTER (Kelmscott HS, Perth, Western Australia) B Bexleyheath 7/11/1962. RHB, LM. Emigrated to Australia with parents at age of four. Debut 1981. HS: 118 v Indians (Canterbury) 1982. HSNW: 45 v Essex (Chelmsford) 1982. HSJPL: 45 v Warwicks (Birmingham) 1982. BBJPL: 4-27 v Somerset (Bath) 1981.

Christopher James TAVARÉ (Sevenoaks School and Oxford) B Orpington 27/10/1954. RHB, RM. Debut 1974. Blue 1975-76-77. Cap 1978. Captain 1983. Tests: 26 between 1980 and 1983. Tours: India and Sri Lanka 1981-82, Australia 1982-83. 1,000 runs (7) – 1,770 runs (av. 53.63) in 1981 best. NatWest Man of the Match Awards: 2. BH Gold Awards: 5 (2 for Combined Universities). HS: 168* v Essex (Chelmsford) 1982. HSTC: 149 v India (Delhi) 1981-82. HSNW: 118* v Yorks (Canterbury) 1981. HSJPL: 136* v Glos (Canterbury) 1978. HSBH: 95 v Surrey (Oval) 1980.

Neil Royston TAYLOR B Orpington 21/7/1959. RHB, OB. Debut 1979 scoring 110 v Sri Lankans (Canterbury) in debut match. 1,000 runs (2): 1,340 runs (av. 34.35) in 1982 best. BH Gold Awards: 4. HS: 155* v Glamorgan (Cardiff) 1983. HSNW: 20 v Essex (Chelmsford) 1982. HSJPL: 74 v Glos (Folkestone) 1982. HSBH: 121 v Sussex (Hove) and v Somerset (Canterbury) 1982.

Derek Leslie UNDERWOOD B Bromley 8/6/1945. RHB, LM. Debut 1963, taking 100 wkts and being the youngest player ever to do so in debut season. Cap 1964 (second youngest Kent player to have received this award). Best Young Cricketer of the Year in 1966. *Wisden* 1968. Benefit (£24,114) in 1975. Awarded MBE in 1981 New Year's Honours List. Took 1,000th wkt in first-class cricket in New Zealand 1970-71 at age of 25 years 264 days – only W. Rhodes (in 1902) and G.A. Lohmann (in 1890) have achieved the feat at a younger age – and 2,000th wkt in 1981). Took 200th wkt in Test cricket against Australia in 1975. Tests: 86 between 1966 and 1981-82. Played in 3 matches against Rest of World in 1970. Tours: Pakistan 1966-67, International XI to Africa and Asia 1967-68, Ceylon and Pakistan 1968-69, Duke of Norfolk to West Indies 1969-70, Australia and New Zealand 1970-71, 1974-75, India, Sri Lanka and Pakistan 1972-73, West Indies 1973-74, International Wanderers to South Africa 1975-76, India, Sri Lanka and Australia 1976-77, Australia and India 1979-80, India and Sri Lanka 1981-82, SAB to South Africa 1981-82. Banned from Test cricket for 3 years. BH Gold Award: 1. 100 wkts (10) – 157 wkts (av. 13.80) in 1966 best. Hat-trick v Sussex (Hove) 1977. HS: 80 v Lancs (Manchester) 1969. HSTC: 45* v Australia (Leeds) 1968. HSGC/NW: 28 v Sussex (Tunbridge Wells) 1963. HSJPL: 22 v Worcs (Dudley) 1969. HSBH: 27 v Surrey (Canterbury) 1983. BB: 9-28 v Sussex (Hastings) 1964 and 9-32 v Surrey (Oval) 1978. BBTC: 8-51 v Pakistan (Lord's) 1974. BBGC/NW: 4-57 v Leics (Canterbury) 1974. BBJPL: 5-14 v Surrey Canterbury) 1983. BBBH: 5-35 v Surrey (Oval) 1976.

Stuart Nicholas Varney WATERTON B Dartford 6/12/1960. RHB, WK. Debut 1980. Did not play in 1983. HS: 40* v Surrey (Maidstone) 1980.

Lindsay Jonathan WOOD B Ruislip (Middlesex) 12/5/1961. LHB, SLA. Debut 1981. Did not play in 1983. BB: 4-124 v Essex (Chelmsford) 1981.

Robert Andrew WOOLMER B Kanpur, India 14/5/1948. RHB, RM. Debut 1968. Cap 1970. Wisden 1975. Played for Natal between 1973-74 and 1975-76 and for Western Province in 1980-81. Benefit 1984. Tests: 19 between 1975 and 1981. Tours: India, Sri Lanka and Australia 1976-77, SAB to South Africa 1981-82. Banned from Test cricket for 3 years. 1,000 runs (5) – 1,749 (av. 47.27) in 1976 best. Hat-trick for MCC v Australians (Lord's) 1975. Gillette Man of the Match Awards: 2. BH Gold Awards: 5. HS: 203 v Sussex (Tunbridge Wells) 1982. HSTC: 149 England v Australia (Oval) 1975. HSGC/NW: 91 v Yorks (Leeds) 1980. HSJPL: 112* v Notts (Nottingham) 1980. HSBH: 79* v Essex (Dartford) 1981. BB: 7-47 v Sussex (Canterbury) 1969. BBGC/NW: 4-28 v Somerset (Taunton) 1979. BBJPL: 6-9 v Derbyshire (Chesterfield) 1979. BBBH: 4-14 v Sussex (Tunbridge Wells) 1972.

County Averages

Schweppes County Championship: Played 24, won 7, drawn 13, lost 4.
All first-class matches: Played 25, won 7, drawn 14, lost 4.

BATTING AND FIELDING

Cap		*M*	*I*	*NO*	*RUNS*	*HS*	*Avge*	*100*	*50*	*Ct*	*St*
1979	C.S. Cowdrey	22	34	10	1364	123	56.83	5	5	27	—
1970	R.A. Woolmer	14	22	1	994	129	47.33	4	5	6	—
1981	M.R. Benson	23	37	3	1515	152*	44.55	4	10	15	—
1978	C.J. Tavaré	11	16	0	700	94	43.75	—	7	10	—
1983	D.G. Aslett	20	36	3	1437	168	43.54	3	8	18	—
1965	A.P.E. Knott	23	30	9	848	92*	40.38	—	6	39	8
—	N.R. Taylor	23	39	6	1275	155*	38.63	5	3	18	—
1983	E.A.E. Baptiste	17	26	5	755	136*	35.95	2	3	10	—
—	S.G. Hinks	6	10	0	253	87	25.30	—	1	2	—
1983	R.M. Ellison	22	21	7	343	63	24.50	—	1	15	—
1970	G.W. Johnson	25	30	13	413	79*	24.29	—	1	28	—
—	L. Potter	6	11	0	258	50	23.45	—	1	2	—
1980	G.W. Dilley	11	7	1	99	29	16.50	—	—	8	—
1964	D.L. Underwood	25	20	6	142	26*	10.14	—	—	5	—
1977	K.B.S. Jarvis	21	13	5	43	9*	5.37	—	—	2	—

Played in two matches: K.D. Masters 0, 1, 0, 0, (2ct); C. Penn 24, (1 ct); S. Marsh 5, 0; S.N.V. Waterton, 8, 3 (3 ct).

BOWLING

	Type	*O*	*M*	*R*	*W*	*Avge*	*Best*	*5 wI*	*10 wM*
R.A. Woolmer	**RM**	86	29	170	10	17.00	3-13	—	—
D.L. Underwood	**LM**	936.3	358	2044	106	19.28	7-55	9	3
G.R. Dilley	**RF**	250.3	67	629	31	20.29	5-70	1	—
E.A.E. Baptiste	**RFM**	376.3	88	1187	50	23.74	5-39	3	—
R.M. Ellison	**RM**	598.4	167	1491	51	29.23	5-73	1	—
G.W. Johnson	**OB**	631.1	166	1652	51	32.39	7-76	2	1
K.B.S. Jarvis	**RFM**	498.5	95	1579	30	52.63	3-32	—	—
C.S. Cowdrey	**RM**	220.2	34	733	12	61.08	3-80	—	—

Also bowled: D.G. Aslett 37-5-218-3; M.R. Benson 5-1-16-0; K.D. Masters 33-4-121-2; C. Penn 35-8-116-2; L. Potter 6-2-14-0; C.J. Tavaré 3-0-3-0; N.R. Taylor 35-9-108-1.

County Records

First-class cricket

Highest innings totals:	For	803-4d v Essex (Brentwood)	1934
	Agst	676 by Australians (Canterbury)	1921
Lowest innings totals:	For	18 v Sussex (Gravesend)	1867
	Agst	16 by Warwicks (Tonbridge)	1913
Highest individual innings:	For	332 W.H. Ashdown v Essex (Brentwood)	1934
	Agst	344 W.G. Grace for MCC (Canterbury)	1876
Best bowling in an innings:	For	10-30 C. Blythe v Northants (Northampton)	1907
	Agst	10-48 C.H.G. Bland for Sussex (Tonbridge)	1899
Best bowling in a match:	For	17-47 C. Blythe v Northants (Northampton)	1907
	Agst	17-106 T.W.J. Goddard for Glos (Bristol)	1939
Most runs in a season:		2,894 (av. 59.06) F.E. Woolley	1928
runs in a career:		47,868 (av. 41.77) F.E. Woolley	1906-1938
100s in a season:		10 by F.E. Woolley	1928 & 1934
100s in a career:		122 by F.E. Woolley	1906-1938
wickets in a season:		262 (av. 14.74) A.P. Freeman	1933
wickets in a career:		3,340 (av. 17.64) A.P. Freeman	1914-1936

RECORD WICKET STANDS

1st	283	A.E. Fagg & P.R. Sunnucks v Essex (Colchester)	1938
2nd	352	W.H. Ashdown & F.E. Woolley v Essex (Brentwood)	1934
3rd	321*	A. Hearne & J.R. Mason v Notts (Nottingham)	1899
4th	297	H.T.W. Hardinge & A.P.F. Chapman v Hants (Southampton)	1926
5th	277	F.E. Woolley & L.E.G. Ames v New Zealanders (Canterbury)	1931
6th	284	A.P.F. Chapman & G.B. Legge v Lancs (Maidstone)	1927
7th	248	A.P. Day & E. Humphreys v Somerset (Taunton)	1908
8th	157	A.L. Hilder & C. Wright v Essex (Gravesend)	1924
9th	161	B.R. Edrich & F. Ridgway v Sussex (Tunbridge Wells)	1949
10th	235	F.E. Woolley & A. Fielder v Worcs (Stourbridge)	1909

One-day cricket

Highest innings totals:	Gillette Cup/ NatWest Trophy	297-3 v Worcs (Canterbury)	1970
	John Player League	281-5 v Warwicks (Folkestone)	1983
	Benson & Hedges Cup	280-3 v Surrey (Oval)	1976
Lowest innings totals:	Gillette Cup/ NatWest Trophy	60 v Somerset (Taunton)	1979
	John Player League	84 v Glos (Folkestone)	1969
	Benson & Hedges Cup	73 v Middlesex (Canterbury)	1979
Highest individual innings:	Gillette Cup/ NatWest Trophy	129 B.W. Luckhurst v Durham (Canterbury)	1974
	John Player League	142 B.W. Luckhurst v Somerset (Weston-super-Mare)	1970
	Benson & Hedges Cup	121 N.R. Taylor v Sussex (Hove)	1982
		121 N.R. Taylor v Somerset (Canterbury)	1982
Best bowling figures:	Gillette Cup/ NatWest Trophy	7-15 A.L. Dixon v Surrey (Oval)	1967
	John Player League	6-9 R.A. Woolmer v Derby (Chesterfield)	1979
	Benson & Hedges Cup	5-21 B.D. Julien v Surrey (Oval)	1973

LANCASHIRE

Formation of present club: 1864.
Colours: Red, green and blue.
Badge: Red rose.
County Champions (8): 1881, 1897, 1904, 1926, 1927, 1928, 1930 and 1934.
Joint Champions (4): 1879, 1882, 1889 and 1950.
Gillette Cup Winners (4): 1970, 1971, 1972 and 1975.
Gillette Cup Finalists (2): 1974 and 1976.
NatWest Trophy Semi-Finalists: 1981.
John Player League Champions (2): 1969 and 1970.
Benson & Hedges Cup Semi-Finalists (3): 1973, 1974 1982 and 1983.
Gillette Man of the Match Awards: 35.
NatWest Man of the Match Awards: 3.
Benson & Hedges Gold Awards: 33.

Secretary: C.D. Hassell, Old Trafford, Manchester M16 0PX.
Cricket Manager: J.D. Bond.
Captain: C.H. Lloyd.
Prospects of Play Telephone No: 061-872 0261.

John ABRAHAMS B Cape Town, South Africa 21/7/1952. LHB, OB. Debut 1973. Cap 1982. 1,000 runs (2): 1,261 (av. 39.40) in 1983 best. HS: 178 v Worcs (Manchester) 1983. HSNW: 51* v Durham (Chester-le-Street) 1983. HSJPL: 79* v Sussex (Horsham) 1983. HSBH: 47 v Leics (Leicester) 1980. BB: 3-27 v Worcs (Manchester) 1981.

Paul John Walter ALLOTT (Durham University) B Altrincham, Cheshire 14/9/1956. RHB, RFM. Debut 1978. Cap 1981. Tests: 5 between 1981 and 1982. Tours: India and Sri Lanka 1981-82; International XI to Jamaica 1982-83. HS: 52* England v Australia (Manchester) 1981. HSC: 41 v Kent (Maidstone) 1983. HSGC/NW: 19* v Worcs (Worcester) 1980. HSJPL: 32* v Yorks (Leeds) 1983. HSBH: 10 v Notts (Nottingham) 1982. BB: 8-48 v Northants (Northampton) 1981. BBNW: 3-22 v Durham (Manchester) 1981. BBJPL: 4-29 v Middlesex (Manchester) 1983. BBBH: 3-34 v Derby (Manchester) 1981.

Mark Robert CHADWICK B Rochdale 9/2/1963. RHB, RM. Debut 1983. HSJPL: 10 v Glos (Bristol) 1983.

Neil Harvey FAIRBROTHER B Warrington 9/9/1963. LHB. Debut 1982. HS: 94* v Warwicks (Birmingham) 1983. HSJPL: 44 v Surrey (Oval) 1983.

Ian FOLLEY B Burnley 9/1/1963. RHB, LM. Debut 1982. HS: 36 v Derby (Manchester) 1982. HSJPL: 11* v Somerset (Manchester) 1983. HSBH: 11* v Notts (Nottingham) 1982. BB: 4-40 v Cambridge U (Cambridge) 1982. BBBH: 4-18 v Middlesex (Lord's) 1982.

Graeme FOWLER B Accrington 20/4/1957. LHB, WK. Debut 1979. Cap 1981. Tours: International XI to Jamaica 1982-83; Australia and New Zealand 1982-83. 1,000 runs (3) - 1,560 runs (av. 39.00) in 1981 best. Tests 6 between 1982 and 1983. Scored 126 and 128* v Warwicks (Southport) 1982. BH Gold Awards: 2. HS: 156* v Yorks (Manchester) 1983. HSTC: 105 v New Zealand (Oval) 1983. HSNW: 57 v Northants (Northampton) 1981. HSJPL: 65 v Worcs (Manchester) 1981. HSBH: 97 v Northants (Manchester) 1983.

Frank Charles HAYES B Preston 6/12/1946. RHB, RM. Debut 1970 scoring 94 and 99 in first two matches. Cap 1972. County Captain 1978 to 1980. Tests: 9 between 1973 and 1976. Tours: D.H. Robins to South Africa 1972-73 and 1975-76, West Indies 1973-74, International Wanderers to South Africa 1975-76, International team to Pakistan 1981-82. Also played for Overseas XI v Board President's XI (Calcutta) 1980-81. 1,000 runs (6) – 1,311 runs (av. 35.43) in 1974 best. Scored 34 in one over (6 4 6 6 6 6) off M.A. Nash v Glamorgan (Swansea) 1977. Benefit 1983. Gillette Man of the Match Awards: 1. BH Gold Awards: 2. HS: 187 v Indians (Manchester) 1974. HSTC: 106* v West Indies (Oval) 1973 in second innings on Test debut. HSGC/NW: 93 v Warwickshire (Birmingham) 1976. HSJPL: 87 v Essex (Manchester) 1982. HSBH: 102 v Minor Counties (North) (Manchester) 1973. Amateur soccer player. Studied at Sheffield University.

Kevin Anthony HAYES (Oxford U) B Mexborough (Yorks) 26/9/1962. No relation to F.C. Hayes. RHB, RM. Debut 1980. Blue 1981-82-83. Secretary 1982. HS: 152 Oxford U v Warwicks (Oxford) 1982. HSC: 62 v Somerset (Taunton) 1982. HSBH: 17 Combined Universities v Essex (Chelmsford) 1981.

David Paul HUGHES B Newton-le-Willows 13/5/1947. RHB, SLA. Debut 1967. Cap 1970. Played for Tasmania in 1975-76 and 1976-77. Testimonial in 1981. Tour: D.H. Robins to South Africa 1972-73. 1,000 runs (2) – 1,303 (av. 48.25) in 1982 best. Gillette Man of the Match: 1. BH Gold Awards: 1. HS: 153 v Glamorgan (Manchester) 1983. HSNW: 71 v Durham (Chester-le-Street) 1983. HSJPL: 87* v Surrey (Oval) 1983. HSBH: 52 v Derbyshire Manchester) 1981. BB: 7-24 v Oxford U (Oxford) 1970. BBGC/NW: 4-61 v Somerset (Manchester) 1972. BBJPL: 6-29 v Somerset (Manchester) 1977. BBBH: 5-23 v Minor Counties (West) Watford) 1978.

Stephen Thomas JEFFERIES B Cape Town 8/12/1959. LHB, LFM. Played for Western Province 1978-79 to 1982-83, Derby 1982. Debut for Lancs 1983. HS: 75* v Essex (Manchester) 1983. HSJPL: 37* v Notts (Manchester) 1983. BB: 8-46 v Notts (Nottingham) 1983.

Clive Hubert LLOYD B Georgetown, British Guiana 31/8/1944. 6ft 4½ins tall. Cousin of L.R. Gibbs. LHB, RM. Wears glasses. Debut 1963-64 for British Guiana. Played for Rest of World XI in 1967 and 1968. Debut for county 1968. Cap 1969. *Wisden* 1970. Testimonial (£27,199) in 1977. Appointed County Captain in 1981. Tests: 90 for West Indies between 1966-67 and 1982-83 captaining West Indies in 54 Tests, the record for all countries. Played in 5 matches for Rest of World 1970 and 2 in 1971-72. Scored 118 on debut v England (Port of Spain) 1967-68, 129 on debut v Australia (Brisbane) 1968-69. Tours: West Indies to India and Ceylon 1966-67, Australia and New Zealand 1968-69, 1979-80 (captain), England 1969, 1973, 1976 (captain), and 1980 (captain), Rest of World to Australia 1971-72 (returning early owing to back injury), World XI to Pakistan 1973-74, India, Sri Lanka and Pakistan 1974-75 (captain), Australia 1975-76 (captain), 1981-82 (captain). Pakistan 1980-81 (captain). 1,000 runs (10) – 1,603 runs (av. 47.14) in 1970 best. Also scored 1,000 runs in 1968-69, 1974-75, 1975-76 and 1980-81. Scored 201* in 120 minutes for West Indies v Glamorgan (Swansea) 1976 to equal record for fastest double-century in first-class cricket. Gillette Man of the Match: 6. NW Man of the Match: 1. BH Gold Award: 1. HS: 242* West Indies v India (Bombay) 1974-75. HSUK: 217* v Warwickshire (Manchester) 1971. HSGC/NW: 126 v Warwickshire (Lord's) 1972.

HSJPL: 134* v Somerset (Manchester) 1970. HSBH: 124 v Warwicks (Manchester) 1981. BB: 4-48 v Leics (Manchester) 1970. BBGC/NW: 3-39 v Somerset (Taunton) 1970. BBJPL: 4-33 v Middlesex (Lord's) 1971. BBBH: 3-23 v Derby (Manchester) 1974.

Leslie Leopold McFARLANE B Portland, Jamaica 19/8/1952. RHB, RM. Played for Northants in 1979. Debut for Lancs 1982. HS: 12* v Somerset (Manchester) 1983. 1982. BB: 6-59 v Warwicks (Southport) 1982. BBJPL: 4-18 v Hants (Portsmouth) 1982.

Christopher MAYNARD B Haslemere (Surrey) 8/4/1958. RHB, WK. Played for Warwicks 1978 to 1982. Specially registered for Lancs in middle of 1982 season. Tour: D.H. Robins to New Zealand 1979-80. 9 dismissals (8 ct 1st) v Somerset (Taunton) 1982. HSNW: 16 v Somerset (Manchester) 1983. HS: 85 Warwicks v Kent (Birmingham) 1979. HSJPL: 46 v Notts (Manchester) 1983. HSBH: 60 v Notts (Nottingham) 1982.

Syed Mohammad NASIR ZAIDI B Karachi 25/3/1961. RHB, LB. Debut 1983. HS: 51 v Somerset (Manchester) 1983. BB: 3-27 v Sussex (Hove) 1983.

Steven Joseph O'SHAUGHNESSY B Bury 9/9/1961. RHB, RM. Debut 1980. BH Gold Award: 1. HS: 105 v Leics (Manchester) 1983. HSNW: 49 v Somerset (Manchester) 1983. HSJPL: 38 v Hants (Southampton) 1980. HSBH: 27 v Yorks (Leeds) 1983. BB: 4-66 v Notts (Nottingham) 1982. BBJPL: 3-23 v Hants (Southampton) 1980.

Neal Victor RADFORD B Luanshya, Northern Rhodesia (now Zambia) 7/6/1957. RHB, RFM. Played for Transvaal 1978-79 to 1982-83. Debut for county 1980. HS: 76* v Derbyshire (Blackpool) 1981. HSNW: 14 v Durham (Chester-le-Street) 1983. HSJPL: 48* v Glamorgan (Cardiff) 1981. HSBH: 14 v Middlesex (Lord's) 1983. BB: 6-41 Transvaal B v Griqualand West (Kimberley) 1980-81. BBUK: 5-107 v Notts (Nottingham) 1981. BBNW: 3-20 v Middlesex (Manchester) 1981. BBJPL: 3-16 v Hants (Manchester) 1981.

Jack SIMMONS B Clayton-le-Moors (Lancs) 28/3/1941. RHB, OB. Debut 1968. Cap 1971. Played for Tasmania from 1972-73 to 1978-79 whilst coaching there and for Overseas XI v Board President's XI (Calcutta) 1980-81. Benefit (£128,000) in 1980. Hat-trick v Notts (Liverpool) 1977. Gillette Man of the Match: 1. BH Gold Awards: 2. HS: 112 v Sussex (Hove) 1970. HSGC/NW: 54* v Essex (Manchester) 1979. HSJPL: 65 v Essex (Manchester) 1980. HSBH: 64 v Derby (Manchester) 1978. BB: 7-59 Tasmania v Queensland (Brisbane) 1978-79. BBUK: 7-64 v Hants (Southport) 1973. BBGC/NW: 5-49 v Worcs (Worcester) 1974. BBJPL: 5-17 v Worcs (Worcester) 1982. BBBH: 4-31 v Yorks (Manchester) 1975. Has played soccer in Lancs Combination.

Gary John SPEAK B Chorley 26/4/1962. RHB, RFM. Debut 1981. Did not play in 1983. HS: 15* v Cambridge U (Cambridge) 1982.

John STANWORTH B Oldham 30/9/1960. RHB, WK. Debut 1983. HS: 31* v Essex (Manchester) 1983.

Timothy John TAYLOR (Stockport GS and Oxford) B Romiley (Cheshire) 28/3/1961. RHB, SLA. Debut for both county and university in 1981. Also played for Minor Counties v Sri Lankans (Reading). Blue 1981-82. HS: 28* Oxford U v Kent (Oxford) 1981. BB: 5-81 Oxford U v Middlesex (Oxford) 1981.

LANCASHIRE

Mark Andrew WALLWORK B Urmston 14/12/1960. RHB, WK. Debut in 1982 (one match v Yorks). Did not play in 1983.

Michael WATKINSON B Westhoughton 1/8/1961. RHB, RM. Debut 1982. HS: 29 v Worcs (Manchester) 1983. HSJPL: 27* v Hants (Manchester) 1983. BB: 6-51 v Sussex (Hove) 1983. BBJPL: 3-31 v Middx (Manchester) 1983. BBBH: 4-39 v Notts (Manchester) 1983.

Roger Graeme WATSON B Rawtenstall 14/1/1964. LHB, OB. Debut 1982. Did not play in 1983. HS: 11 v Somerset (Taunton) 1982.

NB. The following players whose particulars appeared in the 1983 Annual have been omitted: I. Cockbain and D. Lloyd.

County Averages

Schweppes County Championship: Played 24, won 3, drawn 17, lost 4.
All first-class matches: Played 25, won 3, drawn 18, lost 4.

BATTING AND FIELDING

Cap		*M*	*I*	*NO*	*RUNS*	*HS*	*Avge*	*100*	*50*	*Ct*	*St*
1981	G. Fowler	16	26	3	1269	156*	55.17	4	6	4	—
1968	D. Lloyd	10	15	3	507	123	42.25	1	4	8	—
1982	J. Abrahams	24	39	7	1261	178	39.40	3	4	11	—
—	N.H. Fairbrother	16	26	5	759	94*	36.14	—	8	8	—
—	L.L. McFarlane	10	9	8	35	12*	35.00	—	—	1	—
—	S.T. Jefferies	10	12	4	260	75*	32.50	—	1	1	—
1972	F.C. Hayes	20	28	1	866	149	32.07	3	4	13	—
1969	C.H. Lloyd	11	16	1	447	86	29.80	—	3	11	—
—	S.J.O'Shaughnessy	18	28	3	685	105	27.40	2	1	5	—
1971	J. Simmons	23	31	2	679	104	23.41	2	3	17	—
—	J. Stanworth	3	6	2	90	31*	22.50	—	—	2	—
—	S.M. Nasir Zaidi	13	16	6	215	51	21.50	—	1	9	—
—	I. Cockbain	8	15	1	291	52	20.78	—	1	4	—
1970	D.P. Hughes	19	28	2	522	153	20.07	1	3	14	—
—	I. Folley	12	9	4	91	25	18.20	—	—	3	—
—	C. Maynard	22	27	3	417	61*	17.37	—	2	27	2
1981	P.J.W. Allott	18	18	4	225	41	16.07	—	—	4	—
—	K.A. Hayes	5	8	0	103	32	12.87	—	—	1	—
—	M. Watkinson	15	20	4	168	29	10.50	—	—	2	—

Played in one match: M.R. Chadwick 1, 1, (1 ct); N. V. Radford 24, 27.

BOWLING

	Type	*O*	*M*	*R*	*W*	*Avge*	*Best*	*5 wI*	*10 wM*
D. Lloyd	**SLA**	199	60	400	17	23.52	5-22	1	—
S.T. Jefferies	**LRM**	278.1	74	797	32	24.90	8-46	2	1
M. Watkinson	**RM**	319.3	69	929	35	26.54	6-51	2	—
J. Simmons	**OB**	744	214	1807	68	26.57	7-73	5	1
P.J.W. Allott	**RFM**	457.4	131	1178	38	31.00	5-45	1	—
S.M. Nasir Zaidi	**LB**	191.3	48	530	16	33.12	3-27	—	—
S.J. O'Shaughnessy	**RM**	236.2	44	830	25	33.20	4-73	—	—
L.L. McFarlane	**RFM**	216.4	38	742	15	49.46	3-53	—	—
J. Abrahams	**OB**	216	41	658	13	50.61	3-83	—	—
I. Folley	**LFM**	191	58	522	7	74.57	2-37	—	—

Also bowled: N.H. Fairbrother 3-2-1-0; G. Fowler 2-0-7-0; D.P. Hughes 67.5-9-230-2; N.V. Radford 25-2-99-0.

County Records LANCASHIRE

First-class cricket

Highest innings	For	801 v Somerset (Taunton)	1895
totals:	Agst	634 by Surrey (Oval)	1898
Lowest innings	For	25 v Derby (Manchester)	1871
totals:	Agst	22 by Glamorgan (Liverpool)	1924
Highest indi-	For	424 A.C. MacLaren v Somerset (Taunton)	1895
vidual innings:	Agst	315* T.W. Hayward for Surrey (Oval)	1898
Best bowling	For	10-55 J. Briggs v Worcs (Manchester)	1900
in innings:	Agst	10-40 G.O.B. Allen for Middlesex (Lord's)	1929
Best bowling	For	17-91 H. Dean v Yorks (Liverpool)	1913
in a match:	Agst	16-65 G. Giffen for Australians (Manchester)	1886
Most runs in a season:		2,633 (av. 56.02) J.T. Tyldesley	1901
runs in a career:		34,222 (av. 45.20) G.E. Tyldesley	1909-1936
100s in a season:		11 by C. Hallows	1928
100s in a career:		90 by G.E. Tyldesley	1909-1936
wickets in a season:		198 (av. 18.55) E.A. McDonald	1925
wickets in a career:		1,816 (av. 15.12) J.B. Statham	1950-1968

RECORD WICKET STANDS

1st	368	A.C. MacLaren & R.H. Spooner v Glos (Liverpool)	1903
2nd	371	F.B. Watson & G.E. Tyldesley v Surrey (Manchester)	1928
3rd	306	E. Paynter & N. Oldfield v Hants (Southampton)	1938
4th	324	A.C. MacLaren & J.T. Tyldesley v Notts (Nottingham)	1904
5th	249	B. Wood & A. Kennedy v Warwicks (Birmingham)	1975
6th	278	J. Iddon & H.R.W. Butterworth v Sussex (Manchester)	1932
7th	245	A.H. Hornby & J. Sharp v Leics (Manchester)	1912
8th	158	J. Lyon & R.M. Ratcliffe v Warwickshire (Manchester)	1979
9th	142	L.O.S. Poidevin & A. Kermode v Sussex (Eastbourne)	1907
10th	173	J. Briggs & R. Pilling v Surrey (Liverpool)	1885

One-day cricket

Highest innings totals:	Gillette Cup/ NatWest Trophy	304-9 v Leics (Manchester)	1963
	John Player League	255-5 v Somerset (Manchester)	1970
	Benson & Hedges Cup	290-5 v Northants (Manchester)	1983
Lowest innings totals:	Gillette Cup/ NatWest Trophy	59 v Worcs (Worcester)	1963
	John Player League	76 v Somerset (Manchester)	1972
	Benson & Hedges Cup	82 v Yorks (Bradford)	1972
Highest indi- vidual innings:	Gillette Cup/ NatWest Trophy	131 A. Kennedy v Middlesex (Manchester)	1978
	John Player League	134* C.H. Lloyd v Somerset (Manchester)	1970
	Benson & Hedges Cup	124 C.H. Lloyd v Warwicks (Manchester)	1981
Best bowling figures:	Gillette Cup/ NatWest Trophy	5-28 J.B. Statham v Leics (Manchester)	1963
	John Player League	6-29 D.P. Hughes v Somerset (Manchester)	1977
	Benson & Hedges Cup	6-10 C.E.H. Croft v Scotland (Manchester)	1982

LEICESTERSHIRE

Formation of present club: 1879.
Colours: Scarlet and dark green.
Badge: Running fox (gold) on green background.
County Champions: 1975.
Gillette Cup Semi-Finalists: 1977.
NatWest Trophy Third Round: 1981.
John Player League Champions (2): 1974 and 1977.
Benson & Hedges Cup Winners (2): 1972 and 1975.
Benson & Hedges Cup Finalists: 1974.
Fenner Trophy Winners: 1979.
Gillette Man of the Match Awards: 15.
NatWest Man of the Match Awards: 3.
Benson & Hedges Gold Awards: 33.

Secretary/Manager: F.M. Turner, County Ground, Grace Road, Leicester LE2 8AD.
Captain: D.I. Gower.
Prospects of Play Telephone No: Leicester (0533) 836236.

Jonathan Philip AGNEW (Uppingham School) B Macclesfield, Cheshire 4/4/1960. RHB, RF. Debut 1978. Tour: Leics in Zimbabwe 1980-81. HS: 56 v Worcs (Worcester) 1982. BB: 6-70 v Zimbabwe (Salisbury) 1980-81. BBUK: 5-72 v Yorks (Bradford) 1981.

John Christopher BALDERSTONE B Huddersfield 16/11/1940. RHB, SLA. Played for Yorks 1961 to 1970. Debut for Leics 1971. Cap 1973. Tests: 2 in 1976. Tour: Leics in Zimbabwe 1980-81. 1,000 runs (9) – 1,482 (av. 39.00) in 1982 best. Shared 2nd wkt partnership record for county (289*) with D.I. Gower v Essex (Leicester) 1981. Hat-trick v Sussex (Eastbourne) 1976. Testimonial 1984. GC Man of the Match: 2. BH Gold Awards: 8. HS: 178* v Notts (Nottingham) 1977. HSTC: 35 v West Indies (Leeds) 1976. HSGC/NW: 119* v Somerset (Taunton) 1973. HSJPL: 96 v Northants (Leicester) 1976. HSBH: 113* v Glos (Leicester) 1977. BB: 6-25 v Hants (Southampton) 1978. BBGC/NW: 4-33 v Herts (Leicester) 1977. BBJPL: 3-29 v Worcs (Leicester) 1971. Soccer for Huddersfield Town, Carlisle United, Doncaster Rovers and Queen of the South.

Timothy James BOON B Doncaster, Yorks 1/11/1961. RHB, RM. Debut 1980. Tour: Leics in Zimbabwe 1980-81. HS: 90 v Pakistanis (Leicester) 1982. HSC: 83 v Warwicks (Coventry) 1981. HSJPL: 39 v Surrey (Leicester) 1981.

Nigel Edwin BRIERS B Leicester 15/1/1955. RHB. Cousin of N. Briers who played once for county in 1967. Debut 1971 at age of 16 years 103 days. Youngest player ever to appear for county. Cap 1981. Tour: Leics to Zimbabwe 1980-81. 1,000 runs (3): 1289 (av. 40.28) in 1983 best. Shared in 5th wkt partnership record for county, 235 with R.W. Tolchard v Somerset (Leicester) 1979. BH Gold Awards: HS: 201* v Warwicks (Birmingham) 1983. HSNW: 40 v Devon (Leicester) 1983. HSJPL: 119* v Hants (Bournemouth) 1981. HSBH: 71* v Hants (Southampton) 1979.

Ian Paul BUTCHER B Farnborough, Kent 1/7/1962. RHB, WK. Brother of A.R. Butcher of Surrey. Debut 1980. HS: 139 v Notts (Leicester) 1983. HSNW: 12 v Glos (Leicester) 1983. HSJPL: 71 v Northants (Leicester) 1982. HSBH: 47 v Worcs (Worcester) 1982.

Patrick Bernard (Paddy) CLIFT (St George's College, Salisbury) B Salisbury, Rhodesia 14/7/1953. RHB, RM. Played for Rhodesia 1971-72 to 1979-80 and Natal 1980-81 and 1981-82. Debut for county 1975. Cap 1976. Hat-trick v Yorks (Leicester) 1976. HS: 100* v Sussex (Hove) 1983. HSGC/NW: 48* v Worcs (Leicester) 1979. HSJPL: 51* v Somerset (Leicester) 1979. HSBH: 91 v Notts (Leicester) 1980. BB: 8-17 v MCC (Lord's) 1976. BBGC: 3-36 v Worcs (Leicester) 1979. BBJPL: 4-12 v Lancs (Leicester) 1978. BBBH: 4-13 v Minor Counties (East) (Amersham) 1978.

Russell Alan COBB (Trent College) B Leicester 18/5/1961. RHB, LM. Tours: D.H. Robins to New Zealand 1979-80, Leics to Zimbabwe 1980-81. Debut 1980. HS: 63 v Zimbabwe (Leicester) 1982. HSJPL: 24 v Worcs (Leicester) 1981.

Nicholas Grant Billson COOK B Leicester 17/6/1956. RHB, SLA. Debut 1978. Cap 1982. Tests: 2 in 1983. Tours: D.H. Robins XI to New Zealand 1979-80; Leics to Zimbabwe 1980-81. HS: 75 v Somerset (Taunton) 1980. HSTC: 26 v New Zealand (Nottingham) 1983. HSJPL: 13* v Kent (Leicester) 1979 and 13* v Middlesex (Lord's) 1981. BB: 7-63 v Somerset (Taunton) 1982. BBTC: 5-35 v New Zealand (Lord's) 1983.

George John Fitzgerald FERRIS B Urlings Village, Antigua 18/10/1964. RHB, RF. Played for Leeward Islands 1982-83. Debut for county 1983. HS: 26 Leeward Islands v Guyana (Nevis) 1982-83. HSC: 11 v Sussex (Hove) 1983. BB: 7-42 v Glamorgan (Hinckley) 1983.

Michael Anthony GARNHAM B Johannesburg 20/8/1960. RHB, WK. Debut for Glos 1979. Debut for Leics in 1980. HS: 74 v Kent (Leicester) 1981. BH Gold Award: 1. HSGC/NW: 25 v Essex (Leicester) 1980. HSJPL: 79* v Lancs (Leicester) 1982. HSBH: 55 v Derby Leicester) 1982.

David Ivon GOWER (King's School, Canterbury) B Tunbridge Wells 1/4/1957. LHB, OB. Debut 1975. Cap 1977. *Wisden* 1978. Best Young Cricketer of the Year in 1978. Tests: 44 between 1978 and 1982. Tours: D.H. Robins to Sri Lanka 1977-78, Australia 1978-79, Australia and India 1979-80, West Indies 1980-81, India and Sri Lanka 1981-82, Australia 1982-83. 1,000 runs (5) – 1,530 (av. 46.36) in 1982 best. Shared in 2nd wkt partnership record for county, 289* with J.C. Balderstone v Essex (Leicester) 1981. Gillette Man of the Match: 1. BH Gold Awards: 1. HS: 200* England v India (Birmingham) 1979. HSC: 176* v Pakistanis (Leicester) 1982. HSNW: 138* v Glos (Leicester) 1983. HSJPL: 135* v Warwicks (Leicester) 1977. HSBH: 114* v Derby (Derby) 1980. BB: 3-47 v Essex (Leicester) 1977. County captain in 1984.

Kenneth HIGGS B Sandyford (Staffordshire) 14/1/1937. LHB, RM. Debut for Lancs 1958. Cap 1959. *Wisden* 1967. Benefit (£8,390) in 1968. Retired after 1969 Season. Reappeared for Leics in 1972. Cap 1972. Appointed County Vice-Captain in 1973 and County Captain for 1979 relinquishing post at end of season. Is now county coach. Tests: 15 between 1965 and 1968. Shared in 10th wkt partnership of 128 with J.A. Snow v West Indies (Oval) 1966 – 2 runs short of then record 10th wkt partnership in Test cricket. Also shared in 10th wkt partnership record for county, 228 with R. Illingworth v Northants (Leicester) 1977. Tours: Australia and New

Zealand 1965-66, West Indies 1967-68. 100 wkts (5) – 132 wkts (av. 19.42) in 1960 best. Hat-tricks (3) – Lancs v Essex (Blackpool) 1960, Lancs v Yorks (Leeds) 1968 and v Hants (Leicester) 1977. Hat-trick also in Benson & Hedges Cup Final v Surrey (Lord's) 1974. NW Man of the Match: 1. BH Gold Awards: 1. HS: 98 v Northants (Leicester) 1977. HSTC: 63 England v West Indies (Oval) 1966. HSGC/NW: 25 Lancs v Somerset (Taunton) 1966. HSJPL: 17* v Notts (Nottingham) 1975. HSBH: 10 v Surrey (Oval) 1981. BB: 7-19 Lancs v Leics (Manchester) 1965. BBTC: 6-91 v West Indies (Lord's) 1966. BBC: 7-44 v Middlesex (Lord's) 1978. BBGC/NW: 6-20 v Staffs (Longton) 1975. BBJPL: 6-17 v Glamorgan (Leicester) 1973. BBBH: 4-10 v Surrey (Lord's) 1974. Soccer for Port Vale.

Gordon James PARSONS B Slough (Bucks) 17/10/1959. LHB, RM. Debut 1978. Tour: Leics to Zimbabwe 1980-81. HS: 56 v Notts (Leicester) 1983. HSGC/NW: 22 v Essex (Leicester) 1980. HSJPL: 13 v Yorks (Scarborough) 1983. HSBH: 29* v Northants (Leicester) 1983. BB: 5-25 v Essex (Leicester) 1982. BBJPL: 4-19 v Essex (Harlow) 1982. BBBH: 4-33 v Worcs (Leicester) 1981.

Leslie Brian TAYLOR B Earl Shilton 25/10/1953. RHB, RFM. Debut 1977. Cap 1981. Tour: Leics to Zimbabwe 1980-81. Played for Natal in 1981-82 and 1982-83. Hat-trick v Middlesex (Leicester) 1979. HS: 47 v Derby (Derby) 1983. HSJPL: 15* v Somerset (Taunton) 1980. BB: 7-28 v Derby (Leicester) 1981. BBNW: 4-34 v Norfolk (Leicester) 1982. BBJPL: 5-23 v Notts (Nottingham) 1978. BBBH: 6-35 v Worcs (Worcester) 1982.

Peter WILLEY B Sedgefied, County Durham 6/12/1949. RHB, OB. Debut 1966 for Northants aged 16 years 180 days scoring 78 in second innings of first match v Cambridge U (Cambridge). Cap 1971. Benefit (£31,400) in 1981. Joined Leics for 1984. Tests: 20 between 1976 and 1981. Tours: D.H. Robins to South Africa 1972-73 and to Sri Lanka 1977-78, Australia and India 1979-80, West Indies 1980-81, SAB to South Africa 1981-82. Banned from Test cricket for 3 years. Played for Eastern Province 1982-83. 1,000 runs (4) – 1,783 (av. 50.94) in 1982 best. Shared in 4th wkt partnership record for Northants, 370 with R.T. Virgin v Somerset (Northampton) 1976. Gillette Man of Match: 4. NW Man of the Match: 2. BH Gold Awards: 1. HS: 227 Northants v Somerset (Northampton) 1976. HSTC: 102* v West Indies (St. John's) 1980-81. HSGC/NW: 89 Northants v Sussex (Hove) 1979. HSJPL: 107 Northants v Warwicks (Birmingham) 1975 and 107 Northants v Hants (Tring) 1976. HSBH: 71 Northants v Glos (Northampton) 1983. BB: 7-37 Northants v Oxford U (Oxford) 1975. BBGC/NW: 3-37 Northants v Cambs (March) 1975. BBJPL: 4-38 Northants v Leics (Leicester) 1980. BBBH: 3-12 Northants v Minor Counties (East) (Horton) 1977.

NB. The following players whose particulars appeared in the 1983 Annual have been omitted: B.F. Davison, A.M.E. Roberts, J.F. Steele, R.W. Tolchard.

County Averages

Schweppes County Championship: Played 24, won 9, drawn 12, lost 3.
All first-class matches: Played 26, won 9, drawn 13, lost 4.

BATTING AND FIELDING

Cap		*M*	*I*	*NO*	*RUNS*	*HS*	*Avge*	*100*	*50*	*Ct*	*St*
1977	D.I. Gower	15	24	4	849	140	42.45	3	4	12	—
1971	B.F. Davison	26	41	6	1417	123*	40.48	3	8	17	—
1981	N.E. Briers	25	38	6	1289	201*	40.28	1	8	15	—
1973	J.C. Balderstone	25	41	4	1478	112	39.94	3	9	16	—
—	I.P. Butcher	17	30	1	973	139	33.55	3	3	17	—
1976	P.B. Clift	23	33	7	843	100*	32.42	1	2	10	—
1966	R.W. Tolchard	26	35	7	775	80*	27.67	—	4	44	9
—	J.J. Whitaker	10	16	4	305	56*	24.41	—	1	4	—
1981	L.B. Taylor	19	18	6	250	47	20.83	—	—	7	—
1971	J.F. Steele	24	26	9	327	50	19.23	—	1	30	—
—	G.J. Parsons	14	15	3	207	56	17.25	—	1	5	—
—	R.A. Cobb	8	10	0	110	28	11.00	—	—	5	—
1982	N.G.B. Cook	23	20	5	150	32	10.00	—	—	8	—
—	†J.P. Agnew	10	5	0	50	26	10.00	—	—	2	—
—	A.M.E. Roberts	4	3	0	22	15	7.33	—	—	—	—
—	G.J.F. Ferris	13	12	4	38	11	4.75	—	—	1	—
—	T.J. Boon	4	7	0	18	5	2.57	—	—	—	—

Played in one match: J.P. Addison 51, 16.
† *denotes one match as substitute.*

BOWLING

	Type	*O*	*M*	*R*	*W*	*Avge*	*Best*	*5 wI*	*10 wM*
A.M.E. Roberts	**RF**	101.2	19	294	16	18.37	5-26	1	—
L.B. Taylor	**RFM**	529.5	151	1381	69	20.01	7-73	3	1
P.B. Clift	**RM**	619.4	167	1592	83	19.18	5-20	2	—
G.J.F. Ferris	**RF**	360	74	1205	53	22.73	7-42	3	1
N.G.B. Cook	**SLA**	742.5	265	1584	56	28.28	4-53	—	—
G.J. Parsons	**RM**	269	73	823	29	28.37	5-51	1	—
J.F. Steele	**SLA**	520.1	161	1280	40	32.00	4-3	—	—
J.P. Agnew	**RF**	228	41	839	21	39.95	3-34	—	—

Also bowled: J.C. Balderstone 68-22-171-7; N.E. Briers 3.5-2-9-0; I.P. Butcher 2-0-2-1; B.F. Davison 4.4.-0-18-0; D.I. Gower 9-0-102-0; J.J. Whitaker 10-2-88-0.

County Records

First-class cricket

Highest innings totals:	For	701-4d v Worcs (Worcester)	1906
	Agst	739-7d by Notts (Nottingham)	1903
Lowest innings totals:	For	25 v Kent (Leicester)	1912
	Agst	24 by Glamorgan (Leicester)	1971

LEICESTERSHIRE

Highest individual innings:	For	252* S. Coe v Northants (Leicester)	1914
	Agst	341 G.H. Hirst for Yorks (Leicester)	1905
Best bowling in an innings:	For	10-18 G. Geary v Glamorgan (Pontypridd)	1929
	Agst	10-32 H. Pickett for Essex (Leyton)	1958
Best bowling in a match:	For	16-96 G. Geary v Glamorgan (Pontypridd)	1929
	Agst	16-102 C. Blythe for Kent (Leicester)	1909
Most runs in a season:		2,446 (av. 52.04) G.L. Berry	1937
runs in a career:		30,143 (av. 30.32) G.L. Berry	1924-1951
100s in a season:		7 by G.L. Berry, W. Watson and B.F. Davison	1937, 1959 and 1982
100s in a career:		45 by G.L. Berry	1924-1951
wickets in a season:		170 (av. 18.96) J.E. Walsh	1948
wickets in a career:		2,130 (av. 23.19) W.E. Astill	1906-1939

RECORD WICKET STANDS

1st	390	B. Dudleston & J.F. Steele v Derby (Leicester)	1979
2nd	239*	J.C. Balderstone & D.I. Gower v Essex (Leicester)	1981
3rd	316*	W. Watson & A. Wharton v Somerset (Taunton)	1961
4th	270	C.S. Dempster & G.S. Watson v Yorks (Hull)	1937
5th	233	N.E. Briers & R.W. Tolchard v Somerset (Leicester)	1979
6th	262	A.T. Sharpe & G.H.S. Fowke v Derby (Chesterfield)	1911
7th	206	B. Dudleston & J. Birkenshaw v Kent (Canterbury)	1969
8th	164	M.R. Hallam & C.T. Spencer v Essex (Leicester)	1964
9th	160	W.W. Odell & R.T. Crawford v Worcs (Leicester)	1902
10th	228	R. Illingworth & K. Higgs v Northants (Leicester)	1977

One-day cricket

Highest innings totals:	Gillette Cup/ NatWest Trophy	326-6 v Worcs (Leicester)	1979
	John Player League	262-6 v Somerset (Frome)	1970
	Benson & Hedges Cup	327-4 v Warwicks (Coventry)	1972
Lowest innings totals:	Gillette Cup/ NatWest Trophy	56 v Northants (Leicester)	1964
	John Player League	36 v Sussex (Leicester)	1973
	Benson & Hedges Cup	56 v Minor Counties (Wellington)	1982
Highest individual innings:	Gillette Cup/ NatWest Trophy	138* D.I. Gower v Glos. (Leicester)	1983
	John Player League	152 B. Dudleston v Lancs (Manchester)	1975
	Benson & Hedges Cup	158* B.F. Davison v Warwicks (Coventry)	1972
Best bowling figures:	Gillette Cup/ NatWest Trophy	6-20 K. Higgs v Staffs (Longton)	1975
	John Player League	6-17 K. Higgs v Glamorgan (Leicester)	1973
	Benson & Hedges Cup	6-35 L.B. Taylor v Worcs (Worcester)	1982

MIDDLESEX

Formation of present club: 1863.
Colours: Blue.
Badge: Three seaxes.
County Champions (8): 1866, 1903, 1920, 1921, 1947, 1976, 1980 and 1982.
Joint Champions (2): 1949 and 1977.
Gillette Cup Winners (2): 1977 and 1980.
Gillette Cup Finalists: 1975.
NatWest Trophy Semi-final: 1982.
Best Position in John Player League: 2nd in 1982.
Benson & Hedges Cup Winners: 1983.
Gillette Man of the Match Awards: 27.
NatWest Man of the Match Awards: 3.
Benson & Hedges Gold Awards: 29.

Secretary: T.M. Lamb, Lord's Cricket Ground, St. John's Wood Road, London NW8 8QN.
Captain: M.W. Gatting.
Prospects of Play Telephone No: 01-286 8011.

Graham Derek BARLOW B Folkestone 26/3/1950. LHB, RM. Debut 1969. Cap 1976. Tests: 3 in 1976-77 and 1977. Tour: India, Sri Lanka and Australia 1976-77. 1,000 runs (6): 1545 (av. 48.28) in 1983 best. Shared 1st wkt partnership record for county (367*) with W.N. Slack v Kent (Lord's) 1981. GC Man of the Match: 1. NW Man of the Match: 1. BH Gold Awards: 2. HS: 177 v Lancs (Southport) 1981. HSTC: 7* v India (Calcutta) 1976-77. HSNW: 77 v Northants (Northampton) 1983. HSJPL: 114 v Warwicks (Lord's) 1979. HSBH: 129 v Northants (Northampton) 1977. Benefit 1984.

Roland Orlando BUTCHER B East Point, St. Philip, Barbados 14/10/1953. RHB, RM. Debut 1974. Played for Barbados in 1974-75 and Tasmania 1982-83. Cap 1979. Tests: 3 v West Indies in 1980-81. Tours: Middlesex to Zimbabwe 1980-81, West Indies 1980-81, International XI to Pakistan 1981-82 and to Jamaica 1982-83. BH Gold Award: 1. Scored 1,058 runs (av. 43.32) in 1982. HS: 197 v Yorks (Lord's) 1982. HSTC: 32 v West Indies (Kingston) 1980-81. HSGC/NW: 50* v Surrey (Lord's) 1980. HSJPL: 100 v Glos (Lord's) 1983. HSBH: 85 v Surrey (Oval) 1983.

John Donald CARR (Repton School and Oxford) B St. John's Wood, London 15/6/1963. RHB, OB. Son of J.D. Carr (Derbyshire and England). Blue 1983. HS: 18 Oxford U v Northants (Oxford) 1983. HSC: 12* v Leics (Lord's) 1983.

Colin Roy COOK (Merchant Taylor's School, Northwood) B Edgware 11/1/1960. RHB. Debut 1981. HS: 79 v Lancs (Southport) 1981 in debut match. HSJPL: 73 v Glos (Lord's) 1981.

Norman George COWANS B Enfield St. Mary, Jamaica 17/4/1961. RHB, RFM. Debut 1980. Best Young Cricketer of the Year 1982. Tours: Middlesex to Zimbabwe 1980-81, Australia and New Zealand 1982-83. Tests: 8 in 1982-83 and 1983. NW Man of the Match: 1. HS: 36 England v Australia (Perth) 1982-83. HSC: 10 v Oxford U (Oxford) 1981 and 10 v Derbys (Chesterfield) 1983. HSJPL: 14* v Sussex (Hove) 1982. BB: 6-77 England v Australia (Melbourne) 1983. BBC: 5-43 v Notts

(Nottingham) 1983. BBNW: 4-26 v Lancs (Lord's) 1982. BBJPL: 4-44 v Sussex (Hove) 1982. BBBH: 4-33 v Lancs (Lords) 1983.

Wayne Wendell DANIEL B St. Philip, Barbados 16/1/1956. RHB, RF. Played for Barbados 1975-76 to date. Debut for county and cap 1977. Tests: 5 for West Indies in 1975-76 and 1976. Tours: West Indies to England 1976. Young West Indies to Zimbabwe 1981-82. Hat-trick v Lancs (Southport) 1981. Gillette Man of the Match: 2. BH Gold Awards: 2. HS: 53* Barbados v Jamaica (Bridgetown) 1979-80 and 53* v Yorks (Lord's) 1981. HSTC: 11 West Indies v India (Kingston) 1975-76. HSGC/NW: 14 v Lancs (Manchester) 1978. HSJPL: 14 v Kent (Lord's) 1980. HSBH: 20* v Derby (Derby) 1978. BB: 9-61 v Glamorgan (Swansea) 1982. BBTC: 4-53 West Indies v England (Nottingham) 1976. BBGC/NW: 6-15 v Sussex (Hove) 1980. BBJPL: 5-27 v Lancs (Lord's) 1982. BBBH: 7-12 v Minor Counties (East) (Ipswich) 1978 – record for competition.

Paul Rupert DOWNTON (Sevenoaks School) B Farnborough (Kent) 4/4/1957. Son of G. Downton, former Kent player. RHB, WK. Debut for Kent 1977. Cap 1979. Debut for Middlesex in 1980. Cap 1981. Tests: 4 in 1980-81 and 1981. Tours: Pakistan and New Zealand 1977-78, Middlesex to Zimbabwe 1980-81, West Indies 1980-81. HS: 90* v Derby (Uxbridge) 1980. HSTC: 26* v West Indies (Kingston) 1980-81. HSNW: 40* v Glos (Bristol) 1982. HSJPL: 58* v Worcs (Worcester) 1982. HSBH: 11* v Surrey (Oval) 1983.

Phillipe Henri EDMONDS (Cambridge) B Lusaka, Northern Rhodesia (now Zambia) 8/3/1951. RHB, SLA. Debut for Cambridge U and county 1971. Blue 1971-73 (capt in 1973). Cap 1974. Best Young Cricketer of the Year in 1974. Played for Eastern Province in 1975-76. Tests: 23 between 1975 and 1983. Tours: Pakistan and New Zealand 1977-78, Australia 1978-79. Hat-trick v Leics (Leicester) 1981. Benefit 1983. NW Man of the Match: 1. BH Gold Awards: 2. HS: 141* v Glamorgan (Lord's) 1979. HSTC: 64 v India (Lord's) 1982. HSGC/NW: 63* v Somerset (Lord's) 1979. HSJPL: 52 v Somerset (Taunton) 1980. HSBH: 44* v Notts (Newark) 1976. BB: 8-80 v Sussex (Lord's) 1982. BBTC: 7-66 v Pakistan (Karachi) 1977-78. BBNW: 5-12 v Cheshire (Enfield) 1982. BBJPL: 3-19 v Leics (Lord's) 1973. BBBH: 4-11 v Kent (Lord's) 1975. Also played rugby for University and narrowly missed obtaining Blue.

Richard Gary Peter ELLIS (Haileybury College and Oxford) B Paddington 20/2/1960. RHB, OB. Debut for Oxford U 1981. Blue 1981-83. University captain 1982. Debut for Middlesex 1982. HS: 105* v Surrey (Oxford) 1982. HSC: 55 v Sussex (Hove) 1982. HSNW: 15* v Northants (Northampton) 1983. HSJPL: 52 v Northants (Milton Keynes) 1983. HSBH: 32 Combined Universities v Essex (Chelmsford) 1981.

John Ernest EMBUREY B Peckham 20/8/1952. RHB, OB. Debut 1973. Cap 1977. Tests: 22 between 1978 and 1982. Tours: D.H. Robins to Sri Lanka 1977-78, Australia 1978-79, Australia and India 1979-80 (as replacement for G. Miller), Middlesex to Zimbabwe 1980-81, West Indies 1980-81, India and Sri Lanka 1981-82, SAB to South Africa 1981-82. Banned from Test cricket for 3 years. Played for Western Province 1982-83. 103 wkts (av. 17.88) in 1983. BH Gold Awards: HS: 133 v Essex (Chelmsford) 1983. HSTC: 57 v Australia (Manchester) 1981. HSGC/NW: 36* v Lancs (Manchester) 1978. HSJPL: 40* v Leics (Lord's) 1983. HSBH: 44* v Glos (Bristol) 1982. BB: 7-36 v Cambridge U (Cambridge) 1977. BBTC: 6-33 v Sri Lanka (Colombo) 1981-82. BBJPL: 5-36 v Warwicks (Lord's) 1983. BBBH: 3-35 v Kent (Lord's) 1980.

Michael William GATTING B Kingsbury 6/6/1957. RHB, RM. Debut 1975. Cap 1977. Best Young Cricketer of the Year in 1981. Captain 1983. Tests: 24 between 1977-78 and 1983. Tours: Pakistan and New Zealand 1977-78, Middlesex to Zimbabwe 1980-81, West Indies 1980-81, India and Sri Lanka 1981-82. 1,000 runs (5) – 1,651 (av. 58.96) in 1982 best. Gillette Man of the Match: 1. BH Gold Awards: 2. HS: 216 v New Zealanders (Lord's) 1983. HSTC: 81 v New Zealand (Lord's) 1983. HSGC/NW: 95* v Notts (Nottingham) 1980. HSJPL: 85 v Notts (Lord's) 1976 and 85 v Glos (Lord's) 1983. HSBH: 95* v Somerset (Taunton) 1980. BB: 5-34 v Glamorgan (Swansea) 1982. BBJPL: 4-32 v Kent (Lord's) 1978. BBBH: 3-19 v Kent (Lord's) 1980.

Simon Peter HUGHES B Kingston-upon-Thames 20/12/1959. RHB, RFM. Debut 1980. Played for Northern Transvaal 1982-83. Cap 1981. Gillette Man of the Match: 1. HS: 18 v Kent (Maidstone) 1981 and v Worcs (Worcester) 1982. BB: 6-32 v Glos (Bristol) 1983. BBGC/NW: 3-23 v Worcs (Worcester) 1980. BBJPL: 3-37 v Surrey (Oval) 1983.

Kevan David JAMES B Lambeth 18/3/1961. LHB, LM. Debut 1980. Played for Wellington 1982-83. HS: 34 v Northants (Northampton) 1983. HSJPL: 13 v Kent (Canterbury) 1981. BB: 5-28 v Cambridge U (Cambridge) 1983.

Andrew John Trevor MILLER (Haileybury College and Oxford). B Chesham, Bucks. 30/5/1963. LHB, RM. Debut for Oxford U 1982. Debut for county 1983. Blue 1983. 1,002 runs (av. 43.56) in 1983. HS: 127* Oxford U. v Hants (Oxford) 1983. HSC: 86 v Sussex (Hove) 1983.

James Dermot MONTEITH (Royal Belfast Academical Insititute) B Lisburn (Co Antrim, Northern Ireland) 2/6/1943. RHB, SLA. Played for Ireland 1965 to 1983. Debut for county 1981. Had match double of 100 runs and 10 wickets (26 and 78, 7-38 and 5-57) Ireland v Scotland (Cork) 1973. HS: 78 Ireland v Scotland (Cork) 1973. HSC: 36 v Hants (Uxbridge) 1982. HSJPL: 10 v Warwicks (Lord's) 1981. BB: 7-38 Ireland v Scotland (Cork) 1973. BBC: 5-68 v Northants (Northampton) 1981.

Clive Thornton RADLEY B Hertford 13/5/1944. RHB, LB. Debut 1964. Cap 1967. Benefit (£26,000) in 1977. *Wisden* 1978. Tests: 8 in 1977-78 and 1978. Tours: D.H. Robins' to South Africa 1972-73 and 1974-75, Pakistan and New Zealand 1977-78 (as replacement for J.M. Brearley), Australia 1978-79, Middlesex to Zimbabwe 1980-81. 1,000 runs (14) – 1,491 runs (av. 57.34) in 1980 best. Shared in 6th wicket partnership record for county, 227 with F.J. Titmus v South Africans (Lord's) 1965. Gillette Man of the Match: 2. BH Gold Awards: 4. HS: 171 v Cambridge U (Cambridge) 1976. HSTC: 158 v New Zealand (Auckland) 1977-78. HSGC/NW: 105* v Worcs (Worcester) 1975. HSJPL: 133* v Glamorgan (Lord's) 1969. HSBH: 121* v Minor Counties (East) (Lord's) 1976.

Graham David Rose B Tottenham 12/4/1964. RHB, RM. Played in two JPL matches in 1983. HSJPL: 33 v Notts (Cleethorpes) 1983.

Wilfred Norris SLACK B Troumaca, St. Vincent 12/12/1954. LHB, RM. Debut 1977. Cap 1981. Played for Windward Islands 1981-82 and 1982-83. 1,000 runs (3) 1,499 (av. 44.08) in 1982 best. Tours: Middlesex to Zimbabwe 1980-81, International XI to Pakistan 1981-82. Shared 1st wicket partnership record for county, 367* with G.D. Barlow v Kent (Lord's) 1981. HS: 248* v Worcs (Lord's) 1981. HSNW: 60 v Cambridgeshire (Wisbech) 1983. HSJPL: 77 v Somerset (Weston-super-Mare) 1982. HSBH: 60* v Combined Universities (Cambridge) 1982. BB: 3-17 v Leics (Uxbridge) 1982. BBNW: 3-37 v Northants (Northampton) 1983. BBJPL: 5-32 v Leics (Lord's) 1983.

MIDDLESEX

James Frederick SYKES B Shoreditch, London 30/12/1965. RHB, OB. Debut 1983.

Keith Patrick TOMLINS B Kingston-upon-Thames 23/10/1957. RHB, RM. Debut 1977. Cap 1983. Tour: Middlesex to Zimbabwe 1980-81. HS: 146 v Oxford U (Oxford) 1982. HSNW: 80 v Cambridgeshire (Wisbech) 1983. HSJPL: 58 v Warwicks (Birmingham) 1982. BBJPL: 4-24 v Notts (Lord's) 1978.

Neil Fitzgerald WILLIAMS B Hope Well, St. Vincent, WI 2/7/1962. RHB, RFM. Debut 1982. Played for Windward Islands 1982-83. HS: 63 v Worcs (Worcester) 1983. HSJPL: 31* v Notts (Cleethorpes) 1983. HSBH: 13 v Essex (Lord's) 1983. BB: 5-77 v Yorks (Leeds) 1983. BBNW: 4-36 v Derby (Derby) 1983. BBJPL: 4-40 v Derby (Chesterfield) 1983. BBBH: 3-16 v Combined Universities (Cambridge) 1982.

NB. The following players whose particulars appeared in the 1983 Annual have been omitted: R.J. Maru and W.G. Merry.

County Averages

Schweppes County Championship: Played 24, won 11, drawn 8, lost 4, abandoned 1.
All first-class matches: Played 26, won 12, drawn 9, lost 4, abandoned 1.

BATTING AND FIELDING

Cap		*M*	*I*	*NO*	*RUNS*	*HS*	*Avge*	*100*	*50*	*Ct*	*St*
1977	M.W. Gatting	16	24	5	1373	216	72.26	6	4	15	—
1976	G.D. Barlow	23	39	7	1545	132	48.28	4	9	22	—
1981	W.N. Slack	18	28	4	1034	140	43.08	3	6	17	—
—	A.J.T. Miller	6	11	0	465	86	42.27	—	4	—	—
1979	R.O. Butcher	15	19	3	657	179	41.06	2	3	36	—
1983	K.P. Tomlins	20	27	5	670	132*	30.45	1	3	22	—
1967	C.T. Radley	25	38	6	943	119	29.46	1	4	22	—
1977	J.E. Emburey	25	33	5	782	133	27.92	1	3	23	—
—	K.D. James	8	8	2	141	34	23.50	—	—	1	—
—	N.F. Williams	25	25	7	407	63	22.61	—	2	6	—
1981	P.R. Downton	25	30	7	508	87	22.08	—	4	54	5
1974	P.H. Edmonds	17	16	3	145	65	11.15	—	1	15	—
—	R.G.P. Ellis	6	11	0	107	34	9.72	—	—	2	—
1977	W.W. Daniel	17	13	2	88	18	8.00	—	—	3	—
—	N.G. Cowans	11	8	3	34	10	6.80	—	—	2	—
1981	S.P. Hughes	13	10	6	13	4*	3.25	—	—	2	–

Played in three matches: J.D. Carr 9*, 12*, 1*.
Played in one match: J.M. Brearley 17; J.F. Sykes 4.

BOWLING

	Type	*O*	*M*	*R*	*W*	*Avge*	*Best*	*5 wI*	*10 wM*
J.E. Emburey	**OB**	935	325	1842	103	17.88	6-13	4	—
K.D. James	**LM**	89	20	217	11	19.72	5-28	1	—
P.H. Edmonds	**SLA**	733.2	200	1753	88	19.92	6-38	9	2
W.W. Daniel	**RF**	324.3	51	1106	48	23.04	7-61	1	1
S.P. Hughes	**RFM**	268.3	61	910	36	25.27	6-32	2	—
N.G. Cowans	**RF**	161	35	465	18	25.83	5-43	1	—
N.F. Williams	**RFM**	532.2	114	1659	63	26.33	5-77	1	—
M.W. Gatting	**RM**	82.2	25	217	5	43.40	2-26	—	—

Also bowled: G.D. Barlow 2-1-2-0; R.O. Butcher 3-1-11-0; J.D. Carr 15-4-31-0; C.T. Radley 2-0-6-0; W.N. Slack 44-20-84-6; J.F. Sykes 21-6-54-1; K.P. Tomlins 6-2-19-0.

County Records

First-class cricket

Highest innings totals:	For	642-3d v Hants (Southampton)	1923
	Agst	665 by West Indians (Lord's)	1939
Lowest innings totals:	For	20 v MCC (Lord's)	1864
	Agst	31 by Glos (Bristol)	1924
Highest individual innings:	For	331* J.D.B. Robertson v Worcs (Worcester)	1949
	Agst	316* J.B. Hobbs for Surrey (Lord's)	1926
Best bowling in an innings:	For	10-40 G.O.B. Allen v Lancs (Lord's)	1929
	Agst	9-38 R.C. Robertson-Glasgow for Somerset (Lord's)	1924
Best bowling in a match:	For	16-114 { G. Burton v Yorks (Sheffield)	1888
		J.T. Hearne v Lancs (Manchester)	1898
	Agst	16-109 C.W.L. Parker for Glos (Cheltenham)	1930
Most runs in a season:		2,650 (av. 85.48) W.J. Edrich	1947
runs in a career:		40,302 (av. 48.82) E.H. Hendren	1907-1937
100s in a season:		13 by D.C.S. Compton	1947
100s in a career:		119 by E.H. Hendren	1907-1937
wickets in a season:		158 (av. 14.63) F.J. Titmus	1955
wickets in a career:		2,361 (av. 21.27) F.J. Titmus	1949-1982

RECORD WICKET STANDS

1st	367*	G.D. Barlow & W.N. Slack v Kent (Lord's)	1981
2nd	380	F.A. Tarrant & J.W. Hearne v Lancs (Lord's)	1914
3rd	424*	W.J. Edrich & D.C.S. Compton v Somerset (Lord's)	1948
4th	325	J.W. Hearne & E.H. Hendren v Hants (Lord's)	1919
5th	338	R.S. Lucas & T.C. O'Brien v Sussex (Hove)	1895
6th	227	C.T. Radley & F.J. Titmus v South Africans (Lord's)	1965
7th	271*	E.H. Hendren & F.T. Mann v Notts (Nottingham)	1925
8th	182*	M.H.C. Doll & H.R. Murrell v Notts (Lord's)	1913
9th	160*	E.H. Hendren & T.J. Durston v Essex (Leyton)	1927
10th	230	R.W. Nicholls & W. Roche v Kent (Lord's)	1899

One-day cricket

Highest innings totals:	Gillette Cup/ NatWest Trophy	280-8 v Sussex (Lord's)	1965
	John Player League	270-5 v Glos. (Lord's)	1983
	Benson & Hedges Cup	303-7 v Northants (Northampton)	1977
Lowest innings totals:	Gillette Cup/ NatWest Trophy	41 v Essex (Westcliff)	1972
	John Player League	23 v Yorks (Leeds)	1974
	Benson & Hedges Cup	97 v Northants (Lord's)	1976
Highest individual innings:	Gillette Cup/ NatWest Trophy	124* J.M. Brearley v Bucks (Lord's)	1975
	John Player League	133* C.T. Radley v Glamorgan (Lord's)	1969
	Benson & Hedges Cup	129 G.D. Barlow v Northants (Northampton)	1977
Best bowling figures:	Gillette Cup/ NatWest Trophy	6-15 W.W. Daniel v Sussex (Hove)	1980
	John Player League	6-6 R.W. Hooker v Surrey (Lord's)	1969
	Benson & Hedges Cup	7-12 W.W. Daniel v Minor Counties (East) (Ipswich)	1978

NORTHAMPTONSHIRE

Formation of present club: 1878.
Colours: Maroon.
Badge: Tudor Rose.
County Championship Runners-up (4): 1912, 1957, 1965 and 1976.
Gillette Cup Winners: 1976.
Gillette Cup Finalists: 1979.
NatWest Trophy Finalists: 1981.
Best final position in John Player League: 4th in 1974.
Benson & Hedges Cup Winners: 1980.
Fenner Trophy Winners: 1978.
Gillette Man of the Match Awards: 17.
NatWest Man of the Match Awards: 7.
Benson & Hedges Gold Awards: 22.

Secretary: K.C. Turner, County Ground, Wantage Rd, Northampton, NN1 4TJ.
Captain: G. Cook.
Prospects of Play Telephone No: Northampton (0604) 37040.

Robert John BAILEY B Biddulph, Staffordshire 28/10/1963. RHB, OB. Debut 1982. HS: 37* v Oxford U (Oxford) 1983. HSNW: 21 v Wiltshire (Swindon) 1983. HSJPL: 36 v Sussex (Hastings) 1983. BB: 3-33 v Cambridge U (Cambridge) 1983.

Martin John BAMBER B Cheam, Surrey 7/1/1961. RHB, RM. Debut 1982. HS: 77 v Cambridge U (Cambridge) 1983. HSJPL: 71 v Surrey (East Molesey) 1983.

Robin James BOYD-MOSS (Bedford School and Cambridge) B Hattoh, Ceylon 16/12/1959. RHB, SLA. Debut for Cambridge U and County in 1980. Blue 1980-83. 1,000 runs (2). 1,602 runs (av. 44.50) in 1982 best. 100 in each innings twice: 123 & 119 Cambridge U v Warwicks (Cambridge) 1982 and 139 & 124 for Cambridge U v Oxford University (Lord's) 1983 – the only instance in the University Match. HS: 139 as above. HSC: 101 v Leics (Leicester) 1983. HSJPL: 62 v Warwicks (Northampton) 1981. HSBH: 58 Combined Universities v Northants (Northampton) 1980. BB: 5-27 Cambridge U v Oxford U (Lord's) 1983. Rugby Blue.

David John CAPEL B Northampton 6/2/1963. RHB, RM. Debut 1981. HS: 109* v Somerset (Northampton) 1983. HSNW: 27 v Middx (Northampton) 1983. HSJPL: 79 v Kent (Northampton) 1982. HSBH: 28 v Lancs (Manchester) 1983. BBJPL: 4-30 v Yorks (Middlesbrough) 1982. BBBH: 3-24 v Leics (Leicester) 1983.

Geoffrey COOK B Middlesbrough 9/10/1951. RHB, SLA. Debut 1971. Cap 1975. Played for Eastern Province from 1978-79 to 1980-81. Appointed County Captain in 1981. Tests: 7 between 1981-82 and 1982-83. Tours: India and Sri Lanka 1981-82, Australia 1982-83. 1,000 runs (8) – 1,759 runs (av. 43.97) in 1981 best. Gillette Man of Match: 2. NatWest Man of the Match: 2. BH Gold Awards: 3. HS: 172 Eastern Province v Northern Transvaal (Port Elizabeth) 1979-80. HSUK: 155 v Derby (Northampton) 1978. HSTC: 66 v India (Manchester) 1982. HSGC/NW: 114* v Surrey (Northampton) 1979. HSJPL: 85 v Leics (Leicester) 1976. HSBH: 96 v Minor Counties (East) (Northampon) 1978.

Brian James GRIFFITHS B Wellingborough 13/6/1949. RHB, RFM. Debut 1974. Cap 1978. NW Man of the Match: 1. HS: 16 v Glos (Bristol) 1982. HSJPL: 11* v Surrey (Tring) 1982. BB: 8-50 v Glamorgan (Northampton) 1981. BBNW: 5-33 v Yorks (Leeds) 1983. BBJPL: 4-22 v Somerset (Weston-super-Mare) 1977. BBBH: 5-43 v Sussex (Eastbourne) 1979.

Rupert William HANLEY B Port Elizabeth 29/1/1952. RHB, RF. Son of A.W.D. Hanley (Border). Played for Eastern Province in 1970-71 and 1972-73 to 1974-75, Orange Free State in 1975-76 and Transvaal 1976-77 to date. Joined Northants for 1984. Played for D.H. Robins XI v Pakistan 1974. HS: 18 Transvaal B v South African Universities (Potchefstroom) 1982-83. BB: 6-27 Orange Free State v Transvaal B (Stilfontein) 1975-76.

Allan Joseph LAMB B Langebaanweg, Cape Province, South Africa 20/6/1954. RHB, RM. Played for Western Province 1972-73 to 1981-82. Debut for county and cap 1978. *Wisden* 1980. Tests: 15 between 1982 and 1983. Tour: Australia 1982-83. 1,000 runs (5) – 2,049 runs (av. 60.26) in 1981 best. NW Man of the Match: 1. BH Gold Awards 4. HS: 178 v Leics (Leicester) 1979. HSTC: 137* v New Zealand (Nottingham) 1983. HSGC/NW: 101 v Sussex (Hove) 1979. HSJPL: 127* v Worcs (Worcester) 1981. HSBH: 106* v Leics (Leicester) 1983.

Wayne LARKINS B Roxton (Beds) 22/11/1953. RHB, RM. Debut 1972. Cap 1976. Tests: 6 between 1979-80 and 1981. Tours: Australia and India 1979-80, SAB to South Africa 1981-82. Banned from Test cricket for 3 years. Played for Overseas XI v Board President's XI (Calcutta) 1980-82 and for Western Province 1982-83. 1,000 runs (6) – 1,863 (av. 45.43) in 1982 best. Shared in 2nd wkt partnership record for county, 342 with P. Willey v Lancs (Northampton) 1983. Hat-trick in Benson & Hedges Cup v Combined Universities (Northampton) 1980. NW Man of the Match: 1. BH Gold Awards: 4. HS: 252 v Glamorgan (Cardiff) 1983. HSTC: 34 v Australia (Oval) 1981. HSGC/NW: 92* v Leics (Northampton) 1979. HSJPL: 172* v Warwicks (Luton) 1983. HSBH: 132 v Warwicks (Birmingham) 1982. BB: 4-30 v Essex (Wellingborough) 1983. BBJPL: 5-32 v Essex (Ilford) 1978. BBBH: 4-37 v Combined Universities (Northampton) 1980.

Neil Alan MALLENDER B Kirk Sandall (Yorks) 13/8/1961. RHB, RFM. Debut 1980. HS: 71* v Oxford U (Oxford) 1983. HSNW: 11* v Yorks (Leeds) 1983. HSJPL: 22 v Warwicks (Northampton) 1981 and 22 v Somerset (Weston-super-Mare) 1983. BB: 7-41 v Derby (Northampton) 1982. BBNW: 3-34 v Yorks (Leeds) 1983. BBJPL: 5-34 v Middlesex (Tring) 1981. BBBH: 3-12 v Worcs (Worcester) 1983.

George SHARP B West Hartlepool 12/3/1959. RHB, WK. Can also bowl SLA. Debut 1968. Cap 1973. Benefit in 1982. HS: 94 v Lancs (Southport) 1980. HSNW: 41* v Yorks (Leeds) 1983. HSJPL: 51* v Glos (Northampton) 1983. HSBH: 43 v Surrey (Northampton) 1979.

David Stanley STEELE B Stoke-on-Trent 29/9/1941. Elder brother of J.F. Steele of Leics and cousin of B.S. Crump, former Northants player. Wears glasses. RHB, SLA. Debut for Northants 1963. Cap 1965. Benefit (£25,500) in 1975. *Wisden* 1975. Transferred to Derbyshire in 1979 as county captain. Relinquished post during season. Cap 1979. Rejoined Northants 1982. Tests: 8 in 1975 and 1976. 1,000 runs (10) – 1,756 (av. 48.77) in 1975 best. Hat-trick v Glamorgan (Derby) 1980. Had match double of 100 runs and 10 wkts (130, 6-36 and 5-39) v Derbyshire (Northampton) 1978. Gillette Man of the Match: 1. NW Man of the Match: 1 (for

Derbyshire). HS: 140* v Worcs (Worcester) 1971. HSTC: 106 v West Indies (Nottingham) 1976. HSGC/NW: 109 v Cambs (March) 1975. HSJPL: 76 v Sussex (Hove) 1974. HSBH: 71 Derby v Notts (Nottingham) 1980. BB: 8-29 v Lancs (Northampton) 1966. BBNW: 3-23 Derby v Suffolk (Bury St. Edmunds) 1981. BBJPL: 4-21 Derby v Notts (Derby) 1979. BBBH: 3-23 v Scotland (Northampton) 1983.

Alan WALKER B Emsley, Yorks 7/7/1962. LHB, RFM. Debut 1983. HSJPL: 13 v Yorks (Tring) 1983. BB: 4-61 v Notts (Nottingham) 1983.

Duncan James WILD B Northampton 28/11/1962. Son of J. Wild, former Northants player. LHB, RM. Debut 1980. HS: 48 v Cambridge U (Cambridge) 1983. HSJPL: 20* v Lancs (Manchester) 1983.

Richard Grenville WILLIAMS B Bangor, Caernarvonshire 10/8/1957. RHB, OB. Debut 1974 aged 16 years 313 days. Cap 1979. Tour: D.H. Robins' to New Zealand 1979-80. 1,000 runs (5) – 1,305 (av. 43.50) in 1983 best. Scored two centuries in match (109 and 151*) v Warwicks (Northampton) 1979. Hat-trick v Glos (Northampton) 1980. Gillette Man of Match: 1. BH Gold Awards: 2. HS: 175* v Leics (Leicester) 1980. HSGC/NW: 51 v Durham (Northampton) 1977. HSJPL: 82 v Glos (Bristol) 1982. HSBH: 83 v Yorks (Bradford) 1980. BB: 7-73 v Cambridge U (Cambridge) 1980. BBGC/NW: 3-15 v Leics (Northampton) 1979. BBJPL: 5-30 v Warwicks (Luton) 1983.

NB. The following players whose particulars appeared in the 1983 Annual have been omitted: Kapil Dev, T.M. Lamb, P. Willey and T.J. Yardley.

County Averages

Schweppes County Championships: Played 24, won 7, drawn 13, lost 4.
All first-class matches: Played 26, won 8, drawn 14, lost 4.

BATTING AND FIELDING

Cap		*M*	*I*	*NO*	*RUNS*	*HS*	*Avge*	*100*	*50*	*Ct*	*St*
—	J.A. Carse	11	10	8	129	36*	64.50	—	—	—	—
1978	A.J. Lamb	13	21	5	840	119	52.50	3	2	9	—
1971	P. Willey	23	40	8	1546	175*	48.31	4	9	5	—
1982	Kapil Dev	7	10	2	349	120	43.62	1	1	10	—
1979	R.G. Williams	26	40	10	1305	104*	43.50	1	10	9	—
1976	W. Larkins	25	42	0	1774	252	42.23	5	4	15	—
1975	G. Cook	24	41	3	1510	128	39.73	1	11	32	3
1973	G. Sharp	23	24	8	536	98	33.50	—	3	41	5
—	R.J. Boyd-Moss	15	24	2	704	101	32.00	1	5	4	—
—	D.J. Capel	17	24	5	534	109*	28.11	1	3	11	—
—	M.J. Bamber	7	14	1	360	77	27.69	—	2	5	—
1965	D.S. Steele	25	31	6	569	60	22.76	—	3	29	—
—	A. Walker	6	4	3	18	7*	18.00	—	—	3	—
—	D.J. Wild	5	9	0	162	48	18.00	—	—	2	—
—	N.A. Mallender	23	27	9	320	71*	17.77	—	1	7	—
1978	T.M. Lamb	9	10	1	70	34	7.77	—	—	—	—
1978	B.J. Griffiths	22	13	2	27	15	2.45	—	—	2	—

Played in three matches: R.J. Bailey 4, 37*, 32, 16, 4 (5 ct).
Played in one match: S.J. Lines 29 (1 ct); M.W.C. Olley 8 (3 ct).

BOWLING

	Type	*O*	*M*	*R*	*W*	*Avge*	*Best*	*5 wI*	*10 wM*
T.M. Lamb	**RM**	188.2	57	416	21	19.80	4-27	—	—
D.S. Steele	**SLA**	678	255	1460	68	21.47	5-48	2	—
R.G. Williams	**OB**	434.1	148	1036	47	22.04	4-18	—	—
Kapil Dev	**RFM**	161	47	385	16	24.06	4-24	—	—
A. Walker	**RFM**	165.4	30	578	22	26.27	4-61	—	—
B.J. Griffiths	**RFM**	536.2	130	1424	50	28.48	6-92	1	—
N.A. Mallender	**RFM**	524.5	112	1642	56	29.32	6-48	1	—
P. Willey	**OB**	483.5	159	991	32	30.96	4-51	—	—
J.A. Carse	**RFM**	238.5	50	772	22	32.81	5-43	1	—

Also bowled: R.J. Bailey 15-5-35-3; R.J. Boyd-Moss 11-5-15-1; D.J. Capel 65.5-15-226-3; G. Cook 11-3-43-0; A.J. Lamb 1-0-1-0; W. Larkins 30.4-5-74-5; D.J. Wild 36-10-128-2.

County Records

First-class cricket

Highest innings totals:	For	557-6d v Sussex (Hove)	1914
	Agst	670-9d by Sussex (Hove)	1921
Lowest innings totals:	For	12 v Glos (Gloucester)	1907
	Agst	33 by Lancs (Northampton)	1977
Highest individual innings	For	300 R. Subba Row v Surrey (Oval)	1958
	Agst	333 K.S. Duleepsinhji for Sussex (Hove)	1930
Best bowling in an innings:	For	10-127 V.W.C. Jupp v Kent (Tunbridge Wells)	1932
	Agst	10-30 C. Blythe for Kent (Northampton)	1907
Best bowling in a match:	For	15-31 G.E. Tribe v Yorks (Northampton)	1958
	Agst	17-48 C. Blythe for Kent (Northampton)	1907
Most runs in a season:		2198 (av. 51.11) D. Brookes	1952
runs in a career:		28980 (av. 36.13) D. Brookes	1934-1959
100s in a season:		8 by R.A. Haywood	1921
100s in a career:		67 by D. Brookes	1934-1959
wickets in a season:		175 (av. 18.70) G.E. Tribe	1955
wickets in a career:		1097 (av. 21.31) E.W. Clark	1922-1947

RECORD WICKET STANDS

1st	361	N. Oldfield & V. Broderick v Scotland (Peterborough)	1953
2nd	342	W. Larkins & P. Willey v Lancs (Northampton)	1983
3rd	320	L. Livingston & F. Jakeman v South Africans (Northampton)	1951
4th	370	R.T. Virgin & P. Willey v Somerset (Northampton)	1976
5th	347	D. Brookes & D.W. Barrick v Essex (Northampton)	1952
6th	376	R. Subba Row & A. Lightfoot v Surrey (Oval)	1958
7th	229	W.W. Timms & F.A. Walden v Warwicks (Northampton)	1926
8th	155	F.R. Brown & A.E. Nutter v Glamorgan (Northampton)	1952
9th	156	R. Subba Row & S. Starkie v Lancs (Northampton)	1955
10th	148	B.W. Bellamy & J.V. Murdin v Glamorgan (Northampton)	1925

One-day cricket

Highest innings totals:	Gillette Cup/ NatWest Trophy	285-6 v Wilts (Swindon)	1983
	John Player League	298-2 v Warwicks (Luton)	1983
	Benson & Hedges Cup	259-5 v Scotland (Glasgow)	1982
Lowest innings totals:	Gillette Cup/ NatWest Trophy	62 v Leics (Leicester)	1974
	John Player League	41 v Middlesex (Northampton)	1972
	Benson & Hedges Cup	85 v Sussex (Northampton)	1978
Highest individual innings:	Gillette Cup/ NatWest Trophy	114* G. Cook v Surrey (Northampton)	1979
	John Player League	172* W. Larkins v Warwicks (Luton)	1983
	Benson & Hedges Cup	132 W. Larkins v Warwicks (Birmingham)	1982
Best bowling figures:	Gillette Cup/ NatWest Trophy	5-24 J.D.F. Larter v Leics (Leicester)	1964
	John Player League	7-39 A. Hodgson v Somerset (Northampton)	1976
	Benson & Hedges Cup	5-21 Sarfraz Nawaz v Middlesex (Lord's)	1980

NOTTINGHAMSHIRE

Formation of present club: 1841, reorganised 1866.
Colours: Green and gold.
Badge: Coat of Arms of the City of Nottingham.
County Champions (13): 1865, 1868, 1871, 1872, 1875, 1880, 1883, 1884, 1885, 1886, 1907, 1929 and 1981.
Joint Champions (5): 1869, 1873, 1879, 1882 and 1889.
Gillette Cup Semi-Finalists: 1969.
NatWest Trophy Third Round: 1981.
Best final position in John Player League: 5th in 1975 and 1982.
Benson & Hedges Finalists: 1982.
Gillette Man of the Match Awards: 13.
NatWest Man of the Match Awards: 3.
Benson & Hedges Gold Awards: 30.

Secretary: B. Robson, County Cricket Ground, Trent Bridge, Nottingham NG2 6AG.
Cricket Manager: K. Taylor.
Captain: C.E.B. Rice.
Prospects of Play Telephone No: Nottingham (0602) 822753.

John Dennis BIRCH B Nottingham 18/6/1955. RHB, RM. Debut 1973. Cap 1981. 1,000 runs (2) – 1,086 (av. 30.16) in 1983 best. BH Gold Award: 1. HS: 125 v Leics (Nottingham) 1982. HSGC/NW: 32 v Yorks (Bradford) 1978. HSJPL: 92 v Sussex (Nottingham) 1983. HSBH: 85 v Minor Counties (North) (Nottingham) 1979. BB: 6-64 v Hants (Bournemouth 1975. BBJPL: 3-29 v Glamorgan (Swansea) 1976.

Michael Kenneth BORE B Hull 2/6/1947. RHB, LM. Played for Yorks 1969 to 1978. Debut for Notts 1979. Cap 1980. BH Gold Award: 1. HS: 37* Yorks v Notts (Bradford) 1973. HSC: 24* v Yorks (Nottingham) 1980. HSJPL: 28* v Northants (Northampton) 1979. BB: 8-89 v Kent (Folkestone) 1979. BBGC/NW: 3-35 Yorks v Kent (Canterbury) 1971. BBJPL: 4-21 Yorks v Sussex (Middlesbrough) 1971 and v Worcs (Worcester) 1970. BBBH: 6-22 v Leics (Leicester) 1980.

Brian Christopher BROAD B Bristol 29/9/1957. LHB, RM. Debut for Glos 1979. Cap 1981. Joined Notts for 1984. 1,000 runs (3) – 1,153 (av. 28.12) in 1982 best. NW Man of the Match: 1. HS: 145 Glos v Notts (Bristol) 1983. HSNW: 98 v Middlesex (Bristol) 1982. HSJPL: 96 Glos v Yorks (Cheltenham) 1983. HSBH: 53 v Combined Universities (Oxford) 1982.

Kevin Edward COOPER B Hucknall (Notts) 27/12/1957. LHB, RFM. Debut 1976. Cap 1980. HS: 38* v Cambridge U (Cambridge) 1982. HSNW: 11 v Glos (Nottingham) 1982. HSJPL: 12 v Northants (Northampton) 1979. HSBH: 25* v Lancs (Manchester) 1983. BB: 7-33 v Worcs (Worcester) 1983. BBNW: 3-18 v Worcs (Worcester) 1983. BBJPL: 4-25 v Hants (Nottingham) 1976. BBBH: 4-23 v Kent (Canterbury) 1979.

Bruce Nicholas FRENCH B Warsop 13/8/1959. RHB, WK. Debut 1976 aged 16 years 287 days. Cap 1980. HS: 91 v Yorks (Bradford) 1983. HSNW: 33* v Kent (Canterbury) 1981. HSJPL: 25 v Northants (Nottingham) 1978. HSBH: 16 v Surrey (Nottingham) 1981.

NOTTINGHAMSHIRE

Richard John HADLEE B Christchurch, New Zealand 3/7/1951. Youngest son of W.A. Hadlee, former New Zealand Test cricketer, and brother of D.R. Hadlee. LHB, RFM. Played for Canterbury 1971-72 to date. Debut for county and cap 1978. Played for Tasmania in 1979-80. *Wisden* 1981. Tests: 44 for New Zealand between 1972-73 and 1983. Tours: New Zealand to England 1973, 1978 and 1983. Australia 1972-73, 1973-74 and 1980-81, Pakistan and India 1976-77. Took 105 wkts (av. 14.89) in 1981. NW Man of the Match Awards: 1. BH Gold Awards: 5. HS: 142* v Yorks (Bradford) 1981. HSTC: 103 New Zealand v West Indies (Christchurch) 1979-80. HSNW: 38* v Kent (Canterbury) 1981. HSJPL: 100* v Glos (Cheltenham) 1982. HSBH: 70 v Warwicks (Nottingham) 1982. BB: 7-23 New Zealand v India (Wellington) 1975-76 and 7-23 v Sussex (Nottingham) 1979. BBJPL: 6-12 v Lancs (Nottingham) 1980. BBBH: 4-13 Derby (Nottingham) 1980.

Sheikh Basharat HASSAN B Nairobi, Kenya 24/3/1944. RHB, RM, occasional WK. Debut for East African Invitation XI v MCC 1963-64. Played for Coast Invitation XI v Pakistan International Airways 1964. Also played for Kenya against these and other touring sides. Debut for county 1966. Cap 1970. Benefit in 1978. BH Award: 1. 1,000 runs (5) – 1,395 runs (av. 32.44) in 1970 best. Scored century with aid of a runner v Kent (Canterbury) 1977. HS: 182* v Glos (Nottingham) 1977. HSGC/NW: 79 v Hants (Southampton) 1977. HSJPL: 120* v Warwicks (Birmingham) 1981. HSBH: 99* v Warwicks (Nottingham) 1982. BB: 3-33 v Lancs (Manchester) 1976. BBGC/NW: 3-20 v Durham (Chester-le-Street) 1967.

Edward Ernest HEMMINGS B Leamington Spa 20/2/1949. RHB, OB. Played for Warwicks 1966 to 1978. Cap 1974. Debut for Notts 1979. Cap 1980. Hat-trick Warwicks v Worcs (Birmingham) 1977. Tours: D.H. Robins XI to South Africa 1974-75; International XIs to Pakistan 1981-82 and Jamaica 1982-83, Australia 1982-83. Tests: 5 in 1982 and 1982-83. HS: 127 v Yorks (Worksop) 1982. HSTC: 95 v Australia (Sydney) 1982-83. HSGC/NW: 20 Warwicks v Worcs (Birmingham) 1973. HSJPL: 44* Warwicks v Kent (Birmingham) 1971. HSBH: 61* Warwicks v Leics (Birmingham) 1974. BB: 10-175 International XI v West Indies XI (Kingston) 1982-83. BBTC: 3-68 v Australia (Sydney) 1982-83. BBC: 7-23 v Lancs (Nottingham) 1983. BBJPL: 5-22 Warwicks v Northants (Birmingham) 1974. BBBH: 3-18 Warwicks v Oxford and Cambridge Universities (Coventry) 1975.

Michael HENDRICK B Darley Dale (Derbyshire) 22/10/1948. RHB, RFM. Played for Derbyshire 1969 to 1981. Cap 1972. Best Young Cricketer of the Year in 1973. *Wisden* 1977. Benefit (£36,050) in 1980. Debut for Notts 1982. Tests: 30 between 1974 and 1981. Tours: West Indies 1973-74. Australia and New Zealand 1974-75, D.H. Robins to South Africa 1975-76, Pakistan and New Zealand 1977-78, Australia 1978-79, Australia (returned home early through injury) 1979-80. SAB to South Africa 1981-82. Banned from Test cricket for 3 years. Hat-trick Derby v West Indians (Derby) 1980. Gillette Man of the Match: 1 (for Derby). BH Gold Awards: 3 (for Derby). HS: 46 Derby v Essex (Chelmsford) 1973. HSTC: 15 v Australia (Oval) 1977. HSNW: 18 v Worcs (Worcester) 1983. HSJPL: 21 Derby v Warwicks (Buxton) 1974. HSBH: 32 Derby v Notts (Chesterfield) 1973. BB: 8-45 Derby v Warwicks (Chesterfield) 1973. BBTC: 4-28 v India (Birmingham) 1974. BBGC/NW: 4-15 Derby v Middlesex (Chesterfield) 1975. BBJPL: 6-7 Derbyshire v Notts (Nottingham) 1972. BBBH: 6-33 v Northants (Northampton) 1982.

Paul JOHNSON B Newark 24/4/1965. RHB, RM. Debut 1982. HS: 125 v Glos (Bristol) 1983. HSJPL: 44 v Warwicks (Birmingham) 1983.

Robert Andrew PICK B Nottingham 19/11/1963. LHB, RFM. Debut 1983. HS: 25* v Derby (Derby) 1983. HSNW: 34* v Sussex (Hove) 1983.

Derek William RANDALL B Retford 24/2/1951. RHB, RM. Debut 1972. Cap 1973. *Wisden* 1979. Tests: 40 between 1976-77 and 1982-83. Tours: D.H. Robins to South Africa 1975-76, India, Sri Lanka and Australia 1976-77, Pakistan and New Zealand 1977-78, Australia 1978-79, Australia and India 1979-80, Australia 1982-83. 1,000 runs (8) – 1,546 runs (av. 42.94) in 1976 best. Scored two centuries in match (209 and 146) v Middlesex (Nottingham) 1979. Gillete Man of Match: 1. BH Gold Awards: 3. HS: 209 v Middlesex (Nottingham) 1979. HSTC: 174 v Australia (Melbourne) 1976-77. HSGC/NW: 75 v Sussex (Hove) 1979. HSJPL: 107* v Middlesex (Lord's) 1976 and 107 v Essex (Nottingham) 1983. HSBH: 103* v Minor Counties (North) (Nottingham) 1979. BB: 3-15 v MCC (Lord's) 1982. Benefit 1983.

Clive Edward Butler RICE B Johannesburg 23/7/1949. RHB, RFM. Played for Transvaal 1969-70 to date. Played for D.H. Robins XI v West Indians 1973 and Pakistanis 1974. Debut for county and cap 1975. Appointed county captain for 1978, but was relieved of appointment when his signing for World Series Cricket was announced. Re-appointed county captain during 1979 season. *Wisden* 1980. 1,000 runs (9) – 1,871 runs (av. 66.82) in 1978 best. Scored two centuries in match (131* and 114*) v Somerset (Nottingham) 1980. Scored 105* out of innings total of 143 v Hants (Bournemouth) 1981 – lowest innings total in first-class cricket to contain a century. BH Gold Awards: 6 HS: 246 v Sussex (Hove) 1976. HSGC/NW: 71 v Yorks (Bradford) 1978. Scored 157 for Transvaal v Orange Free State (Bloemfontein) 1975-76 in South African Gillete Cup competition. HSJPL: 120* v Glamorgan (Swansea) 1978. HSBH: 130* v Scotland (Glasgow) 1982. BB: 7-62 Transvaal v Western Province (Johannesburg) 1975-76. BBUK: 6-16 v Worcs (Worcester) 1977. BBNW: 6-18 v Sussex (Hove) 1982. BBJPL: 4-15 v Hants (Nottingham) 1980. BBBH: 6-22 v Northants (Northampton) 1981.

Robert Timothy ROBINSON B Sutton-in-Ashfield (Notts) 21/11/1958. RHB, RM. Debut 1978. Cap 1983. Scored 1545 runs (av. 40.65) in 1983. BH Gold Awards: 1. HS: 207 v Warwicks (Nottingham) 1983. HSNW: 44* v Sussex (Hove) 1982. HSJPL: 74 v Hants (Portsmouth) 1983. HSBH: 77* v Worcs (Nottingham) 1981.

Kevin SAXELBY B Worksop 23/2/1959. RHB, RM. Debut 1978. HS: 59* v Derby (Chesterfield) 1982. HSNW: 12 v Worcs (Worcester) 1983. HSJPL: 23* v Middlesex (Cleethorpes) 1983. HSBH: 13* v Lancs (Nottingham) 1982. BB: 4-18 v Hants (Nottingham) 1982. BBJPL: 4-29 v Warwicks (Birmingham) 1983. BBNW: 3-46 v Worcs (Worcester) 1983. BBBH: 3-46 v Yorks (Bradford) 1983.

Christopher William SCOTT B Thorpe-on-the-Hill (Lincs) 23/1/1964. RHB, WK. Debut 1981. HS: 78 v Cambridge U (Cambridge) 1983.

Peter Mark SUCH B Helensburgh, Scotland 12/6/1964. RHB, OB. Debut 1982. BB: 6-123 v Kent (Nottingham) 1983.

NB. The following players whose particulars appeared in the 1983 Annual have been omitted: M.A. Fell and N.J.B. Illingworth.

NOTTINGHAMSHIRE

County Averages

Schweppes County Championship: Played 24, won 3, drawn 11, lost 10.
All first-class matches: Played 25, won 4, drawn 11, lost 10.

BATTING AND FIELDING

Cap		*M*	*I*	*NO*	*RUNS*	*HS*	*Avge*	*100*	*50*	*Ct*	*St*
1983	R.T. Robinson	25	41	3	1545	207	40.65	2	11	6	—
1975	C.E.B.Rice	19	30	2	1026	101*	36.64	2	3	14	—
1981	J.D. Birch	24	38	2	1086	95	30.16	—	8	20	—
1978	R.J. Hadlee	5	4	0	119	103	29.75	1	—	3	—
1973	D.W. Randall	15	22	1	583	94	27.76	—	4	17	—
1970	S.B. Hassan	21	34	1	890	112	26.96	1	5	17	—
—	P. Johnson	16	28	2	612	125	23.53	1	4	9	—
1980	B.N. French	24	38	4	630	91	18.52	—	3	49	3
—	R.A. Pick	6	8	2	84	25*	14.00	—	—	—	—
1980	E.E. Hemmings	23	32	3	377	38	13.00	—	—	11	—
1980	K.E. Cooper	22	27	7	254	30*	12.70	—	—	4	—
1980	M.K. Bore	13	16	5	135	24	12.27	—	—	7	—
—	K. Saxelby	21	28	3	274	35	10.96	—	—	1	—
—	M.A. Fell	5	9	0	93	41	10.33	—	—	4	—
—	M. Hendrick	21	26	13	127	15*	9.76	—	—	18	—
—	N.G.B. Illingworth	3	6	1	49	17	9.80	—	—	3	—
—	P.M. Such	10	15	4	13	5	1.18	—	—	6	—

Played in two matches: C.W. Scott 2, 78 (3 ct 1 st).

BOWLING

	Type	*O*	*M*	*R*	*W*	*Avge*	*Best*	*5 wI*	*10 wM*
R.J. Hadlee	RF	86.2	28	210	13	16.15	5-72	1	—
M. Hendrick	RFM	552.1	190	1122	66	17.00	6-17	4	—
K. Saxelby	RM	410.2	96	1337	50	26.74	5-52	2	—
K.E. Cooper	RFM	579	164	1610	57	28.24	7-33	5	—
E.E. Hemmings	OB	710.4	195	2000	59	33.89	7-23	2	1
P.M. Such	RM	214	44	767	20	38.35	6-123	1	—
M.K. Bore	LM	370.5	108	1040	27	38.51	4-29	—	—
R.A. Pick	RM	134.4	16	500	7	71.42	2-50	—	—

Also bowled: J.D. Birch 1-0-1-0; M.A. Fell 3-0-11-0; N.G.B. Illingworth 37-6-113-1; R.T. Robinson 1-0-1-0.

County Records

First-class cricket

Highest innings	For	739-7d v Leics (Nottingham)	1903
totals:	Agst	706-4d by Surrey (Nottingham)	1947
Lowest innings	For	13 v Yorks (Nottingham)	1901
totals:	Agst	16 by Derby (Nottingham) and Surrey (Oval)	1879 & 1880

Highest individual innings:	For	312* W.W. Keeton v Middlesex (Oval)	1939
	Agst	345 C.G. Macartney for Australians (Nottingham)	1921
Best bowling in an innings:	For	10-66 K. Smales v Glos (Stroud)	1956
	Agst	10-10 H. Verity for Yorks (Leeds)	1932
Best bowling in a match:	For	17-89 F.C.L. Matthews v Northants (Nottingham)	1923
	Agst	17-89 W.G. Grace for Glos (Cheltenham)	1877
Most runs in a season:		2,620 (av. 53.46) W.W. Whysall	1929
runs in a career:		31,592 (av. 35.70) G. Gunn	1902-1932
100s in a season:		9 by W.W. Whysall	1928
		and M.J. Harris	1971
100s in a career:		65 by J. Hardstaff	1930-1955
wickets in a season:		181 (av. 14.96) B. Dooland	1954
wickets in a career:		1,653 (av. 20.34) T. Wass	1896-1920

RECORD WICKET STANDS

1st	391	A.O. Jones & A. Shrewsbury v Glos (Bristol)	1899
2nd	398	W. Gunn & A. Shrewsbury v Sussex (Nottingham)	1890
3rd	369	J.R. Gunn & W. Gunn v Leics (Nottingham)	1903
4th	361	A.O. Jones & J.R. Gunn v Essex (Leyton)	1905
5th	266	A. Shrewsbury & W. Gunn v Sussex (Hove)	1884
6th	303*	F.H. Winrow & P.F. Harvey v Derby (Nottingham)	1947
7th	204	M.J. Smedley & R.A. White v Surrey (Oval)	1967
8th	220	G.F.H. Heane & R. Winrow v Somerset (Nottingham)	1935
9th	165	W. McIntyre & G. Wootton v Kent (Nottingham)	1869
10th	152	E. Alletson & W. Riley v Sussex (Hove)	1911

One-day cricket

Highest innings totals:	Gillette Cup/ NatWest Trophy	271 v Glos (Nottingham)	1968
	John Player League	260-5 v Warwicks (Birmingham)	1976
	Benson & Hedges Cup	269-5 v Derby (Nottingham)	1980
Lowest innings totals:	Gillette Cup/ NatWest Trophy	123 v Yorks (Scarborough)	1969
	John Player League	66 v Yorks (Bradford)	1969
	Benson & Hedges Cup	94 v Lancs (Nottingham)	1975
Highest individual innings:	Gillette Cup/ NatWest Trophy	107 M. Hill v Somerset (Taunton)	1964
	John Player League	120* C.E.B. Rice v Glamorgan (Swansea)	1978
		120* S.B. Hassan v Warwicks (Birmingham)	1981
	Benson & Hedges Cup	130* C.E.B. Rice v Scotland (Glasgow)	1982
Best bowling figures:	Gillette Cup/ NatWest Trophy	6-18 C.E.B. Rice v Sussex (Hove)	1982
	John Player League	6-12 R.J. Hadlee v Lancs (Nottingham)	1980
	Benson & Hedges Cup	6-22 M.K. Bore v Leics (Leicester)	1980
		6-22 C.E.B. Rice v Northants (Northampton)	1981

SOMERSET

Formation of present club: 1875, reorganised 1885.
Colours: Black, silver and maroon.
Badge: Wessex Wyvern.
Best final position in Championship: Third (5): 1892, 1958, 1963, 1966 and 1981.
Gillette Cup Winners: 1979.
Gillette Cup Finalists (2): 1967 and 1978.
NatWest Trophy Winners: 1983
John Player League Champions: 1979.
Benson & Hedges Cup Winners (2): 1981 and 1982.
Gillette Man of the Match Awards: 26.
NatWest Man of the Match Awards: 5.
Benson & Hedges Gold Awards: 33.

Secretary and Chief Executive: A.S. Brown, County Cricket Ground, St. James's Street, Taunton TA1 1JT.
Captain: I.T. Botham.
Prospects of Play Telephone No: Taunton (0823) 70007.

Stephen Charles BOOTH B Leeds (Yorks) 30/10/1963. RHB, SLA. Debut 1983. BB: 4-26 v Middlesex (Lord's) 1983.

Ian Terrence BOTHAM B Haswell (Cheshire) 24/11/1955. RHB, REM. Debut 1974. Cap 1976. Best Young Cricketer of the Year in 1977. *Wisden* 1977. County Captain 1984. Testimonial 1984. Tests: 63 between 1977 and 1983 captaining England in 12 Tests. Tours: Pakistan and New Zealand 1977-78, Australia 1978-79, Australia and India 1979-80, West Indies 1980-81 (Captain), India and Sri Lanka 1981-82, Australia 1982-83. 1,000 runs (3) – 1,241 (av. 44.32) in 1982 best. Took 100 wkts (av. 16.40) in 1978. Became first player ever to score a century and take 8 wkts in innings in a Test match v Pakistan (Lord's) 1978, and to score a century and take 10 wkts in a Test, v India (Bombay) 1979-80. Took 100th wkt in Test cricket in 1979 in record time of 2 years 9 days. Achieved double of 1,000 runs and 100 wkts in Tests in 1979 to create record of fewest Tests (21). Took 200th wkt in 1981 in record time of 4 years 34 days and at youngest age of 25 years 280 days. Became third player in Test cricket to achieve double of 2,000 runs and 200 wkts in 1981-82 in fewest Tests (42), shortest time (4 years 126 days) and youngest age (26 years 7 days). Scored centuries against Australia in 1981 off 87 balls (Leeds) and 86 balls (Manchester). Hat-trick for MCC v Middlesex (Lord's) 1978. Gillette Man of Match: 1. BH Gold Awards: 5. HS: 228 v Glos (Taunton) 1980 in 184 minutes with 10 6's and 27 4's, scoring 182 between lunch and tea, and sharing in 4th wkt partnership record for county, 310 with P.W. Denning. HSTC: 208 v India (Oval) 1982. HSNW: 96* v Middlesex (Lord's) 1983. HSJPL: 106 v Hants (Taunton) 1981. HSBH: 57* v Kent (Taunton) 1981. BB: 8-34 v Pakistan (Lord's) 1978. BBC: 7-61 v Glamorgan (Cardiff) 1978. BBNW: 4-20 v Sussex (Hove) 1983. BBJPL: 4-10 v Yorks (Scarborough) 1979. BBBH: 4-16 v Combined Universities (Taunton) 1978. Soccer for Scunthorpe United.

Martin David CROWE B Auckland 22/9/1962. RHB, RM. Debut for Auckland 1979-80. Played for D.B. Close's XI v Pakistanis (Scarborough) 1982. Joined county for 1984. Son of D.W. Crowe (Wellington). Tours: New Zealand to Australia 1982-83, England 1983. HS: 150 Auckland v Central Districts (New Plymouth) 1981-82. BB: 5-69 Auckland v Central Districts (Napier) 1982-83.

Mark Richard DAVIS B Kilve (Somerset) 26/2/1962. LHB, LFM. Debut 1982. HS: 21* v Leics (Taunton) 1982. HSJPL: 11 v Middlesex (Weston-super-Mare) 1982. BB: 3-36 v Glamorgan (Swansea) 1982.

Peter William DENNING (Millfield School) B Chewton Mendip (Somerset) 16/12/1949. LHB, OB. Debut 1969. Cap 1973. 1,000 runs (6) – 1,222 runs (av. 42.13) in 1979 best. Scored two centuries in match (122 and 107) v Glos (Taunton) 1977. Shared in 4th wkt partnership record for county, 310 with I.T. Botham v Glos (Taunton) 1980. Gillette Man of Match: 4. BH Gold Awards: 3. HS: 184 v Notts (Nottingham) 1980. HSGC/NW: 145 v Glamorgan (Cardiff) 1978. HSJPL: 112* v Warwicks (Birmingham) 1982. HSBH: 129 v Glos (Taunton) 1982. Benefit 1981.

Colin Herbert DREDGE B Frome 4/8/1954. LHB, RM. 6ft 5ins tall. Debut 1976. Cap 1978. Gillette Man of Match: 1 HS: 56* v Yorks (Harrogate) 1977. HSJPL: 25* v Middlesex (Weston-super-Mare) 1982 and 25* v Glamorgan (Bath) 1983. HSBH: 10* v Worcs (Taunton) 1978 and v Glamorgan (Swansea) 1982. BB: 6-37 v Glos (Bristol) 1981. BBGC/NW: 4-23 v Kent (Canterbury) 1978. BBJPL: 5-35 v Middlesex (Lord's) 1981. BBBH: 4-10 v Hants (Bournemouth) 1980.

Nigel Alfred FELTON B Guildford, Surrey 24/10/1960. LHB. Debut 1982. HS: 173* v Kent (Taunton) 1983.

Trevor GARD B West Lambrook, near South Petheron 2/6/1957. RHB, WK. Debut 1976. Cap 1983. BH: Gold Award: 1. HS: 51* v Indians (Taunton) 1979. HSNW: 17 v Shropshire (Wellington) 1983. HSJPL: 14* v Derbyshire (Heanor) 1983. HSBH: 10 v Hants (Taunton) 1983.

Joel GARNER B Barbados 16/12/1952. RHB, RF. 6ft 8ins tall. Played for Barbados 1975-76 to date. Debut for county 1977. Cap 1979. *Wisden* 1979. Tests: 32 for West Indies between 1976-77 and 1982-83 Tours: West Indies to Australia and New Zealand 1979-80, England 1980, Pakistan 1980-81, Australia 1981-82. Gillette Man of Match: 1. BH Gold Awards: 2. HS: 104 West Indians v Glos (Bristol) 1980. HSTC: 60 West Indies v Australia (Brisbane) 1979-80. HSC: 90 v Glos (Bath) 1981. HSGC/NW: 38* v Glamorgan (Cardiff) 1978. HSJPL: 59* v Surrey (Bath) 1982. HSBH: 17 v Sussex (Hove) 1978. BB: 8-31 v Glamorgan (Cardiff) 1977. BBTC: 6-56 West Indies v New Zealand (Auckland) 1979-80. BBGC/NW: 6-29 v Northants (Lord's) 1979. BBJPL: 4-6 v Notts (Bath) 1982. BBBH: 5-14 v Surrey (Lord's) 1981.

Jeremy William LLOYDS (Blundell's School) B Penang, Malaya 17/11/1954. LHB, OB. Debut 1979. Cap 1982. Scored 132* and 102* v Northants (Northampton) 1982. HS: 132* v Northants (Northampton) 1982. HSNW: 28* v Leics (Taunton) 1982 and v Sussex (Hove) 1983. HSJPL: 33 v Surrey (Oval) 1981. HSBH: 51 v Sussex (Taunton) 1983. BB: 7-88 v Essex (Chelmsford) 1982.

Victor James MARKS (Blundell's School and Oxford) B Middle Chinnock 25/6/1955. RHB, OB. Debut for Oxford U and county 1975. Blue 1975-76-77-78 (Captain in 1976-77). Cap 1979. Tour: Australia 1982-83. NW Man of the Match: 2. BH Gold Awards: 3. HS: 105 Oxford U v Worcs (Oxford) 1976. HSTC: 12* v Pakistan (Leeds) 1982. HSC: 98 v Essex (Leyton) 1976. HSNW: 55 v Warwicks (Taunton) 1982. HSJPL: 71* v Surrey (Taunton) 1980. HSBH: 81* v Hants (Bournemouth) 1980. BB: 7-51 v Notts (Nottingham) 1982. BBTC: 3-78 v New Zealand (Oval) 1983. BBNW: 3-30 v Kent (Lord's) 1983. BBJPL: 3-19 v Derby (Taunton) 1979, v Glos (Bristol) 1980 and v Warwicks (Birmingham) 1982. BBBH: 3-25 v Sussex (Taunton) 1982. Half-blue for Rugby Fives.

SOMERSET

Hallam Reynold MOSELEY B Christ Chruch, Barbados 28/5/1948. RHB, RFM. Toured England with Barbados team in 1969 and made debut v Notts (Nottingham). Played for Barbados in 1971-72. Debut for county in 1971. Cap 1972. Testimonial (£24,085) in 1979. Did not play in 1983. HS: 67 v Leics (Taunton) 1972. HSGC/NW: 15 v Lancs (Manchester) 1972. HSJPL: 24 v Notts (Torquay) 1972 and 24 v Hants (Weston-super-Mare) 1975. HSBH: 33 v Hants (Bournemouth) 1973. BB: 6-34 v Derby (Bath) 1975 and 6-35 v Glos (Taunton) 1978. BBGC/NW: 4-31 v Surrey (Taunton) 1974. BBJPL: 5-30 v Middlesex (Lord's) 1973. BBBH: 3-13 v Combined Universities (Taunton 1982.

Richard Leslie OLLIS B Clifton (Glos) 14/1/1961. LHB, RM. Debut 1981. HS: 99* v Glos (Bristol) 1983.

Gary Vincent PALMER B Taunton 1/11/1965. RHB, RM. Debut 1982. HS: 78 v Glos (Bristol) 1983. HSJPL: 13* v Derby (Heanor) 1983. BB: 5-38 v Warwicks (Taunton) 1983.

Nigel Francis Mark POPPLEWELL (Radley College and Cambridge) B Chislehurst (Kent) 8/8/1957. Son of O.B. Popplewell, Q.C., former Cambridge Blue. RHB, RM. Debut for Cambridge U 1977. Blue 1977-78-79 (secretary). Debut for county 1979. Cap 1983. BH Gold Awards: 2. HS: 143 v Glos (Bath) 1983 including 100 in 41 minutes. HSNW: 68* v Lancs (Manchester) 1983. HSJPL: 84 v Glamorgan (Bath) 1983. HSBH: 42 v Kent (Taunton) 1981. BB: 5-33 v Northants (Weston-super-Mare) 1981. BBNW: 3-34 v Middlesex (Lord's) 1983. BBJPL: 3-38 v Glos (Bath) 1983.

Isaac Vivian Alexander RICHARDS B St. John's, Antigua 7/3/1952. RHB, OB. Played for Leeward Islands and Combined Islands 1971-72 to date. Debut for county and cap 1974. *Wisden* 1976. Played for Queensland in 1976-77. Benefit in 1982 (£56,440). Tests: 52 for West Indies between 1974-75 and 1982-83, captaining West Indies in 1 Test in 1980. Tours: West Indies to India, Sri Lanka and Pakistan 1974-75, Australia 1975-76, 1979-80 1981-82, England 1976 and 1980, Pakistan 1980-81. 1,000 runs (10) – 2,161 runs (av. 65.48) in 1977 best. Also scored 1,267 runs (av. 60.33) on 1974-75 tour and 1,107 runs (av. 58.26) on 1975-76 tour, and in 1980-81. Scored 1,710 in 11 Test matches in 1976 including 829 runs in 4 Tests against England. Hat-trick in JPL v Essex (Chelmsford) 1982. Gillette Man of Match: 3. NW Man of the Match: 1. BH Gold Awards: 5. HS: 291 West Indies v England (Oval) 1976. HSC: 241* v Glos (Bristol) 1977. HSGC/NW: 139* v Warwicks (Taunton) 1978. HSJPL: 126* v Glos (Bristol, Imperial Ground) 1975. HSBH: 132* v Surrey (Lord's) 1981. BB: 5-88 West Indians v Queensland (Brisbane) 1981-82. BBUK: 4-55 v Glamorgan (Taunton) 1981. BBJPL: 6-24 v Lancs (Manchester) 1983.

Peter Michael ROEBUCK (Millfield School and Cambridge) B Oxford 6/3/1956. RHB, OB. Debut 1974. Blue 1975-76-77. Cap 1978. 1,000 runs (3) – 1,273 runs (av. 47.14) in 1979 best. BH Gold Awards: 1. HS: 158 Cambridge U v Oxford U (Lord's) 1975. HSC: 131* v New Zealanders (Taunton) 1978. HSGC/NW: 57 v Essex (Taunton) 1978. HSJPL: 105 v Glos (Bath) 1983. HSBH: 53* v Notts (Lord's) 1982. BB: 6-50 Cambridge U v Kent (Canterbury) 1977.

Brian Charles ROSE B Dartford (Kent) 4/6/1950. LHB, LM. Wears spectacles. Debut 1969. Cap 1975. Appointed county captain in 1978. *Wisden* 1979 Tests: 9 between 1977-78 and 1980-81. Tours: Pakistan and New Zealand 1977-78, West Indies 1980-81 (returned through eyesight problem). 1,000 runs (8) – 1,624 runs (av. 46.40) in 1976 best. Scored two centuries in match (124 and 150*) v Worcs

(Worcester) 1980. Gillette Man of Match: 2. BH Gold Awards: 2. HS: 205 v Northants (Weston-super-Mare) 1977. HSTC: 70 v West Indies (Manchester) 1980. HSGC/NW: 128 v Derby (Ilkeston) 1977. HSJPL: 112* v Essex (Ilford) 1980. HSBH: 137* v Kent (Canterbury) 1980. BB: 3-9 v Glos (Taunton) 1975. BBJPL: 3-25 v Lancs (Manchester) 1975. Benefit 1983.

Philip Anthony SLOCOMBE (Millfield School) B Weston-super-Mare 6/9/1954. RHB, RM. Debut 1975. Cap 1978. 1,000 runs (2) – 1,221 runs (av. 38.15) in 1978 best. Scored 106* & 98 v Worcs (Worcester) 1978. HS: 132 v Notts (Taunton) 1975. HSGC/NW: 42 v Surrey (Oval) 1975. HSJPL: 46 v Glamorgan (Bath) 1983. HSBH: 42 v Middlesex (Taunton) 1980. Plays soccer for Weston-super-Mare in Western League.

Peter Hugh L'Estrange WILSON (Wellington College) B Guildford 17/8/1958. 6ft 5in tall. RHB, Played for Surrey 1978 to 1982. Joined Somerset 1983. Played for Northern Transvaal in 1979-80. HS: 29 Northern Transvaal v Transvaal (Pretoria) 1979-80. HSUK: 15 Surrey v Worcs (Guildford) 1979. HSJPL: 18* Surrey v Worcs (Oval) 1979. BB: 5-36 Northern Transvaal v Eastern Province (Pretoria) 1979-80. BBUK: 4-39 Surrey v Warwicks (Oval) 1979. BBGC/NW: 3–59 Surrey v Essex (Colchester) 1978. BBJPL: 4-32 Surrey v Middlesex (Oval) 1979. BBBH: 5-21 Surrey v Combined Universities (Oval) 1979.

Julian George WYATT B Paulton 19/6/1963. RHB, RM. Debut 1983. HS: 82* v Warwicks (Taunton) 1983.

NB. The following players whose particulars appeared in the 1983 Annual have been omitted: N. Russom, D.J.S. Taylor.

County Averages

Schweppes County Championship: Played 24, won 3, drawn 14, lost 7.
All first-class matches: Played 25, won 3, drawn 15, lost 7.

BATTING AND FIELDING

Cap		*M*	*I*	*NO*	*RUNS*	*HS*	*Avge*	*100*	*50*	*Ct*	*St*
1974	I.V.A.Richards	12	20	4	1204	216	75.25	5	3	6	—
1976	I.T. Botham	10	13	0	570	152	43.84	2	1	7	—
1978	P.M. Roebuck	22	38	5	1235	106*	37.42	1	9	9	—
—	J.G. Wyatt	6	12	2	352	82*	35.20	—	3	1	—
—	N.A. Felton	7	12	1	376	173*	34.18	1	1	2	—
1982	J.W. Lloyds	21	35	2	901	100	27.30	1	4	12	—
1979	J. Garner	10	16	6	265	44	26.50	—	—	10	—
—	R.L. Ollis	13	22	2	517	99*	25.85	—	3	3	—
1983	N.F.M. Popplewell	24	39	3	886	143	24.61	1	4	21	—
1979	V.J. Marks	16	25	3	524	44*	23.81	—	—	5	—
1973	P.W. Denning	21	36	3	758	99	22.96	—	4	6	—
1975	B.C. Rose	8	9	0	184	52	20.44	—	1	2	—
1983	T. Gard	25	33	4	457	51	15.75	—	2	42	8
—	P.H.L. Wilson	11	11	7	60	25	15.00	—	—	3	—
1978	P.A. Slocombe	11	17	2	224	66	14.93	—	1	5	—
1978	C.H. Dredge	21	26	5	296	50	14.09	—	1	10	—
—	G.V. Palmer	10	13	2	119	78	10.81	—	1	8	—
—	M.R. Davis	14	17	5	125	20*	10.41	—	—	5	—
—	S.C. Booth	10	12	5	24	9	3.42	—	—	7	—

Played in two matches: D. Breakwell 55*, 4, 13;
Played in one match: N. Russom 8.

BOWLING

	Type	*O*	*M*	*R*	*W*	*Avge*	*Best*	*5 wI*	*10 wM*
J. Garner	**RF**	277	74	708	35	20.22	6-37	1	—
C.H. Dredge	**RM**	492.3	126	1323	48	27.56	5-51	2	—
J.W. Lloyds	**OB**	358.1	98	1079	35	30.82	5-120	1	—
G.V. Palmer	**RM**	208.3	40	630	20	31.50	5-38	1	—
I.T. Botham	**RFM**	119.3	28	388	12	32.33	5-38	1	—
V.J. Marks	**OB**	572.3	179	1620	50	32.40	6-79	3	-
P.H.L. Wilson	**RFM**	248.3	45	837	25	33.48	4-77	—	—
N.F.M. Popplewell	**RM**	232	38	786	23	34.17	4-69	—	—
M.R. Davis	**LFM**	240.4	43	873	25	34.92	4-34	—	—
I.V.A. Richards	**OB**	188	61	462	12	38.50	3-56	—	—
S.C. Booth	**SLA**	286.2	85	849	21	40.42	4-26	—	—

Also bowled: D. Breakwell 49-17-121-4; T. Gard 0.2-0-8-0; R.L. Ollis 1-0-2-0; P.M. Roebuck 5-0-25-0; B.C. Rose 1-0-6-0; N. Russom 5-1-18-0; P.A. Slocombe 2-1-1-0.

County Records

First-class cricket

Highest innings totals:	For	675-9d v Hants (Bath)	1924
	Agst	811 by Surrey (Oval)	1899
Lowest innings totals:	For	25 v Glos (Bristol)	1947
	Agst	22 by Glos (Bristol)	1920
Highest individual innings:	For	310 H. Gimblett v Sussex (Eastbourne)	1948
	Agst	424 A.C. MacLaren for Lancs (Taunton)	1895
Best bowling: in an innings:	For	10-49 E.J. Tyler v Surrey (Taunton)	1895
	Agst	10-35 A. Drake for Yorks (Weston-s-Mare)	1914
Best bowling in a match:	For	16-83 J.C. White v Worcs (Bath)	1919
	Agst	17-137 W. Brearley for Lancs (Manchester)	1905
Most runs in a season:		2,761 (av. 58.74) W.E. Alley	1961
runs in a career:		21,142 (av. 36.96) H. Gimblett	1935-1954
100s in a season:		10 by W.E. Alley	1961
100s in a career:		49 by H. Gimblett	1935-1954
wickets in a season:		169 (av. 19.24) A.W. Wellard	1938
wickets in a career:		2,166 (av. 18.02) J.C. White	1909-1937

RECORD WICKET STANDS

1st	346	H.T. Hewett & L.C.H. Palairet v Yorks (Taunton)	1892
2nd	290	J.C.W. MacBryan & M.D. Lyon v Derby (Buxton)	1924
3rd	300	G. Atkinson & P.B. Wight v Glamorgan (Bath)	1960
4th	310	P.W. Denning & I.T. Botham v Glos (Taunton)	1980
5th	235	J.C. White & C.C.C. Case v Glos (Taunton)	1927
6th	265	W.E. Alley & K.E. Palmer v Northants (Northampton)	1961
7th	240	S.M.J. Woods & V.T. Hill v Kent (Taunton)	1898
8th	172	I.V.A. Richards & I.T. Botham v Leics (Leicester)	1983
9th	183	C. Greetham & H.W. Stephenson v Leics (Weston-super-Mare)	1963
10th	143	J.J. Bridges & H. Gibbs v Surrey (Weston-super-Mare)	1919

One-day cricket

Highest innings totals:	Gillette Cup/ NatWest Trophy	330-4 v Glamorgan (Cardiff)	1978
	John Player League	286-7 v Hants (Taunton)	1981
	Benson & Hedges Cup	307-6 v Glos (Taunton)	1982
Lowest innings totals:	Gillette Cup/ NatWest Trophy	59 v Middlesex (Lord's)	1977
	John Player League	58 v Essex (Chelmsford)	1977
	Benson & Hedges Cup	98 v Middlesex (Lord's)	1982
Highest individual innings:	Gillette Cup/ NatWest Trophy	145 P.W. Denning v Glamorgan (Cardiff)	1978
	John Player League	131 D.B. Close v Yorks (Bath)	1974
	Benson & Hedges Cup	137* B.C. Rose v Kent (Canterbury)	1980
Best bowling figures:	Gillette Cup/ NatWest Trophy	6-29 J. Garner v Northants (Lord's)	1979
	John Player League	6-24 I.V.A. Richards v Lancs (Manchester)	1983
	Benson & Hedges Cup	5-14 J. Garner v Surrey (Lord's)	1981

SURREY

Formation of present club: 1845.
Colours: Chocolate and Silver.
Badge: Prince of Wales' Feathers.
County Champions (18): 1864, 1887, 1888, 1890, 1891, 1892, 1894, 1895, 1899, 1914, 1952, 1953, 1954, 1955, 1956, 1957, 1958 and 1971.
Joint Champions (2): 1889 and 1950.
Gillette Cup Finalists (2): 1965 and 1980.
NatWest Trophy Winners: 1982.
Best final position in John Player League: 5th in 1969 and 1980.
Benson & Hedges Cup Winners: 1974.
Benson & Hedges Cup Finalists (2): 1979 and 1981.
Gillette Man of the Match Awards: 18.
NatWest Trophy Man of the Match Awards: 6.
Benson & Hedges Gold Awards: 32.

Secretary: I.F.B. Scott-Browne, Kennington Oval, London, SE11 5SS.
Cricket manager: M. J. Stewart.
Captain: G.P. Howarth.
Prospects of Play Telephone No: (01) 735 4911.

Christopher Keith BULLEN B Clapham 5/11/1962. RHB, OB. Debut 1982. One match v Oxford U (Oxford) Did not play in 1983.

Alan Raymond BUTCHER B Croydon 7/1/1954. LHB, SLA. Debut 1972. Cap 1975. Played for Overseas XI v Board Presidents XI (Calcutta) 1980-81. Tour: International XI to Jamaica 1982-83. Tests: 1 in 1979. 1,000 runs (5) – 1,713 runs (av. 46.29) in 1980 best. BH Gold Awards: 4. HS: 216 v Cambridge U (Cambridge) 1980. HSTC: 20 v India (Oval) 1979. HSNW: 86* v Warwicks (Lord's) 1982. HSJPL: 113* v Warwicks (Birmingham) 1978. HSBH: 80 v Sussex (Oval) 1982. BB: 6-48 v Hants (Guildford) 1972. BBJPL: 5-19 Glos (Bristol) 1975. BBBH: 3-11 v Lancs (Manchester) 1974.

Sylvester Theophilus CLARKE B Christ Church, Barbados 11/12/1954. RHB, RF. Played for Barbados 1977-78 to 1981-82 and for West Indies XI v International XI (Kingston) 1982-83. Debut for county 1979. Cap 1980. Tests: 11 for West Indies between 1977-78 and 1981-82. Tours: West Indies to India and Sri Lanka 1978-79. Pakistan 1980-81, Australia 1981-82, West Indian "rebels" to South Africa 1982-83. Hat-tricks (2): Barbados v Trinidad (Bridgetown) 1977-78, v Notts (Oval) 1980. NW Man of the Match: 1. BH Gold Awards: 2. HS 100* (in 62 minutes) v Glamorgan (Swansea) 1981. HSTC: 35* West Indies v Pakistan (Faialabad) 1980-81. HSNW: 45* v Leics (Oval) 1981. HSJPL: 34* v Hants (Oval) 1980. HSBH: 39 v Hants (Southampton) 1982. BB: 7-34 West Indian XI v South Africa (Johannesburg) 1982-83. BBUK: 7-53 v Warwicks (Oval) 1983. BBTC: 5-126 West Indies v India (Bangalore) 1978-79. BBGC/NW: 4-38 v Yorks (Oval) 1980. BBJPL: 3-21 v Middlesex (Oval) 1983. BBBH: 5-23 v Kent (Oval) 1980.

Grahame Selvey CLINTON B Sidcup 5/5/1953. LHB, RM. Debut for Kent 1974. Debut for Surrey in 1979. Played for Zimbabwe/Rhodesia in 1979-80. Cap 1980. 1,000 runs (3) – 1,240 runs (av. 37.57) in 1980 best. BH Gold Awards: 2 (1 for Kent). HS: 172* v Oxford U (Oxford) 1982. HSGC/NW: 58 v Essex (Chelmsford) 1980. HSJPL: 105* v Yorks (Scarborough) 1981. HSBH: 79 v Essex (Oval) 1982.

Ian James CURTIS (Whitgift School and Oxford) B Purley 13/5/1959. LHB, SLA/SLC. Debut for Oxford U 1980. Blue 1980 and 1982. Debut for County 1983. HS: 20* Oxford U v Warwicks (Oxford) 1982. BB: 6-28 v Oxford U (Oxford) 1983.

Geoffrey Philip HOWARTH B Auckland 29/3/1951. Younger brother of H.J. Howarth, New Zealand Test cricketer. RHB, OB. Debut for New Zealand under-23 XI v Auckland (Auckland) 1968-69 and has played for Auckland 1972-73 and 1973-74 and Northern Districts 1974-75 to date. Debut for Surrey 1971. Cap 1974. Awarded M.B.E. in 1981 Birthday Honours List. Appointed county captain for 1984. Tests: 34 for New Zealand between 1974-75 and 1983 captaining New Zealand in 17 tests. Tours: D.H. Robins to South Africa 1975-76 and to India 1977-78. New Zealand to Pakistan and India 1976-77, England 1978 and 1983 (captain), Australia 1980-81 (captain) and 1982-83 (captain) 1,000 runs (4) – 1,554 runs (av. 37.90) in 1976 best. Scored two centuries in match (122 and 102) New Zealand v England (Auckland) 1977-78. BH Gold Awards: 1. HS: 183 v Hants (Oval) 1979. HSTC: 147 New Zealand v West Indies (Christchurch) 1979-80. HSGC/NW: 34 v Lancs (Manchester) 1977 and 34 v Northants (Northampton) 1979. HSJPL: 122 v Glos (Oval) 1976. HSBH: 80 v Yorks (Oval) 1974. BB: 5-32 Auckland v Central Districts (Auckland) 1973-74. BBUK: 3-20 v Northants (Northampton) 1976. BBJPL: 4-16 v Warwicks (Byfleet) 1979. Benefit 1983.

Roger David Verdon KNIGHT (Dulwich College and Cambridge) B Streatham 6/9/1946. LHB, RM. Debut for Cambridge U 1967. Blue 1967-68-69-70. Debut for Surrey 1968. Debut for Glos by special registration 1971. Cap 1971. Debut for Sussex in 1976. Cap 1976. Rejoined Surrey for 1978 as county captain. Cap 1978. Relinquished captaincy for 1984. 1,000 runs (12) – 1,350 runs (av. 38.57) in 1974 best. Gillette Man of the Match: 5 (3 for Glos). BH Gold Awards: 5 (1 for Sussex, 2 for Glos). HS: 165* Sussex v Middlesex (Hove) 1976. HSC: 132 v Lancs (Oval) 1980. HSGC/NW: 75 Glos v Glamorgan (Cardiff) 1973. HSJPL: 127 Sussex v Hants (Hove) 1976. HSBH: 117 Sussex v Surrey (Oval) 1977. BB: 6-44 Glos v Northants (Northampton) 1974. BBC: 5-44 v Glos (Cheltenham) 1979. BBGC/NW: 5-39 Glos v Surrey (Bristol) 1971. BBJPL: 5-42 Sussex v Notts (Nottingham) 1977. BBBH: 3-19 Sussex v Surrey (Oval) 1977.

Monte Alan LYNCH B Georgetown, British Guiana 21/5/1958. RHB, RM/OB. Debut 1977. Cap 1982. Played for Guyana 1982-83. 1,000 runs (2) – 1558 (av. 53.72) in 1983 best. Tour: International XI to Pakistan 1981-82. NW Man of the Match: 1. HS: 141* v Glamorgan (Guildford) 1982. HSNW: 129 v Durham (Oval) 1982. HSJPL: 80* v Warwicks (Oval) 1981. HSBH: 67 v Worcs (Worcester) 1979. BB: 3-6 v Glamorgan (Swansea) 1981.

Kevin Scott MACKINTOSH (Kingston-upon-Thames GS) B Surbiton (Surrey) 30/8/1957. RHB, RM. Debut for Notts in 1978. Rejoined Surrey in 1981. HS: 31 v Somerset (Oval) 1982. HSJPL: 12* Notts v Lancs (Nottingham) 1978. BB: 6-61 v Middlesex (Lord's) 1982. BBNW: 3-27 v Durham (Oval) 1982. BBJPL: 4-26 Notts v Glos (Nottingham) 1979.

SURREY

Graham MONKHOUSE B Carlisle 26/4/1955. RHB, RM. Debut 1981. HS: 63* v Somerset (Oval) 1982. HSJPL: 55 v Essex (Southend) 1982. BB: 7-51 v Notts (Oval) 1983. BBNW: 3-26 v Lincolnshire (Sleaford) 1983. BBJPL: 3-22 v Hants (Oval) 1982. Has played soccer for Carlisle United and Workington.

Andrew NEEDHAM B Calow (Derbyshire) 23/3/1957. RHB, OB. Debut 1977. HS: 134* v Lancs (Manchester) 1982. HSJPL: 25* v Middlesex (Oval) 1983. BB: 6-30 v Oxford U (Oval) 1983. BBJPL: 3-41 v Lancs (Manchester) 1982.

Duncan Brian PAULINE B Aberdeen 15/12/1960. RHB, RM. Debut 1979. HS: 115 v Sussex (Oval) 1983. HSNW: 10 v Durham (Oval) 1982. HSJPL: 92 v Worcs (Oval) 1981.

Ian Roger PAYNE (Emanuel School) B Lambeth Hospital, Kennington 9/5/1958. RHB, RM. Debut 1977. BH Gold Awards: 1. HS: 43 v Essex (Oval) 1983. HSNW: 56* v Lincolnshire (Sleaford) 1983. HSJPL: 33* v Glamorgan (Swansea) 1983. BB: 5-13 v Glos (Oval) 1983. BBNW: 5-36 v Lincolnshire (Sleaford) 1983. BBJPL: 5-21 v Derby (Derby) 1982. BBBH: 3-20 v Leics (Oval) 1981.

Patrick Ian POCOCK B Bangor, Caernarvonshire 24/9/1946. RHB, OB. Debut 1964. Cap 1967. Benefit (£18,500) in 1977. Played for Northern Transvaal in 1971-72. Tests: 17 between 1967-68 and 1976. Tours: Pakistan 1966-67, West Indies 1967-68 and 1973-74, Ceylon and Pakistan 1968-69, Ceylon 1969-70, India, Pakistan and Sri Lanka 1972-73. Played for Rest of the World XI v Pakistan XI (Karachi) 1970-71. Took 112 wkts (av. 18.22) in 1967. Took 4 wkts in 4 balls, 5 in 6, 6 in 9, and 7 in 11 (the last two being first-class records) v Sussex (Eastbourne) 1972. Hat-tricks (2): as above and v Worcs (Guildford) 1971. BH Gold Awards: 2. HS: 75* v Notts (Oval) 1968. HSTC: 33 v Pakistan (Hyderabad) 1972-73. HSGC/NW: 14 v Essex (Colchester) 1978. HSJPL: 22 v Notts (Nottingham) 1971. HSBH: 19 v Middlesex (Oval) 1972. BB: 9-57 v Glamorgan (Cardiff) 1979. BBTC: 6-79 v Australia (Manchester) 1968. BBGC/NW: 3-34 v Somerset (Oval) 1975. BBJPL: 4-27 v Essex (Chelmsford) 1974. BBBH: 4-11 v Yorks (Barnsley) 1978.

Clifton James RICHARDS B Penzance 10/8/1958. RHB, WK. Debut 1976. Cap 1978. Tours: D.H. Robins to New Zealand 1979-80, India and Sri Lanka 1981-82. International XI to Jamaica 1982-83. NW Man of the Match: 1. HS: 117* v Notts (Oval) 1982. HSNW: 105* v Lincolnshire (Sleaford) 1983. HSJPL: 52 v Lancs (Manchester) 1982. HSBH: 32 v Leics (Oval) 1981.

Alec James STEWART (Tiffin School) B Merton 8/4/1963. Son of M.J. Stewart, RHB, WK. Debut 1981. HS: 118* v Oxford U (Oval) 1983. HSJPL: 36 v Sussex (Hove) 1983.

David James THOMAS B Solihull (Warwicks) 30/6/1959. LHB, LM. Debut 1977. Cap 1982. Played for Northern Transvaal in 1980-81. HS: 119 v Notts (Oval) 1983. HSNW: 37 v Warwicks (Oval) 1983. HSJPL: 72 v Glamorgan (Swansea) 1983. HSBH: 13 v Kent (Oval) 1980 and 13 v Notts (Nottingham) 1981. BB: 6–84 v Derby (Oval) 1979. BBNW: 3-16 v Durham (Oval) 1982. BBJPL: 4-13 v Sussex (Oval) 1978. BBBH: 3-30 v Leics (Oval) 1981.

Peter Andrew WATERMAN B Hendon, Middlesex 26/3/1961. RHB. RFM. Debut 1983.

NB. The following players whose particulars appeared in the 1983 Annual have been omitted: M.S. Butcher, R.G.L. Cheatle and D.M. Smith.

County Averages

Schweppes County Championship: Played 24, won 7, drawn 13, lost 4.
All first-class matches: Played 25, won 8, drawn 13, lost 4.

BATTING AND FIELDING

Cap		*M*	*I*	*NO*	*RUNS*	*HS*	*Avge*	*100*	*50*	*Ct*	*St*
1982	M.A. Lynch	24	39	10	1558	119	53.72	3	11	15	—
1980	D.M. Smith	13	20	4	748	131*	46.75	2	3	13	—
—	D.B. Pauline	12	21	2	796	115	41.89	1	7	3	—
—	A.J. Stewart	10	17	4	525	118*	40.38	1	2	4	1
1978	R.D.V. Knight	24	38	6	1235	101*	38.59	1	9	28	—
—	D.J. Thomas	23	31	5	937	119	36.03	2	4	9	—
1975	A.R. Butcher	25	44	3	1349	128	32.90	3	6	15	—
1974	G.P. Howarth	4	5	1	123	66	30.75	—	1	1	—
1978	C.J. Richards	25	35	8	751	85*	27.81	—	2	48	7
—	I.R. Payne	10	11	4	167	43	23.85	—	—	11	—
1980	G.S. Clinton	13	22	3	439	105	23.10	1	3	-	-
-	G. Monkhouse	18	18	5	291	46	22.38	—	—	8	—
1980	S.T. Clarke	24	24	4	285	43	14.25	—	—	17	—
1967	P.I. Pocock	23	19	7	110	23	9.16	—	—	8	—
—	A. Needham	9	13	1	88	18	7.33	—	—	2	—
—	I.J. Curtis	13	10	4	22	7	3.66	—	—	3	—

Played in two matches: P.A. Waterman 6*, 0.
Played in one match: R.G.L. Cheadle did not bat (1 ct); M.A. Feltham did not bat; K.S. MacIntosh 18*, 5*.

BOWLING

	Type	*O*	*M*	*R*	*W*	*Avge*	*Best*	*5 wI*	*10 wM*
G. Monkhouse	**RM**	373.3	97	1040	47	22.12	7-51	1	—
S.T. Clarke	**RF**	693.1	183	1773	79	22.44	7-53	4	1
A. Needham	**OB**	164	50	470	19	24.73	6-30	2	—
P.I. Pocock	**OB**	681.2	200	1774	68	26.08	7-79	4	—
D.J. Thomas	**LFM**	547	114	1781	57	31.24	4-22	—	—
I.R. Payne	**RM**	158.5	41	450	12	37.50	5-13	1	—
R.D.V. Knight	**RM**	236	60	677	15	45.13	3-58	—	—
I.J. Curtis	**SLA**	269	82	690	17	40.58	6-28	1	—

Also bowled: A.R. Butcher 44.4-9-210-5; M.A. Feltham 18-5-44-2; M.A. Lynch 7.3-0-47-0; K.S. MacIntosh 15-2-47-0; D.M. Smith 2.2-0-20-0; P.A. Waterman 39-7-151-1.

County Records

First-class cricket

Highest innings totals:	For	811 v Somerset (Oval)	1899
	Agst	705-8d by Sussex (Hastings)	1902
Lowest innings totals:	For	14 v Essex (Chelmsford)	1983
	Agst	16 by MCC (Lord's)	1872
Highest Individual innings:	For	357* R. Abel v Somerset (Oval)	1899
	Agst	300* F. B. Watson for Lancs (Manchester)	1928
		300 R. Subba Row for Northants (Oval)	1958
Best bowling in an innings:	For	10-43 T. Rushby v Somerset (Taunton)	1921
	Agst	10-28 W. P. Howell for Australians (Oval)	1899
Best bowling in a match:	For	16-83 G. A. R. Lock v Kent (Blackheath)	1956
	Agst	15-57 W. P. Howell for Australians (Oval)	1899
Most runs in a season:		3,246 (av. 72.13) T. W. Hayward	1906
runs in a career:		43,554 (av. 49.72) J. B. Hobbs	1905-1934
100s in a season:		13 by T. W. Hayward and	1906
		J. B. Hobbs	1925
100s in a career:		144 by J. B. Hobbs	1905-1934
wickets in a season:		252 (av. 17.87) T. Richardson	1895
wickets in a career:		1,775 (av. 17.88) T. Richardson	1892-1904

RECORD WICKET STANDS

1st	428	J. B. Hobbs & A. Sandham v Oxford U (Oval)	1926
2nd	371	J. B. Hobbs & E. G. Hayes v Hants (Oval)	1909
3rd	353	A. Ducat & E. G. Hayes v Hants (Southampton)	1919
4th	448	R. Abel & T. W. Hayward v Yorks (Oval)	1899
5th	308	J. N. Crawford & F. C. Holland v Somerset (Oval)	1908
6th	298	A. Sandham & H. S. Harrison v Sussex (Oval)	1913
7th	200	T. F. Shepherd & J. W. Hitch v Kent (Blackheath)	1921
8th	204	T. W. Hayward & L. C. Braund v Lancs (Oval)	1898
9th	168	E. R. T. Holmes & E. W. J. Brooks v Hants (Oval)	1936
10th	173	A. Ducat & A. Sandham v Essex (Leyton)	1921

One-day cricket

Highest innings: totals:	GC/Natwest Trophy	297-6 v Lincoln (Sleaford)	1983
	John Player League	270-6 v Worcs (Guildford)	1983
	Benson & Hedges Cup	276-6 v Essex (Oval)	1982
Lowest innings: totals:	GC/NatWest Trophy	74 v Kent (Oval)	1967
	John Player League	64 v Worcs (Worcester)	1978
	Benson & Hedges Cup	122 v Kent (Canterbury)	1983
Highest individual innings:	Gillette Cup/ NatWest Trophy	129 M.A. Lynch v Durham (Oval)	1982
	John Player League	122 G.P. Howarth v Glos (Oval)	1976
	Benson & Hedges Cup	115 G.R.J. Roope v Essex (Chelmsford)	1973
Best bowling figures:	Gillette Cup/ NatWest Trophy	7-33 R.D. Jackman v Yorks (Harrogate)	1970
	John Player League	6-25 Intikhab Alam v Derby (Oval)	1974
	Benson & Hedges Cup	5-21 P.H.L. Wilson v Combined U. (Oval)	1979

SUSSEX

Formation of present club: 1839, reorganised 1857.
Colours: Dark blue, light blue, and gold.
Badge: County Arms of six martlets (in shape of inverted pyramid).
County Championship Runners-up (7): 1902, 1903, 1932, 1933, 1934, 1953 and 1981.
Gillette Cup Winners (3): 1963, 1964 and 1978.
Gillette Cup Finalists (3): 1968, 1970 and 1973.
NatWest Trophy third round (2): 1981 and 1983.
John Player League Winners: 1982.
Benson & Hedges Cup Semi-finalists: 1982.
Gillette Man of the Match Awards: 30.
NatWest Man of the Match Awards: 2.
Benson & Hedges Gold Awards: 29.

Secretary: R. Renold, County Ground, Eaton Road, Hove, BN3 3AN.
Captain: J.R.T. Barclay.
Prospects of Play Telephone No: Brighton (0273) 772766.

John Robert Troutbeck BARCLAY (Eton College) B Bonn, West Germany 22/1/1954. RHB, OB. Debut 1970 aged 16 years 205 days. Cap 1976. Captain 1981. Played for Orange Free State in 1978-79. 1,000 runs (4) – 1,093 (av. 32.14) in 1979 best. Gillette Man of the Match: 1. BH Gold Awards: 2. HS: 119 v Leics (Hove) 1980. HSNW: 48 v Ireland (Dublin) 1983. HSJPL: 48 v Derby (Derby) 1974. HSBH: 93* v Surrey (Oval) 1976. BB: 6-61 v Sri Lankans (Hove) 1979. BBNW: 3-18 v Notts (Hove) 1983. BBJPL: 3-11 v Worcs (Eastbourne) 1978. BBBH: 5-43 v Combined Universities (Oxford) 1979.

Ian James GOULD B Slough (Bucks) 19/8/1957. LHB, WK. Debut for Middlesex 1975. Cap 1977. Played for Auckland in 1979-80. Debut for Sussex in 1981. Cap 1981. Tour: Australia 1982-83. BH Gold Award: 1. HS: 128 Middlesex v Worcs (Worcester) 1978. HSC: 94 v Somerset (Hove) 1982. HSGC/NW: 58 Middlesex v Derby (Derby) 1978. HSJPL: 69* v Hants (Basingstoke) 1981. HSBH: 72 v Kent (Hove) 1982.

Allan Michael GREEN B Pulborough 28/5/1960. RHB, RM. Debut 1980. HS: 99 v Middlesex (Hove) 1982. HSNW: 41 v Notts (Hove) 1982. HSJPL: 19 v Notts (Hove) 1982. HSBH: 30 v Somerset (Taunton) 1983.

Ian Alexander GREIG (Queen's College, Queenstown and Cambridge) B Queenstown, South Africa 8/12/1955. RHB, RM. Younger brother of A.W. Greig. Played for Border in 1974-75 and 1979-80 and for Griqualand West in 1975-76. Debut for Cambridge U 1977. Blue 1977-78-79 (captain). Debut for county 1980. Cap 1981. Tests: 2 in 1982. Had match double of 100 runs and 10 wkts (118*, 6-75, 4-57) v Hants (Hove) 1981. NW Man of the Match: 1. BH Gold Awards: 1. HS: 147* v Oxford U (Oxford) 1983. HSTC: 14 v Pakistan (Birmingham) 1982. HSNW: 82 v Warwicks Birmingham) 1981. HSJPL: 54 v Warwicks (Horsham) 1981. HSBH: 51 v Hants (Hove) 1981. BB. 7-43 v Cambridge U (Cambridge) 1981. BBTC: 4-53 v Pakistan (Birmingham) 1982. BBNW: 4-31 v Warwicks (Birmingham) 1981. BBJPL: 5-42 v Leics (Hove) 1982. BBBH: 5-35 v Hants (Hove) 1981. Blues for rugby 1977-78.

Jerry Richard Percy HEATH B Turner's Hill 26/4/1959. LHB. Debut 1980. HS: 101* v Sri Lankans (Hastings) 1981. HSJPL: 35 v Hants (Hove) 1980.

IMRAN KHAN NIAZI (Aitchison College, Lahore and Oxford) B Lahore, Pakistan 25/11/1952. RHB, RF. Cousin of Majid Jahangir Khan. Debut for Lahore A 1969-70 and has played subsequently for various Lahore teams and Pakistan International Airways. Debut for Worcs 1971. Blue 1973-74-75 (capt. in 1974). Cap 1976. Debut for Sussex by special registration 1977. Cap 1978. Tests: 49 for Pakistan between 1971 and 1983. Captain in 12 Tests. Tours: Pakistan to England 1971, 1974 and 1982, Pakistan to Sri Lanka 1975-76, Australia and West Indies 1976-77, New Zealand and Australia 1978-79, India 1979-80, Australia 1981-82. 1,000 runs (4) – 1,339 runs (av. 41.84) in 1978 best. Scored two centuries in match (117* and 106), Oxford U v Notts (Oxford) 1974. Had match double of 111* and 13–99 (7-53 and 6-46) v Lancs (Worcester) 1976. Gillette Man of Match Awards: 4. (1 for Worcs). NW Man of the Match: 1. BH Gold Awards: 6, (1 for Oxford and Cambridge Universities, 1 for Worcs). HS: 170 Oxford U v Northants (Oxford) 1974. HSC: 167 v Glos (Hove) 1978. HSTC: 123 Pakistan v West Indies (Lahore) 1980-81. HSNW: 114* v Notts (Hove) 1983. HSJPL: 90 v Hants (Southampton) 1983. HSBH: 72 Worcs v Warwicks (Birmingham) 1976. BB: 8-58 Pakistan v Sri Lanka (Faisalabad) 1981-82. BBUK: 7-52 v Glos (Bristol) 1978 and for Pakistan v England (Birmingham) 1982. BBGC/NW: 4-27 v Staffs (Stone) 1978. BBJPL: 5-29 Worcs v Leics (Leicester) 1973. BBBH: 5-8 v Northants (Northampton) 1978. Wisden 1982.

Adrian Nicholas JONES B Woking (Surrey) 22/7/1961. LHB, RFM. Debut 1981. Played for Border 1981-82. HS: 29 v Kent (Hove) 1982. BB: 4-33 v Yorks (Hove) 1981.

Garth Stirling LE ROUX B Cape Town 4/9/1955. RHB, RF. Played for Western Province 1975-76 to date. Debut for county 1978. Cap 1981. Hat-trick v Warwicks (Hove) 1981. HS: 83 v Surrey (Hove) 1982. HSNW: 22 v Ireland (Dublin) 1983. HSJPL: 88 v Glamorgan (Hastings) 1982. HSBH: 46 v Somerset (Taunton) 1982. BB: 8-107 v Somerset (Taunton) 1981. BBNW: 5-35 v Essex (Hove) 1981. BBJPL: 4-18 v Notts (Hove) 1982. BBBH: 4-22 v Hants (Hove) 1983.

· **Gehan Dixon MENDIS** (St Thomas College, Colombo) B Colombo, Ceylon 20/4/1955. RHB, occasional WK. Debut 1974. Cap 1980. Tours: International teams to Pakistan 1981-82 and Jamaica 1982-83. 1,000 runs (4) – 1,624 (av. 40.60) in 1983 best. Gillette Man of Match: 2. BH Gold Awards: 2. HS: 204 v Northants (Eastbourne) 1980. HSGC/NW: 141* v Warwicks (Hove) 1980. HSJPL: 125* v Glos (Hove) 1981. HSBH: 109 v Glos (Hove) 1980.

Paul William Giles PARKER (Cambridge U). B Bulawayo, Rhodesia 15/1/1956. RHB, RM. Debut for both Cambridge U and county 1976. Blue 1976-77-78. Cap 1979. Best Young Cricketer for the Year in 1979. Tests: 1 in 1981. 1,000 runs (5) – 1,412 runs (av. 45.54) in 1981 best. Gillette Man of Match: 2. BH Gold Awards: 3. HS: 215 Cambridge U v Essex (Cambridge) 1976. HSC: 136 v Lancs (Hove) 1981. HSGC/NW: 69 v Lancs (Hove) 1978. HSJPL: 121* v Northants (Hastings) 1983. HSBH: 77 v Hants (Bournemouth) 1982. Selected for University rugby match in 1977, but had to withdraw through injury.

Christopher Paul PHILLIPSON (Ardingly College) B Vrindaban, India 10/2/1952. RHB, RM. Debut 1970. Cap 1980. BH Gold Awards: 2. HS: 87 v Hants (Hove) 1980. HSGC/NW: 70* v Suffolk (Hove) 1980. HSJPL: 71 v Lancs (Hastings) 1979. HSBH: 66* v Surrey (Oval) 1982. BB: 6-56 v Notts (Hove) 1972. BBJPL: 4-25 v Middlesex (Eastbourne) 1972. BBBH: 5-32 v Combined Universities (Oxford) 1977.

Anthony Charles Shackleton PIGOTT (Harrow School) B London 4/6/1958. RHB, RFM. Debut 1978. Cap 1982. Tour: D.H. Robins to New Zealand 1979-80. Played for Wellington 1982-83. Hat-trick v Surrey (Hove) 1978. HS: 63 v Hants (Eastbourne) 1983. HSGC/NW: 30 v Northants (Hove) 1979. HSJPL: 49 v Warwicks (Hove) 1979. BB: 7-74 v Northants (Eastbourne) 1982. BBGC/NW: 3-43 v Notts (Hove) 1979. BBJPL: 5-28 v Surrey (Guildford) 1982. BBBH: 3-33 v Hants. (Bournemouth) 1982.

Dermot Alexander REEVE B Hong Kong 2/4/1963. RHB. RFM. Debut 1983. HS: 42* v Lancs (Hove) 1983. HSNW: 16* v Ireland (Dublin) 1983. BB: 4-15 v Worcs (Worcester) 1983. BBNW: 3-26 v Ireland (Dublin) 1983. BBJPL: 3-25 v Glamorgan (Cardiff) 1983.

David James SMITH B Brighton 28/4/1962. LHB, WK. Debut 1981. HS: 13 v Somerset (Hove) 1983.

Christopher Edward WALLER B Guildford 3/10/1948. RHB, SLA. Debut for Surrey 1967. Cap 1972. Debut for Sussex in 1974. Cap 1976. Benefit 1984. HS: 51* v Cambridge U (Cambridge) 1981. HSGC/NW: 14* v Notts (Nottingham) 1975. HSJPL: 18* v Glamorgan (Hove) 1975. HSBH: 11* v Essex (Chelmsford) 1975. BB: 7-64 Surrey v Sussex (Oval) 1971. BBC: 6-40 v Surrey (Hove) 1975. BBJPL: 4-28 v Essex (Hove) 1976. BBBH: 4-25 v Minor Counties (South) (Hove) 1975.

Alan Peter WELLS B Newhaven 2/10/1961. Younger brother of C.M. Wells. RHB, RM. Debut 1981. Played for Border 1981-82. HS: 92 v Kent (Hove) 1983. HSJPL: 47* v Northants (Hastings) 1981. HSBH: 16 v Hants (Hove) 1983.

Colin Mark WELLS B Newhaven 3/3/1960. Older brother of A.P. Wells. Debut 1979. Cap 1982. RHB, RM. 1,000 runs (2) – 1,248 (av. 32.84) in 1982 best. HS: 135 v Glamorgan (Swansea) 1980. HSNW: 28 v Warwicks (Birmingham) 1981 and v Notts (Hove) 1983. HSJPL: 104* v Warwicks (Hove) 1983. HSBH: 80 v Kent (Hove) 1982. BB: 4-23 v Oxford U (Pagham) 1979. BBJPL: 4-15 v Worcs (Worcester) 1983. BBBH: 4-21 v Middlesex (Lord's) 1980.

Alan WILLOWS B Portslade 24/4/1961. RHB, SLA. Debut 1980. BB: 4-33 v Hants (Southampton) 1980.

SUSSEX

County Averages

Schweppes County Championship: Played 24, won 3, drawn 10, lost 10, abandoned 1.
All first-class matches: Played 25, won 3, drawn 11, lost 10, abandoned 1.

BATTING AND FIELDING

Cap		*M*	*I*	*NO*	*RUNS*	*HS*	*Avge*	*100*	*50*	*Ct*	*St*
1978	Imran Khan	13	25	3	1260	124*	57.27	2	12	6	—
—	D.K. Standing	4	8	3	240	60	48.00	—	2	2	—
1980	G.D. Mendis	24	46	6	1624	133*	40.60	4	8	8	—
1981	I.A. Greig	9	10	1	324	147*	36.00	1	1	2	—
1981	I.J. Gould	18	23	6	474	59*	27.88	—	1	32	13
—	A.P. Wells	16	28	4	665	92	27.70	—	5	11	—
1981	G.S. Le Roux	13	17	1	401	80	25.06	—	1	2	—
1982	C.M. Wells	24	40	6	857	71	25.20	—	5	8	—
1976	J.R.T. Barclay	21	37	3	743	65	21.85	—	3	15	—
1979	P.W.G. Parker	17	27	2	512	79	20.46	—	4	5	—
—	J.R.P. Heath	9	18	2	335	39	20.93	—	—	4	—
—	A.M. Green	16	30	2	552	53	19.71	—	1	10	—
1982	A.C.S. Pigott	23	29	8	408	63	19.42	—	3	14	—
—	R.S. Cowan	5	10	0	154	50	15.40	—	1	2	—
—	D.A. Reeve	17	20	5	192	42*	12.80	—	—	7	—
1976	C.E. Waller	22	23	11	100	21	8.33	—	—	6	—
—	D.J. Smith	5	7	2	22	13	4.40	—	—	9	—
—	A.N. Jones	5	7	3	11	4*	2.75	—	—	—	—

Played in two matches: C.P. Phillipson 18, 23, 28 (1 ct).
Played in one match: A. Willows did not bat.

BOWLING

	Type	*O*	*M*	*R*	*W*	*Avge*	*Best*	*5 wI*	*10 wM*
Imran Khan	**RF**	46.2	12	86	12	7.16	6-6	1	—
G.S. Le Roux	**RF**	362.3	92	950	37	25.67	5-17	2	—
A.C.S. Pigott	**RFM**	582.5	98	1889	72	26.23	6-22	4	—
D.A. Reeve	**RM**	472.1	130	1233	42	29.35	4-15	—	—
C.E. Waller	**SLA**	754	224	1873	53	35.33	6-126	2	—
C.M. Wells	**RM**	376.3	82	1135	32	35.46	4-69	—	—
I.A. Greig	**RM**	185	27	681	17	40.05	4-42	—	—
A.M. Green	**RM**	53.4	9	248	6	41.33	2-30	—	—
J.R.T. Barclay	**OB**	231.3	56	774	17	45.52	3-30	—	—
A.N. Jones	**RFM**	81.4	10	358	6	59.66	2-65	—	—

Also bowled: R.S. Cowan 8-2-27-0; I.J. Gould 2-0-9-0; J.R.P. Heath 8-0-58-0; P.W.G. Parker 4.2-1-30-0; D.K. Standing 4.3-0-32-0; A. Willows 8-3-11-0.

County Records

First-class cricket

Highest innings totals:	For	705-8d v Surrey (Hastings)	1902
	Agst	726 by Notts (Nottingham)	1895
Lowest innings totals:	For	19 v Surrey (Godalming)	1830
		19 v Notts (Hove)	1873
	Agst	18 by Kent (Gravesend)	1867
Highest individual innings:	For	333 by K.S. Duleepsinhji v Northants (Hove)	1930
	Agst	322 E. Paynter for Lancs (Hove)	1937
Best bowling in an innings:	For	10-48 C.H.G. Bland v Kent (Tonbridge)	1899
	Agst	9-11 A.P. Freeman for Kent (Hove)	1922
Best bowling in a match:	For	17-106 G.R. Cox v Warwicks (Horsham)	1926
	Agst	17-67 A.P. Freeman for Kent (Hove)	1922
Most runs in a season:		2850 (av. 64.77) John Langridge	1949
runs in a career:		34152 (av. 37.69) John Langridge	1928-1955
100s in a season:		12 by John Langridge	1949
100s in a career:		76 by John Langridge	1928-1955
wickets in a season:		198 (av. 13.45) M.W. Tate	1925
wickets in a career:		2223 (av. 16.34) M.W. Tate	1912-1937

RECORD WICKET STANDS

1st	490	E.H. Bowley & John Langridge v Middlesex (Hove)	1933
2nd	385	E.H. Bowley & M.W. Tate v Northants (Hove)	1921
3rd	298	K.S. Ranjitsinhji & E.H. Killick v Lancs (Hove)	1901
4th	326*	G. Cox & James Langridge v Yorks (Leeds)	1949
5th	297	J.H. Parks & H.W. Parks v Hants (Portsmouth)	1937
6th	255	K.S. Duleepsinhji & M.W. Tate v Northants (Hove)	1930
7th	344	K.S. Ranjitsinhji & W. Newham v Essex (Leyton)	1902
8th	229*	C.L.A. Smith & G. Brann v Kent (Hove)	1902
9th	178	H.W. Parks & A.F. Wensley v Derby (Horsham)	1930
10th	156	G.R. Cox & H.R. Butt v Cambridge U (Cambridge)	1908

One-day cricket

Highest innings totals:	Gillette Cup/ NatWest Trophy	314-7 v Kent (Tunbridge Wells)	1963
	John Player League	293-4 v Worcs (Horsham)	1980
	Benson & Hedges Cup	305-6 v Kent (Hove)	1982
Lowest innings totals:	Gillette Cup/ NatWest Trophy	49 v Derby (Chesterfield)	1969
	John Player League	61 v Derby (Derby)	1978
	Benson & Hedges Cup	61 v Middlesex (Hove)	1978
Highest individual innings:	Gillette Cup/ NatWest Trophy	141* G.D. Mendis v Warwicks (Hove)	1980
	John Player League	129 A.W. Greig v Yorks (Scarborough)	1976
	Benson & Hedges Cup	117 R.D.V. Knight v Surrey (Oval)	1977
Best bowling figures:	Gillette Cup/ NatWest Trophy	6-30 D.L. Bates v Glos (Hove)	1968
	John Player League	6-14 M.A. Buss v Lancs (Hove)	1973
	Benson & Hedges Cup	5-8 Imran Khan v Northants (Northampton)	1978

WARWICKSHIRE

Formation of club: 1882.
Colours: Blue, gold and silver.
Badge: Bear and ragged staff.
County Champions (3): 1911, 1951 and 1972.
Gillette Cup Winners (2): 1966 and 1968.
Gillette Cup Finalists (2): 1964 and 1972.
NatWest Trophy Finalists: 1982.
John Player League Champions: 1980.
Benson & Hedges Cup Semi-Finalists (4): 1972, 1975, 1976 and 1978.
Gillette Man of the Match Awards: 21.
NatWest Man of the Match Awards: 5.
Benson & Hedges Gold Awards: 28.

Secretary: A.C. Smith, County Ground, Edgbaston, Birmingham B5 7QU.
Cricket Manager: D.J. Brown.
Captain: R.G.D. Willis, MBE.
Prospects of Play Telephone No: (021) 440 3624.

Dennis Leslie AMISS B Birmingham 7/4/1943. RHB, SLC. Debut 1960. Cap 1965. Benefit 1975 (£34,947). Tests: 50 between 1966 and 1977 and 1 match v Rest of the World in 1970. Tours: Pakistan 1966-67, India, Pakistan and Sri Lanka 1972-73, West Indies 1973-74, Australia and New Zealand 1974-75, India, Sri Lanka and Australia 1976-77, International XI in India and Pakistan 1967-68, SAB XI in South Africa 1981-82. Banned for 3 years from Test cricket. Also played for Rest of the World XI v Pakistan XI in Pakistan 1970-71. 1,000 runs (19) – 2,110 (av. 65.93) in 1976 best. Scored 1,120 runs (av. 74.66) in West Indies in 1973-74. Two centuries in a match twice: 155* and 112 v Worcs (Birmingham) 1978 and 109 and 127 v Derby (Derby) 1981. NW Man of the Match: 1. Gillette Man of the Match: 3. BH Gold Awards: 3. HS: 262* England v West Indies (Kingston) 1973-74. HSUK: 232* v Glos (Bristol) 1979. HSNW: 135 v Cambs (Birmingham) 1982. HSJPL: 117* v Sussex (Horsham) 1981. HSBH: 105* v Scotland (Birmingham) 1982. BB: 3-21 v Middlesex (Lord's) 1970.

Mohamed ASIF DIN B Kampala, Uganda 21/9/1960. RHB, LB. Debut 1981. HS: 102 v Middlesex (Coventry) 1982. HSNW: 45 v Surrey (Lord's) 1982. HSJPL: 56* v Hants (Bournemouth) 1982. HSBH: 61 v Notts (Nottingham) 1982. BB: 5-100 v Glamorgan (Birmingham) 1982.

Robin Ian Henry Benbow DYER (Wellington College) B Hertford 22/12/1958. 6ft 4ins tall. RHB, RM. Debut 1981. HS: 93 v Glamorgan (Cardiff) 1983. HSJPL: 43 v Sussex (Hove) 1983.

Anthonie Michal (Yogi) FERREIRA (Hillview High School, Pretoria) B Pretoria, South Africa 13/4/1955. RHB, RM. Played for Northern Transvaal 1974-75 to date. Played for D.H. Robins XI v both Oxford and Cambridge Universities at Eastbourne in 1978. Debut for county 1979. HS: 112* v Indians (Birmingham) 1982. HSGC/NW: 14 v Oxfordshire (Birmingham) 1980. HSJPL: 52 v Hants (Birmingham) 1983. HSBH: 45 v Lancs (Manchester) 1982. BB: 8-38 Northern Transvaal v Transvaal B (Pretoria) 1977-78. BBUK: 5-19 v Middlesex (Birmingham) 1983. BBGC/NW: 4-50 v Notts (Birmingham) 1979. BBJPL: 4-26 v Sussex (Horsham) 1981. BBBH: 4-42 v Scotland (Birmingham) 1982. Cap 1983.

Norman GIFFORD B Ulverston (Lancs) 30/3/1940. LHB, SLA. Played for Worcs 1960-82. Cap 1961. County captain 1971 to 1980. Benefit (£11,047) in 1974 *Wisden* 1974. Awarded MBE in 1978. Second benefit in 1981. Debut for Warwicks 1983. England selector. Tests: 15 between 1964 and 1973. Played in one match for Rest of World v Australia 1971-72. Tours: International team to South Africa and Pakistan 1961-62. Worcs to South Africa 1964-65. Commonwealth to Pakistan 1970-71. Rest of World to Australia 1971-72, International Wanderers to South Africa 1972-73, India, Pakistan and Sri Lanka 1972-73. 100 wkts: (4) – 133 wkts (av. 19.66) in 1961 best. Hat-trick v Derby (Chesterfield) 1965. Took 4 wkts in 6 balls v Cambridge U (Cambridge) 1972. Gillette Man of Match Awards: 1. BH Gold Awards: 2. HS: 89 Worcs v Oxford U (Oxford) 1963. HSTC: 25* v New Zealand (Nottingham) 1973. HSGC/NW: 38 Worcs v Warwicks (Lord's) 1966. HSJPL: 32* v Northants (Luton) 1983. HSBH: 33 Worcs v Kent (Lord's) 1973. BB: 8-28 Worcs v Yorks (Sheffield) 1968. BBTC: 5-55 v Pakistan (Karachi) 1972-73. BBGC/NW: 4-7 Worcs v Surrey (Worcester) 1972. BBJPL: 5-28 Worcs v Northants (Worcester) 1979. BBBH: 6-8 Worcs v Minor Counties (South) (High Wycombe) 1979. Cap 1983.

William HOGG B Ulverston (Lancs) 12/7/1955. RHB, RFM. Debut for Lancs 1976. Debut for Warwicks 1981. HS: 31 v Hants (Birmingham) 1981. BB: 7-84 Lancs v Warwicks (Manchester) 1978. BBC: 4-46 v Northants (Northampton) 1981. BBJPL: 4-23 Lancs v Essex (Ilford) 1979. BBBH: 4-35 Lancs v Hants (Manchester) 1979.

Geoffrey William HUMPAGE B Birmingham 24/4/1954. RHB, WK, RM. Debut 1974. Cap 1976, 1,000 runs (6) – 1,701 runs (av. 50.02) in 1981 best. Scored two centuries in match (146 and 110) v Glos (Gloucester) 1981. BH Gold Awards: 2. HS: 254 v Lancs (Southport) 1982 sharing in English record 4th wkt partnership of 470 with A.I. Kallicharran. HSGC/NW: 58 v Somerset (Taunton) 1978. HSJPL: 108* v Middlesex (Birmingham) 1980. HSBH: 93 v Yorks (Birmingham) 1981. BBJPL: 4-53 v Glos (Moreton-in-Marsh) 1979.

Alvin Isaac KALLICHARRAN B Port Mourant, Berbice, British Guiana 21/3/1949. LHB, OB. 5ft 4ins tall. Played for Guyana 1966-67 to 1980-81. Debut for county 1971. Cap 1972. Played for Queensland in 1977-78 and for Transvaal in 1981-82 and 1982-83. Tests: 66 for West Indies between 1971-72 and 1980-81 scoring 100* and 101 in first two innings in Tests v New Zealand and captaining country in 9 Tests. Tours: West Indies to England 1973, 1976 and 1980, World XI in Pakistan 1973-74, India, Sri Lanka and Pakistan 1974-75, Australia 1975-76, India and Sri Lanka 1978-79 (captain), Australia and New Zealand 1979-80, Pakistan 1980-81, West Indies XI in South Africa 1982-83. 1,000 runs (9) – 2,120 (av. 66.25) in 1982 best. Also scored 1,249 runs (av. 56.77) on 1974-75 tour. NW Man of the Match: 1. BH Gold Awards: 2. HS: 235 v Worcs (Worcester) 1982. HSTC: 187 West Indies v India (Bombay) 1978-79. HSNW: 141* v Somerset (Taunton) 1982. HSJPL: 102* v Notts (Birmingham) 1981. HSBH: 119 v Derby (Birmingham) 1983. BB: 4-48 v Derby (Birmingham) 1978. Benefit 1983. Wisden 1982.

Christopher LETHBRIDGE B Castleford (Yorks) 23/6/1961. RHB, RM. Debut 1981 taking wicket of G. Boycott with his first ball in first-class cricket. HS: 87* v Somerset (Taunton) 1982. HSJPL: 57* v Somerset (Birmingham) 1982. 5-68 v Glamorgan (Cardiff) 1982. BBJPL: 5-47 v Northants (Birmingham) 1982. BBBH: 3-49 v Northants (Birmingham) 1982.

WARWICKSHIRE

Timothy Andrew LLOYD B Oswestry (Shropshire) 5/11/1956. LHB, RM. Debut 1977. Played for Orange Free State in 1978-79 and 1979-80. Cap 1980 NW Man of the Match: 1. BH Gold Awards: 1. 1,000 runs (4) – 1,673 (av. 45.21) in 1983 best. HS: 208* v Glos (Birmingham) 1983. HSGC/NW: 81 v Devon (Birmingham) 1980. HSJPL: 90 v Kent (Birmingham) 1980. HSBH: 60 v Kent (Oval) 1981.

Gordon John LORD B Birmingham 25/4/1961. LHB. SLA. Debut 1983. HS: 61 v Notts (Nottingham) 1983. HSJPL: 40 v Notts (Birmingham) 1983.

William A. MORTON LHB, SLA. Debut for Scotland 1982. BB: 4-40 Scotland v Ireland 1983. HSBH: 11* Scotland v Glos (Glasgow) 1983. BBBH: 3-17 Scotland v Glos (Glasgow) 1983.

Christopher Middleton OLD B Middlesbrough 22/12/1948. LHB, RFM. Debut for Yorks 1966. Cap 1969. Best Young Cricketer of the Year in 1970. *Wisden* 1978. Benefit (£32,916) in 1979. County Captain 1981. Replaced in 1982 and joined Warwicks for 1983. Played for Northern Transvaal in 1981-82 and 1982-83. Tests: 46 between 1972-73 and 1981. Played in 2 matches against Rest of World 1970. Tours: Duke of Norfolk to West Indies 1969-70, India, Pakistan and Sri Lanka 1972-73, West Indies 1973-74 and 1980-81, Australia and New Zealand 1974-75, International Wanderers to South Africa 1975-76, India, Sri Lanka and Australia 1976-77, Pakistan and New Zealand 1977-78, Australia 1978-79. SAB XI to South Africa 1981-82. Banned from Test cricket for 3 years. Scored century in 37 minutes v Warwickshire (Birmingham) 1977 – second fastest ever in first-class cricket. Took 4 wickets in 5 balls, England v Pakistan (Birmingham) 1978. BH Gold Awards: 3 for Yorks. HS: 116 Yorks v Indians (Bradford) 1974. HSTC: 65 v Pakistan (Oval) 1974. HSNW: 55* Yorks v Worcs (Leeds) 1982. HSJPL: 82 Yorks v Somerset (Bath) 1974 and 82* v Somerset (Glastonbury) 1976. HSBH: 78* Yorks v Scotland (Bradford) 1981. BB: 7-20 Yorks v Glos (Middlesbrough) 1969. BBTC: 7-50 v Pakistan (Birmingham) 1978. BBGC/NW: 4-9 Yorks v Durham (Middlesbrough) 1978. BBJPL: 5-53 Yorks v Sussex (Hove) 1971. BBBH: 4-17 Yorks v Derby (Bradford) 1973.

Gladstone Cleopthas SMALL (Moseley School, Birmingham) B St. George. Barbados 18/10/1961. RHB, RFM. Toured New Zealand with D.H. Robins' XI in 1979-80 and made debut v Northern Districts (Hamilton). Debut for county 1980. Toured Pakistan with International XI 1981-82. Cap 1982. HS: 57* v Oxford U (Oxford) 1982. HSNW: 33 v Surrey (Lord's) 1982. HSJPL: 17 v Notts (Birmingham) 1980. HSBH: 19* v Yorks (Birmingham) 1981. BB: 7-68 Yorks (Birmingham) 1982. BBNW: 3-22 v Glamorgan (Cardiff) 1982. BBJPL: 5-29 v Surrey (Birmingham) 1980.

Kenneth David SMITH B Jesmond, Newcastle-upon-Tyne 9/7/1956. RHB. Son of Kenneth D. Smith, former Leics player. Brother of P.A. Smith. Debut 1973. Cap 1978. 1,000 runs (4) 1,582 runs (av. 36.79) in 1980 best. NW Man of the Match: 1. BH Gold Awards: 1. HS: 140 v Worcs (Worcester) 1980. HSNW: 113 v Yorks (Birmingham) 1982. HSJPL: 60 v Glamorgan (Swansea) 1979. HSBH: 84 v Worcs (Worcester) 1980.

Paul Andrew SMITH B Newcastle-upon-Tyne 15/4/1964. Son of K.D. Smith (Leics). Brother of K.D. Smith Junior. RHB, RM. Debut 1982. HS: 114 v Oxford U (Birmingham) 1983. HSJPL: 41 v Essex (Birmingham) 1983. BB: 3-56 v Sussex (Birmingham) 1983. BBJPL: 4-23 v Notts (Birmingham) 1983.

Geoffrey Alan TEDSTONE B Southport, Lancs 19/1/1961. RHB, WK. Debut 1982. HS: 67* v Cambridge U (Cambridge) 1983. HSJPL: 23 v Middlesex (Birmingham) 1982.

Robert George Dylan WILLIS (Guildford RGS) B Sunderland 30/5/1949. RHB, RF. Debut for Surrey 1969. Debut for Warwickshire in 1972. Cap 1972. *Wisden* 1977. Appointed County Captain in 1980. Benefit in 1981. Awarded MBE in 1982 New Year Honours List. Tests: 83 between 1970-71 and 1983, captain in 15 Tests. Tours: Australia and New Zealand 1970-71 (flown out as replacement for A. Ward) and 1974-75, D.H. Robins to South Africa 1972-73. West Indies 1973-74 and 1980-81, India, Sri Lanka and Australia 1976-77, Pakistan and New Zealand 1977-78, Australia 1978-79, Australia and India 1979-80, India and Sri Lanka 1981-82, Australia 1982-83 (captain). Hat-tricks (2) v Derby (Birmingham) 1972 and West Indies (Birmingham) 1976. Also in John Player League v Yorks (Birmingham) 1973. Gillette Man of the Match: 1 (for Surrey). BH Gold Awards: 5 HS: 72 v Indians (Birmingham) 1982. HSTC: 28* v Pakistan (Birmingham) 1982. HSGC/NW: 12* Surrey v Sussex (Oval) 1970. HSJPL: 52* v Derby (Birmingham) 1975. HSBH: 37 v Notts (Nottingham) 1982. BB: 8-32 v Glos (Bristol) 1977. BBTC: 8-43 v Australia (Leeds) 1981. BBGC/NW: 6-49 Surrey v Middlesex (Oval) 1970. BBJPL: 4-12 v Middlesex (Lord's) 1973. BBBH: 7-32 v Yorkshire (Birmingham) 1981. Played soccer (goalkeeper) for Guildford City.

N.B. The following players whose particulars appeared in the 1983 Annual have been omitted: M.S.A. McEvoy, P. Oliver, D.M. Smith, S.P. Sutcliffe and S. Wootton.

County Averages

Schweppes County Championship: Played 24, won 10, drawn 11, lost 3.
All first-class matches; Played 27, won 10, drawn 13, lost 4.

BATTING AND FIELDING

Cap		*M*	*I*	*NO*	*RUNS*	*HS*	*Avge*	*100*	*50*	*Ct*	*St*
1972	A.I. Kallicharran	22	34	4	1637	243*	54.56	6	4	16	—
1980	T.A. Lloyd	23	41	4	1673	208*	45.21	5	5	12	—
1965	D.L. Amiss	26	43	4	1721	164	44.12	3	12	22	—
—	P.A. Smith	13	17	3	458	114	32.71	1	3	1	—
1976	G.W. Humpage	26	42	6	1116	141*	31.00	2	5	20	8
1978	K.D. Smith	27	47	4	1272	109	29.58	2	8	7	—
—	C. Lethbridge	8	7	3	110	73*	27.50	—	1	—	—
1983	A.M. Ferreira	17	24	6	465	66	25.83	—	3	8	—
—	Asif Din	14	21	3	411	65	22.83	—	2	11	—
—	R.H.I.B. Dyer	9	15	3	242	93	20.16	—	1	5	—
1972	R.G.D. Willis	13	13	7	116	37	19.33	—	—	2	—
—	C.M. Old	22	25	4	396	62	18.85	—	1	7	—
—	G.D. Tedstone	13	16	3	243	67*	18.69	—	1	23	4
—	D.A. Thorne	5	7	3	62	23*	15.50	—	—	3	—
1983	N. Gifford	22	21	6	201	39	13.40	—	—	10	—
1982	G.C. Small	6	8	3	62	31	12.40	—	—	2	—
—	W. Hogg	23	18	7	72	27*	6.54	—	—	5	—

Played in three matches; G.J. Lord 61, 29, 1 (1 ct).
Played in two matches: S.P. Sutcliffe did not bat (1 ct); S.H. Wootton 104, 19, 34.
Played in one match: D.M. Smith 100* (1 ct).

WARWICKSHIRE

BOWLING

	Type	O	M	R	W	Avge	Best	5 wI	10 wM
N. Gifford	SLA	1043.4	347	2393	104	23.00	6-22	7	2
C.M. Old	RFM	656.3	152	1824	62	29.41	5-50	2	—
W. Hogg	RFM	385	73	1198	39	30.71	5-63	1	—
A.M. Ferreira	RM	502.4	131	1277	40	31.92	5-19	1	—
G.C. Small	RFM	110.5	19	349	10	34.90	3-13	—	—
R.G.D. Willis	RF	253.2	60	785	21	37.38	3–8	—	—
P.A. Smith	RM	218	29	844	21	40.19	3-56	—	—
C. Lethbridge	RM	70.1	11	268	6	44.66	2-15	—	—
A.I. Kallicharran	OB	135	18	476	8	59.50	2-64	—	—

Also bowled: Asif Din 84.1-14-291-3; G.W. Humpage 16-1-51-1; T.A. Lloyd 8-1-52-0; G.J. Lord 8-3-12-0; D.M. Smith 18-3-44-1; S. P. Sutcliffe 74-17-191-3; D.A. Thorne 45-6-189-2.

County Records

First-class cricket

Highest innings totals:	For	657-6d v Hants (Birmingham)	1899
	Agst	887 by Yorks (Birmingham)	1896
Lowest innings totals:	For	16 v Kent (Tonbridge)	1913
	Agst	15 by Hants (Birmingham)	1922
Highest individual innings:	For	305* F.R. Foster v Worcs (Dudley)	1914
	Agst	316 R.H. Moore for Hants (Bournemouth)	1937
Best bowling in an innings:	For	10-41 J.D. Bannister v Combined Services (Birmingham)	1959
	Agst	10-36 H. Verity for Yorks (Leeds)	1931
Best bowling in a match:	For	15-76 S. Hargreave v Surrey (Oval)	1903
	Agst	17-92 A.P. Freeman for Kent (Folkestone)	1932
Most runs in a season:		2,417 (av. 60.42) M.J.K. Smith	1959
runs in a career:		33,862 (av. 36.18) William Quaife	1894-1928
100s in a season:		8 by R.E.S. Wyatt	1937
		R.B. Kanhai	1972
		and A.I. Kallicharan	1982
100s in a career:		71 by William Quaife	1894-1928
wickets in a season:		180 (av. 15.13) W.E. Hollies	1946
wickets in a career:		2,201 (av. 20.45) W.E. Hollies	1932-1957

RECORD WICKET STANDS

1st	377*	N.F. Horner & K. Ibadulla v Surrey (Oval)	1960
2nd	465*	J.A. Jameson & R.B. Kanhai v Glos (Birmingham)	1974
3rd	327	S. Kinneir & William Quaife v Lancs (Birmingham)	1901
4th	470	A.I. Kallicharan & G.W. Humpage v Lancs (Southport)	1982
5th	268	Walter Quaife & William Quaife v Essex (Leyton)	1900
6th	220	H.E. Dollery & J. Buckingham v Derby (Derby)	1938
7th	250	H.E. Dollery & J.S. Ord v Kent (Maidstone)	1953
8th	228	A.J.W. Croom & R.E.S. Wyatt v Worcs (Dudley)	1925
9th	154	G.W. Stephens & A.J.W. Croom v Derby (Birmingham)	1925
10th	128	F.R. Santall & W. Sanders v Yorks (Birmingham)	1930

One-day cricket

Highest innings totals:	Gillette Cup/ NatWest Trophy	314-6 v Oxfordshire (Birmingham)	1980
	John Player League	265-5 v Northants (Northampton)	1979
	Benson & Hedges Cup	291-5 v Lancs (Manchester)	1981
Lowest innings totals:	Gillette Cup/ NatWest Trophy	109 v Kent (Canterbury)	1971
	John Player League	65 v Kent (Maidstone)	1979
	Benson & Hedges Cup	96 v Leics (Leicester)	1972
Highest individual innings	Gillette Cup/ NatWest Trophy	141* A.I. Kallicharran v Somerset (Taunton)	1982
	John Player League	123* J.A. Jameson v Notts (Nottingham)	1973
	Benson & Hedges Cup	119* R.B. Kanhai v Northants (Northampton)	1975
Best bowling figures:	Gillette Cup/ NatWest Trophy	6-32 K. Ibadulla v Hants (Birmingham)	1965
	John Player League	5-13 D.J. Brown v Worcs (Birmingham)	1970
	Benson & Hedges Cup	7-32 R.G.D. Willis v Yorks (Birmingham)	1981

WORCESTERSHIRE

Formation of present club: 1865.
Colours: Dark Green and Black.
Badge: Shield, *Argent*, bearing *Fess* between three *Pears Sable*.
County Champions (3): 1964, 1965, and 1974.
Gillette Cup Finalists (2): 1963 and 1966.
NatWest Trophy Second Round: 1981 and 1982.
John Player League Champions: 1971.
Benson & Hedges Cup Finalists (2): 1973 and 1976.
Gillette Man of the Match Awards: 18.
NatWest Man of the Match Awards: 1.
Benson & Hedges Gold Awards: 26.

Secretary: M.D. Vockins, County Ground, New Road, Worcester WR2 4QQ.
Captain: P.A. Neale.
Prospects of Play Telephone No: (0905) 422011.

David Andrew BANKS B Brierley Hill, Staffordshire 11/1/1965. RHB, RM. Debut 1983 scoring 100 v Oxford University (Oxford). HS: 100 (see before). HSJPL: 18 v Yorks (Worcester) 1983.

Timothy Stephen CURTIS B Chislehurst (Kent) 15/1/1960. RHB, LB. Debut 1979. Cambridge Blue 1983. HS: 92 Cambridge U v Northants (Cambridge) 1983. HSC: 84 v Kent (Canterbury) 1983. HSNW: 29 v Derby (Derby) 1981. HSJPL: 33* v Middlesex (Lord's) 1981.

Damian Basil D'OLIVEIRA B Cape Town, South Africa 19/10/1960. RHB, RM/OB. Son of Basil D'Oliveira (England and Worcs). Debut 1982. NW Man of the Match: 1. HS: 102 v Middlesex (Worcester) 1983. HSNW: 48 v Notts (Worcester) 1983. HSJPL: 51* v Lancs (Manchester) 1983. HSBH: 13 v Glos (Gloucester) 1983. BBJPL: 3-23 v Derby (Derby) 1983.

Ricardo McDonald ELLCOCK B Bridgetown, Barbados 17/6/1965. RHB, RFM. Debut 1982 aged 17 years 86 days. HS: 36 v Hants (Worcester) 1983. BB: 4-70 v Warwicks (Worcester) 1983. BBNW: 3-49 v Notts (Worcester) 1983. BBJPL: 4-43 v Kent (Canterbury) 1983.

David John HUMPHRIES B Alveley (Shropshire) 6/8/1953. LHB, WK. Debut for Leics 1974. Debut for Worcs in 1977. Cap 1978. Gillette Man of Match: 1. HS: 111* v Warwicks (Worcester) 1978. HSGC/NW: 58 v Glamorgan (Worcester) 1977. HSJPL: 62 v Notts (Dudley) 1977. HSBH: 41 v Yorks (Leeds) 1982.

Richard Keith ILLINGWORTH B Bradford, Yorks 23/8/1963. RHB, SLA. Debut 1982. HS: 55 v Leics (Hereford) 1983. HSJPL: 21 v Middlesex (Worcester) 1982. HSBH: 11* v Leics (Worcester) 1983. BB: 5-26 v Glos (Worcester) 1983. BBJPL: 5-24 v Somerset (Worcester) 1983. BBBH: 3-24 v Leics (Worcester) 1983.

John Darling INCHMORE B Ashington (Northumberland) 22/2/1949. RHB, RFM. Debut 1973. Cap 1976. Played for Northern Transvaal in 1976-77. BH Gold Awards: 2. HS: 113 v Essex (Worcester) 1974. HSNW: 32* v Yorks (Leeds) 1982. HSJPL: 45 v Northants (Worcester) 1981 and 45 v Derby (Chesterfield) 1981. HSBH: 49* v Somerset (Taunton) 1976. BB: 8-58 v Yorks (Worcester) 1977. BBNW: 4-47 v Yorks (Leeds) 1982. BBJPL: 4-9 v Northants (Dudley) 1975. BBBH: 4-21 v Combined Universities (Cambridge) 1980.

KAPIL DEV NIKHANJ B Chandigarh, India 6/1/1959. RHB, RFM. Debut for Haryana in Ranji Trophy 1975-76 aged 16 years 10 months taking 6-39 in debut match v Punjab (Rohtak). Debut for Northants 1981. Joined Worcs for 1984. *Wisden* 1982. Tests: 53 for India between 1978-79 and 1982-83. Captain in 5 Tests. Tours: India to England 1979, Australia and New Zealand 1980-81, West Indies 1982-83. Is youngest player to take 100 wkts in Test cricket (21 years 25 days) and score 1,000 runs (21 years 27 days). Took 100 wkts in 1 year 107 days to beat record held previously by I.T. Botham. Hat-trick North Zone v West Zone (Delhi) 1978-79. HS: 193 Haryana v Punjab (Chandigarh) 1979-80. HSTC: 126* India v West Indies (Delhi) 1978-79. HSUK: 120 v Somerset (Weston-super-Mare) 1983. HSJPL: 75 v Derby (Milton Keynes) 1982. HSBH: 49 v Lancs (Manchester) 1983. BB: 8-38 Haryana v Services (Rohtak) 1977-78. BBTC: 7-56 India v Pakistan (Madras) 1979-80. BBUK: 5-39 Indians v Notts (Nottingham) 1982. BBJPL: 3-23 v Essex (Wellingborough) 1983.

Collis Llewellyn KING B Barbados 11/6/1951. RHB, RM. Played for Barbados 1972-73 to 1981-82, Glamorgan 1977, D.B. Close's XI 1982, Worcs 1983. 9 Tests for West Indies between 1976 and 1980. Tours: West Indies to England 1976 and 1980; Australia and New Zealand 1979-80; International XI to Pakistan 1981-82; West Indians in South Africa 1982-83, 1,320 runs (av. 55.00) in 1976. HS: 163 West Indians v Northants (Northampton) 1976. HSTC: 100* West Indies v New Zealand (Christchurch) 1979-80. HSC: 123 v Somerset (Worcester) 1983. HSJPL: 127 v Surrey (Guildford) 1983. HSBH: 51 v Glos (Gloucester) 1983. BB: 5-91 Barbados v Jamaica (Bridgetown) 1975-76.

Michael Stephen Anthony McEVOY B Jorhat, Assam 25/1/1956. RHB, RM. Played for Essex 1976 to 1981. Debut for Worcs 1983. HS: 103 v Warwicks (Birmingham) 1983. HSJPL: 17 v Warwicks (Birmingham) Northants (Worcester) and Surrey (Guildford) 1983. HSBH: 24 v Glos (Gloucester) 1983. BB: 3-20 Essex v Middlesex (Lord's) 1981.

Peter MOORES B Macclesfield, Cheshire 18/12/1962. RHB, WK. Debut 1983. HS: 30 v Northants (Northampton) 1983. HSJPL: 10* v Notts (Hereford).

Philip Anthony NEALE B Scunthorpe (Lincs) 5/6/1954. RHB, RM. Debut 1975. Cap 1978. Captain 1983. 1,000 runs (5) – 1,521 (av. 41.10) in 1983 best. HS: 163* v Notts (Worcester) 1979. HSGC/NW: 68 v Glos (Bristol) 1976. HSJPL: 102* v Northants (Luton) 1982. HSBH: 128 v Lancs (Manchester) 1980. Soccer for Lincoln City.

Philip John NEWPORT B High Wycombe, Buckinghamshire 11/10/1962. RHB, RFM. Debut 1982. HS: 41* v Warwicks (Birmingham) 1983. BB: 4-76 v Notts (Worcester) 1982.

Joseph Alan ORMROD (Kirkaldy HS) B Ramsbottom (Lancs) 22/12/1942. RHB, OB. Debut 1962. Cap 1966. Benefit (£19,000) in 1977. Tours: Worcs to Jamaica 1965-66, Pakistan 1966-67. 1,000 runs: (12) – 1,535 runs (av. 45.14) in 1978 best. Scored two centuries in match (101 and 131*) v Somerset (Worcester) 1980. Shared in 4th wkt partnership record for county, 281 with Younis Ahmed v Notts (Nottingham) 1979. BH Gold Awards: 4. HS: 204* v Kent (Dartford) 1973. HSGC/NW: 59 v Essex (Worcester) 1975. HSJPL: 110* v Kent (Canterbury) 1975. HSBH: 124* v Glos (Worcester) 1976. BB: 5-27 v Glos (Bristol) 1972. BBJPL: 3-51 v Hants (Worcester) 1972.

Dipak Narshibhai PATEL B Nairobi, Kenya 25/10/1958. Has lived in UK since 1967. RHB, OB. Debut 1976. Cap 1979. 1,000 runs (3) – 1,615 (38.45) in 1983 best. Shared in 6th wkt partnership record for county, 227 with E.J.O. Hemsley v Oxford U (Oxford) 1976. HS: 138 v Warwicks (Worcester) 1981. HSNW: 42 v Derby (Derby) 1981. HSJPL: 125 v Hants (Southampton) 1982. HSBH: 90 v Leics (Worcester) 1982. BB: 7-46 v Lancs (Worcester) 1982. BBJPL: 5-27 v Northants (Worcester) 1983. BBBH: 3-42 v Yorks (Worcester) 1980.

Alan Paul PRIDGEON B Wall Heath (Staffs) 22/2/1954. RHB, RM. Debut 1972. Cap 1980. HS: 34 v Glamorgan (Swansea) 1981. HSGC/NW: 13* v Somerset (Taunton) 1980. HSJPL: 17 v Kent (Worcester) 1982. HSBH: 13* v Leics (Worcester) 1982. BB: 7-35 v Oxford U (Oxford) 1976. BBGC/NW: 3-25 v Somerset (Taunton) 1980. BBJPL: 6-26 v Surrey (Worcester) 1978. BBBH: 3-57 v Warwicks (Birmingham) 1976. Soccer for Ledbury Town in West Midland League.

David Mark SMITH B Balham 9/1/1956. LHB, RM. Debut for Surrey 1973 aged 17 years 4 months whilst still at school. Cap 1980. Scored 1065 (av. 50.71) in 1982. NW Man of the Match: 1. BH Gold Awards: 1. HS: 160 v Worcs (Worcester) 1982. HSNW: 103* v Northants (Oval) 1982. HSJPL: 87* v Hants (Oval) 1980. HSBH: 45* v Northants (Northampton) 1979 and 45* v Hants (Oval) 1980. BB: 3-40 v Sussex (Oval) 1976. BBGC/NW: 3-39 v Derby (Ilkeston) 1976. BBBH: 4-29 v Kent (Oval) 1980.

Alan Esmond WARNER B Birmingham 12/5/1957. RHB, RFM. Debut 1982. HS: 67 v Warwicks (Birmingham) 1982. HSJPL: 14 v Derby (Derby) 1983. HSBH: 24* v Derby (Worcester) 1982. BB: 4-72 v Derby (Derby) 1983. BBJPL: 3-26 v Essex (Worcester) 1983.

Stephen George WATKINS B Hereford 23/3/1959. RHB, RM. Debut 1983. HS: 77 v Oxford U (Oxford) 1983. HSJPL: 24 v Kent (Canterbury) 1983.

Martin John WESTON B Worcester 8/4/1959. RHB, RM. Debut 1979. HS: 115 v Sussex (Hove) 1983. HSNW: 23 v Yorks (Leeds) 1982. HSJPL: 109 v Somerset (Taunton) 1982. HSBH: 56 v Scotland (Aberdeen) 1983. BB: 3-42 v Middlesex (Worcester) 1982.

NB. The following players whose particulars were included in the 1983 Annual have been omitted: S.P. Perryman, M.S. Scott, A.J. Webster, Younis Ahmed.

County Averages

Schweppes County Championship: Played 24, won 2, drawn 11, lost 11.
All first-class matches: Played 27, won 4, drawn 11, lost 12.

BATTING AND FIELDING

Cap		M	I	NO	RUNS	HS	Avge	100	50	Ct	St
1978	P.A. Neale	24	40	3	1521	139	41.10	2	11	9	—
1979	D.N. Patel	26	44	2	1615	112	38.45	3	10	14	—
—	D.A. Banks	7	13	1	363	100	30.25	1	1	3	—
—	M.S. Scott	7	12	2	297	76	29.70	—	3	—	—
—	D.B. D'Oliveira	22	39	2	972	102	26.27	1	5	13	—
1966	J.A. Ormrod	24	41	3	967	84	25.44	—	6	12	—
—	T.S. Curtis	9	17	2	374	84	24.93	—	2	5	—
—	P.J. Newport	4	4	1	72	41*	24.00	—	—	—	—
—	M.J. Weston	22	38	1	862	115	23.29	1	2	9	—
—	M.St.A. McEvoy	16	26	1	569	103	22.76	1	2	17	—
1978	D.J. Humphries	20	30	4	560	59	21.53	—	2	27	9
1976	J.D. Inchmore	20	26	4	377	51	17.13	—	1	5	—
—	P. Moores	7	11	1	154	30	15.40	—	—	11	2
—	A.E. Warner	9	15	5	131	26*	13.10	—	—	3	—
—	R.M. Ellcock	12	18	4	154	36	11.00	—	—	2	—
—	R.K. Illingworth	25	35	6	273	55	9.41	—	1	7	—
1980	A.P. Pridgeon	27	32	10	190	23	8.63	—	—	8	—
—	S.P. Perryman	11	15	6	69	22	7.66	—	—	4	—

Played in two matches: C.L. King 123, 8, 27 (1 ct); Younis Ahmed 10*, 35*.
Played in one match: S.G. Watkins 77, 28.

BOWLING

	Type	O	M	R	W	Avge	Best	5 wI	10 wM
A.E. Warner	**RFM**	210.3	39	608	27	22.51	4-72	—	—
A.P. Pridgeon	**RM**	700	166	1978	72	27.47	5-21	2	—
J.D. Inchmore	**RFM**	488.3	104	1369	47	29.12	5-45	3	—
D.N. Patel	**OB**	685.5	204	1799	49	36.71	5-52	2	—
R.M. Ellcock	**RF**	244	39	931	25	37.24	4-70	—	—
R.K. Illingworth	**SLA**	664.5	172	1830	48	38.12	5-26	1	—
S.P. Perryman	**RM**	253.5	54	750	14	53.57	4-91	—	—
D.B. D'Oliveira	**RM/OB**	69.1	14	262	4	65.50	1-12	—	—

Also bowled: T.S. Curtis 3-1-6-0; C.L. King 15-2-39-1; P.J. Newport 41-3-118-3; M.J. Weston 26.2-6-91-2.

County Records

First-class Cricket

Highest innings	For	633 v Warwicks (Worcester)	1906
totals:	Agst	701-4d by Leics (Worcester)	1906
Lowest innings	For	24 v Yorks (Huddersfield)	1903
totals:	Agst	30 by Hants (Worcester)	1903
Highest indi-	For	311* by G.M. Turner v Warwicks (Worcester)	1982
vidual innings:	Agst	331* J.D.B. Robertson for Middlesex (Worcester)	1949
Best bowling	For	9-23 C.F. Root v Lancs (Worcester)	1931
in an innings:	Agst	10-51 J. Mercer for Glamorgan (Worcester)	1936
Best bowling	For	15-87 A.J. Conway v Glos (Moreton-in-Marsh)	1914
in a match:	Agst	17-212 J.C. Clay for Glamorgan (Swansea)	1937
Most runs in a season:		2654 (av. 52.03) H.H.I. Gibbons	1934
runs in a career:		34490 (av. 34.04) D. Kenyon	1946-1967
100s in a season:		10 by G.M. Turner	1970
100s in a career:		72 by G.M. Turner	1967-1982
wickets in a season:		207 (av. 17.52) C.F. Root	1925
wickets in a career:		2143 (av. 23.73) R.T.D. Perks	1930-1955

RECORD WICKET STANDS

1st	309	F.L. Bowley & H.K. Foster v Derby (Derby)	1901
2nd	274	H.H.I. Gibbons & Nawab of Pataudi v Kent (Worcester)	1933
		H.H.I Gibbons & Nawab of Pataudi v Glam (Worcester)	1934
3rd	314	M.J. Horton & T.W. Graveney v Somerset (Worcester)	1962
4th	281	J.A. Ormrod & Younis Ahmed v Notts (Nottingham)	1979
5th	393	E.G. Arnold & W.B. Burns v Warwicks (Birmingham)	1909
6th	227	E.J.O. Hemsley & D.N. Patel v Oxford U (Oxford)	1976
7th	197	H.H.I. Gibbons & R. Howorth v Surrey (Oval)	1938
8th	145*	F. Chester & W.H. Taylor v Essex (Worcester)	1914
9th	181	J.A. Cuffe & R.D. Burrows v Glos (Worcester)	1907
10th	119	W.B. Burns & G.A. Wilson v Somerset (Worcester)	1906

One-day Cricket

Highest innings:	GC/NatWest Trophy	286-5 v Yorks (Leeds)	1982
	John Player League	307-4 v Derby (Worcester)	1975
	Benson & Hedges Cup	314-5 v Lancs (Manchester)	1980
Lowest innings totals:	Gillette Cup/ NatWest Trophy	98 v Durham (Chester-le-Street)	1968
	John Player League	86 v Yorks (Leeds)	1969
	Benson & Hedges Cup	92 v Oxford & Cambridge Universities (Cambridge)	1975
Highest individual innings:	Gillette Cup/ NatWest Trophy	117* G.M. Turner v Lancs (Worcester)	1971
	John Player League	147 G.M. Turner v Sussex (Horsham)	1980
	Benson & Hedges Cup	143* G.M. Turner v Warwicks (Birmingham)	1976
Best bowling figures:	Gillette Cup/ NatWest Trophy	6-14 J.A. Flavell v Lancs (Worcester)	1963
	John Player League	6-26 A.P. Pridgeon v Surrey (Worcester)	1978
	Benson & Hedges Cup	6-8 N. Gifford v Minor Cos. (South) (High Wycombe)	1979

YORKSHIRE

Formation of present club: 1863, reorganised 1891.
Colours: Oxford blue, Cambridge blue, and gold.
Badge: White rose.
County Champions (31): 1867, 1870, 1893, 1896, 1898, 1900, 1901, 1902, 1905, 1908, 1912, 1919, 1922, 1923, 1924, 1925, 1931, 1932, 1933, 1935, 1937, 1938, 1939, 1946, 1959, 1960, 1962, 1963, 1966, 1967, and 1968.
Joint Champions (2): 1869 and 1949.
Gillette Cup Winners (2): 1965 and 1969.
NatWest Trophy Semi-Final: 1982.
John Player League Winners: 1983.
Benson & Hedges Cup Finalists: 1972.
Fenner Trophy Winners: 1972, 1974 and 1981.
Gillette Man of the Match Awards: 14.
NatWest Man of the Match Awards: 3.
Benson & Hedges Gold Awards: 28.

Secretary: J. Lister, Headingley Cricket Ground, Leeds LS6 3BU.
Cricket Manager: R. Illingworth, CBE.
Captain: D.L. Bairstow.

David Leslie BAIRSTOW B Bradford 1/9/1951. RHB, WK, RM. Debut 1970. Cap 1973. Played for Griqualand West 1976-77 and 1977-78 (captain). Benefit 1982. Appointed county captain for 1984. Tests: 4 between 1979 and 1980-81. Tours: Australia 1979-80, West Indies 1980-81. 1,000 runs (2) – 1,102 (av. 38.00) in 1983 best. Dismissed 11 batsmen (all ct) for Yorks v Derby (Scarborough) 1982 equalling world record for most catches in a match. NW Man of the Match: 1. BH Gold Awards: 4. HS: 145 v Middlesex (Scarborough) 1980. HSTC: 59 v India (Oval) 1979. HSNW: 92 v Worcs (Leeds) 1982. HSJPL: 78 v Surrey (Scarborough) 1981. HSBH: 103* v Derby (Derby) 1981. BB: 3-82 Griqualand West v Transvaal B (Johannesburg) 1976-77. Soccer for Bradford City.

Paul Anthony BOOTH B Huddersfield 5/9/1965. LHB, SLA. Debut 1982 aged 17 years 3 days. Has played two matches without scoring or taking a wicket.

Geoffrey BOYCOTT B Fitzwilliam (Yorks) 21/10/1940. RHB, RM. Plays in contact lenses. Debut for Yorks 1962. Cap 1963. Best Young Cricketer of the Year in 1963. *Wisden* 1964. County captain from 1971 to 1978. Played for Northern Transvaal in 1971-72. Benefit (£20,639) in 1974. Awarded OBE in 1980 Birthday Honours List. Tests: 108 between 1964 and 1981-82 captaining England in 4 Tests in 1977-78. Played in 2 matches against Rest of World in 1970. Tours: South Africa 1964-65, Australia and New Zealand 1965-66 and 1970-71 (returned home early through broken arm injury), West Indies 1967-68, 1973-74 and 1980-81, Ceylon 1969-70, Pakistan and New Zealand 1977-78 (vice-captain), Australia 1978-79, Australia and India 1979-80, India and Sri Lanka 1981-82. SAB to South Africa 1981-82. Banned for 3 years from Test cricket. 1,000 runs (21) – 2,503 runs (av. 100.12) in 1971 best. Only English batsman ever to have an average of 100 for season and repeated the feat in 1979 with 1,538 runs (av. 102.53). Also scored 1,000 runs in South Africa 1964-65 (1,135 runs, av. 56.75), West Indies 1967-68 (1,154, av. 82.42), Australia 1970-71 (1,535 runs, av. 95.93). Scored two centuries in match (103 and 105) v Notts (Sheffield) 1966 and (160* and 116) England v The Rest (Worcester)

1974. Completed 30,000 runs in 1977 and scored his 100th century in Leeds Test of that year – only player to have done so in a Test match. Scored 155 v India (Birmingham) 1979 to become the second batsman to have scored a century in a Test on all six grounds in this country. Gillette Man of Match: 2. BH Gold Awards: 8. HS: 261* MCC v President's XI (Bridgetown) 1973-74. HSUK: 260* v Essex (Colchester) 1970. HSTC: 246* v India (Leeds) 1967. HSGC/NW: 146 v Surrey (Lord's) 1965. HSJPL: 108* v Northants (Huddersfield) 1974. HSBH: 142 v Worcs (Worcester) 1980. BB: 4-14 v Lancs (Leeds) 1979. BBTC: 3-47 England v South Africa (Cape Town 1964-65. BBJPL: 3-15 v Middlesex (Hull) 1983. Testimonial 1984.

Philip CARRICK B Armley, Leeds 16/7/1952. RHB, SLA. Debut 1970. Cap 1976. Played for Eastern Province in 1976-77 and for Northern Transvaal in 1982-83. Tours: D.H. Robins to South Africa 1975-76 and Sri Lanka 1977-78. HS: 131* v Northants (Northampton) 1980. HSNW: 33 v Warwicks (Birmingham) 1982. HSJPL: 39 v Hants (Southampton) 1982. HSBH: 19* v Notts (Bradford) 1979. BB: 8-33 v Cambridge U (Cambridge) 1973. BBNW: 3-27 v Northants (Leeds) 1983. BBJPL: 4-13 v Derby (Bradford) 1983.

Simon John DENNIS B Scarborough 18/10/1960. Nephew of Sir Leonard Hutton and F. Dennis, former Yorkshire player. RHB, LFM. Debut 1980. Played for Orange Free State 1982-83. Cap 1983. HS: 37* Orange Free State v Western Province B (Bloemfontein) 1982-83. HSUK: 17 v Derby (Sheffield) 1983. HSJPL: 16* v Glamorgan (Cardiff) and Derby (Bradford) 1983. BB: 5-35 v Somerset (Sheffield) 1981. BBJPL: 3-19 v Hants (Middlesbrough) 1981.

Stuart David FLETCHER B Keighley 8/6/1964. RHB, RFM. Debut 1983. HS: 12 v Surrey (Scarborough) 1983. BB: 4-71 v Essex (Chelmsford) 1983.

Stuart Neil HARTLEY B Shipley (Yorks) 18/3/1956. RHB, RM. Debut 1978. Acted as captain in a number of matches in 1981. Cap 1981. Played for Orange Free State in 1982-83. HS: 114 v Glos (Bradford) 1982. HSNW: 58 v Worcs (Leeds) 1982. HSJPL: 67* v Hants (Middlesbrough) 1983. HSBH: 48 v Notts (Bradford) 1983. BB: 3-40 v Glos (Sheffield) 1980. BBJPL: 3-31 v Notts (Scarborough) 1980.

Paul William JARVIS B Redcar 29/6/1965. RHB, RFM. Debut 1981 aged 16 years 75 days. Hat-trick in JPL v Derbys (Derby) 1982. HS: 11* v Kent (Sheffield) 1983. BBJPL: 3-24 v Kent (Canterbury) 1982.

James Derek LOVE B Leeds 22/4/1955. RHB, RM. Debut 1975. Cap 1980. 1,000 runs (2) – 1,203 (av. 33.41) in 1981 best. BH Gold Awards: 1. HS: 170* v Worcs (Worcester) 1979. HSGC/NW: 61* v Hants (Southampton) 1980. HSJPL: 90* v Derby (Chesterfield) 1979. HSBH: 118* v Scotland (Bradford) 1981.

Richard Graham LUMB B Doncaster 27/2/1950. RHB, RM. Debut 1970. Cap 1974. Benefit 1983. 1,000 runs (5) – 1,532 runs (av. 41.40) in 1975 best. HS: 159 v Somerset (Harrogate) 1979. HSGC/NW: 56 v Shropshire (Wellington) 1976. HSJPL: 101 v Notts (Scarborough) 1976. HSBH: 90 v Northants (Bradford) 1980.

Ashley Anthony METCALFE B Horsforth 25/12/1963. RHB, OB. Debut 1983 scoring 122 v Notts (Bradford) in only match. HS: 122 as before.

Martyn Douglas MOXON B Barnsley 4/5/1960. RHB, RM. Debut 1981 scoring 116 in second innings of debut match. Played for Griqualand West in 1982-83. NW Man of the Match: 1. HS: 153 v Lancs (Leeds) 1983. HSNW: 78* v Essex (Leeds) 1982. HSJPL: 22 v Surrey (Oval) 1982. HSBH: 22 v Somerset (Leeds) 1981.

Stephen OLDHAM B High Green, Sheffield, Yorks 26/7/1948. RHB, RFM. Played for Yorkshire 1974-79. Debut and cap for Derby 1980. Benson & Hedges Gold Award: 1 (for Yorks). HS: 50 Yorks v Sussex (Hove) 1979. HSC: 35* v Warwicks (Birmingham) 1982. HSJPL: 38* Yorks v Glamorgan (Cardiff) 1977. BB: 7-78 v Warwicks (Birmingham) 1982. BBNW: 3-29 v Notts (Derby) 1981. BBJPL: 5-37 v Lancs (Derby) 1982. BBBH: 5-32 Yorks v Minor Counties (North) (Scunthorpe) 1975. Rejoined Yorks for 1984.

Steven John RHODES (Carlton-Bolling School, Bradford) B Bradford 17/6/1964. Son of W.E. Rhodes who played for Notts from 1961 to 1964. RHB, WK. Debut 1981 aged 17 years 35 days. One match v Sri Lankans (Sheffield). Did not play in 1982 or 1983.

Kevin SHARP B Leeds 6/4/1959. LHB, OB. Debut 1976 Played for Griqualand West in 1981-82 and 1982-83. Cap 1982. Tour: D.H. Robins to New Zealand 1979-80. HS: 139 v Surrey (Scarborough) 1983. HSGC/NW: 25 v Middlesex (Lord's) 1979. HSJPL: 62 v Hants (Southampton) 1982. HSBH: 71 v Worcs (Leeds) 1982.

Arnold SIDEBOTTOM B Barnsley 1/4/1954. RHB, RFM. Debut 1973. Cap 1980. HS: 124 v Glamorgan (Cardiff) 1977. HSGC/NW: 45 v Hants (Bournemouth) 1977. HSJPL: 52* v Norhtants (Middlesbrough) 1982. HSBH: 32 v Notts (Leeds) 1983. BB: 7-18 v Oxford U (Oxford) 1980. BBGC/NW: 4-35 v Kent (Leeds) 1980. BBJPL: 4-24 v Surrey (Scarborough) 1975. BBBH: 3-21 v Minor Counties (North) (Jesmond) 1979. Soccer for Manchester United, Huddersfield Town and Halifax Town.

Graham Barry STEVENSON B Ackworth 16/12/1955. RHB, RM. Debut 1973. Cap 1978. Tests: 2 in 1979-80 and 1980-81. NW Man of the Match: 1. BH Gold Award: 1. Tours: Australia and India 1979-80 (flown out as a replacement for M. Hendrick), West Indies 1980-81. HS: 115* v Warwicks (Birmingham) 1982. HSTC: 27* v India (Bombay) 1979-80. HSNW: 34 v Northants (Leeds) 1983. HSJPL: 56 v Somerset (Scarborough) 1981. HSBH: 16 v Middlesex (Lord's) 1977. BB: 8-57 v Northants (Leeds) 1980. BBTC: 3-111 v West Indies (St. John's) 1980-81. BBNW: 5-27 v Berkshire (Reading) 1983. BBJPL: 5-41 v Leics (Leicester) 1976. BBBH: 5-28 v Kent (Canterbury) 1978.

Ian Geoffrey SWALLOW B Barnsley 18/12/1962. RHB, OB. Debut 1983. HS: 11* v Somerset (Weston-super-Mare) 1983.
NB. The following players whose particulars were included in the 1983 Annual have been omitted. C.W.J. Athey, R. Illingworth, A. Ramage, S. Stuchbury and N.S. Taylor.

P. C. A. 1984—6

YORKSHIRE

County Averages

Schweppes County Championships: Played 24, won 1, drawn 17, lost 5, abandoned 1.

BATTING AND FIELDING

Cap		*M*	*I*	*NO*	*RUNS*	*HS*	*Avge*	*100*	*50*	*Ct*	*St*
1963	G. Boycott	23	40	5	1941	214*	55.45	7	4	17	—
1973	D.L. Bairstow	23	35	6	1102	100*	38.00	1	8	47	8
1980	A. Sidebottom	16	21	7	490	78	35.00	—	2	2	—
—	M.D. Moxon	12	23	0	780	153	33.91	1	4	5	—
1980	J.D. Love	23	38	7	1020	76*	32.90	—	7	8	—
1982	K. Sharp	12	21	1	597	139	29.85	2	1	6	—
1976	P. Carrick	23	32	8	697	83	29.04	—	4	9	—
1980	C.W.J. Athey	20	32	1	758	90	24.45	—	5	15	—
1974	R.G. Lumb	10	15	1	328	60	23.42	—	2	6	—
1978	G.B. Stevenson	20	25	1	396	52	16.50	—	2	4	—
1981	S.N. Hartley	14	19	1	261	69	14.50	—	1	5	—
1955	R. Illingworth	21	16	4	71	16	5.91	—	—	11	—
1983	S.J. Dennis	20	23	8	71	17	4.73	—	—	6	—
—	N.S. Taylor	4	5	0	10	4	2.00	—	—	1	-

Played in three matches: S.D. Fletcher 0*, 12, 11; A. Ramage 32, 0*, 14.
Played in two matches: P.W. Jarvis 5*, 1*, 11*; I.G. Swallow 4, 11*, 4* (1 ct).
Played in one match: P.A. Booth 0, 0; A.A. Metcalfe 122, 7 (1 ct).

BOWLING

	Type	*O*	*M*	*R*	*W*	*Avge*	*Best*	*5 wI*	*10 wM*
G.B. Stevenson	**RM**	460.1	103	1400	56	25.00	5-35	2	—
A. Sidebottom	**RFM**	361	81	1080	39	27.69	5-6	1	—
P. Carrick	**SLA**	848.1	303	1750	62	28.22	7-44	6	1
R. Illingworth	**OB**	411.5	136	951	32	29.71	4-48	—	—
N.S. Taylor	**RFM**	111.1	23	427	14	30.50	5-49	1	—
S.J. Dennis	**LFM**	525.2	117	1600	52	30.76	4-32	—	—

Also bowled: C.W.J. Athey 38-8-110-3; D.L. Bairstow 10-4-27-1; P.A. Booth 17-3-50-0; G. Boycott 23-10-45-1; S.D. Fletcher 55.4-7-186-8; S.N. Hartley 14-3-40-1; P.W. Jarvis 44-8-155-3; J.D. Love 22-5-89-1; A.A. Metcalfe 2-0-6-0; M.D. Moxon 33-3-123-1; A. Ramage 39-4-145-2; I.G. Swallow 30.4-8-82-2.

County Records

First-class cricket

Highest innings totals:	For	887 v Warwicks (Birmingham)	1896
	Agst	630 by Somerset (Leeds)	1901
Lowest innings totals:	For	23 v Hants (Middlesbrough)	1965
	Agst	13 by Notts (Nottingham)	1901
Highest individual innings:	For	341 G.H. Hirst v Leics (Leicester)	1905
	Agst	318* W.G. Grace for Glos (Cheltenham)	1876
Best bowling in an innings:	For	10-10 H. Verity v Notts (Leeds)	1932
	Agst	10-37 C.V. Grimmett for Australians (Sheffield)	1930
Best bowling in a match:	For	17-91 H. Verity v Essex (Leyton)	1933
	Agst	17-91 H. Dean for Lancs (Liverpool)	1913
Most runs in a season:		2883 (av. 80.08) H. Sutcliffe	1932
Most runs in a career:		38561 (av. 50.21) H. Sutcliffe	1919-1945
100s in a season:		12 by H. Sutcliffe	1932
100s in a career:		112 by H. Sutcliffe	1919-1945
wickets in a season:		240 (av. 12.72) W. Rhodes	1900
wickets in a career:		3608 (av. 16.00) W. Rhodes	1898-1930

RECORD WICKET STANDS

1st	555	P. Holmes & H. Sutcliffe v Essex (Leyton)	1932
2nd	346	W. Barber & M. Leyland v Middlesex (Sheffield)	1932
3rd	323*	H. Sutcliffe & M. Leyland v Glamorgan (Huddersfield)	1928
4th	312	G.H. Hirst & D. Denton v Hants (Southampton)	1914
5th	340	E. Wainwright & G.H. Hirst v Surrey (Oval)	1899
6th	276	M. Leyland & E. Robinson v Glamorgan (Swansea)	1926
7th	254	D.C.F. Burton & W. Rhodes v Hants (Dewsbury)	1919
8th	292	Lord Hawke & R. Peel v Warwicks (Birmingham)	1896
9th	192	G.H. Hirst & S. Haigh v Surrey (Bradford)	1898
10th	149	G. Boycott & G.B. Stevenson v Warwicks (Birmingham)	1982

One-day cricket

Highest innings totals:	Gillette Cup/ NatWest Trophy	317-4 v Surrey (Lord's)	1965
	John Player League	257-4 v Hants (Middlesbrough)	1983
	Benson & Hedges Cup	269-6 v Worcs (Worcester)	1980
Lowest innings totals:	Gillette Cup/ NatWest Trophy	76 v Surrey (Harrogate)	1970
	John Player League	74 v Warwicks (Birmingham)	1972
	Benson & Hedges Cup	114 v Kent (Canterbury)	1978
Highest individual innings:	Gillette Cup/ NatWest Trophy	146 G. Boycott v Surrey (Lord's)	1965
	John Player League	119 J.H. Hampshire v Leicestershire (Hull)	1971
	Benson & Hedges Cup	142 G. Boycott v Worcs (Worcester)	1980
Best bowling figures:	Gillette Cup/ NatWest Trophy	6-15 F.S. Trueman v Somerset (Taunton)	1965
	John Player League	7-15 R.A. Hutton v Worcs (Leeds)	1969
	Benson & Hedges Cup	6-27 A.G. Nicholson v Minor Counties (North) (Middlesbrough)	1972

VALETE

The following players appeared for counties in 1983 but are not expected to play in 1984. Their records are included to bring them up to date and in case they do re-appear.

James Paul ADDISON B Leek, Staffs 14/11/1965. RHB, SLA. Debut for Leics. 1983. HS: 51 v New Zealanders (Leicester) 1983. HSJPL: 10 v Warwicks (Birmingham) 1983.

James Alexander CARSE B Salisbury, Rhodesia 13/12/1958. RHB, RFM. Played for Rhodesia 1977-78 to 1979-80, Western Province 1980-81, Eastern Province 1981-82 and 1982-83. Debut for Northants 1983. HS: 44 Zimbabwe Rhodesia v Northern Transvaal (Pretoria) 1979-80. HSUK: 36* v Hants (Northampton) 1983. BB: 6-50 Eastern Province v Northern Transvaal (Port Elizabeth) 1981-82. BBUK: 5-43 v Glamorgan (Cardiff) 1983. BBBH: 3-38 v Glos (Northampton) 1983.

Robert Giles Lenthall CHEATLE (Stowe School) B London 31/7/1953. LHB, SLA. Debut for Sussex 1974. Debut for Surrey 1980. HS: 49 Sussex v Kent (Tunbridge Wells) 1978. HSC: 27* v Sussex (Hove) 1982. HSJPL: 18* Sussex v Warwicks (Hove) 1979. HSBH: 16 Sussex v Somerset (Hove) 1978. BB: 6-32 Sussex v Yorks (Hove) 1979. BBC: 5-28 v Sussex (Oval) 1980. BBJPL: 4-33 Sussex v Glamorgan (Eastbourne) 1977. BBBH: 3-26 v Hants (Oval) 1980.

Ian COCKBAIN B Bootle 19/4/1958. RHB, SLA. Debut for Lancs 1979. HS: 98 v Warwicks (Southport) 1982. HSJPL: 53* v Glos (Manchester) 1982. HSBH: 53 v Worcs (Manchester) 1980.

Brian Fettes DAVISON B Bulawayo, Rhodesia 21/12/1946. RHB, RM. Played for Rhodesia 1967-68 to 1978-79. Debut for Leics 1970 after having played for International Cavaliers. Cap 1971. County Captain in 1980. Played for Tasmania from 1979-80 to 1981-82. Benefit in 1982. 1,000 runs (13) – 1,818 runs (av. 56.81) in 1976 best. Gillette Man of the Match: 1. NW Man of the Match: 1. BH Gold Awards: 6 HS: 189 v Australians (Leicester) 1975. HSGC/NW 99 v Essex (Southend) 1977. HSJPL: 85* v Glamorgan (Cardiff) 1974. HSBH: 158* v Warwicks (Coventry) 1972. BB: 5-52 Rhodesia v Griqualand West (Bulawayo) 1967-68. BBUK: 4-99 v Northants (Leicester) 1970. BBJPL: 4-29 v Glamorgan (Neath) 1971. Has played hockey for Rhodesia.

Mark Andrew FELL B Newark 17/11/1960. RHB, SLA. Debut for Notts 1982. HS: 108 v Essex (Nottingham) 1982. HSJPL: 28 v Warwicks (Nottingham) 1982. HSBH: 26 v Lancs (Nottingham) 1982.

Mark Andrew FELTHAM B Wandsworth 26/6/1963. RHB, RFM. Debut for Surrey 1983. One match v Oxford U.

Alastair James HIGNELL (Denstone College and Cambridge) B Cambridge 4/9/1955. RHB, LB. Debut for Glos 1974. Cap 1977. Blue 1975-76-77-78. Captain 1977-78. 1,000 runs (3) – 1,140 (av. 30.81) in 1976. 100 runs in each innings (108 and 145) Cambridge U v Surrey (Cambridge) 1978. BH Gold Award: 1 for Combined Universities. HS: 149* v Northants (Bristol) 1979. HSGC/NW: 85* v Northants (Bristol) 1977. HSJPL: 70 v Northants (Northampton) 1983. HSBH: 63 Combined Universities v Worcs (Worcester) 1978. Rugby Blue and England international.

Nigel John Bertie ILLINGWORTH (Denstone College) B Chesterfield 23/11/1960. RHB, RM. Debut for Notts 1981. HS: 49 v Cambridge U (Cambridge) 1982. BB: 5-89 v Middlesex (Lord's) 1982. BBJPL: 4-15 v Leics (Nottingham) 1982.

Raymond ILLINGWORTH B Pudsey 8/6/1932. RHB, OB. Debut for Yorks 1951. Cap 1955. *Wisden* 1959. Benefit (£6,604) in 1965. Joined Leics by special registration in 1969 being appointed county captain. Cap 1969. Awarded CBE in 1973 New Years honours list. Benefit 1977. Rejoined Yorks as cricket manager in 1979 and took over captaincy in middle of 1982 season from C.M. Old. Tests: 61 between 1958 and 1973 captaining England in 31 Test matches between 1969 and 1973. Played in 5 matches as captain against Rest of World in 1970. Tours: West Indies 1959-60, Commonwealth to South Africa 1960-61, Australia and New Zealand 1962-63, 1970-71 (captain). 1,000 runs (8) – 1,726 runs (av. 46.64) in 1959 best. Shared in 10th wkt partnership record for county, 228 with K. Higgs v Northants (Leicester) 1977. 100 wkts (10) – 131 wkts (av. 14.36) in 1968 best. Hat-trick v Surrey (Oval) 1975. Doubles (6): 1957, 1959-62 and 1964. Had match double of 100 runs and 10 wkts Yorks v Kent (Dover) 1964 (135 and 14-101). Gillette Man of Match: 1 (for Yorks). BH Gold Awards: 3. HS: 162 Yorks v Indians (Sheffield) 1959. HSTC: 113 v West Indies (Lord's) 1969. HSC: 153* v Essex (Leicester) 1969. HSGC: 59 v Notts (Leicester) 1970. HSJPL: 79 v Yorks (Leicester) 1970. HSBH: 43* v Worcs (Worcester) 1975. BB: 9-42 Yorks v Worcs (Worcester) 1957. BBTC: 6-29 v India (Lord's) 1967. BBC: 8-38 v Glamorgan (Swansea) 1976. BBGC: 5-29 Yorks v Surrey (Lord's) 1965. BBJPL: 5-31 v Yorks (Bradford) 1977. BBBH: 5-20 v Somerset (Leicester) 1974.

Alan JONES B Swansea 4/11/1938. LHB, OB. Debut 1957. Cap 1962. Captain 1976 to 1978. *Wisden* 1977. Testimonial 1980 (£35,000). Played 1 match v Rest of the World in 1970. Played for Western Australia 1963-64, Northern Transvaal 1975-76 and Natal 1976-77. Tours: Glamorgan in West Indies and MCC to Ceylon 1969-70. 1,000 runs (23) – (av. 34.53) in 1966 best. Hundred in each innings 3 times (187* and 105*) v Somerset (Glastonbury) 1963, (132 and 156*) v Yorks (Middlesbrough) 1976 and (147 and 100) v Hants (Swansea) 1978. Shared country record partnership for any wicket (330 for 1st) with R.C. Fredericks v Northants (Swansea) 1972; also 2nd wicket record (*q.v.*). Holds county record aggregate for runs and centuries. GC Man of the Match: 2. BH Gold Awards: 1. HS: 204* v Hants (Basingstoke) 1980. HSGC/NW: 124* v Warwicks (Birmingham) 1976. HSJPL: 110* v Glos (Cardiff) 1978. HSBH: 89 v Worcs (Cardiff) 1979. BBJPL: 3-21 v Northants (Wellingborough) 1975.

Hon. Timothy Michael LAMB (Shrewsbury and Oxford) B Hartford (Cheshire) 24/3/1953. RHB, RM. Debut for Oxford U 1973. Blue 1973-74. Debut for Middlesex 1974. Left county and made debut for Northants 1978. Cap 1978. NW Man of the Match: 1. BH Gold Awards: 1. HS: 77 Middlesex v Notts (Lord's) 1976. HSC: 30* v Glos (Northampton) 1982. HSGC/NW: 12 v Surrey (Oval) 1980. HSJPL: 27 Middlesex v Hants (Basingstoke) 1976. HSBH: 10* v Combined Universities (Northampton) 1980. BB: 7-56 v Cambridge U (Cambridge) 1980. BBGC/NW: 4-52 v Sussex (Hove) 1979. BBJPL: 5-13 v Notts (Northampton) 1979. BBBH: 5-44 Middlesex v Yorks (Lord's) 1975. Middlesex secretary 1984.

Steven John LINES B Luton, Beds 16/3/1963. RHB, RM. Debut for Northants 1983. HS: 29 v Oxford U 1983 (only match).

David LLOYD B Accrington 18/3/1947. LHB, SLA. Debut 1965. Cap 1968. County Captain from 1973 to 1977. Testimonial (£40,171) in 1978. Tests 9 in 1974 and 1974-75. Tours: Australia and New Zealand 1974-75, D.H. Robins to South

Africa 1975-76. 1,000 runs (11) – 1,510 runs (av. 47.18) in 1972 best. Scored two centuries in match (116 and 104*) v Worcs (Southport) 1979. Gillette Man of the Match: 3. NW Man of the Match: 1. BH Gold Awards: 2. HS: 214* England v India (Birmingham) 1974. HSC: 195 v Glos (Manchester) 1973. HSGC/NW: 121* v Glos (Manchester) 1978. HSJPL: 103* v Northants (Bedford) 1971. HSBH: 113 v Minor Counties (North) (Manchester) 1973 and 113 v Scotland (Manchester) 1980. BB: 7-38 v Glos (Lydney) 1966. BBNW: 3-22 v Durham (Manchester) 1981. BBJPL: 3-23 v Glos (Manchester) 1980. BBBH: 4-17 v Notts (Manchester) 1980.

Malcolm Andrew NASH B Abergavenny 9/5/1945. LHB, LM. Debut for Glamorgan 1966. Cap 1969. Captain 1980-81. Benefit 1978 (£18,000). BH Gold Awards: 3. Tour: Glamorgan to West Indies 1969-70. Hat-trick in JPL v Worcs (Worcester) 1975. HS: 130 v Surrey (Oval) 1976. HSGC/NW: 51 v Lincs (Swansea) 1974. HSJPL: 68 v Essex (Purfleet) 1972. HSBH: 103* v Hants (Swansea) 1976. BB: 9-56 v Hants (Basingstoke) 1975. BBNW: 5-31 v Oxfordshire (Oxford) 1981. BBJPL: 6-29 v Worcs (Worcester) 1975. BBBH: 4-12 v Surrey (Cardiff) 1975.

Martin William Charles OLLEY B Romford, Essex 27/11/1963. RHB, WK. Debut for Northants 1983 in one match v Cambridge U.

Stephen Peter PERRYMAN B Yardley, Birmingham 22/10/1955. RHB, RM. Debut 1974 for Warwicks. Cap 1977. Debut for Worcs 1982. BH Gold Award: 1 (for Warwicks). HS: 42 Warwicks v Somerset (Birmingham) 1977. HSJPL: 19* v Kent (Worcester) 1982. HSBH: 18 Warwicks v Essex (Chelmsford) 1979. BB: 7-49 Warwicks v Hants (Bournemouth) 1978. BBGC/NW: 3-35 Warwicks v Middlesex (Lord's) 1977. BBJPL: 4-19 Warwicks v Surrey (Oval) 1975. BBBH: 4-17 Warwicks v Minor Counties (West) (Birmingham) 1978.

Alan RAMAGE B Guisborough 29/11/1957. LHB, RFM. Debut for Yorks 1979. HS: 52 v Glos (Bristol) 1981. HSNW: 14 v Northants (Leeds) 1983. HSJPL: 32* v Middlesex (Lord's) 1982. HSBH: 17* v Combined Universities (Barnsley) 1976. BB: 5-65 v Surrey (Harrogate) 1981. BBGC/NW: 3-33 v Hants (Southampton) 1980. BBJPL: 3-51 v Kent (Canterbury) 1977. BBBH: 3-63 v Warwicks (Leeds) 1980. Has played soccer for Middlesbrough.

Anderson Montgomery Everton ROBERTS B Antigua 29/1/1951. RHB, RF. Played for Leeward Islands and Combined Islands from 1969-70 to date. Debut for Hants 1973. Cap 1974. *Wisden* 1974. Played for New South Wales in 1976-77. Left Hants in 1978. Debut for Leics 1981. Tests: 45 for West Indies between 1973-74 and 1982-83 Tours: West Indies to India, Sri Lanka and Pakistan 1974-75, Australia 1975-76, 1981-82, England 1976 and 1980, Australia and New Zealand 1979-80. Took 100th wkt in Test cricket in 1976 in then record time of 2 years 142 days. Took 119 wkts (av. 13.62) in 1974. Hat-trick for Combined Islands v Jamaica (St. Kitts) 1908-81. BH Gold Awards: 1 (for Hants). HS: 63 Combined Islands v Guyana (Grenada) 1980-81. HSUK: 57 v Essex (Colchester) 1981. HSTC: 54 West Indies v Australia (Melbourne) 1979-80. HSNW: 46 v Somerset (Taunton) 1982. HSJPL: 59* v Somerset (Leicester) 1981. HSBH: 29 Hants v Glos (Bristol) 1975 and 29 v Surrey (Oval) 1981. BB: 8-47 Hants v Glamorgan (Cardiff) 1974. BBC: 8-56 v Glamorgan (Leicester) 1982. BBTC: 7-54 West Indies v Australia (Perth) 1975-76. BBGC/NW: 3-17 Hants v Glamorgan (Southampton) 1975. BBJPL: 5-13 Hants v Sussex (Hove) 1974. BBBH: 4-12 Hants v Somerset (Bournemouth) 1975.

Neil RUSSOM (Cambridge) B Finchley (London) 3/12/1958. RHB, RM. Debut for Cambridge U 1979. Blues 1980-81. Debut for Somerset 1980. BH Gold Awards: 1 (for Combined Universities). HS: 79* Cambridge U v Northants (Cambridge) 1980. HSBH: 22 Combined Universities v Kent (Canterbury) 1981. BB: 4-84 Cambridge U v Leics (Cambridge) 1980. BBBH: 5-40 Combined Universities v Northants (Northampton) 1980.

Mark Stephen SCOTT B Muswell Hill (Middlesex) 10/3/1959. RHB. Debut for Worcs 1981. HS: 109 v Glos (Bristol) 1981. HSNW: 23 v Notts (Worcester) 1983. HSJPL: 42 v Glos (Worcester) 1981.

David Martin SMITH B Coventry 21/1/1962. No relation to K.D. Smith. LHB, SLA. Debut for Warwicks 1981. HS: 100* v Oxford U (Birmingham) 1983.

John William SOUTHERN B King's Cross, London 2/9/1952. RHB, SLA. Debut for Hants 1975. Cap 1978. HS: 61* v Yorks (Bradford) 1979. HSJPL: 15* v Essex (Southampton) 1983. HSBH: 14 v Somerset (Bournemouth) 1980. BB: 6-46 v Glos (Bournemouth) 1975.

Simon Paul SUTCLIFFE (King George V GS, Southport and Oxford) B Watford 22/5/1960. Son of Peter W. Sutcliffe, former national coach, RHB, OB. Debut for Oxford U 1980. Blues 1980-81. University Secretary in 1981. Debut for Warwicks 1981. HS: 20 v Glos (Nuneaton) 1982. BB: 6-19 Oxford U v Warwickshire (Oxford) 1980. BBNW: 3-40 v Cambridgeshire (Birmingham) 1982.

Nicholas Simon TAYLOR B Holmfirth 2/6/1963. RHB, RFM. Son of K. Taylor (England, Yorks and Auckland). Debut for Yorks 1982. BB: 5-49 v Sussex (Leeds) 1983.

David Anthony THORNE B Coventry 12/12/1964. RHB, LM. Debut for Warwicks 1983. HS: 23* v Glos (Cheltenham) 1983. HSJPL: 42 v Glos (Moreton-in-the-Marsh) 1983.

Roger William TOLCHARD (Malvern College) B Torquay 15/6/1946. RHB, WK. Debut for Leics 1965. Cap 1966. Appointed County Captain in 1981. Tests: 4 in 1976-77. Tours: International XI in East Africa, Pakistan, India and Ceylon 1967-68, India, Pakistan and Sri Lanka 1972-73, D.H. Robins to South Africa 1973-74, 1974-75 and 1975-76, Sri Lanka 1977-78, International Wanderers to Rhodesia 1974-75, India, Sri Lanka and Australia 1976-77, Australia 1978-79, Leics to Zimbabwe 1980-81. Played for Overseas XI v Board Presidents XI (Calcutta) 1980-81. Shared in 5th-wicket partnership record for county, 235 with N.E. Briers v Somerset (Leicester) 1979. NW Man of the Match: 1. BH Gold Awards: 4. HS: 126* v Cambridge U (Cambridge) 1970. HSGC/NW: 86* v Glos (Leicester) 1975. HSJPL: 103 v Middlesex (Lord's) 1972 and was dismissed obstructing the field. HSBH: 92* v Worcs (Worcester) 1976. Benefit 1979.

Stephen George WATKINS B Hereford 23/3/1959. RHB, RM. Debut for Worcs 1983. HS: 77 v Oxford U (Oxford) 1983.

Andrew WATTS B Chapeltown, Yorks 4/10/1960. LHB, RM. Debut for Derby 1982. HS: 33* v Northants (Derby) 1983.

John James WHITAKER B Skipton, Yorks 5/5/1962. RHB, OB. Debut for Leics 1983. HS: 56* v Warwicks (Birmingham) 1983. HSJPL: 65* v Surrey (Leicester) 1983.

Wood and Wootton will be found on page 194.

CAMBRIDGE UNIVERSITY

Captain: A. Pollock
Secretary: T.A. Cotterell

Robin James BOYD-MOSS (Bedford School and Magdalene College) – see Northants section.

Thomas Archibald COTTERELL (Downside and Peterhouse) B London 12/5/1963. RHB, SLA. Debut and Blue 1983. HS: 22 v Worcs (Worcester) 1983. BB: 5-89 v Essex (Cambridge) 1983.

Timothy Stephen CURTIS – see Worcs section.

Andrew George DAVIES (Birkenhead School and Robinson) B Altrincham, Cheshire 5/5/1962. RHB, WK. Debut 1982. HS: 13 v Essex (Cambridge).

Simon Jonathon Graham DOGGART (Winchester College and Magdalene) B Winchester, Hants 8/2/1961. LHB, OB. Debut 1980. Blue 1980-81-82-83. Secretary 1982. HS: 70 v Notts (Cambridge) 1983. BB: 3-3 v Notts (Cambridge) 1983. Son of G.H.G. Doggart and grandson of A.G. Doggart, both former Cambridge Blues. Father also played for Sussex and England.

Charles Christopher ELLISON (Tonbridge School and Homerton) B Pembury, Kent 11/2/1962. RHB, RM. Debut 1982. Blue 1982-83. HS: 21 v Notts (Cambridge) 1983. BB: 4-36 v Notts (Cambridge) 1983. Brother of R.M. Ellison of Kent.

Stephen Peter HENDERSON (Downside, Durham U and Magdalene). See Glamorgan section.

Steven Guy Paul HEWITT (Bradford GS and Peterhouse) B Radcliffe, Lancs. 6/4/1963. RHB, WK. Debut and Blue 1983.

Kenneth Ian HODGSON (Oundle and Downing) B Port Elizabeth South Africa 24/2/1960. RHB, RM. Debut 1981. Blue 1981-82-83. HS: 50 v Lancs (Cambridge) 1982. BB: 8-68 v Glamorgan (Cambridge) 1982. Half-Blue for Squash Rackets.

André ODENDAAL B Queenstown, South Africa 4/5/1954. RHB, OB. Debut and Blue 1980. Played for Boland 1980-81 and 1981-82. HS: 61 v Leics (Cambridge) 1980.

Robert William Michael PALMER (Bedford and St Catharine's) B Hong Kong 4/6/1960. RHB, LM. Debut 1981. Blue 1982. HS: 12 v Essex (Cambridge) 1982. BB: 4-96 v Notts (Cambridge) 1982.

Gajanad PATHMANATHAN (Royal College, Colombo; Sri Lanka U; University College Oxford and Darwin) B Colombo 23/1/1954. RHB, LB. Debut for Sri Lankans in 1972-73. Debut for Oxford U 1975. Blue 1975-76-77-78. Debut for Cambridge U and Blue 1983. HS: 82 Oxford U v Northants (Oxford) 1976.

Angus John POLLOCK (Shrewsbury and Trinity) B Liversedge, Yorks 19/4/1962. RHB, RM. Debut 1982. Blue 1982-83. HS: 19 v Lancs (Cambridge). BB: 5-107 v Worcs (Worcester) 1983. Soccer Blue.

Paul Gerrard Peter ROEBUCK (Millfield and Emmanuel) B Bath, Somerset 13/10/1963. Brother of P.M. Roebuck (CU and Somerset). LHB, RFM. Debut 1983. HS: 31* v Leics (Cambridge) 1983.

David William VAREY (Birkenhead School and Pembroke College) B Darlington, Co Durham 15/10/1961. RHB. Debut for Cheshire 1977. Debut for Lancs 2nd XI 1980. Debut 1981. Blue 1982-83. Secretary 1983. HS: 156* v Northants (Cambridge) 1982. Twin brother of J.G. Varey (Oxford).

University Records

Highest Innings Totals:	For	703-9d v Sussex (Hove)	1890
	Agst	703-3 by West Indians (Cambridge)	1950
Lowest Innings Totals:	For	30 v Yorks (Cambridge)	1928
	Agst	32 by Oxford U (Lord's)	1878
Highest Individual Innings:	For	254* K.S. Duleepsinhji v Middlesex (Cambridge)	1927
	Agst	304* E.D. Weekes for West Indies (Cambridge)	1950
Best Bowling in an Innings:	For	10-69 S.M.J. Woods v C.I. Thornton's XI (Cambridge)	1890
	Agst	10-38 S.E. Butler for Oxford U (Lord's)	1871
Best Bowling in a Match:	For	15-88 S.M.J. Woods v C.I. Thornton's XI (Cambridge)	1890
	Agst	15-95 S.E. Butler for Oxford U (Lord's)	1871
Most runs in a season:		1581 (av. 79.05) D.S. Sheppard	1952
runs in a career:		4310 (av.38.48) J.M. Brearley	1961-1968
100s in a season:		7 by D.S. Sheppard	1952
100s in a career:		14 by D.S. Sheppard	1950-1952
wickets in a season:		80 (av. 17.63) O.S. Wheatley	1958
wickets in a career:		208 (av. 21.82) G. Goonesena	1954-1957

RECORD WICKET STANDS

1st	349	J.G. Dewes & D.S. Sheppard v Sussex (Hove)	1950
2nd	429*	J.G. Dewes & G.H.G. Doggart v Essex (Cambridge)	1949
3rd	284	E.T. Killick & G.C. Grant v Essex (Cambridge)	1929
4th	275	R. de W.K. Winlaw & J.H. Human v Essex (Cambridge)	1934
5th	220	R. Subba Row & F.C.M. Alexander v Notts (Nottingham)	1953
6th	245	J.L. Bryan & C.T. Ashton v Surrey (Oval)	1921
7th	289	G. Goonesena & G.W. Cook v Oxford U (Lord's)	1957
8th	145	H. Ashton & A.E.R. Gilligan v Free Foresters (Cambridge)	1920
9th	200	G.W. Cook & C.S. Smith v Lancs (Liverpool)	1957
10th	177	A.E.R. Gilligan & J.H. Naumann v Sussex (Hove)	1919

Averages

All first-class matches: Played 10, won 0, drawn 7, lost 3.

BATTING AND FIELDING

Cap	*M*	*I*	*NO*	*RUNS*	*HS*	*Avge*	*100*	*50*	*Ct*	*St*
†R.J. Boyd-Moss	10	19	0	733	139	38.57	2	2	4	—
†T.S. Curtis	10	20	3	506	92	29.76	—	3	7	—
†K.I. Hodgson	10	15	5	272	47	27.20	—	—	2	—
†S.P. Henderson	10	19	3	409	90	25.56	—	3	9	—
†S.G.J. Doggart	10	18	5	323	70	24.84	—	2	4	—
†G. Pathmanathan	7	13	1	263	64	21.91	—	2	2	—
P.G.P. Roebuck	5	7	3	82	31*	20.50	—	—	1	—
†D.W. Varey	10	20	1	342	65	18.00	—	1	3	—
†C.C. Ellison	4	6	2	49	21	12.25	—	—	4	—
A. Odenaal	3	6	1	56	21*	11.20	—	—	—	—
†T.A. Cotterell	10	12	3	81	22	9.00	—	—	2	—
†A.J. Pollock	10	9	2	38	14*	5.42	—	—	4	—
†S.G.P. Hewitt	6	7	2	9	6	1.80	—	—	6	1

Played in four matches: A.G. Davies 0, 0 (2 ct).
Played in one match: R.W.M. Palmer 0 (1 ct).
†denotes played in Varsity match.

BOWLING

	Type	*O*	*M*	*R*	*W*	*Avge*	*Best*	*5 wI*	*10 wM*
C.C. Ellison	**RM**	56.4	17	153	7	21.85	4-36	—	—
R.J. Boyd-Moss	**SLA**	70	18	217	8	27.12	5-27	1	—
A.J. Pollock	**RM**	230.2	49	750	21	35.71	5-107	1	—
T.A. Cotterell	**SLA**	273	67	758	17	44.58	5-89	1	—
P.G.P. Roebuck	**RM**	75.5	17	269	6	44.83	2-44	—	—
S.J.G. Doggart	**OB**	285.2	60	844	12	70.33	3-3	—	—
K.I. Hodgson	**RM**	297	75	871	12	72.58	4-58	—	—

Also bowled: T.S. Curtis 40-6-144-3; S.P. Henderson 13-3-66-1; R.W.M. Palmer 12-0-75-1.

OXFORD UNIVERSITY

Captain: K.A. Hayes
Secretary: J.D. Carr

John Donald CARR (Repton and Worcester). See Middlesex section.

John Robert CHESSHER (Ipswich School and Lincoln) B Banstead, Surrey 21/8/1962. RHB. Debut 1982. HS: 47 v Northants (Oxford) on debut.

Mark Ronald CULLINAN (Hilton College, Natal; Cape Town U and Worcester) B Johannesburg 3/4/1957. RHB, WK. Debut for South African Universities v Transvaal (Johannesburg) 1979-80. Debut for University and Blue 1983. HS: 27 v Hants (Oxford) 1983.

Roger Michael EDBROOKE (Queen Elizabeth's Hospital, Bristol and Hertford) B Bristol 30/12/1960. RHB, Debut 1982. HS: 84* v Glamorgan (Swansea). Soccer Blue.

Richard Gary Peter ELLIS (Haileybury College and St. Edmund Hall). See Middlesex section.

Jonathan Guy FRANKS (Stamford School and St Edmund Hall) B Stamford, Lincs. 23/9/1962. RHB, WK. Debut 1983. HS: 29 v Worcs (Oxford) 1983.

Russel Philip GIBAUT (De La Salle College, Jersey and Hertford) B St. Saviour, Jersey 5/3/1963. RHB, RM. Debut 1983.

Dominic Stephen HARRISON (Ampleforth and University College) B Tittensor, Staffs 15/1/1963. RHB, WK. Debut 1983.

Kevin Anthony HAYES (Queen Elizabeth's GS, Blackburn and Merton). See Lancs section.

Phillip John HESELTINE (Barnsley & District Holgate GS and Keble) B Skipton, Yorks 21/6/1960. RHB, RM/OB. Debut and Blue 1983. HS: 40 v Worcs (Oxford) 1983.

Mark Philip LAWRENCE (Manchester GS and Merton) B Warrington, Cheshire 6/5/1962. LHB, SLA. Debut 1982. HS: 18 v Middlesex (Oxford) 1982.

Andrew John Trevor MILLER (Haileybury College and St. Edmund Hall). See Middlesex section.

Roger Peter MOULDING (Haberdashers Ashe School, Elstree and Christ Church) B Enfield, Middlesex 3/1/1958. RHB, LB. Debut for Middlesex 1977 (one match). Debut for University 1978. Blue 1978-79-80-81-82-83. Secretary in 1979 and Captain in 1981. HS: 80* v Warwicks (Birmingham) 1983.

Michael David PETCHEY (Latymer Upper School, Sussex U and Christ Church) B London 16/12/1958. RHB, RM. Debut and Blue 1983. HS: 18 v Surrey (Oval) 1983.

Henry Thomas RAWLINSON (Eton College and Christ Church) B Edgware, Middlesex 21/1/1963. RHB, RM. Debut 1982. Blue 1983. HS: 24 v Worcs (Oxford) 1983. BB: 5-123 v Worcs (Oxford) 1983. Brother of J.L. Rawlinson who played for University 1979-80.

Alastair Harold Kurt SMAIL (Bilborough Sixth Form College and Exeter) B Kingston upon Thames 3/7/1964. RHB, LM. Debut 1983. HS: 13* v Surrey (Oval) 1983. BB: 3-49 v Sussex (Oxford) 1983.

Giles John TOOGOOD (North Bromsgrove HS and Lincoln) B West Bromwich, Staffs 19/11/1961. RHB, OB. Debut 1982. Blut 1982-83. HS: 83 v Worcs (Oxford). Captain 1983.

Jonathan Richard TURNBULL (Merchant Taylors' School, Northwood and Jesus) B Northwood, Middlesex 13/11/1962. RHB, RM. Debut 1983. BB: 4-51 v Sussex (Oxford) 1983.

Jonathan Guy VAREY (Birkenhead School and St Edmund Hall) B Darlington, Co Durham 15/10/1961. RHB, RM. Debut 1982. Blue 1982-83. HS: 69* v Northants (Oxford) 1983. BB: 3-69 v Worcs (Oxford) 1983. Twin brother of D.W. Varey (Cambridge).

University Records

Highest Innings	For	651 v Sussex (Hove)	1895
Totals:	Agst	679-7d by Australians (Oxford)	1938
Lowest Innings	For	12 v MCC (Oxford)	1877
Totals:	Agst	24 by MCC (Oxford)	1846
Highest Individual	For	281 K.J. Key v Middlesex (Chiswick Park)	1887
Innings:	Agst	338 W.W. Read for Surrey (Oval)	1888
Best Bowling	For	10-38 S.E. Butler v Cambridge U (Lord's)	1871
in an Innings:	Agst	10-49 W.G. Grace for MCC (Oxford)	1886
Best Bowling	For	15-95 S.E. Butler v Cambridge U (Lord's)	1871
in a Match:	Agst	16-225 J.E. Walsh for Leics (Oxford)	1953
Most runs in a season:		1307 (av. 93.35) Nawab of Pataudi (Snr.)	1931
runs in a career:		3319 (av. 47.41) N.S. Mitchell-Innes	1934-1937
100s in a season:		6 by Nawab of Pataudi (Snr.)	1931
100s in a career:		9 by A.M. Crawley	1927-1930
		Nawab of Pataudi (Snr.)	1928-31
		N.S. Mitchell-Innes	1934-37
		M.P. Donnelly	1946-47
wickets in a season:		70 (av. 18.15) I.A.R. Peebles	1930
wickets in a career:		182 (av. 19.38) R.H.B. Bettington	1920-1923

RECORD WICKET STANDS

1st	338	T. Bowring & H. Teesdale v Gents of England (Oxford)	1908
2nd	226	W.G. Keighley & H.A. Pawson v Cambridge U (Lord's)	1947
3rd	273	F.C. de Saram & N.S. Mitchell-Innes v Glos (Oxford)	1934
4th	276	P.G.T. Kingsley & N.M. Ford v Surrey (Oval)	1930
5th	256*	A.A. Baig & C.A. Fry v Free Foresters (Oxford)	1959
6th	270	D.R. Walsh & S.A. Westley v Warwicks (Oxford)	1969
7th	340	K.J. Key & H. Philipson v Middlesex (Chiswick Park)	1887
8th	160	H. Philipson & A.C.M. Croome v MCC (Lord's)	1889
9th	157	H.M. Garland-Wells & C.K.H. Hill-Wood v Kent (Oxford)	1928
10th	149	F.H. Hollins & B.A. Collins v MCC (Oxford)	1901

Averages

All first-class matches: Played 10, won 0, drawn 5, lost 4, abandoned 1.

BATTING AND FIELDING

Cap	*M*	*I*	*NO*	*RUNS*	*HS*	*Avge*	*100*	*50*	*Ct*	*St*
†R.P. Moulding	8	13	3	448	80*	44.80	—	4	1	—
†A.J.T. Miller	9	15	3	537	127*	44.75	1	3	1	—
†R.G.P. Ellis	9	15	2	551	103*	42.38	1	3	3	—
†J.G. Varey	6	10	3	187	69*	26.71	—	1	1	—
†P.J. Heseltine	6	10	1	176	40	19.55	—	—	5	—
†K.A. Hayes	3	4	0	62	45	15.50	—	—	—	—
J.G. Franks	5	7	0	98	29	14.00	—	—	2	—
†H.T. Rawlinson	8	9	2	91	24	13.00	—	—	2	—
†M.R. Cullinan	8	8	2	55	27	9.16	—	—	14	—
†G.J. Toogood	5	6	0	48	18	8.00	—	—	—	—
†J.D. Carr	6	7	1	45	18	7.50	—	—	5	—
A.H.K. Smail	6	6	1	24	13*	4.80	—	—	1	—
†M.D. Petchey	6	6	0	21	18	3.50	—	—	3	—
J.R. Turnbull	7	7	4	5	5*	1.66	—	—	6	—

Played in two matches: R.M. Edbrooke 0, 71, (1 ct), R.P. Gibaut 7, 0.

Played in one match: J.R. Chessher 0, 11; D.S. Harrison 1, 8 (1 ct); M.P. Lawrence did not bat (1 ct).

BOWLING

	Type	*O*	*M*	*R*	*W*	*Avge*	*Best*	*5 wI*	*10 wM*
K.A. Hayes	**RM**	33.5	10	124	8	15.50	6-58	1	—
J.R. Turnbull	**RM**	130	34	424	12	35.33	4-51	—	—
A.H.K. Smail	**LM**	70	18	222	5	44.40	3-49	—	—
H.T. Rawlinson	**RM**	154.5	31	626	14	44.71	5-123	1	—
J.D. Carr	**OB**	155	45	445	9	49.44	2-59	—	—
M.D. Petchey	**RM**	206.2	36	804	12	67.00	2-70	—	—

Also bowled: R.G.P. Ellis 22-6-82-0; M.P. Lawrence 6-1-36-0; R.P. Moulding 9.4-0-22-0; J.G. Varey 77-10-316-3.

THE FIRST-CLASS UMPIRES FOR 1984

N.B. The abbreviations used below are as for 'The Counties and their Players'.

William Edward ALLEY B Sydney, Australia 3/2/1919. LHB, RM. Played for New South Wales 1945-46 to 1947-48. Subsequently came to England to play League cricket and then for Somerset from 1957 to 1968. *Wisden* 1961. Testimonial (£2,700) in 1961. Tours: India and Pakistan 1949-50, Pakistan 1963-64 with Commonwealth team. Scored 3,019 runs (av. 56.96) in 1961 including 2,761 runs and 10 centuries for county, both being records. Gillette Man of Match Awards: 3. HS: 221* v Warwickshire (Nuneaton) 1961. BB: 8-65 v Surrey (Oval) 1962. Career record: 19,612 runs (av. 31.88), 31 centuries, 768 wkts (av. 22.68). Appointed 1969. Umpired in 10 Tests between 1974 and 1981.

Harold Denis BIRD B Barnsley 19/4/1933. RHB, RM. Played for Yorks from 1956 to 1959 and for Leics from 1960 to 1964. Was subsequently professional at Paignton CC. HS: 181* Yorks v Glamorgan (Bradford) 1959. Career record: 3,315 runs (av. 20.71), 2 centuries. Appointed 1970. Umpired in 26 Tests between 1973 and 1983.

Jack BIRKENSHAW B Rothwell (Yorks) 13/11/1940. LHB, OB. Played for Yorks from 1958 to 1960, for Leics from 1961 to 1980 and for Worcs in 1981. Benefit (£13,000) in 1974. Tests: 5 in 1972-73 and 1973-74. Tours: India, Pakistan and Sri Lanka 1972-73, West Indies 1973-74. Gillette Man of Match Awards: 1 (for Leics). HS: 131 Leics v Surrey (Guildford) 1969. BB: 8-94 Leics v Somerset (Taunton) 1972. Career Record: 12,780 runs (av. 23.57), 4 centuries, 1,073 wkts (av. 27.28). Appointed 1982.

David John CONSTANT B Bradford-on-Avon (Wilts) 9/11/1941. LHB, SLA. Played for Kent from 1961 to 1963 and for Leics from 1965 to 1968. HS: 80 v Glos (Bristol) 1966. Career record: 1,517 runs (av. 19.20), 1 wkt (36.00). Appointed 1969. Umpired in 26 Tests between 1971 and 1983.

Cecil (Sam) COOK B Tetbury (Glos) 23/8/1921. RHB, SLA. Played for Gloucestershire from 1946 to 1964. Benefit (£3,067) in 1957. Took wicket with first ball in first-class cricket. Tests: 1 v SA 1947. HS: 35* v Sussex (Hove) 1957. BB: 9-42 v Yorks (Bristol) 1947. Career record: 1,964 runs (av. 5.39), 1,782 wkts (av. 20.52). Appointed 1971, after having withdrawn from appointment in 1966.

Barry DUDLESTON B Bebington, Cheshire 16/7/1945. RHB, SLA. Played for Leics from 1966 to 1980, Glos from 1980 to 1983. Also played for Rhodesia 1976-77 to 1979-80. HS: 202 Leics v Derby (Leicester) 1979. BB: 4-6 Leics v Surrey (Leicester) 1972. Career record: 14,747 runs (av. 32.48), 32 centuries, 47 wkts (av. 29.04). Appointed 1984.

Peter James EELE B Taunton 27/1/1935. LHB, WK. Played for Somerset between 1958 and 1966. HS: 103* v Pakistan Eaglets (Taunton) 1963. Career record: 612 runs (av. 12.24), 1 century, 106 dismissals (87 ct, 19 st). Appointed 1981.

David Gwilliam Lloyd EVANS B Lambeth, London 27/7/1933. RHB, WK. Played for Glamorgan from 1956 to 1969. Benefit (£3,500) in 1969. HS: 46* v Oxford U (Oxford) 1961. Career record: 2,875 runs (av. 10.53), 558 dismissals (502 ct, 56 st). Appointed 1971. Umpired in 5 Tests between 1981 and 1983.

John Humphrey HARRIS B Taunton 13/2/1936. LHB, RFM. Played for Somerset from 1952 to 1959. HS: 41 v Worcs (Taunton) 1957. Career record: 154 runs (av. 11.00), 19 wkts (av. 32.05). Appointed 1983.

John Wakefield HOLDER B St George Barbados 19/3/1945. RHB, RFM. Played for Hants from 1968 to 1972. HS: 33 v Sussex (Hove) 1971. BB: 7-79 v Glos (Gloucester) 1972. Career record: 374 runs (av. 10.68), 139 wkts (av. 24.56). Appointed 1983.

John Alexander JAMESON B Bombay 30/6/1941. RHB, RM/OB. WK. Played for Warwicks from 1960 to 1976. Tours: International XI to South Africa 1972-73, West Indies 1973-74. HS: 240* v Glos (Birmingham) 1974 sharing world-record 2nd wicket partnership of 465* with R.B. Kanhai. BB: 4-22 v Oxford U (Oxford) 1971. Career record: 18,941 runs (av. 43.17), 33 centuries, 89 wkts (av. 42.49). Appointed 1984.

Arthur JEPSON B Selston (Notts) 12/7/1915. RHB, RFM. Played for Notts from 1938 to 1959. Benefit (£2,000) in 1951. HS: 130 v Worcs (Nottingham) 1950. BB: 8-45 v Leics (Nottingham) 1958. Career record: 6,369 runs (av. 14.31), 1 century, 1,051 wkts (av. 29.08). Soccer (goalkeeper) for Port Vale, Stoke City and Lincoln City. Appointed 1960 and is longest-serving umpire on list. Umpired in 4 Tests between 1966 and 1969.

Raymond JULIEN B Cosby (Leics) 23/8/1936. RHB, WK. Played for Leicestershire from 1953 (debut at age of 16) to 1971, but lost regular place in side to R.W. Tolchard in 1966. HS: 51 v Worcs (Worcester) 1962. Career record: 2,581 runs (av. 9.73), 421 dismissals (382 ct, 39 st). Appointed 1972.

Mervyn John KITCHEN B Nailsea (Somerset) 1/8/1940. LHB, RM. Played for Somerset from 1960 to 1979. Testimonial (£6,000) in 1973. Gillette Man of Match Awards: 2. Benson & Hedges Gold Awards: 1. HS: 189 v Pakistanis (Taunton) 1967. Career record: 15,230 runs (av. 26.25), 17 centuries, 2 wkts (av. 54.50). Appointed 1982.

Barrie LEADBEATER B Harehills, Leeds 14/8/1943. RHB, RM. Played for Yorkshire from 1966 to 1979. Joint benefit in 1980 with G.A. Cope. Gillette Man of Match Awards: 1 (in 1969 Cup Final). HS: 140* v Hants (Portsmouth) 1976. Career record: 5,373 runs (av. 25.34), 1 century, 1 wkt (av. 5.00). Appointed 1981.

Barrie John MEYER B Bournemouth 21/8/1932. RHB, WK. Played for Gloucestershire from 1957 to 1971. Benefit 1971. HS: 63 v Indians (Cheltenham) 1959, v Oxford U (Bristol) 1962 and v Sussex (Bristol) 1964. Career record: 5,367 runs (av. 14.19), 826 dismissals (707 ct, 119 st). Soccer for Bristol Rovers, Plymouth Argyle, Newport County and Bristol City. Appointed 1973. Umpired in 13 Tests between 1978 and 1983.

Donald Osmund OSLEAR B Cleethorpes (Lincs) 3/3/1929. Has not played first-class cricket. Played soccer for Grimsby Town, Hull City and Oldham Athletic. Also played ice hockey. Has umpired in county second XI matches since 1972. Appointed in 1975. Umpired in 4 Tests in 1980 and 1981.

Kenneth Ernest PALMER B Winchester 22/4/1937. RHB, RFM. Played for Somerset from 1955 to 1969. Testimonial (£4,000) in 1968. Tour: Pakistan with Commonwealth team 1963-64. Coached in Johannesburg 1964-65 and was called upon by MCC to play in final Test v South Africa owing to injuries to other bowlers.

Tests: 1 v South Africa 1964-65. HS: 125* v Northants (Northampton) 1961. BB: 9-57 v Notts (Nottingham) 1963. Career record: 7,771 runs (av. 20.66), 2 centuries, 866 wkts (av. 21.34). Appointed 1972. Umpired in 8 Tests between 1978 and 1981.

Roy PALMER B Devizes (Wilts) 12/7/1942. RHB, RFM. Younger brother of K.E. Palmer. Played for Somerset from 1965 to 1970. Gillette Man of Match Awards: 2. HS: 84 v Leics (Taunton) 1967. BB: 6-45 v Middlesex (Lord's) 1967. Career record: 1,037 runs (av. 13.29). 172 wkts (av. 31.62). Appointed 1980.

Nigel Trevor PLEWIS B Nottingham 5/9/1934. Former policeman. Has not played first-class cricket. Umpired in 2nd XI games since 1968. On Minor Counties reserve list 1980, and on list 1981. Appointed 1982.

David Robert SHEPHERD B Bideford (Devon) 27/12/1940. RHB, RM. Played for Gloucestershire from 1965 to 1979, scoring 108 in debut match v Oxford U. Joint benefit in 1978 with J. Davey. Gillette Man of Match Awards: 1. Benson & Hedges Gold Awards: 1. HS: 153 v Middlesex (Bristol) 1968. Career record: 10,672 runs (av. 24.47), 12 centuries, 2 wkts (av. 53.00). Appointed 1981.

Robert Arthur WHITE B Fulham 6/10/1936. LHB, OB. Played for Middlesex 1958 to 1965. Played for Notts 1966 to 1980. Benefit (£11,000) in 1974. HS: 116* Notts v Surrey (Oval) 1967. BB: 7-41 Notts v Derby (Ilkeston) 1971. Career record: 12,452 runs (av. 23.18), 5 centuries, 693 wts (av. 30.50). Appointed 1983.

Alan Geoffrey Thomas WHITEHEAD B Butleigh (Somerset) 28/10/1940. LHB, SLA. Played for Somerset from 1957 to 1961. HS: 15 v Hants (Southampton) 1959 and 15 v Leics (Leicester) 1960. BB: 6-74 v Sussex (Eastbourne) 1959. Career record: 137 runs (av. 5.70), 67 wkts (av. 34.41). Served on Minor Counties list in 1969. Appointed 1970. Tests: 1 in 1982.

Peter Bernard WIGHT B Georgetown, British Guiana 25/6/1930. RHB, OB. Played for British Guiana in 1950-51 and for Somerset from 1953 to 1965. Benefit (£5,000) in 1963. HS: 222* v Kent (Taunton) 1959. BB: 6-29 v Derbyshire (Chesterfield) 1957. Career record: 17,773 runs (av. 33.09), 28 centuries, 68 wkts (av. 32.26). Appointed 1966.

Test Match Panel for 1984: H.D. Bird, D.J. Constant, D.G.L. Evans, B.J. Meyer and D.O. Oslear.

FIRST CLASS AVERAGES 1983

Compiled by Brian Croudy

The following are the averages for all players who appeared in first-class matches played in England in 1983.
†*Indicates left-handed batsman*

BATTING AND FIELDING

	Cap	*M*	*I*	*NO*	*Runs*	*HS*	*Avge*	*100*	*50*	*Ct*	*St*
†Abrahams, J. (La)	1982	24	39	7	1261	178	39.40	3	4	11	—
Acfield, D.L. (Ex)	1970	22	22	13	74	16	8.22	—	—	7	—
Addison, J.P. (Le)	—	1	2	0	67	51	33.50	—	1	—	—
Agnew, J.P. (Le/DBC)	—	11	7	0	55	26	7.85	—	—	3	—
Allott, P.J.W. (La)	1981	18	18	4	225	41	16.07	—	—	4	—
Amiss, D.L. (Wa)	1965	26	43	4	1721	164	44.12	3	12	22	—
Anderson, I.S. (D)	—	21	37	4	1233	112	37.36	1	9	23	—
Asif Din (Wa)	—	14	21	3	411	65	22.83	—	2	11	—
Aslett, D.G. (K)	1983	20	36	3	1437	168	43.54	3	8	18	—
Athey, C.W.J. (Y)	1980	20	32	1	758	90	24.45	—	5	15	—
Bailey, R.J. (No)	—	3	5	1	93	37*	23.25	—	—	5	—
Bainbridge, P. (Gs)	1981	24	43	2	1217	146	29.68	1	6	14	—
Bairstow, D.L. (Y)	1973	23	35	6	1102	100*	38.00	1	8	47	8
Balderstone, J.C. (Le)	1973	25	41	4	1478	112	39.94	3	9	16	—
Bamber, M.J. (No)	—	7	14	1	360	77	27.69	—	2	5	—
Banks, D.A. (Wo)	—	7	13	1	363	100	30.25	1	1	3	—
Baptiste, E.A.E. (K)	1983	17	26	5	755	136*	35.95	2	3	10	—
Barclay, J.R.T. (Sx)	1976	21	37	3	743	65	21.85	—	3	15	—
†Barlow, G.D. (M)	1976	23	39	7	1545	132	48.28	4	9	22	—
Barnett, K.J. (D)	1982	24	40	3	1423	121	38.45	3	9	13	—
Barwick, S.R. (Gm)	—	7	7	4	31	22*	10.33	—	—	1	—
†Benson, M.R. (K)	1981	23	37	3	1515	152*	44.55	4	10	15	—
Birch, J.D. (Nt)	1981	24	38	2	1086	95	30.16	—	8	20	—
Boon, T.J. (Le)	—	4	7	0	18	5	2.57	—	—	—	—
†Booth, P.A. (Y)	—	1	2	0	0	0	—	—	—	—	—
Booth. S.C. (So)	—	10	12	5	24	9	3.42	—	—	7	—
Bore, M.K. (Nt)	1980	13	16	5	135	24	12.27	—	—	7	—
Botham, I.T. (E/So)	1976	14	21	0	852	152	40.57	3	2	10	—
Boycott, G. (Y)	1963	23	40	5	1941	214*	55.45	7	4	17	—
Boyd-Moss, R.J. (CU/No)	—	25	43	2	1437	139	35.04	3	7	8	—
Bracewell, J.G. (NZ)	—	11	16	3	183	38	14.07	—	—	10	—
†Breakwell, D. (So)	1976	2	3	1	72	55*	36.00	—	1	—	—
Brearley, J.M. (M)	1964	1	1	0	17	17	17.00	—	—	—	—
Briers, N.E. (Le)	1981	25	38	6	1289	201*	40.28	1	8	15	—
†Broad, B.C. (Gs)	1981	16	27	2	1061	145	42.44	3	3	6	—
†Butcher, A.R. (Sy)	1975	25	44	3	1349	128	32.90	3	6	15	—
Butcher, I.P. (Le)	—	17	30	1	973	139	33.55	3	3	17	—
Butcher, R.O. (M)	1979	15	19	3	657	179	41.06	2	3	36	—

	Cap	M	I	NO	Runs	HS	Avge	100	50	Ct	St
Cairns, B.L. (NZ)	—	11	14	2	254	60	21.16	—	1	6	—
Capel, D.J. (No)	—	17	24	5	534	109*	28.10	1	3	11	—
Carr, J.D. (OU/M)	—	9	10	4	67	18	11.16	—	—	5	—
Carrick, P. (Y)	1976	23	32	8	697	83	29.04	—	4	9	—
Carse, J.A. (No)	—	11	10	8	129	36*	64.50	—	—	—	—
Chadwick, M.R. (La)	—	1	2	0	2	1	1.00	—	—	1	—
Chatfield, E.J. (NZ)	—	9	8	4	45	13*	11.25	—	—	1	—
†Cheatle, R.G.L. (Sy)	—	1	—	—	—	—	—	—	—	1	—
Chessher, J.R. (OU)	—	1	2	0	11	11	5.50	—	—	—	—
†Childs, J.H. (Gs)	1977	20	18	2	82	19	5.12	—	—	5	—
Clarke, S.T. (Sy)	1980	24	24	4	285	43	14.25	—	—	17	—
Clift, P.B. (Le)	1976	23	33	7	843	100*	32.42	1	2	10	—
†Clinton, G.S. (Sy)	1980	13	22	3	439	105	23.10	1	3	—	—
†Close, D.B. (DBC)	—	1	2	0	52	51	26.00	—	1	—	—
Cobb, R.A. (Le)	—	8	10	0	110	28	11.00	—	—	5	—
Cockbain, I. (La)	—	8	15	1	291	52	20.78	—	1	4	—
Coney, J.V. (NZ)	—	9	17	3	437	68	31.21	—	4	14	—
Cook, G. (No)	1975	24	41	3	1510	128	39.73	1	11	32	3
Cook, N.G.B. (E/Le)	1982	25	24	5	201	32	10.57	—	—	11	—
†Cooper, K.E. (Nt)	1980	22	27	7	254	30*	12.70	—	—	4	—
Corlett, S.C. (Ire)	—	1	1	0	14	14	14.00	—	—	—	—
Cotterell, T.A. (CU)	—	10	12	3	81	22	9.00	—	—	2	—
Cowan, R.S. (Sx)	—	5	10	0	154	50	15.40	—	1	2	—
Cowans, N.G. (E/M)	—	15	15	4	56	10	5.09	—	—	2	—
Cowdrey, C.S. (K)	1979	22	34	10	1364	123	56.83	5	5	27	—
Cowley, N.G. (H)	1978	23	27	9	351	29	19.50	—	—	7	—
Crowe, J.J. (NZ)	—	11	19	2	470	79	27.64	—	3	13	—
Crowe, M.D. (NZ)	—	11	19	5	819	134*	58.50	3	3	13	—
Cullinan, M.R. (OU)	—	8	8	2	55	27	9.16	—	—	14	—
†Cunningham, E.J. (Gs)	—	4	6	1	83	29*	16.60	—	—	4	—
Curtis, I.J. (Sy)	—	13	10	4	22	7	3.66	—	—	3	—
Curtis, T.S. (CU/Wo)	—	19	37	5	880	92	27.50	—	5	12	—
Daniel, W.W. (M)	1977	17	13	2	88	18	8.00	—	—	3	—
Davies, A.G. (CU)	—	4	2	0	0	0	—	—	—	2	—
Davies, T. (Gm)	—	11	15	4	260	69*	23.63	—	2	18	2
†Davis, M.R. (So)	—	14	17	5	125	20*	10.41	—	—	5	—
Davis, W.W. (Gm)	—	15	18	9	135	39*	15.00	—	—	4	—
Davison, B.F. (Le)	1971	26	41	6	1417	123*	40.48	3	8	17	—
†Denning, P.W. (So)	1973	21	36	3	758	99	22.96	—	4	6	—
Dennis, S.J. (Y)	1983	20	23	8	71	17	4.73	—	—	6	—
Dennison, D. (Ire)	—	1	2	0	17	16	8.50	—	—	1	—
Derrick, J. (Gm)	—	5	5	3	52	24*	26.00	—	—	3	—
†Dilley, G.R. (E/K)	1980	12	9	1	114	29	14.25	—	—	9	—
†Doggart, S.J.G. (CU)	—	10	18	5	323	70	24.84	—	2	4	—
D'Oliveira, D.B. (Wo)	—	22	39	2	972	102	26.27	1	5	13	—
Donald, W.A. (Sc)	—	1	2	0	51	45	25.50	—	—	—	—
Doughty, R.J. (Gs)	—	7	11	6	135	32*	27.00	—	—	—	—
Downton, P.R. (M)	1981	25	30	7	508	87	22.08	—	4	54	5
†Dredge, C.H. (So)	1978	21	26	5	296	50	14.09	—	1	10	—
Dudleston, B. (Gs)	—	2	3	1	58	35*	29.00	—	—	—	—
Dyer, R.I.H.B. (Wa)	—	9	15	3	242	93	20.16	—	1	5	—
East, D.E. (Ex)	1982	26	32	4	635	91	22.67	—	3	63	5

	Cap	M	I	NO	Runs	HS	Avge	100	50	Ct	St
East, R.E. (Ex)	1967	21	27	5	420	80*	19.09	—	1	9	—
Edbrooke, R.M. (OU)	—	2	2	0	71	71	35.50	—	1	1	—
†Edgar, B.A. (NZ)	—	11	21	2	742	100	39.05	1	5	6	—
Edmonds, P.H. (E/M)	1974	19	20	4	208	65	13.00	—	1	15	—
Ellcock, R.M. (Wo)	—	12	18	4	154	36	11.00	—	—	2	—
Ellis, R.G.P. (OU/M)	—	15	26	2	658	103*	27.41	1	3	5	—
Ellison, C.C. (CU)	—	4	6	2	49	21	12.25	—	—	4	—
†Ellison, R.M. (K)	1983	22	21	7	343	63	24.50	—	1	15	—
Emburey, J.E. (M)	1977	25	33	5	782	133	27.92	1	3	23	—
Emery, K.S.D. (H)	—	6	1	0	8	8	8.00	—	—	—	—
†Fairbrother, N.H. (La)	—	16	26	5	759	94*	36.14	—	8	8	—
Fell, M.A. (Nt)	—	5	9	0	93	41	10.33	—	—	4	—
Feltham, M.A. (Sy)	—	1	—	—	—	—	—	—	—	—	—
†Felton, N.A. (So)	—	7	12	1	376	173*	34.18	1	1	2	—
Ferreira, A.M. (Wa)	1983	17	24	6	465	66	25.83	—	3	8	—
Ferris, G.J.F. (Le)	—	13	12	4	38	11	4.75	—	—	1	—
Finney, R.J. (D)	—	20	35	2	578	71	17.51	—	3	4	—
Fletcher, K.W.R. (Ex)	1963	25	36	3	1077	151*	32.63	2	5	15	—
Fletcher, S.D. (Y)	—	3	4	2	14	12	7.00	—	—	—	—
Folley, I. (La)	—	12	9	4	91	25	18.20	—	—	3	—
Foster, N.A. (E/Ex)	1983	13	16	4	232	40*	19.33	—	—	6	—
†Fowler, G. (E/La)	1981	18	30	3	1403	156*	51.96	5	6	4	—
†Fowler, W.P. (D)	—	17	26	2	591	91	24.62	—	5	8	—
Francis, D.A. (Gm)	—	23	39	5	903	89*	26.55	—	4	6	—
Franklin, T.J. (NZ)	—	9	18	3	539	98*	35.93	—	2	6	—
Franks, J.G. (OU)	—	5	7	0	98	29	14.00	—	—	2	—
French, B.N. (Nt)	1980	24	38	4	630	91	18.52	—	3	49	3
Gard, T. (So)	1983	25	33	4	457	51	15.75	—	2	42	8
Garner, J. (So)	1979	10	16	6	265	44	26.50	—	—	10	—
Gatting, M.W. (E/M)	1977	18	28	5	1494	216	64.95	6	5	19	—
Gibaut, R.P. (OU)	—	2	2	0	7	7	3.50	—	—	—	—
†Gifford, N. (Wa)	1983	22	21	6	201	39	13.40	—	—	10	—
†Gladwin, C. (Ex)	—	9	14	0	470	89	33.57	—	2	4	—
Goldie, C.F.E. (H)	—	1	2	1	6	6	6.00	—	—	2	1
Golding, A.K. (Ex)	—	1	2	2	8	6*	—	—	—	—	—
Gooch, G.A. (Ex)	1975	26	38	1	1481	174	40.02	4	7	35	—
†Gould, I.J. (Sx)	1981	18	23	6	474	59*	27.88	—	1	32	13
†Gower, D.I. (E/Le)	1977	19	32	5	1253	140	46.40	5	5	18	—
Graveney, D.A. (Gs)	1976	22	28	8	427	94	21.35	—	2	15	—
Gray, E.J. (NZ)	—	9	15	3	280	72	23.33	—	1	7	—
Green, A.M. (Sx)	—	16	30	2	552	53	19.71	—	1	10	—
Greenidge, C.G. (H)	1972	15	27	5	1438	154	65.36	4	9	21	—
Greig, I.A. (Sx)	1981	9	10	1	324	147*	36.00	1	1	2	—
Griffiths, B.J. (No)	1978	22	13	2	27	15	2.45	—	—	2	—
†Hadlee, R.J. (NZ/Nt)	1978	13	15	2	596	103	45.84	1	5	6	—
Haggo, D.J. (Sc)	—	1	2	0	9	9	4.50	—	—	1	—
Halliday, M. (Ire)	—	1	1	1	0	0*	—	—	—	—	—
Hampshire, J.H. (D/DBC)	1982	15	21	2	601	85	31.63	—	4	5	—
Hardie, B.R. (Ex)	1974	25	37	2	1042	129	29.77	1	6	30	—
Harper, R.A. (DBC)	—	1	2	0	12	7	6.00	—	—	—	—
Harrison, D.S. (OU)	—	1	2	0	9	8	4.50	—	—	1	—

	Cap	M	I	NO	Runs	HS	Avge	100	50	Ct	St
†Harrison, G.D. (Ire)	—	1	2	1	107	86	107.00	—	1	—	—
Hartley, S.N. (Y)	1981	14	19	1	261	69	14.50	—	1	5	—
Hassan, S.B. (Nt)	1970	21	34	1	890	112	26.96	1	5	17	—
Hayes, F.C. (La)	1972	20	28	1	866	149	32.07	3	4	13	—
Hayes, K.A. (OU/La)	—	8	12	0	165	45	13.75	—	—	1	—
†Heath, J.R.P. (Sx)	—	9	18	2	335	39	20.93	—	—	4	—
Hemmings, E.E. (Nt)	1980	23	32	3	377	38	13.00	—	—	11	—
†Henderson, S.P. (CU/Gm)	—	20	35	5	820	135*	27.33	1	4	15	—
Hendrick, M. (Nt)	—	21	26	13	127	15*	9.76	—	—	18	—
Heseltine, P.J. (OU)	—	6	10	1	176	40	19.55	—	—	5	—
Hewitt, S.G.P. (CU)	—	6	7	2	9	6	1.80	—	—	6	1
Hignell, A.J. (Gs)	1977	20	37	6	1044	109*	33.67	2	6	6	—
Hill, A. (D)	1976	24	40	5	1311	137*	37.45	4	6	3	—
†Hinks, S.G. (K)	—	6	10	0	253	87	25.30	—	1	2	—
Hodgson, K.I. (CU)	—	10	15	5	272	47	27.20	—	—	2	—
Hogg, W. (Wa)	—	23	18	7	72	27*	6.54	—	—	5	—
Holding, M.A. (D)	—	6	5	1	90	63	22.50	—	1	2	—
Holmes, G.C. (Gm)	—	3	6	2	116	46	29.00	—	—	1	—
Hopkins, J.A. (Gm)	1977	25	43	2	1123	116	27.39	2	3	16	—
Howarth, G.P. (NZ/Sy)	1974	15	23	2	820	144	39.04	1	6	13	—
Hughes, D.P. (La)	1970	19	28	2	522	153	20.07	1	3	14	—
Hughes, M.G. (Ex)	—	1	2	0	10	10	5.00	—	—	—	—
Hughes, S.P. (M)	1981	13	10	6	13	4*	3.25	—	—	2	—
Humpage, G.W. (Wa)	1976	26	42	6	1116	141*	31.00	2	5	20	8
†Humphries, D.J. (Wo)	1978	20	30	4	560	59	21.53	—	2	27	9
Illingworth, N.J.B. (Nt)	—	3	6	1	49	17	9.80	—	—	3	—
Illingworth, R. (Y)	1955	21	16	4	71	16	5.91	—	—	11	—
Illingworth, R.K. (Wo)	—	25	35	6	273	55	9.41	—	1	7	—
Imran Khan (Sx)	1978	13	25	3	1260	124*	57.27	2	12	6	—
Inchmore, J.D. (Wo)	1976	20	26	4	377	51	17.13	—	1	5	—
Jackson, P.B. (Ire)	—	1	1	0	1	1	1.00	—	—	2	1
†James, K.D. (M)	—	8	8	2	141	34	23.50	—	—	1	—
Jarvis, K.B.S. (K)	1977	21	13	5	43	9*	5.37	—	—	2	—
Jarvis, P.W. (Y)	—	2	3	3	17	11*	—	—	—	—	—
Javed Miandad (Gm)	1980	5	6	0	114	89	19.00	—	1	5	—
†Jefferies, S.T. (La)	—	10	12	4	260	75*	32.50	—	1	1	—
Jesty, T.E. (H)	1971	20	30	5	1072	187	42.88	1	5	12	—
Johnson, G.W. (K)	1970	25	30	13	413	79*	24.29	—	1	28	—
Johnson, P. (Nt)	—	16	28	2	612	125	23.53	1	4	9	—
Johnston, R.I. (Ire)	—	1	2	1	16	14*	16.00	—	—	—	—
†Jones, A. (Gm)	1962	22	37	2	1059	105	30.25	1	5	7	—
†Jones, A.L. (Gm)	1983	23	40	7	1036	99	31.39	—	8	15	—
†Jones, A.N. (Sx)	—	5	7	3	11	4*	2.75	—	—	—	—
Jones, E.W. (Gm)	1967	15	18	5	256	39	19.69	—	—	24	1
†Kallicharran, A.I. (Wa)	1972	22	34	4	1637	243*	54.56	6	4	16	—
Kapil Dev (No)	1982	7	10	2	349	120	43.62	1	1	10	—
Kennedy, I.G. (Sc)	—	1	2	0	15	12	7.50	—	—	—	—
Ker, A.B.M. (Sc)	—	1	2	1	47	27*	47.00	—	—	1	—
Ker, J.E. (Sc)	—	1	1	0	0	0	—	—	—	1	—
King, C.L. (Wo/DBC)	—	3	5	0	184	123	36.80	1	—	3	—

	Cap	M	I	NO	Runs	HS	Avge	100	50	Ct	St
Kirti Azad (DBC)	—	1	2	0	16	15	8.00	—	—	2	—
†Knight, R.D.V. (Sy)	1978	24	38	6	1235	101*	38.59	1	9	28	—
Knott, A.P.E. (K)	1965	23	30	9	848	92*	40.38	—	6	39	8
Lamb, A.J. (E/No)	1978	17	29	7	1232	137*	56.00	5	3	19	—
Lamb, T.M. (No)	1978	9	10	1	70	34	7.77	—	—	—	—
Larkins, W. (No)	1976	25	42	0	1774	252	42.23	5	4	15	—
Lawrence, D.V. (Gs)	—	8	9	4	22	9	4.40	—	—	1	—
†Lawrence, M.P. (OU)	—	1	—	—	—	—	—	—	—	1	—
Lees, W.K. (NZ)	—	6	9	4	136	42*	27.20	—	—	12	—
Le Roux, G.S. (Sx)	1981	13	17	1	401	80	25.06	—	1	2	—
Lethbridge, C. (Wa)	—	8	7	3	110	73*	27.50	—	1	—	—
Lever, J.K. (Ex)	1970	18	17	3	211	44	15.07	—	—	7	—
Lilley, A.W. (Ex)	—	2	4	0	70	61	17.50	—	1	3	—
Lines, S.J. (No)	—	1	1	0	29	29	29.00	—	—	1	—
Lloyd, B.J. (Gm)	1982	14	12	2	135	38	13.50	—	—	4	—
†Lloyd, C.H. (La)	1969	11	16	1	447	86	29.80	—	3	11	—
†Lloyd, D. (La)	1968	10	15	3	507	123	42.25	1	4	8	—
†Lloyd, T.A. (Wa)	1980	23	41	4	1673	208*	45.21	5	5	12	—
†Lloyds, J.W. (So)	1982	21	35	2	901	100	27.30	1	4	12	—
†Lord, G.J. (Wa)	—	3	3	0	91	61	30.33	—	1	1	—
Love, J.D. (Y)	1980	23	38	7	1020	76*	32.90	—	7	8	—
Lumb, R.G. (Y)	1974	10	15	1	328	60	23.42	—	2	6	—
Lynch, M.A. (Sy)	1982	24	39	10	1558	119	53.72	3	11	15	—
McEvoy, M.S.A. (Wo)	—	16	26	1	569	103	22.76	1	2	17	—
McEwan, K.S. (Ex)	1974	26	39	5	2176	189*	64.00	8	8	19	—
McFarlane, L.L. (La)	—	10	9	8	35	12*	35.00	—	—	1	—
McIntyre, E.J. (Sc)	—	1	2	1	1	1	1.00	—	—	—	—
Mackintosh, K.S. (Sy)	—	1	2	2	23	18*	—	—	—	—	—
McPate, W.A. (Sc)	—	1	1	1	5	5*	—	—	—	—	—
Maher, B.J.M. (D)	—	8	12	2	150	52	15.00	—	1	13	3
Mallender, N.A. (No)	—	23	27	9	320	71*	17.77	—	1	7	—
Malone, S.J. (H)	—	22	16	6	47	12	4.70	—	—	4	—
Marks, V.J. (So)	1979	17	27	3	530	44*	22.08	—	—	5	—
Marsh, S. (K)	—	1	2	0	5	5	2.50	—	—	—	—
Marshall, M.D. (H)	1981	16	16	4	563	112	46.91	2	2	6	—
†Masters, K.D. (K)	—	2	4	0	1	1	0.25	—	—	2	—
Maynard, C. (La)	—	22	27	3	417	61*	17.37	—	2	27	2
Mendis, G.D. (Sx)	1980	24	46	6	1624	133*	40.60	4	8	8	—
Metcalfe, A.A. (Y)	—	1	2	0	129	122	64.50	1	—	1	—
†Miller, A.J.T. (OU/M)	—	15	26	3	1002	127*	43.56	1	7	1	—
Miller, G. (D)	1976	21	30	7	699	84	30.39	—	4	13	—
Moir, D.G. (D)	—	17	21	3	224	53	12.44	—	1	14	—
Monkhouse, G. (Sy)	—	18	18	5	291	46	22.38	—	—	8	—
Monteith, J.D. (Ire)	—	1	1	0	0	0	—	—	—	3	—
Moores, P. (Wo)	—	7	11	1	154	30	15.40	—	—	11	2
†Morris, H. (Gm)	—	8	14	3	228	34	20.72	—	—	7	—
Morris, J.E. (D)	—	10	20	1	361	58	19.00	—	1	4	—
Mortensen, O.H. (D)	—	18	23	15	76	14*	9.50	—	—	5	—
Morton, W.A. (Sc)	—	1	1	0	5	5	5.00	—	—	3	—
Moulding, R.P. (OU)	—	8	13	3	448	80*	44.80	—	4	1	—
Moxon, M.D. (Y)	—	12	23	0	780	153	33.91	1	4	5	—

	Cap	M	I	NO	Runs	HS	Avge	100	50	Ct	St
Mushtaq Mohammad (DBC)	—	1	2	1	70	60*	70.00	—	1	1	—
†Nash, M.A. (Gm)	1969	5	2	1	29	27*	29.00	—	—	3	—
Nasir Zaidi S.M. (La)	—	13	16	6	215	51	21.50	—	1	9	—
Neale, P.A. (Wo)	1978	24	40	3	1521	139	41.10	2	11	9	—
Needham, A. (Sy)	—	9	13	1	88	18	7.33	—	—	2	—
Newman, P.G. (D)	—	7	5	0	14	12	2.80	—	—	3	—
Newport, P.J. (Wo)	—	4	4	1	72	41*	24.00	—	—	—	—
Nicholas, M.C.J. (H)	1982	26	43	5	1418	158	37.31	3	6	26	—
Odendaal, A. (CU)	—	3	6	1	56	21*	11.20	—	—	—	—
†Old, C.M. (Wa)	—	22	25	4	396	62	18.85	—	1	7	—
Oldham, S. (D)	1980	15	17	4	177	39	13.61	—	—	3	—
Olley, M.W.C. (No)	—	1	1	0	8	8	8.00	—	—	3	—
†Ollis, R.L. (So)	—	13	22	2	517	99*	25.85	—	3	3	—
Ontong, R.C. (Gm)	1979	26	43	9	1310	112	38.52	3	7	14	—
Ormrod, J.A. (Wo)	1966	24	41	3	967	84	25.44	—	6	12	—
O'Shaughnessy, S.J. (La)	—	18	28	3	685	105	27.40	2	1	5	—
Palmer, G.V. (So)	—	10	13	2	119	78	10.81	—	1	8	—
Palmer, R.W.M. (CU)	—	1	1	0	0	0	—	—	—	1	—
Parker, P.W.G. (Sx)	1979	17	27	2	512	79	20.48	—	4	5	—
Parks, R.J. (H)	1982	25	15	2	180	52	13.84	—	1	51	9
†Parsons, G.J. (Le)	—	14	15	3	207	56	17.25	—	1	5	—
Patel, D.N. (Wo)	1979	26	44	2	1615	112	38.45	3	10	14	—
Pathmanathan, G. (CU)	—	7	13	1	263	64	21.91	—	2	2	—
Pauline, D.B. (Sy)	—	12	21	2	796	115	41.89	1	7	3	—
Payne, I.R. (Sy)	—	10	11	4	167	43	23.85	—	—	11	—
†Penn, C. (K)	—	2	1	0	24	24	24.00	—	—	1	—
Perryman, S.P. (Wo)	—	11	15	6	69	22	7.66	—	—	4	—
Petchey, M.D. (OU)	—	6	6	0	21	18	3.50	—	—	3	—
Phillip, N. (Ex)	1978	19	26	0	413	80	15.88	—	1	8	—
Phillipson, C.P. (Sx)	1980	2	3	0	69	28	23.00	—	—	1	—
†Pick, R.A. (Nt)	—	6	8	2	84	25*	14.00	—	—	—	—
Pigott, A.C.S. (Sx)	1982	23	29	8	408	63	19.42	—	3	14	—
Pocock, N.E.J. (H)	1980	26	35	8	755	60*	27.96	—	6	30	—
Pocock, P.I. (Sy)	1967	23	19	7	110	23	9.16	—	—	8	—
Pollock, A.J. (CU)	—	10	9	2	38	14*	5.42	—	—	4	—
Pont, K.R. (Ex)	1976	21	27	4	802	125*	34.86	2	4	3	—
Popplewell, N.F.M. (So)	1983	24	39	3	886	143	24.61	1	4	21	—
Potter, L. (K)	—	6	11	0	258	50	23.45	—	1	2	—
Pridgeon, A.P. (Wo)	1980	27	32	10	190	23	8.63	—	—	8	—
Pringle, D.R. (Ex)	1982	17	21	4	586	102*	34.47	1	2	12	—
Prior, J.A. (Ire)	—	1	2	0	55	55	27.50	—	1	—	—
Racionzer, T.B. (Sc)	—	1	2	0	118	115	59.00	1	—	—	—
Radford, N.V. (La)	—	1	2	0	51	27	25.50	—	—	—	—
Radley, C.T. (M)	1967	25	38	6	943	119	29.46	1	4	22	—
†Ramage, A. (Y)	—	3	3	1	46	32	23.00	—	—	—	—
Randall, D.W. (E/Nt)	1973	18	28	2	777	94	29.88	—	6	20	—
Rawlinson, H.T. (OU)	—	8	9	2	91	24	13.00	—	—	2	—
Reeve, D.A. (Sx)	—	17	20	5	192	42*	12.80	—	—	7	—
Rice, C.E.B. (Nt)	1975	19	30	2	1026	101*	36.64	2	3	14	—

	Cap	M	I	NO	Runs	HS	Avge	100	50	Ct	St
Richards, C.J. (Sy)	1978	25	35	8	751	85*	27.81	—	2	48	7
Richards, I.V.A. (So)	1974	12	20	4	1204	216	75.25	5	3	6	—
Roberts, A.M.E. (Le)	—	4	3	0	22	15	7.33	—	—	—	—
Robinson, R.T. (Nt)	1983	25	41	3	1545	207	40.65	2	11	6	—
†Roebuck, P.G.P. (CU)	—	5	7	3	82	31*	20.50	—	—	1	—
Roebuck, P.M. (So)	1978	22	38	5	1235	106*	37.42	1	9	9	—
Romaines, P.W. (Gs)	1983	23	41	4	1286	135	34.75	3	4	9	—
†Rose, B.C. (So)	1975	8	9	0	184	52	20.44	—	1	2	—
Rowe, C.J.C. (Gm)	1983	22	33	2	721	82	23.25	—	3	8	—
†Russell, R.C. (Gs)	—	24	32	9	507	64*	22.04	—	3	46	17
Russom, N. (So)	—	1	1	0	8	8	8.00	—	—	—	—
†Sadiq Mohammad (DBC)	—	1	2	0	35	35	17.50	—	—	2	—
Sainsbury, G.E. (Gs)	—	23	23	8	70	13	4.66	—	—	—	—
Saxelby, K. (Nt)	—	21	28	3	274	35	10.96	—	—	1	—
Scott, C.W. (Nt)	—	2	2	0	80	78	40.00	—	1	3	1
Scott, M.S. (Wo)	—	7	12	2	297	76	29.70	—	3	—	—
Selvey, M.W.W. (Gm)	1983	24	24	3	250	63	11.90	—	1	5	—
Sharp, G. (No)	1973	23	24	8	536	98	33.50	—	3	41	5
Sharp, K. (Y)	1982	12	21	1	597	139	29.85	2	1	6	—
Shepherd, J.N. (Gs)	1983	23	34	6	1025	168	36.60	2	6	16	—
Short, J.F. (Ire)	—	1	2	0	40	30	20.00	—	—	1	—
Sidebottom, A. (Y)	1980	16	21	7	490	78	35.00	—	2	2	—
Simmons, J. (La)	1971	23	31	2	679	104	23.41	2	3	17	—
†Slack, W.N. (M)	1981	18	28	4	1034	140	43.08	3	6	17	—
Slocombe, P.A. (So)	1978	11	17	2	224	66	14.93	—	1	5	—
Smail, A.H.K. (OU)	—	6	6	1	24	13*	4.80	—	—	1	—
Small, G.C. (Wa)	1982	6	8	3	62	31	12.40	—	—	2	—
Smith, C.L. (E/H)	1981	23	39	3	1923	193	53.41	6	8	19	—
†Smith, D.J. (Sx)	—	5	7	2	22	13	4.40	—	—	9	—
†Smith, D.M. (Sy)	1980	13	20	4	748	131*	46.75	2	3	13	—
†Smith, D.M. (Wa)	—	1	1	1	100	100*	—	1	—	1	—
Smith, I.D.S. (NZ)	—	8	12	3	104	32*	11.55	—	—	18	2
Smith, K.D. (Wa)	1978	27	47	4	1272	109	29.58	2	8	7	—
Smith, P.A. (Wa)	—	13	17	3	458	114	32.71	1	3	1	—
Smith, R.A. (H)	—	7	12	3	434	104*	48.22	3	—	1	—
†Snedden, M.C. (NZ)	—	10	9	0	154	35	17.11	—	—	—	—
Southern, J.W. (H)	1978	15	13	5	146	45*	18.25	—	—	8	—
Standing, D.K. (Sx)	—	4	8	3	240	60	48.00	—	2	2	—
Stanworth, J. (La)	—	3	6	2	90	31*	22.50	—	—	2	—
Steele, D.S. (No)	1965	25	31	6	569	60	22.76	—	3	29	—
Steele, J.F. (Le)	1971	24	26	9	327	50	19.23	—	1	30	—
Stephenson, F.D. (Gs/DBC)	—	3	3	0	41	21	13.66	—	—	2	—
Stevenson, G.B. (Y)	1978	20	25	1	396	52	16.50	—	2	4	—
Stevenson, K. (H)	1979	7	9	3	77	25	12.83	—	—	2	—
Stewart, A.J. (Sy)	—	10	17	4	525	118*	40.38	1	2	4	1
Stovold, A.W. (Gs)	1976	23	42	3	1671	181	42.84	4	8	16	—
Such, P.M. (Nt)	—	10	15	4	13	5	1.18	—	—	6	—
Sutcliffe, S.P. (Wa)	—	2	—	—	—	—	—	—	—	1	—
Swallow, I.G. (Y)	—	2	3	2	19	11*	19.00	—	—	1	—
Swan, R.G. (Sc)	—	1	2	0	44	39	22.00	—	—	2	—
Sykes, J.F. (M)	—	1	1	0	4	4	4.00	—	—	—	—

	Cap	M	I	NO	Runs	HS	Avge	100	50	Ct	St
Tavaré, C.J. (E/K)	1978	15	24	0	1030	109	42.91	1	9	12	—
Taylor, L.B. (Le)	1981	19	18	6	250	47	20.83	—	—	7	—
Taylor, N.R. (K)	—	23	39	6	1275	155*	38.63	5	3	18	—
Taylor, N.S. (Y)	—	4	5	0	10	4	2.00	—	—	1	—
Taylor, R.W. (E/D/DBC)	1962	21	30	7	366	41*	15.91	—	—	49	2
Tedstone, G.A. (Wa)	—	13	16	3	243	67*	18.69	—	1	23	4
Terry, V.P. (H)	1983	20	33	6	1096	115	40.59	3	4	15	—
†Thomas, D.J. (Sy)	—	23	31	5	937	119	36.03	2	4	9	—
Thomas, J.G. (Gm)	—	9	9	1	96	23	12.00	—	—	1	—
Thorne, D.A. (Wa)	—	5	7	3	62	23*	15.50	—	—	3	—
Tolchard, R.W. (Le)	1966	26	35	7	775	80*	27.67	—	4	44	9
Tomlins, K.P. (M)	1983	20	27	5	670	132*	30.45	1	3	22	—
Toogood, G.J. (OU)	—	5	6	0	48	18	8.00	—	—	—	—
Tracy, S.R. (NZ, Gs)	—	3	3	0	4	4	1.33	—	—	—	—
Tremlett, T.M. (H)	1983	24	19	5	263	59	18.78	—	1	18	—
Tunnicliffe, C.J. (D)	1977	17	25	0	461	91	18.44	—	2	3	—
Turnbull, J.R. (OU)	—	7	7	4	5	5*	1.66	—	—	6	—
†Turner, D.R. (H)	1970	12	17	3	598	122*	42.71	1	3	3	—
Turner, S. (Ex)	1970	15	19	2	177	30	10.41	—	—	7	—
Underwood, D.L. (K)	1964	25	20	6	142	26*	10.14	—	—	5	—
Varey, D.W. (CU)	—	10	20	1	342	65	18.00	—	1	3	—
Varey, J.G. (OU)	—	6	10	3	187	69*	26.71	—	1	1	—
†Walker, A. (No)	—	6	4	3	18	7*	18.00	—	—	3	—
Waller, C.E. (Sx)	1976	22	23	11	100	21	8.33	—	—	6	—
Warke, S.J.S. (Ire)	—	1	2	0	108	63	54.00	—	1	—	—
Warner, A.E. (Wo)	—	9	15	5	131	26*	13.10	—	—	3	—
Warner, C.J. (Sc)	—	1	2	0	81	70	40.50	—	1	—	—
Waterman, P.A. (Sy)	—	2	2	1	6	6*	6.00	—	—	—	—
Waterton, S.N.V. (K)	—	1	2	0	11	8	5.50	—	—	3	—
Watkins, S.G. (Wo)	—	1	2	0	105	77	52.50	—	1	—	—
Watkinson, M. (La)	—	15	20	4	168	29	10.50	—	—	2	—
†Watts, A. (D)	—	2	2	1	39	33*	39.00	—	—	—	—
Wells, A.P. (Sx)	—	16	28	4	665	92	27.70	—	5	11	—
Wells, C.M. (Sx)	1982	24	40	6	857	71	25.20	—	5	8	—
Weston, M.J. (Wo)	—	22	38	1	862	115	23.29	1	2	9	—
Whitaker, J.J. (Le)	—	10	16	4	305	56*	25.41	—	1	4	—
Whitney, M.R. (DBC)	—	1	2	1	6	5*	6.00	—	—	2	—
†Wild, D.J. (No)	—	5	9	0	162	48	18.00	—	—	2	—
Wilkins, A.H. (Gm)	—	14	15	3	185	54	15.41	—	1	3	—
Willey, P. (No)	1971	23	40	8	1546	175*	48.31	4	9	5	—
Williams, N.F. (M)	—	25	25	7	407	63	22.61	—	2	6	—
Williams, R.G. (No)	1979	26	40	10	1305	104*	43.50	1	10	9	—
Willis, R.G.D. (E/Wa)	1972	17	20	9	183	37	16.63	—	—	6	—
Willows, A. (Sx)	—	1	—	—	—	—	—	—	—	—	—
Wills, R.T. (Ire)	—	1	2	0	4	3	2.00	—	—	—	—
Wilson, P.H.L. (Sx)	—	11	11	7	60	25	15.00	—	—	3	—
Wood, B. (D)	1980	3	2	0	22	18	11.00	—	—	—	—
Woolmer, R.A. (K)	1970	14	22	1	994	129	47.33	4	5	6	—
†Wootton, S.H. (Wa)	—	2	3	0	157	104	52.33	1	—	—	—
Wright, A.J. (Gs)	—	10	17	2	380	56*	25.33	—	2	5	—
†Wright, J.G. (NZ/D)	1977	11	13	0	605	136	46.53	1	4	6	—

	Cap	M	I	NO	Runs	HS	Avge	100	50	Ct	St
Wyatt, J.G. (So)	—	6	12	2	352	82*	35.20	—	3	1	—
†Younis Ahmed (Wo)	1979	2	2	2	45	35*	—	—	—	—	—
Zaheer Abbas (Gs)	1975	12	19	0	867	116	45.63	3	4	3	—
Extras					12160					59	2
Total		5149	7249	1212	186996	252	30.98	262	820	3385	142

BOWLING

	Type	O	M	R	W	Avge	Best	5 wI	10 wM
Abrahams, J. (La)	OB	216	41	658	13	50.61	3-83	—	—
Acfield, D.L. (Ex)	OB	497.1	143	1222	43	28.41	7-100	2	1
Agnew, J.P. (Le/DBC)	RF	248	42	930	23	40.43	3-34	—	—
Allott, P.J.W. (La)	RFM	457.4	131	1178	38	31.00	5-45	1	—
Anderson, I.S. (D)	OB	28	4	146	1	146.00	1-45	—	—
Asif Din (Wa)	LB	84.1	14	291	3	97.00	2-77	—	—
Aslett, D.G. (K)	LB	37	5	218	3	72.66	1-28	—	—
Athey, C.W.J. (Y)	RM	38	8	110	3	36.66	1-17	—	—
Bailey, R.J. (No)	OB	15	5	35	3	11.66	3-33	—	—
Bainbridge, P. (Gs)	RM	416.4	106	1199	30	39.96	4-67	—	—
Bairstow, D.L. (Y)	RM	10	4	27	1	27.00	1-18	—	—
Balderstone, J.C. (Le)	SLA	68	22	171	7	24.42	2-10	—	—
Baptiste, E.A.E. (K)	RFM	376.3	88	1187	50	23.74	5-39	3	—
Barclay, J.R.T. (Sx)	OB	231.3	56	774	17	45.52	3-30	—	—
Barlow, G.D. (M)	RM	2	1	2	0	—	—	—	—
Barnett, K.J. (D)	LB	3	0	13	0	—	—	—	—
Barwick, S.R. (Gm)	RM	129.3	21	532	11	48.36	8-42	1	—
Benson, M.R. (K)	OB	5	1	16	0	—	—	—	—
Birch, J.D. (Nt)	RM	1	0	1	0	—	—	—	—
Booth, P.A. (Y)	SLA	17	3	50	0	—	—	—	—
Booth, S.C. (So)	SLA	286.2	85	849	21	40.42	4-26	—	—
Bore, M.K. (Nt)	LM	370.5	108	1040	27	38.51	4-29	—	—
Botham, I.T. (E/So)	RFM	232.2	55	728	22	33.09	5-38	1	—
Boycott, G. (Y)	RM	23	10	45	1	45.00	1-15	—	—
Boyd-Moss, R.J. (CU/No)	SLA	81	23	232	9	25.77	5-27	1	—
Bracewell, J.G. (NZ)	OB	325.5	73	1095	41	26.70	6-111	3	—
Breakwell, D. (So)	SLA	49	17	121	4	30.25	3-44	—	—
Briers, N.E. (Le)	RM	3.5	2	9	0	—	—	—	—
Butcher, A.R. (Sy)	SLA	44.4	9	210	5	42.00	4-123	—	—
Butcher, I.P. (Le)	—	2	0	2	1	2.00	1-2	—	—
Butcher, R.O. (M)	RM	3	1	11	0	—	—	—	—
Cairns, B.L. (NZ)	RM	341.1	101	877	32	27.40	7-46	2	1
Capel, D.J. (No)	RM	65.5	15	226	3	75.33	2-35	—	—
Carr, J.D. (OU/M)	OB	170	49	476	9	52.88	2-59	—	—
Carrick, P. (Y)	SLA	848.1	303	1750	62	28.22	7-44	6	1

	Type	O	M	R	W	Avge	Best	5 wI	10 wM
Carse, J.A. (No)	**RFM**	238.5	50	722	22	32.81	5-43	1	—
Chatfield, E.J. (NZ)	**RM**	303.3	79	818	28	29.21	6-40	2	—
Childs, J.H. (Gs)	**SLA**	664.5	200	1761	48	36.68	6-81	2	—
Clarke, S.T. (Sy)	**RF**	693.1	183	1773	79	22.44	7-53	4	1
Clift, P.B. (Le)	**RM**	619.4	167	1592	83	19.18	5-20	2	—
Close, D.B. (DBC)	**OB**	1.4	0	5	1	5.00	1-5	—	—
Coney, J.V. (NZ)	**RM**	124.5	40	339	14	24.21	3-19	—	—
Cook, G. (No)	**SLA**	11	3	43	0	—	—	—	—
Cook, N.G.B. (E/Le)	**SLA**	878.1	321	1859	73	25.46	5-35	2	—
Cooper, K.E. (Nt)	**RFM**	579	164	1610	57	28.24	7-33	5	—
Corlett, S.C. (Ire)	**RM**	45	14	93	6	15.50	5-40	1	—
Cotterell, T.A. (CU)	**SLA**	273	67	758	17	44.58	5-89	1	—
Cowan, R.S. (Sx)	**RM**	8	2	27	0	—	—	—	—
Cowans, N.G. (E/M)	**RF**	286	60	912	30	30.40	5-43	1	—
Cowdrey, C.S. (K)	**RM**	220.2	34	733	12	61.08	3-80	—	—
Cowley, N.G. (H)	**OB**	440.3	147	1053	41	25.68	4-10	—	—
Crowe, M.D. (NZ)	**RM**	76	12	284	12	23.66	3-21	—	—
Cunningham, E.J. (Gs)	**OB**	49	10	181	4	45.25	2-55	—	—
Curtis, I.J. (Sy)	**SLA**	269	82	690	17	40.58	6-28	1	—
Curtis, T.S. (CU/Wo)	**LB**	43	7	150	3	50.00	2-58	—	—
Daniel, W.W. (M)	**RF**	324.3	51	1106	48	23.04	7-61	1	1
Davis, M.R. (So)	**LFM**	240.4	43	873	25	34.92	4-34	—	—
Davis, W.W. (Gm)	**RFM**	452.4	110	1389	52	26.71	7-70	3	—
Davison, B.F. (Le)	**RM**	4.4	0	18	0	—	—	—	—
Dennis, S.J. (Y)	**LFM**	525.2	117	1600	52	30.76	4-32	—	—
Derrick, J. (Gm)	**RM**	8	1	31	0	—	—	—	—
Dilley, G.R. (E/K)	**RF**	276.3	73	681	31	21.96	5-70	1	—
Doggart, S.J.G. (CU)	**OB**	285.2	60	844	12	70.33	3-3	—	—
D'Oliveira, D.B. (Wo)	**RM/OB**	69.1	14	262	4	65.50	1-12	—	—
Donald, W.A. (Sc)	**RM**	22	7	49	1	49.00	1-46	—	—
Doughty, R.J. (Gs)	**RM**	89.5	11	351	6	58.50	2-43	—	—
Dredge, C.H. (So)	**RM**	492.3	126	1323	48	27.56	5-51	2	—
Dudleston, B. (Gs)	**SLA**	27.5	4	164	4	41.00	3-83	—	—
East, R.E. (Ex)	**SLA**	338	96	889	25	35.56	5-45	1	—
Edgar, B.A. (NZ)	—	5	0	17	1	17.00	1-17	—	—
Edmonds, P.H. (E/M)	**SLA**	820.3	230	1974	92	21.45	6-38	9	2
Ellcock, R.M. (Wo)	**RF**	244	39	931	25	37.24	4-70	—	—
Ellis, R.G.P. (OU/M)	**OB**	22	6	82	0	—	—	—	—
Ellison, C.C. (CU)	**RM**	56.4	17	153	7	21.85	4-36	—	—
Ellison, R.M. (K)	**RM**	598.4	167	1491	51	29.23	5-73	1	—
Emburey, J.E. (M)	**OB**	935	325	1842	103	17.88	6-13	4	—
Emery, K.S.D. (H)	**RFM**	94	28	262	5	52.40	3-34	—	—
Fairbrother, N.H. (La)	—	3	2	1	0	—	—	—	—
Fell, M.A. (Nt)	**SLA**	3	0	11	0	—	—	—	—
Feltham, M.A. (Sy)	**RM**	18	5	44	2	22.00	1-19	—	—
Ferreira, A.M. (Wa)	**RM**	502.4	131	1277	40	31.92	5-19	1	—
Ferris, G.J.F. (Le)	**RF**	360	74	1205	53	22.73	7-42	3	1
Finney, R.J. (D)	**LM**	281.5	43	970	30	32.33	5-58	1	—
Fletcher, K.W.R. (Ex)	**LB**	8.3	0	57	0	—	—	—	—
Fletcher, S.D. (Y)	**RM**	55.4	7	186	8	23.25	4-71	—	—

	Type	O	M	R	W	Avge	Best	5 wI	10 wM
Folley, I. (La)	**LFM**	191	58	522	7	74.57	2-37	—	—
Foster, N.A. (E/Ex)	**RM**	417	78	1216	52	23.38	6-46	1	—
Fowler, G. (E/La)	—	2	0	7	0	—	—	—	—
Fowler, W.P. (D)	**LM**	60	13	214	2	107.00	1-26	—	—
Francis, D.A. (Gm)	—	4	0	25	0	—	—	—	—
Gard, T. (So)	—	0.2	0	8	0	—	—	—	—
Garner, J. (So)	**RF**	277	74	708	35	20.22	6-37	1	—
Gatting, M.W. (E/M)	**RM**	89.2	28	230	5	46.00	2-26	—	—
Gifford, N. (Wa)	**SLA**	1043.4	347	2393	104	23.00	6-22	7	2
Gladwin, C. (Ex)	—	3	0	11	0	—	—	—	—
Golding, A.K. (Ex)	**SLA**	28	3	97	2	48.50	1-44	—	—
Gooch, G.A. (Ex)	**RM**	212	46	572	11	52.00	3-40	—	—
Gould, I.J. (Sx)	**RM**	2	0	9	0	—	—	—	—
Gower, D.I. (E/Le)	—	9	0	102	0	—	—	—	—
Graveney, D.A. (Gs)	**SLA**	512.1	156	1198	37	32.37	6-88	2	—
Gray, E.J. (NZ)	**SLA**	143	40	398	16	24.87	4-24	—	—
Green, A.M. (Sx)	**RM**	53.4	9	248	6	41.33	2-30	—	—
Greig, I.A. (Sx)	**RM**	185	27	681	17	40.05	4-42	—	—
Griffiths, B.J. (No)	**RFM**	536.2	130	1424	50	28.48	6-92	1	—
Hadlee, R.J. (NZ/Nt)	**RF**	431.3	123	1065	49	21.73	6-53	3	—
Halliday, M. (Ire)	**OB**	60	25	109	5	21.80	4-44	—	—
Hampshire, J.H. (D/DBC)	**LB**	2	0	4	0	—	—	—	—
Harper, R.A. (DBC)	**OB**	28	8	81	5	16.20	3-36	—	—
Harrison, G.D. (Ire)	**RFM**	24	11	40	2	20.00	2-30	—	—
Hartley, S.N. (Y)	**RM**	14	3	40	1	40.00	1-15	—	—
Hayes, K.A. (OU/La)	**RM**	33.5	10	124	8	15.50	6-58	1	—
Heath, J.R.P. (Sx)	—	8	0	58	0	—	—	—	—
Hemmings, E.E. (Nt)	**OB**	710.4	195	2000	59	33.89	7-23	2	1
Henderson, S.P. (CU/Gm)	**RM**	21	3	131	3	43.66	2-48	—	—
Hendrick, M. (Nt)	**RFM**	552.1	190	1122	66	17.00	6-17	4	—
Hignell, A.J. (Gs)	**LB**	7	1	46	0	—	—	—	—
Hill, A. (D)	**OB**	6.2	3	15	0	—	—	—	—
Hodgson, K.I. (CU)	**RM**	297	75	871	12	72.58	4-58	—	—
Hogg, W. (Wa)	**RFM**	385	73	1198	39	30.71	5-63	1	—
Holding, M.A. (D)	**RF**	169	41	451	21	21.47	5-48	3	—
Hopkins, J.A. (Gm)	—	4	0	23	0	—	—	—	—
Howarth, G.P. (NZ/Sy)	**OB**	17	4	41	1	41.00	1-36	—	—
Hughes, D.P. (La)	**SLA**	67.5	9	230	2	115.00	1-24	—	—
Hughes, M.G. (Ex)	**RFM**	31.2	2	162	6	27.00	4-71	—	—
Hughes, S.P. (M)	**RFM**	268.3	61	910	36	25.27	6.32	2	—
Humpage, G.W. (Wa)	**RM**	16	1	51	1	51.00	1-38	—	—
Illingworth, N.J.B. (Nt)	**RM**	37	6	113	1	113.00	1-51	—	—
Illingworth, R. (Y)	**OB**	411.5	136	951	32	29.71	4-48	—	—
Illingworth, R.K. (Wo)	**SLA**	664.5	172	1830	48	38.12	5-26	1	—
Imran Khan (Sx)	**RF**	46.2	12	86	12	7.16	6-6	1	—
Inchmore, J.D. (Wo)	**RFM**	488.3	104	1369	47	29.12	5-45	3	—
James, K.D. (M)	**LM**	89	20	217	11	19.72	5-28	1	—

	Type	O	M	R	W	Avge	Best	5 wI	10 wM
Jarvis, K.B.S. (K)	RFM	498.5	95	1579	30	52.63	3-32	—	—
Jarvis, P.W. (Y)	RFM	44	8	155	3	51.66	1-28	—	—
Javed Miandad (Gm)	LBG	2	0	11	0	—	—	—	—
Jefferies, S.T. (La)	LFM	278.1	74	797	32	24.90	8-46	2	1
Jesty, T.E. (H)	RM	256.5	70	804	21	38.28	3-48	—	—
Johnson, G.W. (K)	OB	631.1	166	1652	51	32.39	7-76	2	1
Jones, A.L. (Gm)	—	3	0	25	0	—	—	—	—
Jones, A.N. (Sx)	RFM	81.4	10	358	6	59.66	2-65	—	—
Kallicharran, A.I. (Wa)	OB	135	18	476	8	59.50	2-64	—	—
Kapil Dev (No)	RFM	161	47	385	16	24.06	4-24	—	—
Ker, J.E. (Sc)	RM	23	4	63	3	21.00	3-45	—	—
King, C.L. (Wo/DBC)	RM	18	2	57	1	57.00	1-26	—	—
Kirti Azad (DBC)	OB	19	5	71	2	35.50	1-20	—	—
Knight, R.D.V. (Sy)	RM	236	60	677	15	45.13	3-58	—	—
Lamb, A.J. (E/No)	RM	1	0	1	0	—	—	—	—
Lamb, T.M. (No)	RM	188.2	57	416	21	19.80	4-27	—	—
Larkins, W. (No)	RM	30.4	5	74	5	14.80	4-30	—	—
Lawrence, D.V. (Gs)	RFM	157	21	613	7	87.57	3-62	—	—
Lawrence, M.P. (OU)	SLA	6	1	36	0	—	—	—	—
Le Roux, G.S. (Sx)	RF	362.3	92	950	37	25.67	5-17	2	—
Lethbridge, C. (Wa)	RM	70.1	11	268	6	44.66	2-15	—	—
Lever, J.K. (Ex)	LFM	569	137	1726	106	16.28	7-55	8	3
Lloyd, B.J. (Gm)	OB	288.5	47	876	21	41.71	4-93	—	—
Lloyd, D. (La)	SLA	199	60	400	17	23.52	5-22	1	—
Lloyd, T.A. (Wa)	RM	8	1	52	0	—	—	—	—
Lloyds, J.W. (So)	OB	358.1	98	1079	35	30.82	5-120	1	—
Lord, G.J. (Wa)	SLA	8	3	12	0	—	—	—	—
Love, J.D. (Y)	RM	22	5	89	1	89.00	1-46	—	—
Lynch, M.A. (Sy)	RM/OB	7.3	0	47	0	—	—	—	—
McEwan, K.S. (Ex)	OB	7	0	28	1	28.00	1-8	—	—
McFarlane, L.L. (La)	RFM	216.4	38	742	15	49.46	3-53	—	—
McIntyre, E.J. (Sc)	OB	5	2	24	0	—	—	—	—
Mackintosh, K.S. (Sy)	RM	15	2	47	0	—	—	—	—
McPate, W.A. (Sc)	RFM	17	6	45	1	45.00	1-8	—	—
Mallender, N.A. (No)	RFM	524.5	112	1642	56	29.32	6-48	1	—
Malone, S.J. (H)	RM	547.1	123	1797	48	37.43	4-39	—	—
Marks, V.J. (So)	OB	615.3	199	1698	53	32.03	6-79	3	—
Marshall, M.D. (H)	RF	532.5	143	1327	80	16.58	7-29	5	1
Masters, K.D. (K)	RM	33	4	121	2	60.50	2-26	—	—
Metcalfe, A.A. (Y)	OB	2	0	6	0	—	—	—	—
Miller, G. (D)	OB	492.5	132	1278	37	34.54	5-71	2	—
Moir, D.G. (D)	SLA	462.5	121	1385	40	34.62	5-44	2	—
Monkhouse, G. (Sy)	RM	373.3	97	1040	47	22.12	7-51	1	—
Monteith, J.D. (Ire)	SLA	51	15	110	3	36.66	2-88	—	—
Morris, H. (Gm)	—	3.5	0	23	0	—	—	—	—
Morris, J.E. (D)	RM	2	2	0	0	—	—	—	—
Mortensen, O.H. (D)	RFM	518.3	108	1605	66	24.31	6-27	3	1
Morton, W.A. (Sc)	SLA	45	12	134	7	19.14	4-40	—	—
Moulding, R.P. (OU)	LB	9.4	0	22	0	—	—	—	—
Moxon, M.D. (Y)	RM	33	3	123	1	123.00	1-25	—	—

	Type	O	M	R	W	Avge	Best	5 wI	10 wM
Mushtaq Mohammad (DBC)	**LBG**	24	1	96	1	96.00	1-58	—	—
Nash, M.A. (Gm)	**LM**	91	29	250	4	62.50	1-12	—	—
Nasir Zaidi S.M. (La)	**LB**	191.3	48	530	16	33.12	3-27	—	—
Needham, A. (Sy)	**OB**	164	50	470	19	24.73	6-30	2	—
Newman, P.G. (D)	**RFM**	88.5	20	321	7	45.85	3-0	—	—
Newport, P.J. (Wo)	**RFM**	41	3	118	3	39.33	3-40	—	—
Nicholas, M.C.J. (H)	**RM**	274.2	74	774	27	28.66	5-45	1	—
Old, C.M. (Wa)	**RFM**	656.3	152	1824	62	29.41	5-50	2	—
Oldham, S. (D)	**RFM**	387.2	85	1120	31	36.12	4-56	—	—
Ollis, R.L. (So)	**RM**	1	0	2	0	—	—	—	—
Ontong, R.C. (Gm)	**RM**	644	131	2053	56	36.66	6-64	3	—
O'Shaughnessy, S.J. (La)	**RM**	236.2	44	830	25	33.20	4-73	—	—
Palmer, G.V. (So)	**RM**	208.3	40	630	20	31.50	5-38	1	—
Palmer, R.W.M. (CU)	**LM**	12	0	75	1	75.00	1-48	—	—
Parker, P.W.G. (Sx)	**RM**	4.2	1	30	0	—	—	—	—
Parsons, G.J. (Le)	**RM**	269	73	823	29	28.37	5-51	1	—
Patel, D.N. (Wo)	**OB**	685.5	204	1799	49	36.71	5-52	2	—
Payne, I.R. (Sy)	**RM**	158.5	41	450	12	37.50	5-13	1	—
Penn, C. (K)	**RFM**	35	8	116	2	58.00	1-18	—	—
Perryman, S.P. (Wo)	**RM**	253.5	54	750	14	53.57	4-91	—	—
Petchey, M.D. (OU)	**RM**	206.2	36	804	12	67.00	2-70	—	—
Phillip, N. (Ex)	**RFM**	477.2	88	1409	69	20.42	6-4	5	—
Pick, R.A. (Nt)	**RM**	134.4	16	500	7	71.42	2-50	—	—
Pigott, A.C.S. (Sx)	**RFM**	582.5	98	1889	72	26.23	6-22	4	—
Pocock, N.E.J. (H)	**LM**	29	3	138	1	138.00	1-31	—	—
Pocock, P.I. (Sy)	**OB**	681.2	200	1774	68	26.08	7-79	4	—
Pollock, A.J. (CU)	**RM**	230.2	49	750	21	35.71	5-107	1	—
Pont, K.R. (Ex)	**RM**	74	17	211	5	42.20	3-51	—	—
Popplewell, N.F.M. (So)	**RM**	232	38	786	23	34.17	4-69	—	—
Potter, L. (K)	**LM**	6	2	14	0	—	—	—	—
Pridgeon, A.P. (Wo)	**RM**	700	166	1978	72	27.47	5-21	2	—
Pringle, D.R. (Ex)	**RM**	288.4	54	928	41	22.63	7-32	2	—
Prior, J.A. (Ire)	**RM**	8	4	24	0	—	—	—	—
Racionzer, T.B. (Sc)	**OB**	16.2	7	47	2	23.50	2-11	—	—
Radford, N.V. (La)	**RFM**	25	2	99	0	—	—	—	—
Radley, C.T. (M)	**LB**	2	0	6	0	—	—	—	—
Ramage, A. (Y)	**RFM**	39	4	145	2	72.50	2-67	—	—
Rawlinson, H.T. (OU)	**RM**	154.5	31	626	14	44.71	5-123	1	-
Reeve, D.A. (Sx)	**RM**	472.1	130	1233	42	29.35	4-15	—	—
Richards, I.V.A. (So)	**OB**	188	61	462	12	38.50	3-56	—	—
Roberts, A.M.E. (Le)	**RF**	101.2	19	294	16	18.37	5-26	1	—
Robinson, R.T. (Nt)	**RM**	1	0	1	0	—	—	—	—
Roebuck, P.G.P. (CU)	**RM**	75.5	17	269	6	44.83	2-44	—	—
Roebuck, P.M. (So)	**OB**	5	0	25	0	—	—	—	—
Rose, B.C. (So)	**LM**	1	0	6	0	—	—	—	—
Rowe, C.J.C. (Gm)	**OB**	473.4	91	1572	38	41.36	4-29	-	-
Russom, N. (So)	**RM**	5	1	18	0	—	—	—	—

	Type	O	M	R	W	Avge	Best	5 wI	10 wM
Sainsbury, G.E. (Gs)	LM	625.4	150	1937	58	33.39	6-66	3	—
Saxelby, K. (Nt)	RM	410.2	96	1337	50	26.74	5-52	2	—
Selvey, M.W.W. (Gm)	RFM	629.4	138	2003	62	32.30	6-47	3	—
Shepherd, J.N. (Gs)	RM	776.1	209	2047	67	30.55	7-50	3	—
Sidebottom, A. (Y)	RFM	361	81	1080	39	27.69	5-6	1	—
Simmons, J. (La)	OB	744	214	1807	68	26.57	7-73	5	1
Slack, W.N. (M)	RM	44	20	84	6	14.00	1-1	—	—
Slocombe, P.A. (So)	RM	2	1	1	0	—	—	—	—
Smail, A.H.K. (OU)	LM	70	18	222	5	44.40	3-49	—	—
Small, G.C. (Wa)	RFM	110.5	19	349	10	34.90	3-13	—	—
Smith, C.L. (E/H)	OB	167	44	547	17	32.17	3-35	—	—
Smith, D.M. (Sy)	RM	2.2	0	20	0	—	—	—	—
Smith, D.M. (Wa)	SLA	18	3	44	1	44.00	1-44	-	-
Smith, P.A. (Wa)	RM	218	29	844	21	40.19	3-56	—	—
Smith, R.A. (H)	LB	2	0	19	0	—	—	—	—
Snedden, M.C. (NZ)	RM	236.2	37	845	30	28.16	5-68	1	—
Southern, J.W. (H)	SLA	369.5	115	966	27	35.77	5-60	2	—
Standing, D.K. (Sc)	OB	4.3	0	32	0	—	—	—	—
Steele, D.S. (No)	SLA	678	255	1460	68	21.47	5-48	2	—
Steele, J.F. (Le)	SLA	520.1	161	1280	40	32.00	4-3	—	—
Stephenson, F.D. (Gs/DBC)	RF	74.4	18	230	14	16.42	5-56	1	—
Stevenson, G.B. (Y)	RM	460.1	103	1400	56	25.00	5-35	2	—
Stevenson, K. (H)	RFM	187.5	39	656	21	31.23	5-81	1	—
Such, P.M. (Nt)	RM	214	44	767	20	38.35	6-123	1	—
Sutcliffe, S.P. (Wa)	OB	74	17	191	3	63.66	2-50	—	—
Swallow, I.G. (Y)	OB	30.4	8	82	2	41.00	1-15	—	—
Swan, R.G. (Sc)	—	0.4	0	0	0	—	—	—	—
Sykes, J.F. (M)	OB	21	6	54	1	54.00	1-32	—	—
Tavaré, C.J. (E/K)	RM	3	0	3	0	—	—	—	—
Taylor, L.B. (Le)	RFM	529.5	151	1381	69	20.01	7-73	3	1
Taylor, N.R. (K)	OB	35	9	108	1	108.00	1-30	—	—
Taylor, N.S. (Y)	RFM	111.1	23	427	14	30.50	5-49	1	—
Thomas, D.J. (Sy)	LFM	547	114	1781	57	31.24	4-22	—	—
Thomas, J.G. (Gm)	RM	144.5	34	529	19	27.84	5-78	2	—
Thorne, D.A. (Wa)	LM	45	6	189	2	94.50	1-21	—	—
Tomlins, K.P. (M)	RM	6	2	19	0	—	—	—	—
Tracy, S.R. (NZ/Gs)	RFM	54.1	10	170	10	17.00	5-29	1	—
Tremlett, T.M. (H)	RM	600.2	198	1346	63	21.36	6-82	1	—
Tunnicliffe, C.J. (D)	LFM	428.4	94	1372	39	35.17	4-30	—	—
Turnbull, J.R. (OU)	RM	130	34	424	12	35.33	4-51	—	—
Turner, S. (Ex)	RM	282.1	76	624	27	23.11	5-30	1	—
Underwood, D.L. (K)	LM	936.3	358	2044	106	19.28	7-55	9	3
Varey, J.G. (OU)	RM	77	10	316	3	105.33	3-69	—	—
Walker, A. (No)	RFM	165.4	30	578	22	26.27	4-61	—	—
Waller, C.E. (Sx)	SLA	754	224	1873	53	35.33	6-126	2	—
Warner, A.E. (Wo)	RFM	210.3	39	608	27	22.51	4-72	-	-
Waterman, P.A. (Sy)	RM	39	7	151	1	151.00	1-64	—	—
Watkinson, M. (La)	RM	319.3	69	929	35	26.54	6-51	2	—

P. C. A. 1984—7

	Type	O	M	R	W	Avge	Best	5 wI	10 wM
Watts, A. (D)	**RM**	22	4	87	1	87.00	1-28	—	—
Wells, C.M. (Sx)	**RM**	376.3	82	1135	32	35.46	4-69	—	—
Weston, M.J. (Wo)	**RM**	26.2	6	91	2	45.50	1-15	—	—
Whitaker, J.J. (Le)	**OB**	10	2	88	0	—	—	—	—
Whitney, M.R. (DBC)	**LFM**	18	4	60	2	30.00	1-12	—	—
Wild, D.J. (No)	**RM**	36	10	128	2	64.00	2-62	—	—
Wilkins, A.H. (Gm)	**LM**	205	24	820	12	68.33	2-25	—	—
Willey, P. (No)	**OB**	483.5	159	991	32	30.96	4-51	—	—
Williams, N.F. (M)	**RFM**	532.2	114	1659	63	26.33	5-77	1	—
Williams, R.G. (No)	**OB**	434.1	148	1036	47	22.04	4-18	—	—
Willis, R.G.D. (E/Wa)	**RF**	376.5	98	1058	41	25.80	5-35	1	—
Willows, A. (Sx)	**SLA**	8	3	11	0	—	—	—	—
Wilson, P.H.L. (So)	**RFM**	248.3	45	837	25	33.48	4-77	—	—
Wood, B. (D)	**RM**	20	4	74	0	—	—	—	—
Woolmer, R.A. (K)	**RM**	86	29	170	10	17.00	3-13	—	—
Wright, A.J. (Gs)	**RM**	1	0	3	0	—	—	—	—
Zaheer Abbas (Gs)	**OB**	26	7	79	0	—	—	—	—
Extras				12160	154				
Total	—	61569.5	15733	186996	6037	30.98	8-42	220	23

VALETE *(continued from page 167)*.

Barry WOOD B Ossett, Yorks 26/12/1942. RHB, RM. Brother of R. Wood (Yorks 1952-56). Debut for Yorks 1964. Played for Lancs 1966-79. Cap 1968. Played for Eastern Province 1971-72 and 1973-74. Debut for Derby and cap 1980. Captain 1981. Tests: 12 between 1972 and 1978. Tours: India, Pakistan and Sri Lanka 1972-73, New Zealand 1974-75, International Wanderers in Rhodesia 1975-76. 1,000 runs (8): 1,492 (av. 38.25) in 1971 best. Gillette Man of the Match: 6 (for Lancs). Benson & Hedges Gold Awards: 11 (10 for Lancs). HS: 198 Lancs v Glamorgan (Liverpool) 1976. HSC: 153 v Worcs (Chesterfield) 1981. HSTC: 90 v Australia (Oval) 1972. HSGC/NW: 116 Lancs v Kent (Canterbury) 1979. HSJPL: 90* Lancs v Notts (Manchester) 1977 and v Hants (Southampton) 1980. HSBH: 106 v Worcs (Worcester) 1982. BB: 7-52 Lancs v Middlesex (Manchester) 1968. BBC: 3-22 v Sussex (Derby) 1980. BBGC/NW: 4-17 Lancs v Hants (Manchester) 1975. BBJPL: 5-19 Lancs v Kent (Manchester) 1971. BBBH: 5-12 Lancs v Derby (Stockport) 1976.

Simon Howard WOOTTON B Perivale (Middlesex) 24/2/1959. LHB, SLA. Debut for Warwicks 1981. HS: 104 v Cambridge U (Cambridge) 1983. HSJPL: 28* v Lancs (Manchester) 1982. HSBH: 33 v Kent (Oval) 1981.

The fastest century in NatWest.

NatWest have installed 300 Rapid Cash Tills inside branches in the London area for those who want a quick century.

The Rapid Cash Till certainly lives up to its name.

You can draw up to £100 in just 15 seconds. You can make as many withdrawals a day as you like up to a limit agreed with your branch.

You can keep a check on your money because each withdrawal is accompanied by a slip showing how much you've taken out.

All you need to use a Rapid Cash Till is a Servicecard.

The same card that you can use at over 1,400 of our Servicetills and Midland AutoBanks. So if you want a fast century, track down your nearest Rapid Cash Till. Nothing beats it.

NatWest
The Action Bank

LEADING CAREER AVERAGES

The following are the abbreviated figures of the leading batsmen and bowlers based on their career averages, and fielders and wicket-keepers based on the number of their catches and dismissals. The figures are complete to the end of the 1983 season and the full career records will be found in the main tables overleaf. The qualification for inclusion for batsmen and bowlers is 100 innings and 100 wickets respectively. Only those players likely to play first-class county cricket in 1984 have been included.

BATTING AND BOWLING

BATSMEN	*Runs*	*Avge*	*100s*	BOWLERS	*Wkts*	*Avge*
Zaheer Abbas	32,307	53.66	105	J. Garner	595	17.90
A.J. Lamb	13,542	51.10	34	M.D. Marshall	614	18.23
I.V.A. Richards	22,630	49.73	69	R.J. Hadlee	815	19.76
C.H. Lloyd	28,660	48.82	74	W.W. Daniel	592	20.41
A.I. Kallicharran	25,240	45.23	65	M. Hendrick	762	20.60
C.G. Greenidge	24,255	43.86	54	A.M.E. Roberts	824	20.85
D.L. Amiss	36,879	43.28	85	S.T. Clarke	507	21.01
M.W. Gatting	10,219	41.37	22	C.E.B. Rice	679	21.50
C.L. Smith	5,124	40.66	13	Imran Khan	995	22.10
K.S. McEwan	19,716	40.31	53	J.E. Emburey	745	22.80
C.J. Tavaré	12,058	40.05	23	N. Gifford	1824	22.82

FIELDING AND WICKET-KEEPING

FIELDERS	*Ct*	WICKET-KEEPERS	*Total*	*Ct*	*St*
K.W.R. Fletcher	564	R.W. Taylor	1,594	1,424	170
D.S. Steele	517	A.P.E. Knott	1,260	1,129	131
C.T. Radley	464	E.W. Jones	933	840	93
J.H. Hampshire	426	D.L. Bairstow	840	731	109

TEST MATCH AVERAGES
ENGLAND v NEW ZEALAND 1983
(continued from page 26)
NEW ZEALAND BOWLING

	Overs	*Mdns*	*Runs*	*Wkts*	*Avge*	*Best*	*5 wI*	*10 wM*
J.V. Coney	63	26	115	5	23.00	2-21	—	—
R.J. Hadlee	232	65	559	21	26.61	6-53	2	—
M.C. Snedden	36	8	109	4	27.25	3-69	—	—
B.L. Cairns	184	52	461	16	28.81	7-74	1	1
M.D. Crowe	21	1	58	2	29.00	2-35	—	—
E.J. Gray	48	12	128	4	32.00	3-73	—	—
J.G. Bracewell	123	28	364	10	36.40	4-108	—	—
E.J. Chatfield	153	37	440	11	40.00	5-95	1	—
G.P. Howarth	3	2	1	0	—	—	—	—

CAREER RECORDS

Compiled by Geoffrey Saulez

The following career records are for all players who appeared in first-class cricket during the 1983 season. Some players who did not appear for their counties in 1983, but who may do so in 1984, are also included.

Aggregates of 1,000 runs overseas are preceded by a + sign, e.g. D.L. Amiss 19+1.

BATTING AND FIELDING

	M	*I*	*NO*	*Runs*	*HS*	*Avge*	*100s*	*1000 runs in season*	*Ct*	*St*
Abrahams, J.	168	255	34	6077	178	27.49	6	2	108	—
Acfield, D.L.	352	355	182	1504	42	8.69	—	—	116	—
Addison, J.P.	1	2	0	67	51	33.50	—	—	—	—
Agnew, J.P.	58	56	7	444	56	9.06	—	—	19	—
Allott, P.J.W.	93	86	25	809	52*	13.26	—	—	26	—
Amiss, D.L.	555	954	102	36879	262*	43.28	85	19+1	358	—
Anderson, I.S.	73	112	20	2425	112	26.35	2	1	62	—
Asif Din	59	92	9	2144	102	25.83	1	—	36	—
Aslett, D.G.	38	68	8	2419	168	40.31	4	1	31	—
Athey, C.W.J.	163	268	21	6803	134	27.54	11	2	150	2
Bailey, R.J.	5	8	1	110	37*	15.71	—	—	6	—
Bainbridge, P.	100	171	27	4320	146	30.00	5	3	51	—
Bairstow, D.L.	334	482	92	9498	145	24.35	4	2	731	109
Balderstone, J.C.	331	520	53	16093	178*	34.46	26	9	183	—
Bamber, M.J.	8	16	1	418	77	27.86	—	—	5	—
Banks, D.A.	7	13	1	363	100	30.25	1	—	3	—
Baptiste, E.A.E.	51	78	13	1759	136*	27.06	2	—	33	—
Barclay, J.R.T.	224	379	35	8623	119	25.06	9	4	182	—
Barlow, G.D.	207	330	52	9947	177	35.78	19	6	118	—
Barnett, K.J.	106	158	19	4154	121	29.88	5	1	59	—
Barwick, S.R.	27	29	14	177	24	11.80	—	—	8	—
Benson, M.R.	69	116	13	3926	152*	38.11	9	3	33	—
Birch, J.D.	146	219	33	4951	125	26.61	4	2	109	—
Boon, T.J.	38	63	6	1150	90	20.17	—	—	10	—
Booth, P.A.	2	3	1	0	0*	0.00	—	—	—	—
Booth, S.C.	10	12	5	24	9	3.42	—	—	7	—
Bore, M.K.	148	149	51	828	37*	8.44	—	—	49	—
Botham, I.T.	226	351	25	10701	228	32.82	23	3	214	—
Boycott, G.	555	925	139	44210	261*	56.24	139	21+3	237	—
Boyd-Moss, R.J.	81	139	11	3987	139	31.14	8	2	34	—
Bracewell, J.G.	51	82	12	1449	62	20.70	—	—	40	—
Brassington, A.J.	122	150	43	856	35	8.00	—	—	207	47
Breakwell, D.	231	306	64	4792	100*	19.80	1	—	81	—
Brearley, J.M.	455	768	102	25185	312*	37.81	45	11	418	12
Briers, N.E.	143	228	23	6056	201*	29.54	9	3	59	—
Broad, B.C.	89	159	9	4804	145	32.02	8	3	35	—
Bullen, C.K.	1	—	—	—	—	—	—	—	—	—

	M	I	NO	Runs	HS	Avge	100s	1000 runs in season	Ct	St
Butcher, A.R.	224	378	36	11278	216*	32.97	22	5	103	—
Butcher, I.P.	25	41	4	1211	139	32.72	3	—	22	—
Butcher, R.O.	153	238	18	6491	197	29.50	10	1	188	1
Cairns, B.L.	119	185	22	3389	110	20.79	1	—	73	—
Capel, D.J.	32	48	10	1031	109*	27.13	1	—	20	—
Carr, J.D.	9	10	4	67	18	11.16	—	—	5	—
Carrick, P.	241	305	59	5426	131*	22.05	3	—	119	—
Carse, J.A.	39	49	20	367	44	12.65	—	—	10	—
Chadwick, M.R.	1	2	0	2	1	1.00	—	—	1	—
Chatfield, E.J.	81	75	34	377	24*	9.19	—	—	29	—
Cheatle, R.G.L.	60	44	18	338	49	13.00	—	—	54	—
Chessher, J.R.	4	6	1	78	47	15.60	—	—	—	—
Childs, J.H.	158	145	70	523	34*	6.97	—	—	61	—
Clarke, S.T.	133	146	24	1858	100*	15.22	1	—	68	—
Clift, P.B.	228	327	73	6073	100*	23.90	1	—	120	—
Clinton, G.S.	131	224	23	5854	172*	29.12	9	3	39	—
Close, D.B.	783	1220	170	34911	198	33.24	52	20	811	1
Cobb, R.A.	41	63	1	1193	63	19.24	—	—	24	—
Cockbain, I.	46	78	9	1456	98	21.10	—	—	22	—
Coney, J.V.	104	180	30	4632	120*	30.88	4	—	125	—
Cook, C.R.	9	15	2	287	79	22.07	—	—	7	—
Cook, G.	320	563	39	16079	172	30.68	24	8	333	3
Cook, N.G.B.	121	118	36	993	75	12.10	—	—	71	—
Cooper, K.E.	135	138	30	996	38*	9.22	—	—	44	—
Corlett, S.C.	29	41	7	520	60	15.29	—	—	24	—
Cotterell, T.A.	10	12	3	81	22	9.00	—	—	2	—
Cowan, R.S.	28	52	5	1406	143*	29.91	3	—	17	1
Cowans, N.G.	39	41	7	201	36	5.91	—	—	17	—
Cowdrey, C.S.	138	197	34	5124	123	31.43	6	1	123	—
Cowley, N.G.	182	264	38	4725	109*	20.90	2	—	72	—
Crowe, J.J.	49	90	10	2554	157	31.92	5	—	52	—
Crowe, M.D.	46	77	12	2731	150	42.01	8	—	49	—
Cullinan, M.R.	9	9	2	60	27	8.57	—	—	16	—
Cunningham, E.J.	8	12	3	109	29*	12.11	—	—	4	—
Curtis, I.J.	30	29	13	76	20*	4.75	—	—	7	—
Curtis, T.S.	38	68	11	1404	92	24.63	—	—	19	—
Daniel, W.W.	176	156	67	1138	53*	12.78	—	—	41	—
Davies, A.G.	5	4	0	17	13	4.25	—	—	5	—
Davies, T.	23	33	8	558	69*	22.32	—	—	46	4
Davis, M.R.	23	29	7	190	21*	8.63	—	—	9	—
Davis, W.W.	49	61	25	432	60	12.00	—	—	15	—
Davison, B.F.	415	680	64	24608	189	39.94	48	13	311	—
Denning, P.W.	264	439	41	11221	184	28.19	8	6	129	—
Dennis, S.J.	38	42	16	209	37*	8.03	—	—	11	—
Dennison, D.	1	2	0	17	16	8.50	—	—	1	—
Derrick, J.	5	5	3	52	24*	26.00	—	—	3	—
Dilley, G.R.	110	115	40	1158	81	15.44	—	—	52	—
Doggart, S.J.G.	35	50	11	878	70	22.51	—	—	14	—
D'Oliveira, D.B.	26	46	3	1037	102	24.11	1	—	15	—

	M	I	NO	Runs	HS	Avge	100s	1000 runs in season	Ct	St
Donald, W.A.	5	8	1	126	45	18.00	—	—	1	—
Doughty, R.J.	13	18	7	210	32*	19.09	—	—	2	—
Downton, P.R.	142	160	28	2437	90*	18.46	—	—	305	42
Dredge, C.H.	138	158	50	1535	56*	14.21	—	—	58	—
Dudleston, B.	295	501	47	14747	202	32.48	32	8	234	7
Dyer, R.I.H.B.	16	24	4	323	93	16.15	—	—	8	—
East, D.E.	63	81	15	1304	91	19.75	—	—	159	19
East, R.E.	406	515	112	7148	113	17.73	1	—	254	—
Edbrooke, R.M.	3	4	1	171	84*	57.00	—	—	1	—
Edgar, B.A.	94	171	13	6128	161	38.78	11	—	68	1
Edmonds, P.H.	282	368	64	5966	141*	19.62	2	—	266	—
Ellcock, R.M.	13	20	5	167	36	11.13	—	—	2	—
Ellis, R.G.P.	37	68	3	1943	105*	29.89	2	—	19	—
Ellison, C.C.	11	13	6	105	21	15.00	—	—	5	—
Ellison, R.M.	36	43	16	759	63	28.11	—	—	21	—
Emburey, J.E.	213	253	61	3986	133	20.76	2	—	196	—
Emery, K.S.D.	30	27	15	45	18*	3.75	—	—	3	—
Fairbrother, N.H.	17	26	5	759	94*	36.14	—	—	8	—
Fell, M.A.	15	27	0	408	108	15.11	1	—	13	—
Feltham, M.A.	1	—	—	—	—	—	—	—	—	—
Felton, N.A.	15	24	1	722	173*	31.39	1	—	6	—
Ferreira, A.M.	119	180	29	4109	112*	27.21	2	—	58	—
Ferris, G.J.F.	15	16	6	67	26	6.70	—	—	2	—
Finney, R.J.	21	36	2	617	71	18.14	—	—	5	—
Fletcher, K.W.R.	626	1025	146	33957	228*	38.63	59	19	564	—
Fletcher, S.D.	3	4	2	14	12	7.00	—	—	—	—
Folley, I.	29	24	8	256	36	16.00	—	—	6	—
Foster, N.A.	20	22	7	306	40*	20.40	—	—	6	—
Fowler, G.	85	142	9	5144	156*	38.67	14	3	47	5
Fowler, W.P.	27	44	5	875	91	22.43	—	—	17	—
Francis, D.A.	136	234	36	4911	142*	24.80	3	1	60	—
Franklin, T.J.	35	65	5	1863	136	31.05	3	—	18	—
Franks, J.G.	5	7	0	98	29	14.00	—	—	2	—
French, B.N.	144	189	38	2606	91	17.25	—	—	302	30
Gard, T.	43	49	10	618	51*	15.84	—	—	67	16
Garner, J.	134	151	36	2049	104	17.81	1	—	91	—
Garnham, M.A.	34	49	8	875	74	21.34	—	—	62	13
Gatting, M.W.	192	291	44	10219	216	41.37	22	5	175	—
Gibaut, R.P.	2	2	0	7	7	3.50	—	—	—	—
Gifford, N.	592	691	216	6503	89	13.69	—	—	292	—
Gladwin, C.	10	15	0	523	89	34.86	—	—	4	—
Goldie, C.F.E.	21	24	3	302	77	14.38	—	—	32	7
Golding, A.K.	1	2	2	8	6*	—	—	—	—	—
Gooch, G.A.	259	435	35	15789	205	39.47	37	7+1	240	—
Gould, I.J.	160	218	30	4253	128	22.62	1	—	320	56
Gower, D.I.	209	334	32	11886	200*	39.35	24	5	125	—
Graveney, D.A.	239	325	82	4657	119	19.16	2	—	116	—
Gray, E.J.	68	108	20	2398	126	27.25	2	—	53	—

	M	I	NO	Runs	HS	Avge	100s	1000 runs in season	Ct	St
Green, A.M.	34	62	3	1435	99	24.32	—	—	18	—
Greenidge, C.G.	347	598	45	24255	273*	43.86	54	12	371	—
Greig, I.A.	97	131	14	2926	147*	25.00	3	—	58	—
Griffiths, B.J.	136	102	35	207	16	3.08	—	—	27	—
Hadlee, R.J.	197	276	45	6228	142*	26.96	7	—	103	—
Haggo, D.J.	1	2	0	9	9	4.50	—	—	1	—
Halliday, M.	10	9	4	75	30	15.00	—	—	4	—
Hampshire, J.H.	556	892	108	27267	183*	34.77	42	15	424	—
Hardie, B.R.	234	383	44	11502	162	33.92	14	8	214	—
Harper, R.A.	20	31	1	382	38	12.73	—	—	30	—
Harrison, D.	1	2	0	9	8	4.50	—	—	1	—
Harrison, G.D.	1	2	1	107	86	107.00	—	—	—	—
Hartley, P.J.	3	4	1	31	16	12.00	—	—	1	—
Hartley, S.N.	79	123	17	2533	114	23.89	2	—	35	—
Hassan, S.B.	312	517	49	13786	182*	29.45	14	5	281	1
Hayes, F.C.	271	420	58	13007	187	35.93	23	6	176	—
Hayes, K.A.	29	47	3	1059	152	24.06	1	—	8	—
Heath, J.R.P.	17	31	4	611	101*	22.62	1	—	6	—
Hemmings, E.E.	298	412	88	6600	127*	20.37	1	—	143	—
Henderson, S.P.	53	87	12	1818	209*	24.24	2	—	39	—
Hendrick, M.	264	267	109	1601	46	10.13	—	—	174	—
Heseltine, P.J.	6	10	1	176	40	19.55	—	—	5	—
Hewitt, S.G.P.	6	7	2	9	6	1.80	—	—	6	1
Hignell, A.J.	170	289	36	7459	149*	29.48	11	3	150	—
Hill, A.	199	349	35	9233	160*	29.40	13	3	72	—
Hinks, S.G.	8	14	1	288	87	22.15	—	—	3	—
Hodgson, K.I.	27	34	9	633	50	25.32	—	—	4	—
Hogg, W.	96	90	25	394	31	6.06	—	—	19	—
Holding, M.A.	105	133	23	1521	67	13.82	—	—	40	—
Holmes, G.C.	54	85	22	1396	100*	22.15	1	—	19	—
Hopkins, J.A.	213	376	22	9805	230	27.69	14	6	155	1
Howarth, G.P.	280	486	38	15111	183	33.72	30	4	195	—
Hughes, D.P.	325	415	81	7495	153	22.44	6	2	221	—
Hughes, M.G.	10	12	5	48	17	6.85	—	—	2	—
Hughes, S.P.	50	50	25	130	18	5.20	—	—	11	—
Humpage, G.W.	197	320	37	9987	254	35.28	18	6	341	41
Humphries, D.J.	152	219	36	4410	111*	24.09	2	—	255	53
Illingworth, N.J.B.	15	20	5	207	49	13.80	—	—	8	—
Illingworth, R.	787	1073	213	24134	162	28.06	22	8	446	—
Illingworth, R.K.	36	51	10	464	55	11.31	—	—	12	—
Imran Khan	286	445	69	13105	170	34.85	22	4	93	—
Inchmore, J.D.	169	205	41	2687	113	16.38	1	—	54	—
Jackson, P.B.	3	4	1	96	46	32.00	—	—	4	1
James, K.D.	13	14	5	190	34	21.11	—	—	3	—
Jarvis, K.B.S.	182	125	52	234	14*	3.20	—	—	44	—
Jarvis, P.W.	9	8	5	29	11*	9.66	—	—	5	—
Javed Miandad	263	424	69	18407	311	51.85	51	4+7	256	3

	M	I	NO	Runs	HS	Avge	100s	1000 runs in season	Ct	St
Jefferies, S.T.	49	59	14	1197	75*	26.60	—	—	16	—
Jesty, T.E.	341	540	71	14345	187	30.58	22	6	197	1
Johnson, G.W.	349	543	68	11823	168	24.89	11	3	279	—
Johnson, P.	20	35	3	702	125	21.93	1	—	9	—
Johnston, R.I.	3	5	2	86	34	28.66	—	—	3	—
Jones, A.	645	1168	72	36049	204*	32.89	56	23	288	—
Jones, A.L.	101	179	16	3672	99	22.52	—	1	56	—
Jones. A.N.	16	20	8	73	29	6.08	—	—	1	—
Jones, E.W.	405	591	119	8341	146*	17.67	3	—	840	93
Kallicharran, A.I.	385	624	66	25240	243*	45.23	65	9+1	254	—
Kapil Dev	131	182	18	4834	193	29.47	8	—	83	—
Kennedy, I.G.	1	2	0	15	12	7.50	—	—	—	—
Ker, A.B.M.	3	5	1	170	65	42.50	—	—	3	—
Ker, J.E.	7	10	3	113	50	16.14	—	—	3	—
King, C.L.	99	160	22	5386	163	39.02	13	1	87	—
Kirti Azad	49	66	5	2327	186	38.14	6	—	33	—
Knight, R.D.V.	363	633	56	18264	165*	31.65	28	12	275	—
Knott, A.P.E.	478	699	127	17431	156	30.47	17	2	1129	131
Lamb, A.J.	190	325	60	13542	178	51.10	34	5	138	—
Lamb, T.M.	160	163	61	1274	77	12.49	—	—	40	—
Larkins, W.	231	395	24	12640	252	34.07	29	6	111	—
Lawrence, D.V.	10	9	4	22	9	4.40	—	—	1	—
Lawrence, M.P.	5	5	2	20	18	6.66	—	—	1	—
Lees, W.K.	106	184	32	3616	152	23.78	4	—	207	28
Leiper, R.J.	2	4	0	53	49	13.25	—	—	2	—
le Roux, G.S.	128	162	47	2908	83	25.28	—	—	53	—
Lethbridge, C.	32	38	9	625	87*	21.55	—	—	10	—
Lever, J.K.	418	431	164	2885	91	10.80	—	—	159	—
Lilley, A.W.	30	48	2	1175	100*	25.54	1	—	16	—
Lines, S.J.	1	1	0	29	29	29.00	—	—	1	—
Lloyd, B.J.	147	184	47	1631	48	11.90	—	—	87	—
Lloyd, C.H.	447	674	87	28660	242*	48.82	74	10+4	345	—
Lloyd, D.	407	652	74	19269	214*	33.33	38	11	334	—
Lloyd, T.A.	138	244	28	7775	208*	35.99	13	4	83	—
Lloyds, J.W.	80	132	10	3224	132*	26.42	4	—	62	—
Lord, G.J.	3	3	0	91	61	30.33	—	—	1	—
Love, J.D.	143	236	36	6301	170*	31.50	10	2	78	—
Lumb, R.G.	235	389	28	11189	159	30.99	20	5	129	—
Lynch, M.A.	109	187	24	5035	141*	30.88	9	2	67	—
McEvoy, M.S.A.	59	100	2	1940	103	19.79	1	—	59	—
McEwan, K.S.	322	534	45	19716	218	40.31	53	10	290	7
McFarlane, L.L.	31	21	11	74	12*	7.40	—	—	7	—
McIntyre, E.J.	2	3	1	7	6	3.50	—	—	1	—
Mackintosh, K.S.	33	33	17	303	31	18.93	—	—	14	—
McPate, W.A.	1	1	1	5	5*	—	—	—	—	—
Maher, B.J.M.	20	26	8	205	52	11.38	—	—	32	5
Mallender, N.A.	69	70	26	568	71*	12.90	—	—	27	—
Malone, S.J.	45	38	14	174	23	7.25	—	—	9	—

	M	I	NO	Runs	HS	Avge	100s	1000 runs in season	Ct	St
Marks, V.J.	179	275	38	6234	105	26.30	1	—	78	—
Marsh, S.	3	3	1	15	10*	7.50	—	—	6	—
Marshall, M.D.	145	186	24	3552	116*	21.92	4	—	56	—
Maru, R.J.	16	16	3	147	25	11.30	—	—	14	—
Masters, K.	2	4	0	1	1	0.25	—	—	2	—
Maynard, C.	64	76	12	1211	85	18.92	—	—	86	12
Mendis, G.D.	158	284	25	8724	204	33.68	14	4	74	1
Metcalfe, A.A.	1	2	0	129	122	64.50	1	—	1	—
Metson, C.P.	1	1	1	38	38*	—	—	—	1	—
Miller, A.J.T.	16	28	3	1022	127*	40.88	1	1	1	—
Miller, G.	250	372	61	8496	98*	27.31	—	—	172	—
Moir, D.G.	44	49	5	456	53	10.36	—	—	39	—
Monkhouse, G.	30	34	14	465	63*	23.25	—	—	13	—
Monteith, J.D.	27	38	5	435	78	13.18	—	—	23	—
Moores, P.	7	11	1	154	30	15.40	—	—	11	2
Morris, H.	13	22	6	462	63	28.87	—	—	8	—
Morris, J.E.	11	22	1	379	58	18.04	—	—	4	—
Mortensen, O.H.	18	23	15	76	14*	9.50	—	—	5	—
Morton, W.A.	2	2	0	8	5	4.00	—	—	3	—
Moseley, H.R.	213	217	94	1533	67	12.46	—	—	78	—
Moulding, R.P.	47	79	9	1344	80*	19.20	—	—	17	—
Moxon, M.D.	31	58	1	1888	153	33.12	4	—	17	—
Mushtaq Mohammad	500	840	104	31044	303*	42.17	72	12+3	346	—
Nash, M.A.	336	469	67	7129	130	17.73	2	—	148	—
Nasir Zaidi, S.M.	13	16	6	215	51	21.50	—	—	9	—
Neale, P.A.	173	298	34	8808	163*	33.36	14	5	71	—
Needham, A.	36	48	9	497	134*	12.74	1	—	14	—
Newman, P.G.	45	46	11	371	39*	10.60	—	—	13	—
Newport, P.J.	7	9	2	110	41*	15.71	—	—	1	—
Nicholas, M.C.J.	94	160	23	4444	206*	32.43	9	2	61	—
Odendaal, A.	22	37	3	659	61	19.38	—	—	16	—
Old, C.M.	353	434	85	7241	116	20.74	6	—	205	—
Oldham, S.	118	90	37	555	50	10.47	—	—	35	—
Olley, M.W.C.	1	1	0	8	8	8.00	—	—	3	—
Ollis, R.L.	16	28	2	579	99*	22.26	—	—	5	—
Ontong, R.C.	209	355	37	8547	152*	26.87	14	3	97	—
Ormrod, J.A.	473	799	92	21952	204*	31.04	31	12	386	—
O'Shaughnessy, S.J.	47	70	14	1559	105	27.83	2	—	11	—
Palmer, G.V.	11	15	2	152	78	11.69	—	—	8	—
Palmer, R.W.M.	11	9	5	20	12	5.00	—	—	4	—
Parker, P.W.G.	178	303	44	8559	215	33.04	18	5	109	—
Parks, R.J.	80	87	18	1093	64*	15.84	—	—	182	23
Parsons, G.J.	78	93	22	1019	56	14.35	—	—	25	—
Patel, D.N.	163	254	18	6515	138	27.60	12	3	101	—
Pathmanathan, G.	44	77	3	1553	82	20.98	—	—	35	—
Pauline, D.B.	26	42	3	1044	115	26.76	1	—	5	—
Payne, I.R.	27	34	5	308	43	10.62	—	—	26	—
Penn, C.	9	9	4	78	30	15.60	—	—	5	—

	M	I	NO	Runs	HS	Avge	100s	1000 runs in season	Ct	St
Perryman, S.P.	156	162	68	872	43	9.27	—	—	58	—
Petchey, M.D.	6	6	0	21	18	3.50	—	—	3	—
Phillip, N.	202	299	35	6278	134	23.78	1	—	66	—
Phillipson, C.P.	167	225	61	3046	87	18.57	—	—	135	—
Pick, R.A.	6	8	2	84	25*	14.00	—	—	—	—
Pigott, A.C.S.	81	94	20	1131	63	15.28	—	—	35	—
Pocock, N.E.J.	114	168	20	3476	164	23.48	2	—	111	—
Pocock, P.I.	481	517	132	4431	75*	11.50	—	—	167	—
Pollock, A.J.	17	17	4	101	19	7.76	—	—	4	—
Pont, K.R.	179	274	40	6061	125*	25.90	7	—	86	—
Popplewell, N.F.M.	103	148	23	2890	143	23.12	2	—	73	—
Potter, L.	21	38	3	1132	118	32.34	2	—	10	—
Pridgeon, A.P.	163	162	68	821	34	8.73	—	—	48	—
Pringle, D.R.	93	133	28	3307	127*	31.49	6	—	44	—
Prior, J.A.	3	5	0	99	55	19.80	—	—	1	—
Racionzer, T.B.	44	78	9	1494	115	21.65	1	—	35	—
Radford, N.V.	55	65	14	1073	76*	21.03	—	—	28	—
Radley, C.T.	474	758	106	22829	171	35.01	39	14	464	—
Ramage, A.	23	22	9	219	52	16.84	—	—	1	—
Randall, D.W.	291	496	43	16296	209	35.97	26	8	200	—
Rawlinson, H.T.	12	15	2	121	24	9.30	—	—	3	—
Reeve, D.A.	17	20	5	192	42*	12.80	—	—	7	—
Rhodes, S.J.	1	—	—	—	—	—	—	—	—	—
Rice, C.E.B.	312	501	74	17056	246	39.94	30	9	242	—
Richards, C.J.	161	197	46	3214	117*	21.28	1	—	302	44
Richards, I.V.A.	298	490	35	22630	291	49.73	69	10+3	282	1
Roberts, A.M.E.	208	266	60	3074	63	14.92	—	—	49	—
Robinson, R.T.	82	142	17	4085	207	32.68	4	1	39	—
Roebuck, P.G.	5	7	3	82	31*	20.50	—	—	1	—
Roebuck, P.M.	182	305	48	8288	158	32.24	6	3	96	—
Romaines, P.W.	43	74	7	1951	185	29.11	4	1	15	—
Rose, B.C.	228	379	40	11340	205	33.45	22	8	113	—
Rowe, C.J.C.	169	266	41	6018	147*	26.74	6	2	61	—
Russell, R.C.	29	39	11	589	64*	21.03	—	—	57	20
Russom, N.	25	34	14	641	79*	32.05	—	—	6	—
Sadiq Mohammad	373	657	39	23140	203	37.44	48	7+3	316	—
Sainsbury, G.E.	26	25	10	72	13	4.80	—	—	1	—
Saxelby, K.	43	52	11	475	59*	11.58	—	—	8	—
Scott, C.W.	5	6	1	125	78	25.00	—	—	7	2
Scott, M.S.	32	60	3	1383	109	24.26	1	—	9	—
Selvey, M.W.W.	263	260	80	2294	67	12.74	—	—	70	—
Sharp, G.	284	371	80	5975	98	20.53	—	—	533	85
Sharp, K.	96	161	13	4546	139	30.71	8	—	36	—
Shepherd, J.N.	397	572	99	12469	170	26.36	10	2	277	—
Short, J.F.	10	17	2	518	114	34.53	1	—	10	—
Sidebottom, A.	122	138	32	2306	124	21.75	1	—	34	—
Simmons, J.	344	420	112	7205	112	23.39	5	—	269	—
Slack, W.N.	104	173	15	5582	248*	35.32	8	3	72	—
Slocombe, P.A.	139	233	29	5640	132	27.64	7	2	65	—

	M	I	NO	Runs	HS	Avge	100s	1000 runs in season	Ct	St
Smail, A.H.K.	6	6	1	24	13*	4.80	—	—	1	—
Small, G.C.	68	82	18	687	57*	10.73	—	—	19	—
Smith, C.L.	81	142	16	5124	193	40.66	13	2	50	—
Smith, D.J.	11	12	2	26	13	2.60	—	—	15	—
Smith, D.M. (Sy)	141	215	48	5220	160	31.25	8	1	96	—
Smith, D.M. (Wa)	4	5	2	148	100*	49.33	1	—	2	—
Smith, I.D.S.	56	88	7	1788	145	22.07	3	—	127	10
Smith, K.D.	171	297	27	7922	140	29.34	9	4	66	—
Smith, P.A.	23	33	4	841	114	29.00	1	—	8	—
Smith, R.A.	25	44	7	1266	104*	34.21	3	—	9	—
Snedden, M.C.	45	50	12	775	69	20.39	—	—	21	—
Southern, J.W.	164	179	71	1653	61*	15.30	—	—	59	—
Speak, G.J.	5	6	4	27	15*	13.50	—	—	3	—
Standing, D.K.	4	8	3	240	60	48.00	—	—	2	—
Stanworth, J.	3	6	2	90	31*	22.50	—	—	2	—
Steele, D.S.	475	773	111	21707	140*	32.79	30	10	517	—
Steele, J.F.	331	535	65	13669	195	29.08	20	6	360	—
Stephenson, F.D.	23	32	2	601	165	20.03	1	—	14	—
Stevenson, G.B.	167	204	30	3626	115*	20.83	2	—	67	—
Stevenson, K.	146	167	58	1046	33	9.59	—	—	48	—
Stewart, A.J.	12	21	4	560	118*	32.94	1	11	1	—
Stovold, A.W.	224	400	22	11768	212*	31.13	13	5	220	43
Such, P.M.	18	24	7	16	5	0.94	—	—	13	—
Sutcliffe, S.P.	38	47	11	141	20	3.91	—	—	6	—
Swallow, I.G.	2	3	2	19	11*	19.00	—	—	1	—
Swan, R.G.	4	8	1	180	66	25.71	—	—	3	—
Sykes, J.F.	1	1	0	4	4	4.00	—	—	—	—
Tavaré, C.J.	201	339	38	12058	168*	40.05	23	7	199	—
Taylor, L.B.	129	110	48	636	47	10.25	—	—	32	—
Taylor, N.R.	69	120	16	3517	155*	33.81	9	2	46	—
Taylor, N.S.	8	6	1	10	4	2.00	—	—	2	—
Taylor, R.W.	609	843	159	11521	100	16.84	1	—	1424	170
Taylor, T.J.	14	17	7	115	28*	11.50	—	—	2	—
Tedstone, G.A.	16	21	5	288	67*	18.00	—	—	27	5
Terry, V.P.	39	62	10	1465	115	28.17	3	1	24	—
Thomas, D.J.	87	118	24	1947	119	20.71	2	—	31	—
Thomas, J.G.	24	31	4	355	84	13.14	—	—	8	—
Thorne, D.A.	5	7	3	62	23*	15.50	—	—	3	—
Tolchard, R.W.	483	680	189	15288	126*	31.13	12	—	912	125
Tomlins, K.P.	65	90	12	2166	146	27.76	3	—	49	—
Toogood, G.J.	14	24	4	440	83	22.00	—	—	4	—
Tracy, S.R.	8	9	1	17	5	2.12	—	—	5	—
Trembath, C.R.	2	1	1	8	8*	—	—	—	1	—
Tremlett, T.M.	87	120	18	2078	88	20.37	—	—	47	—
Tunnicliffe, C.J.	150	176	30	2092	91	14.32	—	—	65	—
Turnbull, J.R.	7	7	4	5	5*	1.66	—	—	6	—
Turner, D.R.	332	544	49	14070	181*	28.42	21	6	165	—
Turner, S.	342	489	95	9064	121	23.00	4	—	213	—
Underwood, D.L.	580	606	168	4132	80	9.43	—	—	238	—

	M	I	NO	Runs	HS	Avge	100s	1000 runs in season	Ct	St
Varey, D.W.	22	42	5	971	156*	26.24	1	—	11	—
Varey, J.G.	13	22	8	426	69*	30.42	—	—	3	—
Walker, A.	6	4	3	18	7*	18.00	—	—	3	—
Waller, C.E.	229	236	94	1388	51*	9.77	—	—	118	—
Wallwork, M.A.	1	—	—	—	—	—	—	—	3	—
Warke, S.J.S.	2	3	0	112	63	37.33	—	—	1	—
Warner, A.E.	20	32	7	418	67	16.72	—	—	5	—
Warner, C.J.	7	12	1	268	70	24.36	—	—	5	—
Waterman, P.A.	2	2	1	6	6*	6.00	—	—	—	—
Waterton, S.N.V.	14	16	2	171	40*	12.21	—	—	25	4
Watkins, S.G.	1	2	0	105	77	52.50	—	—	—	—
Watkinson, M.	16	20	4	168	29	10.50	—	—	2	—
Watson, R.G.	1	2	0	15	11	7.50	—	—	—	—
Watts, A.	3	3	1	39	33*	19.50	—	—	1	—
Wells, A.P.	23	40	7	976	92	29.57	—	—	14	—
Wells, C.M.	88	141	19	3726	135	30.54	5	2	28	—
Weston, M.J.	46	79	3	1703	115	22.40	1	—	18	—
Whitaker, J.J.	10	16	4	305	56*	25.41	—	—	4	—
Whitney, M.R.	31	28	8	74	28*	3.70	—	—	19	—
Wild, D.J.	19	28	5	403	48	17.52	—	—	4	—
Wilkins, A.H.	107	124	29	902	70	9.49	—	—	34	—
Willey, P.	365	601	91	15134	227	29.67	24	4	141	—
Williams, N.F.	41	43	13	653	63	21.76	—	—	10	—
Williams, R.G.	162	259	32	6918	175*	30.47	12	5	62	—
Willis, R.G.D.	293	317	137	2606	72	14.47	—	—	126	—
Willows, A.	5	3	1	5	4	2.50	—	—	—	—
Wills, R.T.	3	5	0	95	48	19.00	—	—	—	—
Wilson, P.H.L.	57	48	25	261	29	11.34	—	—	10	—
Wood, B.	357	591	75	17453	198	33.82	30	8	283	—
Wood, L.J.	2	2	0	5	5	2.50	—	—	—	—
Woolmer, R.A.	342	531	72	15344	203	33.42	33	5	234	1
Wootton, S.H.	11	16	2	364	104	26.00	1	—	4	—
Wright, A.J.	20	36	4	779	65	24.34	—	—	8	—
Wright, J.G.	201	349	25	12952	190	39.97	31	5	119	—
Wyatt, J.G.	6	12	2	352	82*	35.20	—	—	1	—
Younis Ahmed	392	658	100	21753	221*	38.98	36	11	219	—
Zaheer Abbas	408	682	80	32307	274	53.66	105	11+6	254	—

BOWLING

Players who have not bowled in first-class cricket are omitted from this list.

	Runs	*Wkts*	*Avge*	*BB*	*5 wI*	*10 wM*	*100 wkts in season*
Abrahams, J.	2225	43	51.74	3-27	—	—	—
Acfield, D.L.	22846	830	27.52	8-55	30	4	—
Agnew, J.P.	4033	125	32.26	6-70	2	—	—
Allott, P.J.W.	6522	224	29.11	8-48	9	—	—
Amiss, D.L.	718	18	39.88	3-21	—	—	—
Anderson, I.S.	836	15	55.73	4-35	—	—	—
Asif Din	1790	28	63.92	5-100	1	—	—
Aslett, D.G.	561	10	56.10	4-119	—	—	—
Athey, C.W.J.	1060	21	50.47	3-38	—	—	—
Bailey, R.J.	35	3	11.66	3-33	—	—	—
Bainbridge, P.	3926	104	37.75	6-59	2	—	—
Bairstow, D.L.	208	6	34.66	3-82	—	—	—
Balderstone, J.C.	7880	305	25.83	6-25	5	—	—
Baptiste, E.A.E.	3620	128	28.28	5-37	4	—	—
Barclay, J.R.T.	7935	257	30.87	6-61	7	1	—
Barlow, G.D.	54	3	18.00	1-6	—	—	—
Barnett, K.J.	1365	18	75.83	4-76	—	—	—
Barwick, S.R.	1646	50	32.92	8-42	2	—	—
Benson, M.R.	72	0	—	—	—	—	—
Birch, J.D.	1836	38	48.31	6-64	1	—	—
Boon, T.J.	57	0	—	—	—	—	—
Booth, P.A.	72	0	—	—	—	—	—
Booth, S.C.	849	21	40.42	4-26	—	—	—
Bore, M.K.	10445	346	30.18	8-89	8	—	—
Botham, I.T.	19430	777	25.00	8-34	44	7	1
Boycott, G.	1405	45	31.22	4-14	—	—	—
Boyd-Moss, R.J.	1231	32	38.46	5-27	1	—	—
Bracewell, J.G.	4641	196	23.67	7-9	15	3	—
Brassington, A.J.	10	0	—	—	—	—	—
Breakwell, D.	13008	422	30.82	8-39	12	1	—
Brearley, J.M.	192	3	64.00	1-6	—	—	—
Briers, N.E.	343	10	34.30	2-11	—	—	—
Broad, B.C.	656	11	59.63	2-14	—	—	—
Bullen, C.K.	29	0	—	—	—	—	—
Butcher, A.R.	3920	99	39.59	6-48	1	—	—
Butcher, I.P.	2	1	2.00	1-2	—	—	—
Butcher, R.O.	76	0	—	—	—	—	—
Cairns, B.L.	10224	394	25.94	8-46	23	5	—
Capel, D.J.	664	9	73.77	2-14	—	—	—
Carr, J.D.	476	9	52.88	2-59	—	—	—
Carrick, P.	17701	612	28.97	8-33	30	3	—
Carse, J.A.	2904	87	33.37	6-50	3	—	—
Chatfield, E.J.	7242	365	19.84	8-24	20	7	—
Cheatle, R.G.L.	3303	104	31.75	6-32	6	—	—
Childs, J.H.	12728	406	31.34	9-56	21	2	—
Clarke, S.T.	10654	507	21.01	7-34	29	4	—
Clift, P.B.	15230	627	24.29	8-17	20	1	—

	Runs	Wkts	Avge	BB	5 wI	10 wM	100 wkts in season
Clinton, G.S.	97	4	24.25	2-8	—	—	—
Close, D.B.	30841	1168	26.40	8-41	43	3	2
Cobb, R.A.	5	0	—	—	—	—	—
Cockbain, I.	14	0	—	—	—	—	—
Coney, J.V.	2332	80	29.15	6-17	1	—	—
Cook, G.	570	14	40.71	3-47	—	—	—
Cook, N.G.B.	9207	354	26.00	7-63	16	1	—
Cooper, K.E.	8937	320	27.92	7-33	11	—	—
Corlett, S.C.	2028	65	31.20	7-82	4	—	—
Cotterell, T.A.	758	17	44.58	5-89	1	—	—
Cowan, R.S.	798	9	88.66	2-75	—	—	—
Cowans, N.G.	2619	99	26.45	6-77	5	—	—
Cowdrey, C.S.	1943	45	43.17	3-17	—	—	—
Cowley, N.G.	9313	271	34.36	6-48	4	—	—
Crowe, J.J.	19	1	19.00	1-10	—	—	—
Crowe, M.D.	728	28	26.00	5-69	1	—	—
Cunningham, E.J.	194	4	48.50	2-55	—	—	—
Curtis, I.J.	2073	50	41.46	6-28	2	—	—
Curtis, T.S.	172	4	43.00	2-58	—	—	—
Daniel, W.W.	12088	592	20.41	9-61	26	7	—
Davis, M.R.	1354	37	36.59	4-34	—	—	—
Davis, W.W.	4906	183	26.80	7-70	9	1	—
Davison, B.F.	2635	82	32.13	5-52	1	—	—
Denning, P.W.	96	1	96.00	1-4	—	—	—
Dennis, S.J.	3199	111	28.81	5-35	3	—	—
Derrick, J.	31	0	—	—	—	—	—
Dilley, G.R.	7431	259	28.69	6-66	9	1	—
Doggart, S.J.G.	2223	34	65.38	3-3	—	—	—
D'Oliveira, D.B.	262	4	65.50	1-12	—	—	—
Donald, W.A.	64	1	64.00	1-46	—	—	—
Doughty, R.J.	939	23	40.82	6-43	1	—	—
Dredge, C.H.	9499	327	29.04	6-37	11	—	—
Dudleston, B.	1365	47	29.04	4-6	—	—	—
Dyer, R.I.H.B.	2	0	—	—	—	—	—
East, R.E.	25886	1008	25.68	8-30	49	10	—
Edgar, B.A.	26	1	26.00	1-17	—	—	—
Edmonds, P.H.	23152	944	24.52	8-80	43	8	—
Ellcock, R.M.	1021	28	36.46	4-70	—	—	—
Ellis, R.G.P.	264	4	66.00	2-40	—	—	—
Ellison, C.C.	467	12	38.91	4-36	—	—	—
Ellison, R.M.	2068	71	29.12	5-73	1	—	—
Emburey, J.E.	16986	745	22.80	7-36	42	8	1
Emery, K.S.D.	2231	88	25.35	6-51	3	1	—
Fairbrother, N.H.	1	0	—	—	—	—	—
Fell, M.A.	157	1	157.00	1-20	—	—	—
Feltham, M.A.	44	2	22.00	1-19	—	—	—
Ferreira, A.M.	9626	308	31.25	8-38	11	1	—
Ferris, G.J.F.	1315	56	23.48	7-42	3	1	—

	Runs	Wkts	Avge	BB	5 wI	10 wM	100 wkts in season
Finney, R.J.	1010	31	32.58	5-58	1	—	—
Fletcher, K.W.R.	2224	50	44.48	5-41	1	—	—
Fletcher, S.D.	186	8	23.25	4-71	—	—	—
Folley, I.	1280	34	37.64	4-40	—	—	—
Foster, N.A.	1811	68	26.63	6-46	1	—	—
Fowler, G.	75	2	37.50	2-43	—	—	—
Fowler, W.P.	661	9	73.44	2-44	—	—	—
Francis, D.A.	31	0	—	—	—	—	—
Franklin, T.J.	10	0	—	—	—	—	—
Gard, T.	8	0	—	—	—	—	—
Garner, J.	10654	595	17.90	8-31	36	7	—
Gatting, M.W.	2355	92	25.59	5-34	2	—	—
Gifford, N.	41637	1824	22.82	8-28	86	14	4
Gladwin, C.	11	0	—	—	—	—	—
Golding, A.K.	97	2	48.50	1-44	—	—	—
Gooch, G.A.	3610	99	36.46	7-14	2	—	—
Gould, I.J.	35	0	—	—	—	—	—
Gower, D.I.	180	4	45.00	3-47	—	—	—
Graveney, D.A.	15562	540	28.81	8-85	25	4	—
Gray, E.J.	4404	167	26.37	6-53	2	—	—
Green, A.M.	522	12	43.50	2-30	—	—	—
Greenidge, C.G.	438	16	27.37	5-49	1	—	—
Greig, I.A.	5899	214	27.56	7-43	7	2	—
Griffiths, B.J.	9908	348	28.47	8-50	10	—	—
Hadlee, R.J.	16109	815	19.76	7-23	47	6	1
Halliday, M.	594	27	22.00	5-39	1	—	—
Hampshire, J.H.	1637	30	54.56	7-52	2	—	—
Hardie, B.R.	80	2	40.00	2-39	—	—	—
Harper, R.A.	2001	72	27.79	5-33	4	—	—
Harrison, G.D.	40	2	20.00	2-30	—	—	—
Hartley, P.J.	215	2	107.50	2-45	—	—	—
Hartley, S.N.	1193	27	44.18	3-40	—	—	—
Hassan, S.B.	407	6	67.83	3-33	—	—	—
Hayes, F.C.	15	0	—	—	—	—	—
Hayes, K.A.	253	8	31.62	6-58	1	—	—
Heath, J.R.P.	58	0	—	—	—	—	—
Hemmings, E.E.	24415	838	29.13	10-175	38	10	—
Hendersen, S.P.	185	3	61.66	2-48	—	—	—
Hendrick, M.	15699	762	20.60	8-45	29	3	—
Hignell, A.J.	230	3	76.66	2-13	—	—	—
Hill, A.	152	5	30.40	3-5	—	—	—
Hinks, S.G.	5	0	—	—	—	—	—
Hodgson, K.I.	2093	55	38.05	8-68	1	1	—
Hogg, W.	6437	222	28.99	7-84	6	1	—
Holding, M.A.	9129	380	24.02	8-92	23	3	—
Holmes, G.C.	1017	26	39.11	5-86	1	—	—
Hopkins, J.A.	50	0	—	—	—	—	—
Howarth, G.P.	3378	109	30.99	5-32	1	—	—
Hughes, D.P.	17967	605	29.69	7-24	20	2	—

	Runs	Wkts	Avge	BB	5 wI	10 wM	100 wkts in season
Hughes, M.G.	1332	35	38.05	4-69	—	—	—
Hughes, S.P.	3938	149	26.42	6-32	6	—	—
Humpage, G.W.	387	8	48.37	2-13	—	—	—
Illingworth, N.J.B.	694	16	43.37	5-89	1	—	—
Illingworth, R.	42023	2072	20.28	9-42	104	11	10
Illingworth, R.K.	2641	66	40.01	5-26	1	—	—
Imran Khan	21999	995	22.10	8-58	56	11	—
Inchmore, J.D.	12007	420	28.58	8-58	18	1	—
James, K.D.	388	21	18.47	5-28	1	—	—
Jarvis, K.B.S.	13930	471	29.57	8-97	14	3	—
Jarvis, P.W.	663	11	60.27	2-24	—	—	—
Javed Miandad	5924	181	32.72	7-39	6	—	—
Jefferies, S.T.	4573	176	25.98	8-46	6	1	—
Jesty, T.E.	14397	536	26.86	7-75	18	—	—
Johnson, G.W.	15838	516	30.69	7-76	19	3	—
Johnston, R.I.	3	0	—	—	—	—	—
Jones, A.	333	3	111.00	1-24	—	—	—
Jones, A.L.	42	0	—	—	—	—	—
Jones, A.N.	849	29	29.27	4-33	—	—	—
Jones, E.W.	5	0	—	—	—	—	—
Kallicharran, A.I.	3152	67	47.04	5-45	1	—	—
Kapil Dev	11656	418	27.88	8-38	24	2	—
Ker, J.E.	244	8	30.50	3-45	—	—	—
King, C.L.	3621	115	31.48	5-91	1	—	—
Kirti Azad	2263	89	25.42	7-63	3	—	—
Knight, R.D.V.	12327	342	36.04	6-44	4	—	—
Knott, A.P.E.	87	2	43.50	1-5	—	—	—
Lamb, A.J.	93	4	23.25	1-1	—	—	—
Lamb, T.M.	10459	361	28.97	7-56	10	—	—
Larkins, W.	1175	32	36.71	4-30	—	—	—
Lawrence, D.V.	773	9	85.88	3-62	—	—	—
Lawrence, M.P.	402	2	201.00	1-32	—	—	—
Lees, W.K.	63	1	63.00	1-34	—	—	—
le Roux, G.S.	9807	496	19.77	8-107	27	3	—
Lethbridge, C.	1746	42	41.57	5-68	1	—	—
Lever, J.K.	31850	1342	23.73	8-49	65	9	3
Lilley, A.W.	10	0	—	—	—	—	—
Lloyd, B.J.	10133	247	41.02	8-70	3	—	—
Lloyd, C.H.	4104	114	36.00	4-48	—	—	—
Lloyd, D.	7172	237	30.26	7-38	5	1	—
Lloyd, T.A.	699	8	87.37	2-29	—	—	—
Lloyds, J.W.	3937	119	33.08	7-88	6	1	—
Lord, G.J.	12	0	—	—	—	—	—
Love, J.D.	233	1	233.00	1-46	—	—	—
Lynch, M.A.	574	11	52.18	3-6	—	—	—
McEvoy, M.S.A.	103	3	34.33	3-20	—	—	—

	Runs	Wkts	Avge	BB	5 wI	10 wM	100 wkts in season
McEwan, K.S.	309	4	77.25	1-0	—	—	—
McFarlane, L.L.	2257	55	41.03	6-59	1	—	—
McIntyre, E.J.	39	0	—	—	—	—	—
Mackintosh, K.S.	2092	59	35.45	6-61	1	—	—
McPate, W.A.	45	1	45.00	1-8	—	—	—
Mallender, N.A.	5065	163	31.07	7-41	5	1	—
Malone, S.J.	3378	99	34.12	7-55	2	1	—
Marks, V.J.	13381	395	33.87	7-51	17	—	—
Marshall, M.D.	11199	614	18.23	8-71	38	6	1
Maru, R.J.	766	23	33.30	4-30	—	—	—
Masters, K.D.	121	2	60.50	2-26	—	—	—
Mendis, G.D.	11	0	—	—	—	—	—
Metcalfe, A.A.	6	0	—	—	—	—	—
Miller, G.	15536	606	25.63	8-70	27	6	—
Moir, D.G.	3742	122	30.67	6-63	6	—	—
Monkhouse, G.	1659	66	25.13	7-51	1	—	—
Monteith, J.D.	1836	92	19.95	7-38	7	1	—
Morris, H.	23	0	—	—	—	—	—
Morris, J.E.	0	0	—	—	—	—	—
Mortensen, O.H.	1605	66	24.31	6-27	3	1	—
Morton, W.A.	216	9	24.00	4-40	—	—	—
Moseley, H.R.	13668	557	24.53	6-34	16	1	—
Moulding, R.P.	22	0	—	—	—	—	—
Moxon, M.D.	174	1	174.00	1-25	—	—	—
Mushtaq Mohammad	22758	936	24.31	7-18	39	2	—
Nash, M.A.	25698	993	25.87	9-56	45	5	—
Nasir Zaidi, S.M.	530	16	33.12	3-27	—	—	—
Neale, P.A.	190	1	190.00	1-15	—	—	—
Needham, A.	2138	51	41.92	6-30	3	—	—
Newman, P.G.	3329	101	32.96	5-51	1	—	—
Newport, P.J.	356	9	39.55	4-76	—	—	—
Nicholas, M.C.J.	859	29	29.62	5-45	1	—	—
Old, C.M.	23309	1012	23.03	7-20	35	1	—
Oldham, S.	8114	251	32.32	7-78	4	—	—
Ollis, R.L.	2	0	—	—	—	—	—
Ontong, R.C.	13658	443	30.83	7-60	16	2	—
Ormrod, J.A.	1094	25	43.76	5-27	1	—	—
O'Shaughnessy, S.J.	1955	64	30.54	4-66	—	—	—
Palmer, G.V.	687	20	34.35	5-38	1	—	—
Palmer, R.W.M.	954	16	59.62	4-96	—	—	—
Parker, P.W.G.	501	8	62.62	2-23	—	—	—
Parks, R.J.	0	0	—	—	—	—	—
Parsons, G.J.	5340	164	32.56	5-25	2	—	—
Patel, D.N.	8704	239	36.41	7-46	10	—	—
Pathmanathan, G.	26	0	—	—	—	—	—
Pauline, D.B.	22	0	—	—	—	—	—
Payne, I.R.	1025	23	44.56	5-13	1	—	—
Penn, C.	443	9	49.22	2-11	—	—	—

	Runs	Wkts	Avge	BB	5 wI	10 wM	100 wkts in season
Perryman, S.P.	11337	358	31.66	7-49	19	3	—
Petchey, M.D.	804	12	67.00	2-70	—	—	—
Phillip, N.	15058	619	24.32	7-33	27	2	—
Phillipson, C.P.	5213	153	34.07	6-56	4	—	—
Pick, R.A.	500	7	71.42	2-50	—	—	—
Pigott, A.C.S.	5864	216	27.14	7-74	10	1	—
Pocock, N.E.J.	335	4	83.75	1-4	—	—	—
Pocock, P.I.	37368	1443	25.89	9-57	56	6	1
Pollock, A.J.	1233	35	35.22	5-107	2	—	—
Pont, K.R.	2689	83	32.39	5-17	2	—	—
Popplewell, N.F.M.	3914	95	41.20	5-33	1	—	—
Potter, L.	47	2	23.50	1-9	—	—	—
Pridgeon, A.P.	12277	351	34.97	7-35	6	1	—
Pringle, D.R.	5528	196	28.20	7-32	5	1	—
Prior, J.A.	80	0	—	—	—	—	—
Racionzer, T.B.	52	2	26.00	2-11	—	—	—
Radford, N.V.	4632	154	30.07	6-41	6	1	—
Radley, C.T.	117	6	19.50	1-0	—	—	—
Ramage, A.	1649	44	37.47	5-65	1	—	—
Randall, D.W.	142	3	47.33	3-15	—	—	—
Rawlinson, H.T.	1061	19	55.84	5-123	1	—	—
Reeve, D.A.	1233	42	29.35	4-15	—	—	—
Rice, C.E.B.	14601	679	21.50	7-62	20	1	—
Richards, C.J.	24	0	—	—	—	—	—
Richards, I.V.A.	5728	136	42.11	5-88	1	—	—
Roberts, A.M.E.	17181	824	20.85	8-47	43	6	1
Robinson, R.T.	94	2	47.00	1-22	—	—	—
Roebuck, P.G.P.	269	6	44.83	2-44	—	—	—
Roebuck, P.M.	2004	42	47.71	6-50	1	—	—
Romaines, P.W.	9	0	—	—	—	—	—
Rose, B.C.	224	6	37.33	3-9	—	—	—
Rowe, C.J.C.	4771	116	41.12	6-46	3	1	—
Russom, N.	1744	42	41.52	4-84	—	—	—
Sadiq Mohammad	7371	231	31.90	7-34	8	—	—
Sainsbury, G.E.	2205	66	33.40	6-66	3	—	—
Saxelby, K.	2631	101	26.04	5-52	2	—	—
Scott, M.S.	37	0	—	—	—	—	—
Selvey, M.W.W.	19585	747	26.21	7-20	37	4	1
Sharp, G.	68	1	68.00	1-47	—	—	—
Sharp, K.	47	0	—	—	—	—	—
Shepherd, J.N.	29710	1083	27.43	8-40	52	2	—
Sidebottom, A.	7009	285	24.59	7-18	11	2	—
Simmons, J.	20838	759	27.45	7-59	26	3	—
Slack, W.N.	386	18	21.44	3-17	—	—	—
Slocombe, P.A.	54	3	18.00	1-2	—	—	—
Smail, A.H.K.	222	5	44.40	3-49	—	—	—
Small, G.C.	4939	143	34.53	7-68	2	—	—
Smith, C.L.	952	21	45.33	3-35	—	—	—
Smith, D.M. (Sy)	1463	27	54.18	3-40	—	—	—

	Runs	Wkts	Avge	BB	5 wI	10 wM	100 wkts in season
Smith, D.M. (Wa)	201	2	100.50	1-44	—	—	—
Smith, I.D.S.	6	0	—	—	—	—	—
Smith, K.D.	3	0	—	—	—	—	—
Smith, P.A.	1380	31	44.51	3-56	—	—	—
Smith, R.A.	25	0	—	—	—	—	—
Snedden, M.C.	3706	149	24.87	7-49	5	1	—
Southern, J.W.	12283	412	29.81	6-46	17	—	—
Speak, G.J.	230	1	230.00	1-78	—	—	—
Standing, D.K.	32	0	—	—	—	—	—
Steele, D.S.	13411	562	23.86	8-29	24	3	—
Steele, J.F.	12762	496	25.72	7-29	12	—	—
Stephenson, F.D.	1873	95	19.71	6-19	6	1	—
Stevenson, G.B.	12789	459	27.86	8-57	18	2	—
Stevenson, K.	10536	355	29.67	7-22	16	—	—
Stovold, A.W.	86	2	43.00	1-0	—	—	—
Such, P.M.	1504	45	33.42	6-123	2	—	—
Sutcliffe, S.P.	4020	96	41.87	6-19	2	—	—
Swallow, I.G.	82	2	41.00	1-15	—	—	—
Swan, R.G.	0	0	—	—	—	—	—
Sykes, J.F.	54	1	54.00	1-32	—	—	—
Tavare, C.J.	275	2	137.50	1-20	—	—	—
Taylor, L.B.	9336	390	23.93	7-28	12	1	—
Taylor, N.R.	234	5	46.80	2-58	—	—	—
Taylor, N.S.	720	22	32.72	5-49	1	—	—
Taylor, R.W.	52	0	—	—	—	—	—
Taylor, T.J.	1272	37	34.37	5-81	2	—	—
Terry, V.P.	39	0	—	—	—	—	—
Thomas, D.J.	6386	185	34.51	6-84	2	—	—
Thomas, J.G.	1530	52	29.42	5-61	3	—	—
Thorne, D.A.	189	2	94.50	1-21	—	—	—
Tolchard, R.W.	34	1	34.00	1-4	—	—	—
Tomlins, K.P.	308	4	77.00	2-28	—	—	—
Toogood, G.J.	22	0	—	—	—	—	—
Tracy, S.R.	666	22	30.27	5-29	1	—	—
Trembath, C.R.	219	6	36.50	5-91	1	—	—
Tremlett, T.M.	3587	143	25.08	6-82	3	—	—
Tunnicliffe, C.J.	10265	319	32.17	7-36	6	—	—
Turnbull, J.R.	424	12	35.33	4-51	—	—	—
Turner, D.R.	323	9	35.88	2-7	—	—	—
Turner, S.	20275	787	25.76	6-26	27	1	—
Underwood, D.L.	44014	2224	19.79	9-28	148	45	10
Varey, D.W.	4	0	—	—	—	—	—
Varey, J.G.	866	6	144.33	3-69	—	—	—
Walker, A.	578	22	26.27	4-61	—	—	—
Waller, C.E.	16081	557	28.87	7-64	20	1	—
Warner, A.E.	1315	46	28.58	4-72	—	—	—
Waterman, P.A.	151	1	151.00	1-64	—	—	—

	Runs	Wkts	Avge	BB	5 wI	10 wM	100 wkts in season
Watkinson, M.	974	36	27.05	6-51	2	—	—
Watts, A.	118	1	118.00	1-28	—	—	—
Wells, A.P.	42	0	—	—	—	—	—
Wells, C.M.	2584	67	38.56	4-23	—	—	—
Weston, M.J.	445	8	55.62	3-42	—	—	—
Whitaker, J.J.	88	0	—	—	—	—	—
Whitney, M.R.	3083	103	29.93	5-29	4	—	—
Wild, D.J.	616	9	68.44	2-15	—	—	—
Wilkins, A.H.	7511	243	30.90	8-57	9	—	—
Willey, P.	15639	530	29.50	7-37	20	3	—
Williams, N.F.	2845	103	27.62	5-77	1	—	—
Williams, R.G.	6877	214	32.13	7-73	6	—	—
Willis, R.G.D.	21226	865	24.53	8-32	34	2	—
Willows, A.	253	8	31.62	4-33	—	—	—
Wilson, P.H.L.	3218	105	30.64	5-36	1	—	—
Wood, B.	9160	298	30.73	7-52	8	—	—
Wood, L.J.	182	4	45.50	4-124	—	—	—
Woolmer, R.A.	10817	415	26.06	7-47	12	1	—
Wootton, S.H.	7	0	—	—	—	—	—
Wright, A.J.	3	0	—	—	—	—	—
Wright, J.G.	67	1	67.00	1-4	—	—	—
Younis Ahmed	1605	39	41.15	4-10	—	—	—
Zaheer Abbas	939	25	37.56	5-15	1	—	—

THE 1983 FIRST-CLASS SEASON STATISTICAL HIGHLIGHTS

Compiled by Brian Croudy

HIGHEST INNINGS TOTALS

634-7	Middlesex v Essex at Chelmsford
544-9d	New Zealanders v Somerset at Taunton
529-8d	Northamptonshire v Glamorgan at Cardiff
528	Somerset v Leicestershire at Leicester
470-8d	Warwickshire v Kent at Folkestone
462	Somerset v Kent at Taunton
454-7d	Hampshire v Derbyshire at Derby
451-9d	Surrey v Worcestershire at Worcester
449-6d	Nottinghamshire v Warwickshire at Nottingham
446-6d	England v New Zealand at the Oval (1st Test)
440	Lancashire v Worcestershire at Manchester
439-4d	Northamptonshire v Derbyshire at Derby
438-3d	Leicestershire v Warwickshire at Birmingham
437-9d	Kent v Derbyshire at Chesterfield
434-5d	Yorkshire v Nottinghamshire at Worksop
432-7	Yorkshire v Hampshire at Southampton
429-8d	Lancashire v Glamorgan at Manchester
424-5d	Kent v Yorkshire at Sheffield
422	Kent v Glamorgan at Canterbury
420	England v New Zealand at Nottingham (4th Test)
420	Hampshire v Yorkshire at Southampton
419-8d	Middlesex v Derbyshire at Uxbridge
417-2	Warwickshire v Glamorgan at Birmingham
414-2	Warwickshire v Gloucestershire at Birmingham
413-8d	Essex v Worcestershire at Colchester
410-6	Hampshire v Essex at Southend
408-4d	Yorkshire v Glamorgan at Middlesborough
408-6	Sussex v Somerset at Taunton
407	Worcestershire v Derbyshire at Derby
405-5d	Northamptonshire v Somerset at Weston-Super-Mare
404-6d	Hampshire v Nottinghamshire at Bournemouth
402-6d	Worcestershire v Warwickshire at Birmingham

LOWEST INNINGS TOTALS

14	Surrey v Essex at Chelmsford
53	Nottinghamshire v Derbyshire at Derby
65	Lancashire v Nottinghamshire at Nottingham
69	Worcestershire v Nottinghamshire at Worcester
76	Somerset v Hampshire at Bournemouth
78 74	Middlesex v Warwickshire at Birmingham
79	Derbyshire v Leicestershire at Derby
81	Northamptonshire v Essex at Ilford
82	Gloucestershire v Essex at Colchester
83	Hampshire v Yorkshire at Southampton
83	Middlesex v Essex at Chelmsford

84	Worcestershire v Essex at Colchester
86	Nottinghamshire v Lancashire at Nottingham
86	Somerset v Hampshire at Taunton
87	Kent v Middlesex at Dartford
92	Derbyshire v Essex at Derby
93	Middlesex v Somerset at Lord's
97	Cambridge University v Nottinghamshire at Cambridge
98	Nottinghamshire v Northamptonshire at Nottingham

DOUBLE CENTURIES

252	W. Larkins for Northamptonshire v Glamorgan at Cardiff
243*	A.I. Kallicharran for Warwickshire v Glamorgan at Birmingham
236	W. Larkins for Northamptonshire v Derbyshire at Derby
216	M.W. Gatting for Middlesex v New Zealanders at Lord's
216	I.V.A. Richards for Somerset v Leicestershire at Leicester
214*	G. Boycott for Yorkshire v Nottinghamshire at Worksop
209*	A.I. Kallicharran for Warwickshire v Lancashire at Birmingham
208*	T.A. Lloyd for Warwickshire v Gloucestershire at Birmingham
207	R.T. Robinson for Nottinghamshire v Warwickshire at Nottingham
201*	N.E. Briers for Leicestershire v Warwickshire at Birmingham

OPENING BATSMAN CARRYING HIS BAT

124* (230)	T.A. Lloyd for Warwickshire v Surrey at the Oval
112* (233)	G. Boycott for Yorkshire v Derbyshire at Sheffield
109* (240)	J.A. Hopkins for Glamorgan v Derbyshire at Swansea
103* (161)	R.G.P. Ellis for Oxford University v Glamorgan at Oxford
100* (198)	J.C. Balderstone for Leicestershire v Worcestershire at Hereford
63* (136)	J.A. Ormrod for Worcestershire v Derbyshire at Derby
44* (83)	G.A. Barlow for Middlesex v Essex at Chelmsford

CENTURY IN EACH INNINGS

168 & 119	D.G. Aslett for Kent v Derbyshire at Chesterfield
102 & 152*	M.R. Benson for Kent v Warwickshire at Birmingham
163 & 141*	G. Boycott for Yorkshire v Nottinghamshire at Bradford
139 & 124	R.J. Boyd-Moss for Cambridge University v Oxford University at Lord's
104 & 100*	C.G. Greenidge for Hampshire v Lancashire at Liverpool

CENTURY BEFORE LUNCH

G. Boycott for Yorkshire v Nottinghamshire at Bradford
G.A. Gooch for Essex v Cambridge University at Cambridge
W. Larkins for Nottinghamshire v Glamorgan at Cardiff (also included 100 between lunch and tea)

CENTURY ON DEBUT

100	D.A. Banks for Worcestershire v Oxford University at Oxford
122	A.A. Metcalfe for Yorkshire v Nottinghamshire at Bradford

BROTHERS SCORING A HUNDRED IN SAME INNINGS

C.L. Smith (100) & R.A. Smith (100*) for Hampshire v Lancashire at Bournemouth

HIGHEST PARTNERSHIPS

342	2nd	W. Larkins and P. Willey for Northamptonshire v Lancashire at Northampton (County Record)
321	3rd	T.E. Jesty and C.L. Smith for Hampshire v Derbyshire at Derby
318	3rd	C.T. Radley and M.W. Gatting for Middlesex v New Zealanders at Lord's
308	2nd	T.A. Lloyd and A.I. Kallicharran for Warwickshire v Glamorgan at Birmingham
293	2nd	T.A. Lloyd and A.I. Kallicharran for Warwickshire v Lancashire at Birmingham
290	2nd	D.R. Turner and M.C.J. Nicholas for Hampshire v Oxford University at Oxford
289	2nd	D.L. Amiss and T.A. Lloyd for Warwickshire v Gloucestershire at Birmingham
269	3rd	C.L. Smith and M.C.J. Nicholas for Hampshire v Essex at Southend
268	6th	J.N. Shepherd and D.A. Graveney for Gloucestershire v Warwickshire at Birmingham
263	1st	G.A. Gooch and B.R. Hardie for Essex v Cambridge University at Cambridge
248	5th	M.W. Gatting and J.E. Emburey for Middlesex v Essex at Chelmsford
248	1st	G. Boycott and A.A. Metcalfe for Yorkshire v Nottinghamshire at Bradford
245	3rd	G. Fowler and D.P. Hughes for Lancashire v Glamorgan at Manchester
242	3rd	W. Larkins and P. Willey for Northamptonshire v Glamorgan at Cardiff
228	5th	C.S. Cowdrey and E.A.E. Baptiste for Kent v Yorkshire at Sheffield
224	3rd	G. Boycott and K. Sharp for Yorkshire v Gloucestershire at Cheltenham
223	1st	G. Fowler and C.J. Tavaré for England v New Zealand at the Oval (1st Test)
222	2nd	G. Fowler and F.C. Hayes for Lancashire v Yorkshire at Manchester
221	4th	P.W. Romaines and J.N. Shepherd for Gloucestershire v Kent at Bristol
211	3rd	W. Larkins and R.J. Boyd-Moss for Northamptonshire v Derbyshire at Derby
210	2nd	G.A. Barlow and C.T. Radley for Middlesex v Essex at Chelmsford
210	3rd	G.P. Howarth and M.D. Crowe for New Zealand v Essex at Chelmsford
210	6th	D.A. Francis and S.P. Henderson for Glamorgan v Warwickshire at Birmingham
207	3rd	A.I. Kallicharran and D.L. Amiss for Warwickshire v Surrey at the Oval
201	1st	G. Fowler and S.J. O'Shaughnessy for Lancashire v Leicestershire at Manchester
172	8th	I.V.A. Richards and I.T. Botham for Somerset v Leicestershire at Leicester

EIGHT WICKETS IN AN INNINGS

8-42	S.R. Barwick for Glamorgan v Worcestershire at Worcester
8-46	S.T. Jefferies for Lancashire v Nottinghamshire at Nottingham

THIRTEEN OR MORE WICKETS IN A MATCH

14-158 (7-103 & 7-55) D.L. Underwood for Kent v Worcestershire at Canterbury
13-161 (7-88 & 6-73) D.L. Underwood for Kent v Nottinghamshire at Nottingham

HAT-TRICKS

D.A. Graveney for Gloucestershire v Leicestershire at Leicester
Imran Khan for Sussex v Warwickshire at Birmingham
M.D. Marshall for Hampshire v Somerset at Taunton
N. Phillip for Essex v Northamptonshire at Wellingborough

SIX CATCHES IN A MATCH BY A FIELDER

K.P. Tomlins for Middlesex v Hampshire at Uxbridge
A.J. Lamb for England v New Zealand at Lord's (3rd Test)

SIX DISMISSALS AND OVER IN AN INNINGS BY A WICKET-KEEPER

6 C. Maynard for Lancashire v Glamorgan at Swansea
6 R.W. Taylor for Derbyshire v Yorkshire at Sheffield

EIGHT DISMISSALS AND OVER IN A MATCH BY A WICKET-KEEPER

9 (9c) D.E. East for Essex v Sussex at Hove
8 (8c) R.J. Parks for Hampshire v Somerset at Bournemouth
8 (8c) C. Maynard for Lancashire v Glamorgan at Swansea

FIRST TO TARGETS

1000 runs: K.S. McEwan on June 22nd
2000 runs: K.S. McEwan on August 25th
100 wkts: J.E. Emburey on September 2nd

OUTSTANDING ANALYSIS

4.3-1-6-6 Imran Khan for Sussex v Warwickshire at Birmingham

MOST EXTRAS CONCEDED IN AN INNINGS

52 by Northamptonshire v Leicestershire at Leicester
50 by Kent v Warwickshire at Folkestone

FIRST-CLASS CRICKET RECORDS

COMPLETE TO END OF 1983 SEASON

Highest Innings Totals

1107	Victoria v New South Wales (Melbourne)	1926-27
1059	Victoria v Tasmania (Melbourne)	1922-23
951-7d	Sind v Baluchistan (Karachi)	1973-74
918	New South Wales v South Australia (Sydney)	1900-01
912-8d	Holkar v Mysore (Indore)	1945-46
910-6d	Railways v Dera Ismail Khan (Lahore)	1964-65
903-7d	England v Australia (Oval)	1938
887	Yorkshire v Warwickshire (Birmingham)	1896
849	England v West Indies (Kingston)	1929-30

NB. There are 22 instances of a side making 800 runs or more in an innings, the last occasion being 951-7 declared by Sind as above.

Lowest Innings Totals

12*	Oxford University v MCC and Ground (Oxford)	1877
12	Northamptonshire v Gloucestershire (Gloucester)	1907
13	Auckland v Canterbury (Auckland)	1877-78
13	Nottinghamshire v Yorkshire (Nottingham)	1901
14	Surrey v Essex (Chelmsford)	1983
15	MCC v Surrey (Lord's)	1839
15*	Victoria v MCC (Melbourne)	1903-04
15*	Northamptonshire v Yorkshire (Northampton)	1908
15	Hampshire v Warwickshire (Birmingham)	1922
16	MCC and Ground v Surrey (Lord's)	1872
16	Derbyshire v Nottinghamshire (Nottingham)	1879
16	Surrey v Nottinghamshire (Oval)	1880
16	Warwickshire v Kent (Tonbridge)	1913
16	Trinidad v Barbados (Bridgetown)	1941-42
16	Border v Natal (East London)	1959-60

**Batted one man short*

NB. There are 26 instances of a side making less than 20 in an innings, the last occasion being 16 and 18 by Border v Natal at East London in 1959-60. The total of 34 is the lowest by one side in a match.

Highest Aggregates in a Match

2376	(38)	Bombay v Maharashtra (Poona)	1948-49
2078	(40)	Bombay v Holkar (Bombay)	1944-45
1981	(35)	South Africa v England (Durban)	1938-39
1929	(39)	New South Wales v South Australia (Sydney)	1925-26
1911	(34)	New South Wales v Victoria (Sydney)	1908-09
1905	(40)	Otago v Wellington (Dunedin)	1923-24

In England the highest are:

1723	(31)	England v Australia (Leeds) 5 day match	1948
1601	(29)	England v Australia (Lord's) 4 day match	1930
1507	(28)	England v West Indies (Oval) 5 day match	1976
1502	(28)	MCC v New Zealanders (Lord's)	1927
1499	(31)	T.N. Pearce's XI v Australians (Scarborough)	1961
1496	(24)	England v Australia (Nottingham) 4 day match	1938
1494	(37)	England v Australia (Oval) 4 day match	1934
1492	(33)	Worcestershire v Oxford U (Worcester)	1904
1477	(32)	Hampshire v Oxford U (Southampton)	1913
1477	(33)	England v South Africa (Oval) 4 day match	1947
1475	(27)	Northamptonshire v Surrey (Northampton)	1920

Lowest Aggregate in a Match

105	(31)	MCC v Australia (Lord's)	1878
134	(30)	England v The B's (Lord's)	1831
147	(40)	Kent v Sussex (Sevenoaks)	1828
149	(30)	England v Kent (Lord's)	1858
150	(30)	Cambridge Town v MCC (Chatteris)	1832
151	(30)	Canterbury v Otago (Christchurch)	1866-67
153	(37)	MCC v Sussex (Lord's)	1843
153	(31)	Otago v Canterbury (Dunedin)	1896-97
156	(30)	Nelson v Wellington (Nelson)	1885-86
158	(22)	Surrey v Worcestershire (Oval)	1954

Wickets that fell are given in parentheses.

Tie Matches

Due to the change of law made in 1948 for tie matches, a tie is now a rarity. The law states that only if the match is played out and the scores are equal is the result a tie.

The most recent tied matches are as follows:

Yorkshire (351-4d & 113) v Leicestershire (328 & 136) at Huddersfield 1954
Sussex (172 & 120) v Hampshire (153 & 139) at Eastbourne 1955
Victoria (244 & 197) v New South Wales (281 & 160) at Melbourne (St. Kilda) 1956-57
(The first tie in Sheffield Shield cricket)
T.N. Pearce's XI (313-7d & 258) v New Zealanders (268 & 303-8d) at Scarborough 1958
Essex (364-6d & 176-8d) v Gloucestershire (329 & 211) at Leyton 1959
Australia (505 & 232) v West Indies (453 & 284) at Brisbane 1960-61
(The first tie in Test cricket)
Bahawalpur (123 & 282) v Lahore B (127 & 278) at Bahawalpur 1961-62
Middlesex (327-5d & 123-9d v Hampshire (277 & 173) at Portsmouth 1967
England XI (312-8d & 190-3d) v England Under-25 XI (320-9d & 182) at Scarborough 1968
Yorkshire (106-9d & 207) v Middlesex (102 & 211) at Bradford 1973
Sussex (245 & 173-5d) v Essex (200-8d & 218) at Hove 1974
South Australia (431 & 171-7d) v Queensland (340-8d & 262) at Adelaide 1976-77
England XI (296-6d & 104) v Central Districts (198 & 202) at New Plymouth 1977-78
Peshawar (139 & 188) v Allied Bank (240 & 87) at Peshawar 1979-80
Victoria (230-5d & 245) v New Zealanders (301-9d & 174-3d) at Melbourne 1982-83

Highest Individual Scores

499	Hanif Mohammad, Karachi v Bahawalpur (Karachi)	1958-59
452*	D.G. Bradman, New South Wales v Queensland (Sydney)	1929-30
443*	B.B. Nimbalkar, Maharashtra v Kathiawar (Poona)	1948-49
437	W.H. Ponsford, Victoria v Queensland (Melbourne)	1927-28
429	W.H. Ponsford, Victoria v Tasmania (Melbourne)	1922-23
428	Aftab Baloch, Sind v Baluchistan (Karachi)	1973-74
424	A.C. MacLaren, Lancashire v Somerset (Taunton)	1895
385	B. Sutcliffe, Otago v Canterbury (Christchurch)	1952-53
383	C.W. Gregory, New South Wales v Queensland (Brisbane)	1906-07
369	D.G. Bradman, South Australia v Tasmania (Adelaide)	1935-36
365*	C. Hill, South Australia v New South Wales (Adelaide)	1900-01
365*	G.S. Sobers, West Indies v Pakistan (Kingston)	1957-58
364	L. Hutton, England v Australia (Oval)	1938
359*	V.M. Merchant, Bombay v Maharashtra (Bombay)	1943-44
359	R.B. Simpson, New South Wales v Queensland (Brisbane)	1963-64
357*	R. Abel, Surrey v Somerset (Oval)	1899
357	D.G. Bradman, South Australia v Victoria (Melbourne)	1935-36
356	B.A. Richards, South Australia v Western Australia (Perth)	1970-71
355	B. Sutcliffe, Otago v Auckland (Dunedin)	1949-50
352	W.H. Ponsford, Victoria v New South Wales (Melbourne)	1926-27
350	Rashid Israr, Habib Bank v National Bank (Lahore)	1976-77

NB. There are 93 instances of a batsman scoring 300 or more in an innings, the last occasion being 311 by G.M. Turner for Worcestershire v Warwickshire (Worcester) 1982.*

Most Centuries in a Season

18	D.C.S. Compton	1947
16	J.B. Hobbs	1925
15	W.R. Hammond	1938
14	H. Sutcliffe	1932

Most Centuries in an Innings

6	for Holkar v Mysore (Indore)	1945-46
5	for New South Wales v South Australia (Sydney)	1900-01
5	for Australia v West Indies (Kingston)	1954-55

Most Centuries in Successive Innings

6	C.B. Fry	1901
6	D.G. Bradman	1938-39
6	M.J. Procter	1970-71
5	E.D. Weekes	1955-56

Two Double Centuries in a Match

A.E. Fagg, 244 and 202* for Kent v Essex (Colchester)	1938

A Double Century and a Century in a Match

C.B. Fry, 125 and 229, Sussex v Surrey (Hove)	1900
W.W. Armstrong, 157* and 245, Victoria v South Australia (Melbourne)	1920-21
H.T.W. Hardinge, 207 and 102* for Kent v Surrey (Blackheath)	1921
C.P. Mead, 113 and 224, Hampshire v Sussex (Horsham)	1921
K.S. Duleepsinhji, 115 and 246, Sussex v Kent (Hastings)	1929
D.G. Bradman, 124 and 225, Woodfull's XI v Ryder's XI (Sydney)	1929-30
B. Sutcliffe, 243 and 100*, New Zealanders v Essex (Southend)	1949
M.R. Hallam, 210* and 157, Leicestershire v Glamorgan (Leicester)	1959
M.R. Hallam, 203* and 143* Leicestershire v Sussex (Worthing)	1961
Hanumant Singh, 109 and 213*, Rajasthan v Bombay (Bombay)	1966-67
Salahuddin, 256 and 102*, Karachi v East Pakistan (Karachi)	1968-69
K.D. Walters, 242 and 103, Australia v West Indies (Sydney)	1968-69
S.M. Gavaskar, 124 and 220, India v West Indies (Port of Spain)	1970-71
L.G. Rowe, 214 and 100*, West Indies v New Zealand (Kingston)	1971-72
G.S. Chappell, 247* and 133, Australia v New Zealand (Wellington)	1973-74
L. Baichan, 216* and 102, Berbice v Demerara (Georgetown)	1973-74
Zaheer Abbas, 216* and 156*, Gloucestershire v Surrey (Oval)	1976
Zaheer Abbas, 230* and 104*, Gloucestershire v Kent (Canterbury)	1976
Zaheer Abbas, 205* and 108*, Gloucestershire v Sussex (Cheltenham)	1977
Saadat Ali, 141 and 222, Income Tax v Multan (Multan)	1977-78
Talat Ali, 214* and 104, Pakistan International Airways v Punjab (Lahore)	1978-79
Shafiq Ahmed, 129 and 217*, National Bank v Muslim Commercial Bank (Karachi)	1978-79
D.W. Randall, 209 and 146, Nottinghamshire v Middlesex (Nottingham)	1979
Zaheer Abbas, 215* and 150*, Gloucestershire v Somerset (Bath)	1981
Qasim Omar, 210* and 110, Muslim Commercial Bank v Lahore (Lahore)	1982-83

Two Centuries in a Match on Most Occasions

8 Zaheer Abbas 7 W.R. Hammond 6 J.B. Hobbs, G.M. Turner

Most Centuries

J.B. Hobbs, 197 (175 in England); E.H. Hendren, 170 (151); W.R. Hammond, 167 (134); C.P. Mead, 153 (145); H. Sutcliffe, 149 (135); F.E. Woolley, 145 (135); G. Boycott, 139 (112); L. Hutton, 129 (105); W.G. Grace 126 (125); D.C.S. Compton, 123 (92); T.W. Graveney, 122 (91); D.G. Bradman, 117 (41); M.C. Cowdrey, 107 (80); A. Sandham, 107 (87); Zaheer Abbas, 105 (58); T.W. Hayward, 104 (100); J.H. Edrich, 103 (90); G.M. Turner, 103 (78); L.E.G. Ames, 102 (89); G.E. Tyldesley, 102 (94).

Highest Individual Batting Aggregate in a Season

Runs		*Season*	*M*	*Innings*	*NO*	*HS*	*Avge*	*100s*
3,816	D.C.S. Compton	1947	30	50	8	246	90.85	18
3,539	W.J. Edrich	1947	30	52	8	267*	80.43	12

NB. The feat of scoring 3,000 runs in a season has been achieved on 28 occasions, the last instance being by W.E. Alley (3,019 runs, av. 59.96) in 1961.
Since the reduction of the matches in the County Championship in 1969, the highest aggregate in a season is 2,554 runs (av. 75.11) by Zaheer Abbas in 1976.

Partnerships for First Wicket

561	Waheed Mirza and Mansoor Akhtar, Karachi Whites v Quetta (Karachi)	1976-77
555	H. Sutcliffe and P. Holmes, Yorkshire v Essex (Leyton)	1932
554	J.T. Brown and J. Tunnicliffe, Yorkshire v Derbyshire (Chesterfield)	1898
490	E.H. Bowley and J.G. Langridge, Sussex v Middlesex (Hove)	1933
456	W.H. Ponsford and E.R. Mayne, Victoria v Queensland (Melbourne)	1923-24
451*	S. Desai and R.M.H. Binny, Karnataka v Kerala (Chikmagalur)	1977-78
428	J.B. Hobbs and A. Sandham, Surrey v Oxford U (Oval)	1926
424	J.F.W. Nicholson and I.J. Siedle, Natal v Orange Free State (Bloemfontein)	1926-27
421	S.M. Gavaskar and G.A. Parkar, Bombay v Bengal (Bombay)	1981-82
418	Kamal Najamuddin and Khalid Alvi, Karachi v Railways (Karachi)	1980-81
413	V. Mankad and P. Roy, India v New Zealand (Madras)	1955-56
405	C.P.S. Chauhan and M. Gupte, Maharashtra v Vidarbha (Poona)	1972-73

Partnerships for Second Wicket

465*	J.A. Jameson and R.B. Kanhai, Warwickshire v Gloucestershire (Birmingham)	1974
455	K.V. Bhandarkar and B.B. Nimbalkar, Maharashtra v Kathiawar (Poona)	1948-49
451	D.G. Bradman and W.H. Ponsford, Australia v England (Oval)	1934
446	C.C. Hunte and G.S. Sobers, West Indies v Pakistan (Kingston)	1957-58
429*	J.G. Dewes and G.H.G. Doggart, Cambridge U v Essex (Cambridge)	1949
426	Arshad Pervez and Mohsin Khan, Habib Bank v Income Tax Department (Lahore)	1977-78
398	W. Gunn and A. Shrewsbury, Nottinghamshire v Sussex (Nottingham)	1890

Partnerships for Third Wicket

456	Aslam Ali and Khalid Irtiza, United Bank v Multan (Karachi)	1975-76
451	Mudassar Nazar and Javed Miandad, Pakistan v India (Hyderabad)	1982-83
445	P.E. Whitelaw and W.N. Carson, Auckland v Otago (Dunedin)	1936-37
434	J.B. Stollmeyer and G.E. Gomez, Trinidad v British Guiana (Port of Spain)	1946-47
424*	W.J. Edrich and D.C.S. Compton, Middlesex v Somerset (Lord's)	1948
410	R.S. Modi and L. Amarnath, India v Rest (Calcutta)	1946-47
399	R.T. Simpson and D.C.S. Compton, MCC v NE Transvaal (Benoni)	1948-49

Partnerships for Fourth Wicket

577	Gul Mahomed and V.S. Hazare, Baroda v Holkar (Baroda)	1946-47
574*	C.L. Walcott and F.M.M. Worrell, Barbados v Trinidad (Port of Spain)	1945-46
502*	F.M.M. Worrell and J.D.C. Goddard, Barbados v Trinidad (Bridgetown)	1943-44
470	A.I. Kallicharran and G.W. Humpage, Warwickshire v Lancashire (Southport)	1982
448	R. Abel and T.W. Hayward, Surrey v Yorkshire (Oval)	1899
424	I.S. Lee and S.O. Quin, Victoria v Tasmania (Melbourne)	1933-34
411	P.B.H. May and M.C. Cowdrey, England v West Indies (Birmingham)	1957
410	G. Abraham and B. Pandit, Kerala v Andhra (Palghat)	1959-60
402	W. Watson and T.W. Graveney, MCC v British Guiana (Georgetown)	1953-54
402	R.B. Kanhai and K. Ibadulla, Warwickshire v Nottinghamshire (Nottingham)	1968

Partnerships for Fifth Wicket

405	D.G. Bradman and S.G. Barnes, Australia v England (Sydney)	1946-47
397	W. Bardsley and C. Kellaway, New South Wales v South Australia (Sydney)	1920-21
393	E.G. Arnold and W.B. Burns, Worcestershire v Warwickshire (Birmingham)	1909
360	U.M. Merchant and M.N. Raiji, Bombay v Hyderabad (Bombay)	1947-48
355	Altaf Shah and Tanq Bashir, HBFC v Multan (Multan)	1976-77

Partnerships for Sixth Wicket

487*	G.A. Headley and C.C. Passailaigue, Jamaica v Lord Tennyson's XI (Kingston)	1931-32
428	W.W. Armstrong and M.A. Noble, Australians v Sussex (Hove)	1902
411	R.M. Poore and E.G. Wynyard, Hampshire v Somerset (Taunton)	1899
376	R. Subba Row and A. Lightfoot, Northamptonshire v Surrey (Oval)	1958
371	V.M. Merchant and R.S. Modi, Bombay v Maharashtra (Bombay)	1943-44

Partnerships for Seventh Wicket

347	D.S. Atkinson and C.C. Depeiza, West Indies v Australia (Bridgetown)	1954-55
344	K.S. Ranjitsinhji and W. Newham, Sussex v Essex (Leyton)	1902
340	K.J. Key and H. Philipson, Oxford U v Middlesex (Chiswick Park)	1887
336	F.C.W. Newman and C.R. Maxwell, Cahn's XI v Leicestershire (Nottingham)	1935
335	C.W. Andrews and E.C. Bensted, Queensland v New South Wales (Sydney)	1934-35

Partnerships for Eighth Wicket

433	V.T. Trumper and A. Sims, Australians v Canterbury (Christchurch)	1913-14
292	R. Peel and Lord Hawke, Yorkshire v Warwickshire (Birmingham)	1896
270	V.T. Trumper and E.P. Barbour, New South Wales v Victoria (Sydney)	1912-13
263	D.R. Wilcox and R.M. Taylor, Essex v Warwickshire (Southend)	1946
255	E.A.V. Williams and E.A. Martindale, Barbados v Trinidad (Bridgetown)	1935-36

Partnerships for Ninth Wicket

283	A.R. Warren and J. Chapman, Derbyshire v Warwickshire (Blackwell)	1910
251	J.W.H.T. Douglas and S.N. Hare, Essex v Derbyshire (Leyton)	1921
245	V.S. Hazare and N.D. Nagarwalla, Maharashtra v Baroda (Poona)	1939-40
239	H.B. Cave and I.B. Leggat, Central Districts v Otago (Dunedin)	1952-53
232	C. Hill and E. Walkley, South Australia v New South Wales (Adelaide)	1900-01

Partnerships for Tenth Wicket

307	A.F. Kippax and J.E.H. Hooker, New South Wales v Victoria (Melbourne)	1928-29
249	C.T. Sarwate and S.N. Bannerjee, Indians v Surrey (Oval)	1946
235	F.E. Woolley and A. Fielder, Kent v Worcestershire (Stourbridge)	1909
230	R.W. Nicholls and W. Roche, Middlesex v Kent (Lord's)	1899
228	R. Illingworth and K. Higgs, Leicestershire v Northamptonshire (Leicester)	1977
218	F.H. Vigar and T.P.B. Smith, Essex v Derbyshire (Chesterfield)	1947

BOWLING

Most Wickets in a Season

W		*Season*	*M*	*O*	*M*	*R*	*Avge*
304	A.P. Freeman	1928	37	1976.1	423	5489	18.05
298	A.P. Freeman	1933	33	2039	651	4549	15.26

NB. The feat of taking 250 wickets in a season has been achieved on 12 occasions, the last instance being by A.P. Freeman in 1933 as above. 200 or more wickets in a season have been taken on 59 occasions, the last instance being by G.A.R. Lock (212 wkts, avge 12.02) in 1957.

The most wickets taken in a season since the reduction of County Championship matches in 1969 are as follows.

W		*Season*	*M*	*O*	*M*	*R*	*Avge*
134	M.D. Marshall	1982	22	822	225	2108	15.73
131	L.R. Gibbs	1971	23	1024.1	295	2475	18.89
121	R.D. Jackman	1980	23	746.2	220	1864	15.40

NB. 100 wickets in a season have been taken on 36 occasions since 1969.

All Ten Wickets in an Innings

The feat has been achieved on 71 occasions.
On three occasions: A.P. Freeman, 1929, 1930 and 1931.
On two occasions: J.C. Laker, 1956, H. Verity, 1931 and 1932, V.E. Walker, 1859 and 1865.
Instances since the war:
W.E. Hollies, Warwickshire v Nottinghamshire (Birmingham) 1946; J.M. Sims of Middlesex playing for East v West (Kingston) 1948; J.K.R. Graveney, Gloucestershire v Derbyshire (Chesterfield) 1949; T.E. Bailey, Essex v Lancashire (Clacton) 1949; R. Berry, Lancashire v Worcestershire (Blackpool) 1953; S.P. Gupte, Bombay v Pakistan Services (Bombay), 1954-55; J.C. Laker, Surrey v Australians (Oval) 1956; J.C. Laker, England v Australia (Manchester) 1956; G.A.R. Lock, Surrey v Kent (Blackheath) 1956; K. Smales, Nottinghamshire v Gloucestershire (Stroud) 1956; P. Chatterjee, Bengal v Assam (Jorhat) 1956-57; J.D. Bannister, Warwickshire v Combined Services (Birmingham) 1959; A.J.G. Pearson, Cambridge U v Leicestershire (Loughborough) 1961; N.I. Thomson, Sussex v Warwickshire (Worthing) 1964; P.J. Allan, Queensland v Victoria (Melbourne) 1965-66; I. Brayshaw, Western Australia v Victoria (Perth) 1967-68; Shahid Mahmood, Karachi Whites v Khairpur (Karachi) 1969-70; E.E. Hemmings, International XI v West Indies XI (Kingston) 1982-83.

Nineteen Wickets in a Match

J.C. Laker 19-90 (9-37 and 10-53), England v Australia (Manchester) 1956.

Seventeen Wickets in a Match

In addition to Laker's 19 wickets the feat has been achieved on 18 occasions. Instances between the two wars were: A.P. Freeman (for 67 runs), Kent v Sussex (Hove) 1922; F.C.L. Matthews (89 runs), Nottinghamshire v Northamptonshire (Nottingham) 1923; C.W.L. Parker (56 runs), Gloucestershire v Essex (Gloucester 1925; G.R. Cox (106 runs), Sussex v Warwickshire (Horsham) 1926; A.P. Freeman (92 runs), Kent v Warwickshire (Folkestone)1932; H. Verity (91 runs), Yorkshire v Essex (Leyton) 1933; J.C. Clay (212 runs), Glamorgan v Worcestershire (Swansea) 1937; T.W.J. Goddard (106 runs), Gloucestershire v Kent (Bristol) 1939. There has been no instance since the last war.

Most Hat-tricks in a Career

7 D.V.P. Wright.
6 T.W.J. Goddard, C.W.L. Parker.
5 S. Haigh, V.W.C. Jupp, A.E.G. Rhodes, F.A. Tarrant.

The 'Double' Event

3,000 runs and 100 wickets: J.H. Parks, 1937.
2,000 runs and 200 wickets: G.H. Hirst, 1906.
2,000 runs and 100 wickets: F.E. Woolley (4), J.W. Hearne (3), G.H. Hirst (2), W. Rhodes (2), T.E. Bailey, D.E. Davies, W.G. Grace, G.L. Jessop, V.W.C. Jupp, James Langridge, F.A. Tarrant, C.L. Townsend, L.F. Townsend.
1,000 runs and 200 wickets: M.W. Tate (3), A.E. Trott (2), A.S. Kennedy.
Most 'Doubles': W. Rhodes (16), G.H. Hirst (14), V.W.C. Jupp (10).
'Double' in first season: D.B. Close, 1949. At the age of 18, Close is the youngest player ever to perform this feat.
The feat of scoring 1,000 runs and taking 100 wickets has been achieved on 302 occasions, the last instance being F.J. Titmus in 1967.

FIELDING

Most catches in a season:	78 W.R. Hammond	1928
	77 M.J. Stewart	1957
Most catches in a match:	10 W.R. Hammond, Gloucestershire v Surrey (Cheltenham)	1928
Most catches in an innings:	7 M.J. Stewart, Surrey v Northamptonshire (Northampton)	1957
	7 A.S. Brown, Gloucestershire v Nottinghamshire (Nottingham)	1966

WICKET-KEEPING

Most dismissals in a season:	127 (79ct, 48st), L.E.G. Ames	1929

NB. The feat of making 100 dismissals in a season has been achieved on 12 occasions, the last instance being by R. Booth (100 dismissals–91ct, 9st) in 1964.

Most dismissals in a match:	12 E. Pooley (8 ct, 4 st) Surrey v Sussex (Oval)	1868
	12 D. Tallon (9 ct, 3 st), Queensland v New South Wales (Sydney)	1938-39
	12 H.B. Taber (9 ct, 3 st), New South Wales v South Australia (Adelaide)	1968-69
Most catches in a match:	11 A. Long, Surrey v Sussex (Hove)	1964
	11 R.W. Marsh, Western Australia v Victoria (Perth)	1975-76
	11 D.L. Bairstow, Yorkshire v Derbyshire (Scarborough)	1982
Most dismissals in an innings:	8 A.T.W. Grout (8 ct), Queensland v W. Australia (Brisbane)	1959-60

TEST CRICKET RECORDS

(including India v Pakistan and West Indies and Australia v Pakistan 1983–84)

HIGHEST INNINGS TOTALS

903-7d	England v Australia (Oval)	1938
849	England v West Indies (Kingston)	1929-30
790-3d	West Indies v Pakistan (Kingston)	1957-58
758-8d	Australia v West Indies (Kingston)	1954-55
729-6d	Australia v England (Lord's)	1930
701	Australia v England (Oval)	1934
695	Australia v England (Oval)	1930
687-8d	West Indies v England (Oval)	1976
681-8d	West Indies v England (Port of Spain)	1953-54
674	Australia v India (Adelaide)	1947-48
668	Australia v West Indies (Bridgetown)	1954-55
659-8d	Australia v England (Sydney)	1946-47
658-8d	England v Australia (Nottingham)	1938
657-8d	Pakistan v West Indies (Bridgetown)	1957-58
656-8d	Australia v England (Manchester)	1964
654-5	England v South Africa (Durban)	1938-39
652	Pakistan v India (Faisalabad)	1982-83
652-8d	West Indies v England (Lord's)	1973
650-6d	Australia v West Indies (Bridgetown)	1964-65

The highest innings for the countries not mentioned above are:

644-7d	India v West Indies (Kanpur)	1978-79
622-9d	South Africa v Australia (Durban)	1969-70
551-9d	New Zealand v England (Lord's)	1973
454	Sri Lanka v Pakistan (Faisalabad)	1981-82

LOWEST INNINGS TOTALS

26	New Zealand v England (Auckland)	1954-55
30	South Africa v England (Port Elizabeth)	1895-96
30	South Africa v England (Birmingham)	1924
35	South Africa v England (Cape Town)	1898-99
36	Australia v England (Birmingham)	1902
36	South Africa v Australia (Melbourne)	1931-32
42	Australia v England (Sydney)	1887-88
42	New Zealand v Australia (Wellington)	1945-46
42†	India v England (Lord's)	1974
43	South Africa v England (Cape Town)	1888-89
44	Australia v England (Oval)	1896
45	England v Australia (Sydney)	1886-87
45	South Africa v Australia (Melbourne)	1931-32
47	South Africa v England (Cape Town)	1888-89
47	New Zealand v England (Lord's)	1958

†*Batted one man short*

The lowest innings for the countries not mentioned above are:

76	West Indies v Pakistan (Dacca)	1958-59
62	Pakistan v Australia (Perth)	1981-82
93	Sri Lanka v New Zealand (Wellington)	1982-83

HIGHEST INDIVIDUAL INNINGS

365*	G.S. Sobers, West Indies v Pakistan (Kingston)	1957-58
364	L. Hutton, England v Australia (Oval)	1938
337	Hanif Mohammad, Pakistan v West Indies (Bridgetown)	1957-58
336*	W.R. Hammond, England v New Zealand (Auckland)	1932-33
334	D.G. Bradman, Australia v England (Leeds)	1930
325	A. Sandham, England v West Indies (Kingston)	1929-30
311	R.B. Simpson, Australia v England (Manchester)	1964
310*	J.H. Edrich, England v New Zealand (Leeds)	1965
307	R.M. Cowper, Australia v England (Melbourne)	1965-66
304	D.G. Bradman, Australia v England (Leeds)	1934
302	L.G. Rowe, West Indies v England (Bridgetown)	1973-74
299*	D.G. Bradman, Australia v South Africa (Adelaide)	1931-32
291	I.V.A. Richards, West Indies v England (Oval)	1976
287	R.E. Foster, England v Australia (Sydney)	1903-04
285*	P.B.H. May, England v West Indies (Birmingham)	1957
280*	Javed Miandad, Pakistan v India (Hyderabad)	1982-83
278	D.C.S. Compton, England v Pakistan (Nottingham)	1954
274	R.G. Pollock, South Africa v Australia (Durban)	1969-70
274	Zaheer Abbas, Pakistan v England (Birmingham)	1971
270*	G.A. Headley, West Indies v England (Kingston)	1934-35
270	D.G. Bradman, Australia v England (Melbourne)	1936-37
268	G.N. Yallop, Australia v Pakistan (Melbourne)	1983-84
266	W.H. Ponsford, Australia v England (Oval)	1934
262*	D.L. Amiss, England v West Indies (Kingston)	1973-74
261	F.M.M. Worrell, West Indies v England (Nottingham)	1950
260	C.C. Hunte, West Indies v Pakistan (Kingston)	1957-58
259	G.M. Turner, New Zealand v West Indies (Georgetown)	1971-72
258	T.W. Graveney, England v West Indies (Nottingham)	1957
258	S.M. Nurse, West Indies v New Zealand (Christchurch)	1968-69
256	R.B. Kanhai, West Indies v India (Calcutta)	1958-59
256	K.F. Barrington, England v Australia (Manchester)	1964
255*	D.J. McGlew, South Africa v New Zealand (Wellington)	1952-53
254	D.G. Bradman, Australia v England (Leeds)	1930
251	W.R. Hammond, England v Australia (Sydney)	1928-29
250	K.D. Walters, Australia v New Zealand (Christchurch)	1976-77
250	S.F.A.F. Bacchus, West Indies v India (Kanpur)	1978-79

The highest individual innings for other countries are:

236*	S.M. Gavaskar, India v West Indies (Madras)	1983-84
157	S. Wettimuny, Sri Lanka v Pakistan (Faisalabad)	1981-82

HIGHEST RUN AGGREGATES IN A TEST RUBBER

R		*Season*	*T*	*I*	*NO*	*HS*	*Avge*	*100s*	*50s*
974	D.G. Bradman (A v E)	1930	5	7	0	334	139.14	4	—
905	W.R. Hammond (E v A)	1928-29	5	9	1	251	113.12	4	—
834	R.N. Harvey (A v SA)	1952-53	5	9	0	205	92.66	4	3
829	I.V.A. Richards (WI v E)	1976	4	7	0	291	118.42	3	2
827	C.L. Walcott (WI v A)	1954-55	5	10	0	155	82.70	5	2
824	G.S. Sobers (WI v P)	1957-58	5	8	2	365*	137.33	3	3
810	D.G. Bradman (A v E)	1936-37	5	9	0	270	90.00	3	1
806	D.G. Bradman (A v SA)	1931-32	5	5	1	299*	201.50	4	—
779	E.D. Weekes (WI v I)	1948-49	5	7	0	194	111.28	4	2
774	S.M. Gavaskar (I v WI)	1970-71	4	8	3	220	154.80	4	3
761	Mudassar Nazar (P v I)	1982-83	6	8	2	231	126.83	4	1
758	D.G. Bradman (A v E)	1934	5	8	0	304	94.75	2	1
753	D.C.S. Compton (E v SA)	1947	5	8	0	208	94.12	4	2

RECORD WICKET PARTNERSHIPS – ALL TEST CRICKET

1st	413	V. Mankad & P. Roy, I v NZ (Madras)	1955-56
2nd	451	W.H. Ponsford & D.G. Bradman, A v E (Oval)	1934
3rd	451	Mudassar Nazar & Javed Miandad, P v I (Hyderabad)	1982-83
4th	411	P.B.H. May & M.C. Cowdrey, E v WI (Birmingham)	1957
5th	405	S.G. Barnes & D.G. Bradman, A v E (Sydney)	1946-47
6th	346	J.H.W. Fingleton & D.G. Bradman, A v E (Melbourne	1936-37
7th	347	D.S. Atkinson & C.C. Depeiza, WI v A (Bridgetown)	1954-55
8th	246	L.E.G. Ames & G.O.B. Allen, E v NZ (Lord's)	1931
9th	190	Asif Iqbal & Intikhab Alam, P v E (Oval)	1967
10th	151	B.F. Hastings & R.O. Collinge, NZ v P (Auckland)	1972-73

WICKET PARTNERSHIPS OF OVER 300

451	2nd	W.H. Ponsford & D.G. Bradman, A v E (Oval)	1934
451	3rd	Mudassar Nazar & Javed Miandad, P v I (Hyderabad)	1982-83
446	2nd	C.C. Hunte & G.S. Sobers, WI v P (Kingston)	1957-58
413	1st	V. Mankad & P. Roy, I v NZ (Madras)	1955-56
411	4th	P.B.H. May & M.C. Cowdrey, E v WI (Birmingham)	1957
405	5th	S.G. Barnes & D.B. Bradman, A v E (Sydney)	1946-47
399	4th	G.S. Sobers & F.M.M. Worrell, WI v E (Bridgetown)	1959-60
388	4th	W.H. Ponsford & D.G. Bradman, A v E (Leeds)	1934
387	1st	G.M. Turner & T.W. Jarvis, NZ v WI (Georgetown)	1971-72
382	2nd	L. Hutton & M. Leyland, E v A (Oval)	1938
382	1st	W.M. Lawry & R.B. Simpson, A v WI (Bridgetown)	1964-65
370	3rd	W.J. Edrich & D.C.S. Compton, E v SA (Lord's)	1947
369	2nd	J.H. Edrich & K.F. Barrington, E v NZ (Leeds)	1965
359	1st	L. Hutton & C. Washbrook, E v SA (Johannesburg)	1948-49
350	4th	Mushtaq Mohammad & Asif Iqbal, P v NZ (Dunedin)	1972-73
347	7th	D.S. Atkinson & C.C. Depeiza, WI v A (Bridgetown)	1954-55
346	6th	J.H.W. Fingleton & D.G. Bradman, A v E (Melbourne)	1936-37
344*	2nd	S.M. Gavaskar & D.B. Vengsarkar, I v WI (Calcutta)	1978-79
341	3rd	E.J. Barlow & R.G. Pollock, SA v A (Adelaide)	1963-64
338	3rd	E.D. Weekes & F.M.M. Worrell, WI v E (Port of Spain)	1953-54
336	4th	W.M. Lawry & K.D. Walters, A v WI (Sydney)	1968-69
323	1st	J.B. Hobbs & W. Rhodes, E v A (Melbourne)	1911-12
319	3rd	A. Melville & A.D. Nourse, SA v E (Nottingham)	1947
316†	3rd	G.R. Viswanath & Yashpal Sharma, I v E (Madras)	1981-82
308	7th	Waqar Hasan & Imtiaz Ahmed, P v NZ (Lahore)	1955-56
303	3rd	I.V.A. Richards & A.I. Kallicharran, WI v E (Nottingham)	1976
301	2nd	A.R. Morris & D.G. Bradman, A v E (Leeds)	1948

† 415 runs were added for this wicket in two separate partnerships. D.B. Vengsarkar retired hurt and was replaced by Yashpal Sharma after 99 runs had been added.

Hat-tricks are on page 244

NINE OR TEN WICKETS IN AN INNINGS

10-53	J.C. Laker, England v Australia (Manchester)	1956
9-28	G.A. Lohmann, England v South Africa (Johannesburg)	1895-96
9-37	J.C. Laker, England v Australia (Manchester)	1956
9-69	J.M. Patel, India v Australia (Kanpur)	1959-60
9-86	Sarfraz Nawaz, Pakistan v Australia (Melbourne)	1978-79
9-95	J.M. Noreiga, West Indies v India (Port of Spain)	1970-71
9-102	S.P. Gupte, India v West Indies (Kanpur)	1958-59
9-103	S.F. Barnes, England v South Africa (Johannesburg)	1913-14
9-113	H.J. Tayfield, South Africa v England (Johannesburg)	1956-57
9-121	A.A. Mailey, Australia v England (Melbourne)	1920-21

FIFTEEN OR MORE WICKETS IN A MATCH

19-90	J.C. Laker, England v Australia (Manchester)	1956
17-159	S.F. Barnes, England v South Africa (Johannesburg)	1913-14
16-137	R.A.L. Massie, Australia v England (Lord's)	1972
15-28	J. Briggs, England v South Africa (Cape Town)	1888-89
15-45	G.A. Lohmann, England v South Africa (Port Elizabeth)	1895-96
15-99	C. Blythe, England v South Africa (Leeds)	1907
15-104	H. Verity, England v Australia (Lord's)	1934
15-124	W. Rhodes, England v Australia (Melbourne)	1903-04

HIGHEST WICKET AGGREGATES IN A TEST RUBBER

Wkts		*Season*	*Tests*	*Balls*	*Mdns*	*Runs*	*Avge*	*5 wI*	*10 M*
49	S.F. Barnes (E v SA)	1913–14	4	1356	56	536	10.93	7	3
46	J.C. Laker (E v A)	1956	5	1703	127	442	9.60	4	2
44	C.V. Grimmett (A v SA)	1935-36	5	2077	140	642	14.59	5	3
42	T.M. Alderman (A v E)	1981	6	1950	76	893	21.26	4	—
41	R.M. Hogg (A v E)	1978-79	6	1740	60	527	12.85	5	2
40	Imran Khan (P v I)	1982-83	6	1339	69	558	13.95	4	2
39	D.K. Lillee (A v E)	1981	6	1870	81	870	22.30	2	1
39	A.V. Bedser (E v A)	1953	5	1591	58	682	17.48	5	1
38	M.W. Tate (E v A)	1924-25	5	2528	62	881	23.18	5	1
37	W.J. Whitty (A v SA)	1910-11	5	1395	55	632	17.08	2	—
37	H.J. Tayfield (SA v E)	1956-57	5	2280	105	636	17.18	4	1
36	A.E.E. Vogler (SA v E)	1909-10	5	1349	33	783	21.75	4	1
36	A.A. Mailey (A v E)	1920-21	5	1465	27	946	26.27	4	2
35	G.A. Lohmann (E v SA)	1895-96	3	520	38	203	5.80	4	2
35	B.S. Chandrasekhar (I v E)	1972-73	5	1747	83	662	18.91	4	—

MOST WICKET-KEEPING DISMISSALS IN AN INNINGS

7 (7 ct)	Wasim Bari, Pakistan v New Zealand (Auckland)	1978-79
7 (7 ct)	R.W. Taylor, England v India (Bombay)	1979-80
6 (6 ct)	A.T.W. Grout, Australia v South Africa (Johannesburg)	1957-58
6 (6 ct)	D.T. Lindsay, South Africa v Australia (Johannesburg)	1966-67
6 (6 ct)	J.T. Murray, England v India (Lord's)	1967
6 (5 ct, 1 st)	S.M.H. Kirmani, India v New Zealand (Christchurch)	1975-76

MOST WICKET-KEEPING DISMISSALS IN A MATCH

10 (10 ct)	R.W. Taylor, England v India (Bombay)	1979-80

MOST WICKET-KEEPING DISMISSALS IN A SERIES

28 (28 ct)	R.W. Marsh, Australia v England	1982-83
26 (23 ct, 3 st)	J.H.B. Waite, South Africa v New Zealand	1961-62
26 (26 ct)	R.W. Marsh, Australia v West Indies	1975-76

HIGHEST WICKET AGGREGATES

Wkts			*Tests*	*Balls*	*Runs*	*Avge*	*5 wI*	*10 wM*
355	D.K. Lillee	(A)	70	18467	8493	23.92	23	7
309	L.R. Gibbs	(WI)	79	27115	8989	29.09	18	2
307	F.S. Trueman	(E)	67	15178	6625	21.57	17	3
305	R.G.D. Willis	(E)	83	16042	7471	24.49	16	—
297	D.L. Underwood	(E)	86	21860	7674	25.83	17	6
277	I.T. Botham	(E)	63	14727	6876	24.82	20	4
266	B.S. Bedi	(I)	67	21364	7637	28.71	14	1
252	J.B. Statham	(E)	70	16056	6261	24.84	9	1
248	R. Benaud	(A)	63	19108	6704	27.03	16	1
247	Kapil Dev	(I)	62	13342	6844	27.70	18	2
246	G.D. McKenzie	(A)	60	17681	7328	29.78	16	3
242	B.S. Chandrasekhar	(I)	58	15963	7199	29.74	16	2
236	A.V. Bedser	(E)	51	15918	5876	24.89	15	3
235	G.S. Sobers	(WI)	93	21599	7999	34.03	6	—
232	Imran Khan	(P)	51	12551	5316	22.91	16	4
228	R.R. Lindwall	(A)	61	13650	5251	23.03	12	—
216	C.V. Grimmett	(A)	37	14513	5231	24.21	21	7
202	A.M.E. Roberts	(WI)	47	11135	5174	25.61	11	2
202	J.A. Snow	(E)	49	12021	5387	26.66	8	1
200	R.J. Hadlee	(NZ)	44	11355	5164	25.82	15	3
197	J.R. Thomson	(A)	49	10199	5326	27.03	8	—
193	J.C. Laker	(E)	46	12027	4101	21.24	9	3
192	W.W. Hall	(WI)	48	10421	5066	26.38	9	1
189	S.F. Barnes	(E)	27	7873	3106	16.43	24	7
189	E.A.S. Prasanna	(I)	49	14353	5742	30.38	10	2
186	A.K. Davidson	(A)	44	11587	3819	30.53	14	2
181	M.A. Holding	(WI)	42	9476	4357	24.07	11	2

MOST TEST APPEARANCES FOR EACH COUNTRY

NB. The abandoned match at Melbourne in 1970–71 is excluded from these figures.

England		Australia	
M.C. Cowdrey	114	R.W. Marsh	96
G. Boycott	108	G.S. Chappell	87
A.P.E. Knott	95	R.N. Harvey	79
T.G. Evans	91	I.M. Chappell	75
D.L. Underwood	86	K.D. Walters	74
W.R. Hammond	85	D.K. Lillee	70
R.G.D. Willis	83	W.M. Lawry	67
K.F. Barrington	82	I.R. Redpath	66
T.W. Graveney	79	R. Benaud	63
L. Hutton	79	R.B. Simpson	62

South Africa		India	
J.H.B. Waite	50	S.M. Gavaskar	99
A.W. Nourse	45	G.R. Viswanath	91
B. Mitchell	42	S.M.H. Kirmani	78
H.W. Taylor	42	D.B. Vengsarkar	69
T.L. Goddard	41	B.S. Bedi	67
R.A. McLean	40	Kapil Dev	62
H.J. Tayfield	37	P.R. Umrigar	59
D.J. McGlew	34	B.S. Chandrasekhar	58
A.D. Nourse	34	S. Venkataraghavan	57
E.J. Barlow	30	C.G. Borde	55
		V.L. Manjrekar	55

West Indies		Pakistan	
C.H. Lloyd	96		
G.S. Sobers	93	Wasim Bari	81
L.R. Gibbs	79	Zaheer Abbas	66
R.B. Kanhai	79	Majid Khan	63
A.I. Kallicharran	66	Javed Miandad	60
D.L. Murray	62	Asif Iqbal	58
R.C. Fredericks	59	Mushtaq Mohammad	57
I.V.A. Richards	58	Hanif Mohammad	55
F.M.M. Worrell	51	Sarfraz Nawaz	52
W.W. Hall	48	Imran Khan	51
E.D. Weekes	48	Wasim Raja	50

New Zealand

B.E. Congdon	61	G.M. Turner	41
J.R. Reid	58	G.T. Dowling	39
M.G. Burgess	50	J.M. Parker	36
R.J. Hadlee	44	R.O. Collinge	35
B. Sutcliffe	42	G.P. Howarth	34

Most Centuries in Succession in Test Matches

5	E.D. Weekes, West Indies	1947-48 and 1948-49
4	J.H.W. Fingleton, Australia	1935-36 and 1936-37
4	A. Melville, South Africa	1938-39 and 1947

HIGHEST WICKET-KEEPING DISMISSAL AGGREGATES

Total		*Tests*	*Ct*	*St*
355	R.W. Marsh (A)	96	343	12
269	A.P.E. Knott (E)	95	250	19
228	Wasim Bari (P)	81	201	27
219	T.G. Evans (E)	91	173	46
189	D.L. Murray (WI)	62	181	8
187	A.T.W. Grout (A)	51	163	24
179	S.M.H. Kirmani (I)	78	145	34
162	R.W. Taylor (E)	51	155	7
141	J.H.B. Waite (SA)	50	124	17
130	W.A.S. Oldfield (A)	54	78	52
114	J.M. Parks (E)	46	103	11

N.B. Parks's figures include 2 catches as a fielder.

MOST CATCHES

Total		Tests
122	G.S. Chappell (A)	87
120	M.C. Cowdrey (E)	114
110	W.R. Hammond (E)	85
110	R.B. Simpson(A)	62

HIGHEST RUN AGGREGATES

Runs			Tests	Inns	NO	HS	Avge	100s	50s
8394	S.M. Gavaskar	(I)	99	174	14	236*	52.46	30	36
8114	G. Boycott	(E)	108	193	23	246*	47.72	22	42
8032	G.S. Sobers	(WI)	93	160	21	365*	57.78	26	30
7624	M.C. Cowdrey	(E)	114	188	15	182	44.06	22	38
7249	W.R. Hammond	(E)	85	140	16	336*	58.45	22	24
7110	G.S. Chappell	(A)	87	151	19	247*	53.86	24	31
6996	D.G. Bradman	(A)	52	80	10	334	99.94	29	13
6971	L. Hutton	(E)	79	138	15	364	56.67	19	33
6806	K.F. Barrington	(E)	82	131	15	256	58.67	20	35
6734	C.H. Lloyd	(WI)	96	157	12	242*	46.44	18	34
6227	R.B. Kanhai	(WI)	79	137	6	256	47.53	15	28
6149	R.N. Harvey	(A)	79	137	10	205	48.41	21	24
6080	G.R. Viswanath	(I)	91	155	10	222	41.93	14	35
5807	D.C.S. Compton	(E)	78	131	15	278	50.06	17	28
5410	J.B. Hobbs	(E)	61	102	7	211	56.94	15	28
5357	K.D. Walters	(A)	74	125	14	250	48.26	15	33
5345	I.M. Chappell	(A)	75	136	10	196	42.42	14	26
5234	W.M. Lawry	(A)	67	123	12	210	47.15	13	27
5138	J.H. Edrich	(E)	77	127	9	310*	43.54	12	24
4882	T.W. Graveney	(E)	79	123	13	258	44.38	11	20
4869	R.B. Simpson	(A)	62	111	7	311	46.81	10	27
4737	I.R. Redpath	(A)	66	120	11	171	43.45	8	31
4717	I.V.A. Richards	(WI)	58	89	4	291	55.49	15	20
4555	H. Sutcliffe	(E)	54	84	9	194	60.73	16	23
4552	Zaheer Abbas	(P)	66	106	8	274	46.44	11	18
4537	P.B.H. May	(E)	66	106	9	285*	46.77	13	22
4519	Javed Miandad	(P)	60	95	14	280*	55.79	11	25
4502	E.R. Dexter	(E)	62	102	8	205	47.89	9	27
4455	E.D. Weekes	(WI)	48	81	5	207	58.61	15	19
4399	A.I. Kallicharran	(WI)	66	109	10	187	44.43	12	21
4389	A.P.E. Knott	(E)	95	149	15	135	32.75	5	30
4334	R.C. Fredericks	(WI)	59	107	7	169	42.49	8	26
4119	K.J. Hughes	(A)	61	106	6	213	41.19	9	22

TEST CAREER RECORDS

(the following series in 1983–84 are included: India v Pakistan; India v West Indies; Australia v Pakistan)

Compiled by Brian Heald

ENGLAND

BATTING AND FIELDING

	M	I	NO	Runs	HS	Avge	100	50	Ct	St
P.J.W. Allott	5	6	2	119	52*	29.75	—	1	2	—
C.W.J. Athey	3	6	0	17	9	2.83	—	—	2	—
D.L. Amiss	50	88	10	3612	262*	46.30	11	11	24	—
D.L. Bairstow	4	7	1	125	59	20.83	—	1	12	1
I.T. Botham	63	100	3	3548	208	36.57	12	14	72	—
A.R. Butcher	1	2	0	34	20	17.00	—	—	—	—
R.O. Butcher	3	5	0	71	22	14.20	—	—	3	—
G. Cook	7	13	0	203	66	15.61	—	2	9	—
N.G.B. Cook	2	4	0	51	26	12.75	—	—	3	—
N.G. Cowans	8	14	2	90	36	7.50	—	—	3	—
G.R. Dilley	17	27	7	328	56	16.40	—	2	5	—
P.R. Downton	4	7	1	59	26*	9.83	—	—	8	—
P.H. Edmonds	23	28	6	430	64	19.54	—	2	23	—
J.E. Emburey	22	33	6	326	57	12.07	—	1	15	—
K.W.R. Fletcher	59	96	14	3272	216	39.90	7	19	54	—
N.A. Foster	1	2	0	13	10	6.50	—	—	1	—
G. Fowler	6	12	0	436	105	36.33	1	3	2	—
M.W. Gatting	24	42	3	918	81	23.53	—	7	21	—
G.A. Gooch	42	75	4	2540	153	35.77	4	15	36	—
D.I. Gower	53	93	8	3742	200*	44.02	7	19	34	—
I.A. Greig	2	4	0	26	14	6.50	—	—	—	—
E.E. Hemmings	5	10	1	198	95	22.00	—	1	4	—
M. Hendrick	30	35	15	128	15	6.40	—	—	25	—
A.P.E. Knott	95	149	15	4389	135	32.75	5	30	250	19
A.J. Lamb	15	29	3	1061	137*	40.80	3	5	16	—
W. Larkins	6	11	0	176	34	16.00	—	—	3	—
J.K. Lever	20	29	4	306	53	12.24	—	1	11	—
V.J. Marks	2	4	1	25	12*	8.33	—	—	—	—
G. Miller	32	47	4	1171	98*	27.23	—	7	15	—
C.M. Old	46	66	9	845	65	14.82	—	2	22	—
P.W.G. Parker	1	2	0	13	13	6.50	—	—	—	—
D.R. Pringle	7	11	2	166	47*	18.44	—	—	—	—
D.W. Randall	40	68	5	2073	174	32.90	5	11	28	—
B.C. Rose	9	16	2	358	70	25.57	—	2	4	—
C.L. Smith	2	4	0	78	43	19.50	—	—	2	—
G.B. Stevenson	2	2	1	28	27*	28.00	—	—	—	—
C.J. Tavaré	26	48	1	1620	149	34.46	2	12	17	—
R.W. Taylor	51	74	12	1073	97	17.03	—	3	155	7
D.L. Underwood	86	116	35	937	45*	11.56	—	—	44	—
P. Willey	20	38	5	923	102*	27.96	2	4	3	—
R.G.D. Willis	83	117	51	775	28*	11.74	—	—	37	—
R.A. Woolmer	19	34	2	1059	149	33.09	3	2	10	

BOWLING

	Balls	Runs	Wkts	Avge	Best	5 wI	10 wM
P.J.W. Allott	696	414	6	69.00	2-17	—	—
I.T. Botham	14727	6876	277	24.82	8-34	20	4
A.R. Butcher	12	9	0	—	—	—	—
G. Cook	42	27	0	—	—	—	—
N.G.B. Cook	812	275	17	16.17	5-35	2	—
N.G. Cowans	1392	843	23	36.65	6-77	1	—
G.R. Dilley	2908	1453	45	32.38	4-24	—	—
P.H. Edmonds	5220	1733	59	29.37	7-66	2	—
J.E. Emburey	4981	1696	56	30.28	6-33	2	—
K.W.R. Fletcher	285	193	2	96.50	1-6	—	—
N.A. Foster	168	75	1	75.00	1-35	—	—
M.W. Gatting	134	52	0	—	—	—	—
G.A. Gooch	937	348	8	43.50	2-12	—	—
D.I. Gower	12	2	1	2.00	1-1	—	—
I.A. Greig	188	114	4	28.50	4-53	—	—
E.E. Hemmings	1468	558	12	46.50	3-68	—	—
M. Hendrick	6208	2248	87	25.83	4-28	—	—
A.J. Lamb	6	0	0	—	—	—	—
J.K. Lever	4115	1785	67	26.64	7-46	3	1
V.J. Marks	300	109	4	27.25	3-78	—	—
G. Miller	4981	1717	59	29.10	5-44	1	—
C.M. Old	8858	4020	143	28.17	7-50	4	—
D.R. Pringle	1091	495	11	45.00	2-16	—	—
D.W. Randall	16	3	0	—	—	—	—
C.L. Smith	72	31	2	15.50	2-31	—	—
G.B. Stevenson	312	183	5	36.60	3-111	—	—
C.J. Tavaré	12	11	0	—	—	—	—
R.W. Taylor	12	6	0	—	—	—	—
D.L. Underwood	21860	7674	297	25.83	8-51	17	6
P. Willey	1067	441	6	73.50	2-73	—	—
R.G.D. Willis	16042	7471	305	24.49	8-43	16	—
R.A. Woolmer	546	299	4	74.75	1-8	—	—

NEW ZEALAND

BATTING AND FIELDING

	M	I	NO	Runs	HS	Avge	100	50	Ct	St
S.L. Boock	12	19	6	37	8	2.84	—	—	8	—
B.P. Bracewell	5	10	2	17	8	2.12	—	—	1	—
J.G. Bracewell	8	13	2	85	28	7.72	—	—	6	—
B.L. Cairns	32	51	7	739	52*	16.79	—	1	23	—
E.J. Chatfield	10	14	7	60	13*	8.57	—	—	—	—
J.V. Coney	24	42	6	1146	84	31.83	—	10	28	—
J.J. Crowe	4	7	0	81	36	11.57	—	—	3	—
M.D. Crowe	7	12	0	183	46	15.25	—	—	8	—
B.A. Edgar	24	43	2	1481	161	36.12	3	8	13	—
G.N. Edwards	8	15	0	377	55	25.13	—	3	7	—
T.J. Franklin	1	2	0	9	7	4.50	—	—	—	—
E.J. Gray	2	4	0	38	17	9.50	—	—	—	—
R.J. Hadlee	44	77	11	1601	103	24.25	1	8	22	—

	M	I	NO	Runs	HS	Avge	100	50	Ct	St
G.P. Howarth	34	62	5	2014	147	35.33	6	8	22	—
W.K. Lees	21	37	4	778	152	23.57	1	1	52	7
P.E. McEwan	3	6	0	56	21	9.33	—	—	3	—
J.F.M. Morrison	17	29	0	656	117	22.62	1	3	9	—
J.M. Parker	36	63	2	1498	121	24.55	3	5	30	—
J.F. Reid	4	7	1	269	123*	44.83	1	1	2	—
I.D.S. Smith	9	13	3	108	20	10.80	—	—	29	—
M.C. Snedden	9	10	2	120	32	15.00	—	—	2	—
G.B. Troup	12	15	6	43	13*	4.77	—	—	2	—
G.M. Turner	41	73	6	2991	259	44.64	7	14	42	—
P.N. Webb	2	3	0	11	5	3.66	—	—	2	—
J.G. Wright	25	44	1	1223	141	28.67	2	5	12	—

BOWLING

	Balls	Runs	Wkts	Avge	Best	5 wI	10 wM
S.L. Boock	2107	706	19	37.15	5-67	1	—
B.P. Bracewell	838	456	10	45.60	3-110	—	—
J.G. Bracewell	1575	654	21	31.14	5-75	1	—
B.L. Cairns	8005	3096	97	31.91	7-74	5	1
E.J. Chatfield	2445	1073	29	37.00	5-95	1	—
J.V. Coney	1515	486	15	32.40	3-28	—	—
M.D. Crowe	153	72	2	36.00	2-35	—	—
E.J. Gray	288	128	4	32.00	3-73	—	—
R.J. Hadlee	11355	5164	200	25.82	7-23	15	3
G.P. Howarth	518	236	3	78.66	1-13	—	—
W.K. Lees	5	4	0	—	—	—	—
J.F.M. Morrison	264	71	2	35.50	2-52	—	—
J.M. Parker	40	24	1	24.00	1-24	—	—
M.C. Snedden	1530	690	23	30.00	3-21	—	—
G.B. Troup	2601	1114	34	32.76	6-95	1	1
G.M. Turner	12	5	0	—	—	—	—
J.G. Wright	6	2	0	—	—	—	—

WEST INDIES

BATTING AND FIELDING

	M	I	NO	Runs	HS	Avge	100	50	Ct	St
E.A.E. Baptiste	1	1	0	6	6	6.00	—	—	—	—
W.W. Daniel	8	9	3	36	11	6.00	—	—	3	—
W.W. Davis	7	8	4	53	19	13.25	—	—	5	—
P.J. Dujon	14	19	2	853	110	50.17	1	5	43	1
J. Garner	32	40	6	424	60	12.47	—	1	26	—
H.A. Gomes	33	50	5	1819	126	40.42	5	8	10	—
C.G. Greenidge	47	80	7	3373	194	46.20	7	23	45	—
R.A. Harper	2	2	0	0	0	0.00	—	—	3	—
D.L. Haynes	35	55	2	1940	184	36.60	4	10	19	—
M.A. Holding	42	56	8	602	58*	12.54	—	3	12	—
C.H. Lloyd	96	157	12	6734	242*	46.44	18	34	72	—
A.L. Logie	8	10	0	230	130	23.00	1	1	2	—
M.D. Marshall	23	29	2	444	92	16.44	—	2	8	—
R. Nanan	1	2	0	16	8	8.00	—	—	2	—
I.V.A. Richards	58	89	4	4717	291	55.49	15	20	64	—
R.B. Richardson	1	2	0	26	26	13.00	—	—	—	—
A.M.E. Roberts	47	62	11	762	68	14.94	—	3	9	—

BOWLING

	Balls	Runs	Wkts	Avge	Best	5 wI	10 wM
E.A.E. Baptiste	102	66	1	66.00	1-58	—	—
W.W. Daniel	1376	713	29	24.58	5-39	1	—
W.W. Davis	1383	737	18	40.94	3-21	—	—
J. Garner	7326	2861	131	21.83	6-56	2	—
H.A. Gomes	1639	647	10	64.70	2-20	—	—
C.G. Greenidge	26	4	0	—	—	—	—
R.A. Harper	300	124	1	124.00	1-108	—	—
D.L. Haynes	18	8	1	8.00	1-2	—	—
M.A. Holding	9476	4357	181	24.07	8-92	11	2
C.H. Lloyd	1716	622	10	62.20	2-13	—	—
M.D. Marshall	4592	2200	88	25.00	6-37	3	—
R. Nanan	216	91	4	22.75	2-37	—	—
I.V.A. Richards	2158	800	14	57.14	2-20	—	—
A.M.E. Roberts	11135	5174	202	25.61	7-54	11	2

SRI LANKA

BATTING AND FIELDING

	M	I	NO	Runs	HS	Avge	100	50	Ct	St
R.G. de Alwis	2	4	0	15	9	3.75	—	—	1	—
A.L.F. de Mel	6	12	2	154	34	15.40	—	—	5	—
D.S. de Silva	8	16	2	364	61	26.00	—	2	3	—
R.L. Dias	6	12	0	543	109	45.25	1	5	3	—
E.R.N.S. Fernando	3	6	0	73	46	12.16	—	—	—	—
Y. Goonasekera	2	4	0	48	23	12.00	—	—	6	—
R.P.W. Guneratne	1	2	2	0	0*	—	—	—	—	—
R.S.A. Jayasekera	1	2	0	2	2	1.00	—	—	—	—
S. Jeganathan	2	4	0	19	8	4.75	—	—	—	—
V.B. John	2	4	2	11	8*	5.50	—	—	1	—
R.S. Madugalle	8	16	1	431	91*	28.73	—	3	5	—
L.R.D. Mendis	6	12	0	450	105	37.50	2	2	4	—
A. Ranatunga	5	10	0	266	90	26.60	—	2	1	—
R.J. Ratnayake	3	6	0	58	30	7.66	—	—	1	—
J.R. Ratnayeke	5	10	2	102	29*	13.75	—	—	—	—
S.A.R. Silva	1	2	0	8	8	4.00	—	—	2	—
M.D. Wettimuny	2	4	0	28	17	7.00	—	—	2	—
S. Wettimuny	7	14	1	514	157	39.53	1	3	3	—
R.G.C.E. Wijesuriya	1	2	0	3	3	1.50	—	—	—	—

BOWLING

	Balls	Runs	Wkts	Avge	Best	5 wI	10 wM
A.L.F. de Mel	1293	905	25	36.20	5-68	1	—
D.S. de Silva	2008	969	27	35.88	5-59	1	—
R.P.W. Guneratne	102	84	0	—	—	—	—
S. Jeganathan	30	12	0	—	—	—	—
V.B. John	272	143	8	17.87	5-60	1	—
A. Ranatunga	120	84	1	84.00	1-72	—	—
R.J. Ratnayake	588	360	7	51.42	4-81	—	—
J.R. Ratnayeke	761	450	9	50.00	3-93	—	—
S. Wettimuny	12	21	0	—	—	—	—
R.G.C.E. Wijesuriya	144	105	0	—	—	—	—

INDIA

BATTING AND FIELDING

	M	I	NO	Runs	HS	Avge	100	50	Ct	St
M. Amarnath	42	72	5	2660	120	39.70	7	16	34	—
Arun Lal	4	7	0	164	63	23.42	—	2	5	—
R. Bhatt	2	3	1	6	6	3.00	—	—	—	—
R.M.H. Binny	17	28	3	605	83*	24.20	—	4	7	—
C.P.S. Chauhan	40	68	2	2084	97	31.57	—	16	38	—
D.R. Doshi	33	38	10	129	20	4.60	—	—	10	—
A.D. Gaekwad	35	62	4	1776	201	30.62	2	8	13	—
S.M. Gavaskar	99	174	14	8394	236*	52.46	30	36	85	—
K.D. Ghavri	39	57	14	913	86	21.23	—	2	16	—
Kapil Dev	62	92	8	2483	126*	29.55	3	13	24	—
S.M.H. Kirmani	78	113	20	2418	101*	26.00	1	11	145	34
Kirti Azad	7	12	0	135	24	11.25	—	—	3	—
S. Madan Lal	37	59	16	1000	74	23.25	—	5	15	—
A. Malhotra	6	9	1	199	72*	24.87	—	1	2	—
Maninder Singh	12	14	4	54	15	5.40	—	—	3	—
S.V. Nayak	2	3	1	19	11	9.50	—	—	1	—
G.A. Parkar	1	2	0	7	6	3.50	—	—	1	—
S.M. Patil	25	41	4	1363	174	36.83	3	7	11	—
P. Roy	2	3	1	71	60*	35.50	—	1	1	—
B.S. Sandhu	8	11	4	214	71	30.57	—	2	1	—
T.A. Sekar	2	1	1	0	0*	—	—	—	—	—
R.J. Shastri	27	41	6	1083	128	30.94	2	5	10	—
R. Shukla	1	—	—	—	—	—	—	—	—	—
N.S. Sidhu	2	3	0	39	20	13.00	—	—	1	—
L. Sivaramakrishnan	1	1	0	17	17	17.00	—	—	—	—
K. Srikkanth	6	9	0	147	65	16.33	—	1	2	—
T.E. Srinivasan	1	2	0	48	29	24.00	—	—	—	—
D.B. Vengsarkar	69	113	10	3970	159	38.54	8	22	45	—
S. Venkataraghavan	57	76	12	748	64	11.68	—	2	44	—
G.R. Viswanath	91	155	10	6080	222	41.93	14	35	63	—
N.S. Yadav	18	23	6	236	43	13.88	—	—	6	—
Yashpal Sharma	37	59	11	1606	140	33.45	2	9	16	—

BOWLING

	Balls	Runs	Wkts	Avge	Best	5 wI	10 wM
M. Amarnath	3072	1525	27	56.48	4-63	—	—
Arun Lal	7	6	0	—	—	—	—
R. Bhatt	438	151	4	37.75	2-65	—	—
R.M.H. Binny	1769	1021	24	42.54	3-18	—	—
C.P.S. Chauhan	174	106	2	53.00	1-4	—	—
D.R. Doshi	9322	3502	114	30.71	6-102	6	—
A.D. Gaekwad	160	107	0	—	—	—	—
S.M. Gavaskar	346	177	1	177.00	1-34	—	—
K.D. Ghavri	7042	3656	109	33.54	5-33	4	—
Kapil Dev	13342	6844	247	27.70	9-83	18	2
S.M.H. Kirmani	18	13	1	13.00	1-9	—	—
Kirti Azad	750	373	3	124.33	2-84	—	—
S. Madan Lal	5710	2704	67	40.35	5-23	4	—

	Balls	Runs	Wkts	Avge	Best	5 wI	10 wM
A. Malhotra	6	0	0	—	—	—	—
Maninder Singh	2328	970	15	64.66	4-85	—	—
S.V. Nayak	231	132	1	132.00	1-16	—	—
S.M. Patil	645	240	9	26.66	2-28	—	—
B.S. Sandhu	1020	557	10	55.70	3-87	—	—
T.A. Sekar	204	129	0	—	—	—	—
R.J. Shastri	6003	2368	62	38.19	5-75	2	—
R. Shukla	294	152	2	76.00	2-82	—	—
L. Sivaramakrishnan	150	95	0	—	—	—	—
K. Srikkanth	36	10	0	—	—	—	—
D.B. Vengsarkar	47	36	0	—	—	—	—
S. Venkataraghavan	14877	5634	156	36.11	8-72	3	1
G.R. Viswanath	70	46	1	46.00	1-11	—	—
N.S. Yadav	3810	1787	50	35.74	5-131	1	—
Yashpal Sharma	30	17	1	17.00	1-6	—	—

AUSTRALIA

BATTING AND FIELDING

	M	I	NO	Runs	HS	Avge	100	50	Ct	St
T.M. Alderman	16	21	11	51	12*	5.10	—	—	16	—
A.R. Border	56	97	17	3968	162	49.60	11	23	65	—
R.J. Bright	16	27	5	303	33	13.77	—	—	8	—
G.S. Chappell	87	151	19	7110	247*	53.86	24	31	122	—
T.M. Chappell	3	6	1	79	27	15.80	—	—	2	—
W.M. Darling	14	27	1	697	91	26.80	—	6	5	—
J. Dyson	27	52	7	1282	127*	28.48	2	5	10	—
A.M.J. Hilditch	9	18	0	452	85	25.11	—	4	9	—
T.G. Hogan	2	2	0	10	8	5.00	—	—	1	—
R.M. Hogg	30	43	8	284	36	8.11	—	—	5	—
D.W. Hookes	14	24	2	923	143*	41.95	1	7	6	—
K.J. Hughes	61	106	6	4119	213	41.19	9	22	45	—
B.M. Laird	21	40	2	1341	92	35.28	—	11	16	—
G.F. Lawson	18	27	5	313	57*	14.22	—	2	5	—
D.K. Lillee	70	90	24	905	73*	13.71	—	1	23	—
J.N. Maguire	1	1	0	4	4	4.00	—	—	2	—
R.W. Marsh	96	150	13	3633	132	26.51	3	16	343	12
G.R.J. Matthews	2	2	1	97	75	97.00	—	1	—	—
L.S. Pascoe	14	19	9	106	30*	10.60	—	—	2	—
W.B. Phillips	5	7	1	362	159	60.33	1	1	7	—
C.G. Rackemann	3	1	0	4	4	4.00	—	—	1	—
G.M. Ritchie	3	6	1	206	106*	41.20	1	—	1	—
S.J. Rixon	10	19	3	341	54	21.. 1	—	2	31	4
P.R. Sleep	4	8	0	124	64	15.50	—	1	—	—
J.R. Thomson	49	69	16	641	49	12.09	—	—	19	—
P.M. Toohey	15	29	1	893	122	31.87	1	7	9	—
D.M. Wellham	4	7	0	221	103	31.57	1	—	1	—
K.C. Wessels	10	16	1	783	179	52.20	3	1	10	—
D.F. Whatmore	7	13	0	293	77	22.53	—	2	13	—
M.R. Whitney	2	4	0	4	4	1.00	—	—	—	—
J.M. Wiener	6	11	0	281	93	25.54	—	2	4	—
G.M. Wood	42	81	5	2554	126	33.60	7	11	32	—

	M	I	NO	Runs	HS	Avge	100	50	Ct	St
R.D. Woolley	1	—	—	—	—	—	—	—	5	—
K.J. Wright	10	18	5	219	55*	16.84	—	1	31	4
G.N. Yallop	38	68	3	2753	268	42.35	8	9	22	—
B. Yardley	33	54	4	978	74	19.56	—	4	31	—

BOWLING

	Balls	Runs	Wkts	Avge	Best	5 wI	10 wM
T.M. Alderman	4111	1890	66	28.63	6-135	4	—
A.R. Border	1444	531	15	35.40	3-20	—	—
R.J. Bright	3598	1343	37	36.29	7-87	3	1
G.S. Chappell	5327	1913	47	40.70	5-61	1	—
T.G. Hogan	440	223	7	31.85	5-66	1	—
R.M. Hogg	6090	2660	103	25.82	6-74	5	2
D.W. Hookes	78	35	0	—	—	—	—
K.J. Hughes	85	28	0	—	—	—	—
B.M. Laird	18	12	0	—	—	—	—
G.F. Lawson	4112	1982	83	23.87	7-81	7	1
D.K. Lillee	18467	8493	355	23.92	7-83	23	7
J.N. Maguire	246	137	3	45.66	3-111	—	—
R.W. Marsh	72	54	0	—	—	—	—
G.R.J. Matthews	448	219	5	43.80	2-48	—	—
L.S. Pascoe	3403	1668	64	26.06	5-59	1	—
C.G. Rackemann	512	273	18	15.16	6-86	2	1
P.R. Sleep	589	382	3	127.33	1-16	—	—
J.R. Thomson	10199	5326	197	27.63	6-46	8	—
P.M. Toohey	2	4	0	—	—	—	—
K.C. Wessels	12	2	0	—	—	—	—
D.F. Whatmore	30	11	0	—	—	—	—
M.R. Whitney	468	246	5	49.20	2-50	—	—
J.M. Wiener	78	41	0	—	—	—	—
G.N. Yallop	192	116	1	116.00	1-21	—	—

PAKISTAN

BATTING AND FIELDING

	M	I	NO	Runs	HS	Avge	100	50	Ct	St
Abdul Qadir	24	30	4	354	45	13.61	—	—	6	—
Ashraf Ali	2	3	2	132	58	132.00	—	1	4	2
Azhar Khan	1	1	0	14	14	14.00	—	—	—	—
Azim Hafeez	8	11	3	45	18	5.62	—	—	1	—
Azmat Rana	1	1	0	49	49	49.00	—	—	—	—
Ehteshamuddin	5	3	1	2	2	1.00	—	—	2	—
Ejaz Fakih	2	4	0	63	34	15.75	—	—	—	—
Haroon Rashid	23	36	1	1217	153	34.77	3	5	16	—
Imran Khan	51	77	12	2023	123	31.12	2	7	16	—
Iqbal Qasim	37	42	12	278	56	9.26	—	1	27	—
Jalaluddin	3	2	2	1	1*	—	—	—	—	—
Javed Miandad	60	95	14	4519	280*	55.79	11	25	51	1
Majid Khan	63	106	5	3931	167	38.92	8	19	70	—
Mansoor Akhtar	13	22	3	484	111	25.47	1	2	7	—
Mohammad Nazir	14	18	10	144	29*	18.00	—	—	4	—

	M	I	NO	Runs	HS	Avge	100	50	Ct	St
Mohsin Khan	30	48	5	1974	200	45.90	6	5	22	—
Mudassar Nazar	43	66	5	2526	231	41.40	6	11	31	—
Qasim Omar	6	10	1	342	113	38.00	1	1	3	—
Rashid Khan	3	4	3	118	59	118.00	—	1	1	—
Rizwan-uz-Zaman	3	6	0	112	42	18.66	—	—	1	—
Sadiq Mohammad	41	74	2	2579	166	35.81	5	10	28	—
Saleem Yousuf	1	1	0	4	4	4.00	—	—	5	2
Salim Malik	13	16	2	453	107	32.35	2	2	13	—
Sarfraz Nawaz	52	67	10	917	55	16.08	—	3	26	—
Shafiq Ahmed	6	10	1	99	27*	11.00	—	—	—	—
Shoaib Mohammad	2	3	1	21	9	10.50	—	—	—	—
Sikander Bakht	26	35	12	146	22*	6.34	—	—	7	—
Tahir Naqqash	14	17	5	299	57	24.91	—	1	2	—
Taslim Arif	6	10	2	501	210*	62.62	1	2	6	3
Tauseef Ahmed	6	3	1	23	18	11.50	—	—	3	—
Wasim Bari	81	112	26	1366	85	15.85	—	6	201	27
Wasim Raja	50	80	12	2546	125	37.44	3	16	17	—
Zaheer Abbas	66	106	8	4552	274	46.44	11	18	33	—

BOWLING

	Balls	Runs	Wkts	Avge	Best	5 wI	10 wM
Abdul Qadir	6320	2929	77	38.03	7-142	4	1
Azhar Khan	18	2	1	2.00	1-1	—	—
Azim Hafeez	1809	1045	29	36.03	5-100	2	—
Ehteshamuddin	940	375	16	23.43	5-47	1	—
Ejaz Fakih	156	85	1	85.00	1-76	—	—
Haroon Rashid	8	3	0	—	—	—	—
Imran Khan	12551	5316	232	22.91	8-58	16	4
Iqbal Qasim	9444	3473	115	30.20	7-49	4	2
Jalaluddin	516	244	7	34.85	3-77	—	—
Javed Miandad	1422	661	17	38.88	3-74	—	—
Majid Khan	3584	1456	27	53.92	4-45	—	—
Mohammad Nazir	3262	1123	34	33.02	7-99	3	—
Mohsin Khan	86	30	0	—	—	—	—
Mudassar Nazar	2970	1313	32	41.03	6-32	1	—
Qasim Omar	6	0	0	—	—	—	—
Rashid Khan	546	263	6	43.03	3-129	—	—
Rizwan-uz-Zaman	102	39	3	13.00	3-26	—	—
Sadiq Mohammad	199	98	0	—	—	—	—
Salim Malik	36	20	2	10.00	1-3	—	—
Sarfraz Nawaz	13102	5439	163	33.36	9-86	4	1
Shafiq Ahmed	8	1	0	—	—	—	—
Sikander Bakht	4870	2411	67	35.98	8-69	3	1
Tahir Naqqash	2600	1317	31	42.48	5-40	2	—
Taslim Arif	30	28	1	28.00	1-28	—	—
Tauseef Ahmed	1446	620	23	26.95	4-58	—	—
Wasim Bari	8	2	0	—	—	—	—
Wasim Raja	3342	1532	45	34.04	4-50	—	—
Zaheer Abbas	284	93	1	93.00	1-14	—	—

YOUNG CRICKETER OF THE YEAR

At the end of each season the members of the Cricket Writers' Club select by ballot the player they consider the best young cricketer of the season.

The selections to date are:

1950 R. Tattersall (Lancashire)
1951 P.B.H. May (Surrey)
1952 F.S. Trueman (Yorkshire)
1953 M.C. Cowdrey (Kent)
1954 P.J. Loader (Surrey)
1955 K.F. Barrington (Surrey)
1956 B. Taylor (Essex)
1957 M.J. Stewart (Surrey)
1958 A.C.D. Ingleby-Mackenzie (Hampshire)
1959 G. Pullar (Lancashire)
1960 D.A. Allen (Gloucestershire)
1961 P.H. Parfitt (Middlesex)
1962 P.J. Sharpe (Yorkshire)
1963 G. Boycott (Yorkshire)
1964 J.M. Brearley (Middlesex)
1965 A.P.E. Knott (Kent)
1966 D.L. Underwood (Kent)
1967 A.W. Greig (Sussex)
1968 R.H.M. Cottam (Hampshire)
1969 A. Ward (Derbyshire)
1970 C.M. Old (Yorkshire)
1971 J. Whitehouse (Warwickshire)
1972 D.R. Owen-Thomas (Surrey)
1973 M. Hendrick (Derbyshire)
1974 P.H. Edmonds (Middlesex)
1975 A. Kennedy (Lancashire)
1976 G. Miller (Derbyshire)
1977 I.T. Botham (Somerset)
1978 D.I. Gower (Leicestershire)
1979 P.W.G. Parker (Sussex)
1980 G.R. Dilley (Kent)
1981 M.W. Gatting (Middlesex)
1982 W.G. Cowans (Middlesex)

NB. An additional award was made in 1980 to C.W.J. Athey (Yorkshire) as the best young batsman of the year.

SCORING OF POINTS IN THE BRITANNIC CHAMPIONSHIP

The scheme is as follows:

(a) For a win, 16 points, plus any points scored in the first innings.
(b) In a tie, each side to score 8 points, plus any points scored in the first innings.
(c) If the scores are equal in a drawn match, the side batting in the fourth innings to score 8 points, plus any points scored in the first innings.
(d) First innings points (awarded only for performances in the first 100 overs of each innings and retained whatever the result of the match).
  (i) A maximum of 4 batting points to be available as follows: 150 to 199 runs – 1 point; 200 to 249 runs – 2 points; 250 to 299 runs – 3 points; 300 runs or over – 4 points.
  (ii) A maximum of 4 bowling points to be available as follows: 3-4 wickets taken – 1 point; 5-6 wickets taken – 2 points; 7-8 wickets taken – 3 points; 9-10 wickets taken – 4 points.
(e) If play starts when less than eight hours playing time remains and a one innings match is played, no first innings points shall be scored. The side winning on the one innings to score 12 points.
(f) The side which has the highest aggregate of points gained at the end of the season shall be the Champion County. Should any sides in the Britannic Championship Table be equal on points, the side with most wins will have priority.

Test Cricket Records *(continued from page 230)*

HAT-TRICKS

F.R. Spofforth	Australia v England (Melbourne)	1878-79
W. Bates	England v Australia (Melbourne)	1882-83
J. Briggs	England v Australia (Sydney)	1891-92
G.A. Lohmann	England v South Africa (Port Elizabeth)	1895-96
J.T. Hearne	England v Australia (Leeds)	1899
H. Trumble	Australia v England (Melbourne)	1901-02
H. Trumble	Australia v England (Melbourne)	1903-04
T.J. Matthews (2)*	Australia v South Africa (Manchester)	1912
M.J.C. Allom†	England v New Zealand (Christchurch)	1929-30
T.W.J. Goddard	England v South Africa (Johannesburg)	1938-39
P.J. Loader	England v West Indies (Leeds)	1957
L.F. Kline	Australia v South Africa (Cape Town)	1957-58
W.W. Hall	West Indies v Pakistan (Lahore)	1958-59
G.M. Griffin	South Africa v England (Lord's)	1960
L.R. Gibbs	West Indies v Australia (Adelaide)	1960-61
P.J. Petherick	New Zealand v Pakistan (Lahore)	1976-77

**In each innings.* †*Four wickets in five balls.*

PRINCIPAL FIXTURES 1984

**Including play on Sunday*

Wednesday 18 April

Cambridge: Cambridge U v Leics

Saturday 21 April

Cambridge: Cambridge U v Essex
Oxford: Oxford U v Notts

Wednesday 25 April

Lord's: MCC v Essex
Cambridge: Cambridge U v Hants
Oxford: Oxford U v Glam

Saturday 28 April

Britannic County Championship
Chesterfield: *Derbys v Leics
Bristol: *Glos v Kent
Southampton: *Hants v Essex
Lord's: Middx v Glam
Trent Bridge: *Notts v Surrey
Taunton: * Somerset v Yorks
Edgbaston: *Warwicks v Northants
Worcester: *Worcs v Sussex
Other match
Oxford U v Lancs

Sunday 29 April

John Player Special League
Leicester: Leics v Derbys

Wednesday 2 May

Britannic County Championship
Canterbury: Kent v Essex
Old Trafford: Lancs v Derbys
Trent Bridge: Notts v Leics
The Oval: Surrey v Northants
Worcester: Worcs v Glam
Other matches
Cambridge: Cambridge U v Sussex
Oxford: Oxford U v Somerset

Saturday 5 May

Benson & Hedges Cup
Chelmsford: Essex v Glos
Swansea: Glam v Somerset
Southampton: Hants v Combined U
Lord's: Middx v Kent
Northampton: Northants v Scotland
Trent Bridge: Notts v Worcs
Headingley: Yorks v Leics
Bowdon: Minor Counties v Lancs
Britannic County Championship
Edgbaston: Warwicks v Surrey

Sunday 6 May

John Player Special League
Chelmsford: Essex v Notts
Swansea: Glam v Glos
Southampton: Hants v Sussex
Lord's: Middx v Kent
Edgbaston: Warwicks v Surrey
Bradford: Yorks v Worcs

Wednesday 9 May

Britannic County Championship
Derby: Derby v Glam
Southampton: Hants v Glos
Old Trafford: Lancs v Kent
Leicester: Leics v Worcs
Northampton: Northants v Essex
Hove: Sussex v Surrey
Headingley: Yorks v Notts
Other matches
Cambridge: Cambridge U v Warwicks
Oxford: Oxford U v Middx

Saturday 12 May

Benson & Hedges Cup
Bristol: Glos v Hants
Canterbury: Kent v Glam
Old Trafford: Lancs v Notts
Leicester: *Leics v Warwicks
Taunton: Somerset v Sussex
Worcester: Worcs v Derbys
Scotland v Yorks
Oxford: Combined U v Surrey

Sunday 13 May

John Player Special League
Old Trafford: Lancs v Northants
Lord's: Middx v Essex
Taunton: Somerset v Hants
The Oval: Surrey v Glam
Worcester: Worcs v Notts

Tuesday 15 May

Benson & Hedges Cup
Derby: Derbys v Notts
Chelmsford: Essex v Surrey

Bristol: Glos v Combined U
Canterbury: Kent v Somerset
Leicester: Leics v Northants
Lord's: Middx v Sussex
Edgbaston: Warwicks v Yorks
Worcester: Worcs v Minor Counties

Thursday 17 May

Benson & Hedges Cup
Old Trafford: Lancs v Worcs
Northampton: Northants v Warwicks
Taunton: Somerset v Middx
The Oval: Surrey v Hants
Hove: Sussex v Glam
Glasgow (Hamilton Cres.): Scotland v Leics
Shrewsbury: Minor Counties v Derbys
Cambridge: Combined U v Essex

Saturday 19 May

Benson & Hedges Cup
Derby: Derbys v Lancs
Cardiff: Glam v Middx
Southampton: Hants v Essex
Trent Bridge: Notts v Minor Counties
The Oval: Surrey v Glos
Hove: Sussex v Kent
Edgbaston: Warwicks v Scotland
Bradford: Yorks v Northants
Britannic County Championship
Leicester: Leics v Somerset
Tourist Match
Worcester: *Worcs v West Indies
Other Match
Oxford: Oxford U v MCC (three days)

Sunday 20 May

John Player Special League
Derby: Derbys v Lancs
Cardiff: Glam v Middx
Canterbury: Kent v Surrey
Leicester: Leics v Somerset
Northampton: Northants v Warwicks
Hove: Sussex v Glos
Hull: Yorks v Notts

Wednesday 23 May

Britannic County Championship
Chesterfield: Derbys v Surrey
Chelmsford: Essex v Notts
Cardiff: Glam v Glos
Lord's: Middx v Northants
Hove: Sussex v Hants
Nuneaton (Griff and Coton): Warwicks v Lancs
Worcester: Worcs v Leics
Tourist Match
Taunton: Somerset v West Indies

Saturday 26 May

Britannic County Championship
Derby: Derbys v Notts
Chelmsford: Essex v Surrey
Canterbury: Kent v Hants
Leicester: Leics v Northants
Lord's: Middx v Sussex
Taunton: Somerset v Glos
Edgbaston: Warwicks v Worcs
Headingley: *Yorks v Lancs
Tourist Match
Swansea: *Glam v West Indies
Other Match
Oxford: Oxford U v Free Foresters (three days)

Sunday 27 May

John Player Special League
Chelmsford: Essex v Surrey
Bristol: Glos v Somerset
Leicester: Leics v Sussex
Lord's: Middx v Northants
Trent Bridge: Notts v Derbys
Edgbaston: Warwicks v Worcs

Tuesday 29 May

Tourist Match
Liverpool: Lancs v West Indies (one day)

Wednesday 30 May

Britannic County Championship
Southampton: Hants v Somerset
Dartford: Kent v Middx
Northampton: Northants v Lancs
The Oval: Surrey v Glam
Edgbaston: Warwicks v Notts
Worcester: Worcs v Essex
Sheffield: Yorks v Sussex
Other Match
Oxford: Oxford U v Glos

Thursday 31 May

Texaco Cup
Old Trafford: England v West Indies (First 'One-day International')

Saturday 2 June

Texaco Cup
Trent Bridge: England v West Indies (Second 'One-day International')
Britannic County Championship
Derby: Derbys v Middx
Swansea: Glam v Worcs
Bournemouth: Hants v Notts
Canterbury: Kent v Glos
Old Trafford: Lancs v Surrey
Hinckley: Leics v Essex
Horsham: Sussex v Nothants
Middlesbrough: Yorks v Somerset
Other Match
Belfast (Ormeau): *Ireland v MCC

Sunday 3 June

John Player Special League
Derby: Derbys v Middx
Southampton: Hants v Notts
Canterbury: Kent v Glos
Old Trafford: Lancs v Surrey
Hinckley: Leics v Essex
Horsham: Sussex v Northants
Worcester: Worcs v Glam
Middlesbrough: Yorks v Somerset

Monday 4 June

Texaco Trophy
Lord's: England v West Indies (Third 'One-day International')

Wednesday 6 June

Benson & Hedges Cup Quarter-Finals

Thursday 7 June

Tourist Match
Oxford: Combined U v West Indies (two days)

Saturday 9 June

Britannic County Championship
Ilford: Essex v Warwicks
Gloucester: Glos v Derbys
Tunbridge Wells: Kent v Yorks
Old Trafford: Lancs v Sussex
Trent Bridge: Notts v Glam
Bath: Somerset v Middx
The Oval: Surrey v Leics
Worcester: Worcs v Hants
Tourist Match
Milton Keynes: *Northants v West Indies

Sunday 10 June

John Player Special League
Ilford: Essex v Warwicks
Gloucester: Glos v Derbys
Canterbury: Kent v Yorks
Old Trafford: Lancs v Sussex
Trent Bridge: Notts v Glam
Bath: Somerset v Middx
The Oval: Surrey v Leics
Worcester: Worcs v Hants

Wednesday 13 June

Britannic County Championship
Ilford: Essex v Derbys
Gloucester: Glos v Worcs
Basingstoke: Hants v Yorks
Tunbridge Wells: Kent v Sussex
Leicester: Leics v Warwicks
Lord's: Middx v Surrey
Bath: Somerset v Lancs
Other Match
Cambridge U v Glam

Thursday 14 June

CORNHILL INSURANCE TEST SERIES
Edgbaston: ENGLAND v WEST INDIES (First Test Match)

Saturday 16 June

Britannic County Championship
Chelmsford: Essex v Northants
Cardiff: Glam v Lancs
Southampton: Hants v Leics
Lord's: Middx v Warwicks
Trent Bridge: Notts v Glos
Guildford: Surrey v Sussex
Harrogate: Yorks v Derbys
Other Matches
Worcester: Worcs v Cambridge U
Oxford: Oxford U v Kent

Sunday 17 June

John Player Special League
Chesterfield: Derbys v Yorks
Chelmsford: Essex v Northants
Cardiff: Glam v Lancs
Basingstoke: Hants v Leics

Lord's: Middx v Warwicks
Trent Bridge: Notts v Glos
Bath: Somerset v Kent
Guildford: Surrey v Sussex

Wednesday 20 June

Benson & Hedges Cup Semi-Finals
Other Matches
Harrogate: Tilcon Trophy (three days)

Thursday 21 June

Tourist Match
Dublin (Rathmines): Ireland v West Indies (two days)

Saturday 23 June

Britannic County Championship
Derby: Derbys v Kent
Bristol: Glos v Hants
Old Trafford: Lancs v Worcs
Leicester: Leics v Notts
Northampton: Northants v Yorks
The Oval: Surrey v Middx
Hove: Sussex v Glam
Edgbaston: Warwicks v Somerset
Tourist Match
Chelmsford: *Essex v West Indies

Sunday 24 June

John Player Special League
Derby: Derbys v Kent
Bristol: Glos v Hants
Old Trafford: Lancs v Worcs
Leicester: Leics v Notts
Luton: Northants v Yorks
The Oval: Surrey v Middx
Hove: Sussex v Glam
Edgbaston: Warwicks v Somerset

Wednesday 27 June

Britannic County Championship
Chesterfield: Derbys v Essex
Swansea: Glam v Middx
Bournemouth: Hants v Sussex
Old Trafford: Lancs v Glos
Northampton: Northants v Warwicks
Trent Bridge: Notts v Yorks
Taunton: Somerset v Leics
Hereford: Worcs v Kent
Other Match
Surrey v Cambridge U

Thursday 28 June

CORNHILL INSURANCE TEST SERIES
Lord's: ENGLAND v WEST INDIES (Second Test Match)

Saturday 30 June

Britannic County Championship
Swansea: Glam v Leics
Liverpool: Lancs v Middx
Northampton: Northants v Somerset
The Oval: Surrey v Hants
Hastings: Sussex v Kent
Edgbaston: Warwicks v Glos
Worcester: Worcs v Derbys
Headingley: Yorks v Essex
Other Match
Portsmouth: *Combined Services v Oxford U (three days)
Trent Bridge: Notts v Cambridge U

Sunday 1 July

John Player Special League
Swansea: Glam v Leics
Old Trafford: Lancs v Middx
Northampton: Northants v Somerset
The Oval: Surrey v Hants
Hastings: Sussex v Kent
Edgbaston: Warwicks v Glos
Worcester: Worcs v Derbys
Headingley: Yorkshire v Essex

Wednesday 4 July

NatWest Bank Trophy First Round
Kendal (Netherfield): Cumberland v Derbys
Darlington (Feethams): Durham v Northants
Chelmsford: Essex v Scotland
Swansea: Glam v Notts
Herts v Somerset
Canterbury: Kent v Berks
Old Trafford: Lancs v Bucks
Norwich (Lakenham): Norfolk v Hants
Jesmond: Northd v Middx
Telford (St. Georges): Shropshire v Yorks
Stone: Staffs v Glos
The Oval: Surrey v Ireland
Hove: Sussex v Devon
Edgbaston: Warwicks v Oxon

Swindon (County Gd): Wilts v Leics
Worcester: Worcs v Suffolk
Other Match
Lord's: Oxford v Cambridge

Thursday 5 July

Tourist Match
Colwyn Bay: League Cricket Conference v West Indies (two days)

Saturday 7 July

Britannic County Championship
Chesterfield: Derbys v Warwicks
Southend: Essex v Glam
Maidstone: Kent v Lancs
Uxbridge: Middx v Worcs
Northampton: Northants v Surrey
Trent Bridge: Notts v Sussex
Taunton: Somerset v Hants
Bradford: Yorks v Glos
Tourist Match
Leicester: *Leics v West Indies

Sunday 8 July

John Player Special League
Derby: Derbys v Warwicks
Southend: Essex v Glam
Maidstone: Kent v Lancs
Lord's: Middx v Worcs
Northampton: Northants v Surrey
Trent Bridge: Notts v Sussex
Scarborough: Yorks v Glos

Wednesday 11 July

Britannic County Championship
Southend: Essex v Lancs
Cardiff: Glam v Yorks
Southampton: Hants v Northants
Maidstone: Kent v Derbys
Leicester: Leics v Sussex
Uxbridge: Middx v Glos
Trent Bridge: Notts v Somerset
Worcester: Worcs v Warwicks

Thursday 12 July

CORNHILL INSURANCE TEST SERIES
Headingley: ENGLAND v WEST INDIES (Third Test Match)

Saturday 14 July

Britannic County Championship
Cardiff: Glam v Somerset
Bristol: Glos v Essex
Portsmouth: Hants v Lancs
Lord's: Middx v Yorks
Northampton: Northants v Kent
Trent Bridge: Notts v Worcs
The Oval: Surrey v Derbys
Edgbaston: Warwicks v Sussex

Sunday 15 July

John Player Special League
Cardiff: Glam v Somerset
Bristol: Glos v Essex
Portsmouth: Hants v Lancs
Lord's: Middx v Yorks
Tring: Northants v Kent
East Molesey (Imber Court): Surrey v Derbys
Edgbaston: Warwicks v Sussex
Worcester: Worcs v Leics
Other Match
Dublin (Malahide): Ireland v Wales

Wednesday 18 July

NatWest Bank Trophy Second Round
Northampton or Chester-le-Street: Durham or Northants v Worcs or Suffolk
Chelmsford or Glasgow (Titwood): Essex or Scotland v Surrey or Ireland
Cardiff or Trent Bridge: Glam or Notts v Northd or Middx
Norwich (Lakenham) or Southampton: Norfolk or Hants v Kent or Berks
Bristol or Stone: Staffs or Glos v Lancs or Bucks
Hove or Torquay: Sussex or Devon v Herts or Somerset
Edgbaston or Oxford (Morris Motors): Warwicks or Oxon v Shropshire or Yorks
Swindon (County Gd) or Leicester: Wilts or Leics v Cumberland or Derbys

Thursday 19 July

Tourist Match
West Bromwich (Dartmouth): MCCA v West Indies (two days)

Saturday 21 July

Lord's: BENSON & HEDGES CUP FINAL
Tourist Match
Derby: *Derbys (or Warwicks if Derbys in B & H Cup Final) v West Indies

Sunday 22 July

John Player Special League
Bournemouth: Hants v Yorks
Canterbury: Kent v Essex
Leicester: Leics v Glos
Trent Bridge: Notts v Northants
Taunton: Somerset v Lancs
Worcester: Worcs v Sussex

Wednesday 25 July

Britannic County Championship
Buxton: Derbys v Lancs
Bristol: Glos v Leics
Northampton: Northants v Middx
Taunton: Somerset v Glam
The Oval: Surrey v Kent
Edgbaston: Warwicks v Hants
Scarborough: Yorks v Worcs
Tourist Match
Cleethorpes: Notts v Sri Lanka

Thursday 26 July

CORNHILL INSURANCE TEST SERIES
Old Trafford: ENGLAND v WEST INDIES (Fourth Test Match)

Saturday 28 July

Britannic County Championship
Chelmsford: Essex v Worcs
Swansea: Glam v Derbys
Bristol: Glos v Northants
Lord's: Middx v Hants
Trent Bridge: Notts v Lancs
Hove: Sussex v Somerset
Edgbaston: Warwicks v Kent
Sheffield: Yorks v Leics
Tourist Match
The Oval: *Surrey v Sri Lanka

Sunday 29 July

John Player Special League
Chelmsford: Essex v Worcs
Ebbw Vale: Glam v Derbys
Bristol: Glos v Northants
Lord's: Middx v Hants
Trent Bridge: Notts v Lancs
Hove: Sussex v Somerset
Edgbaston: Warwicks v Kent
Bradford: Yorks v Leics

Wednesday 1 August

NatWest Bank Trophy Quarter-Finals
Tourist Match
Trent Bridge: Notts v West Indies (Provided Notts not in NatWest Trophy Quarter-finals)

Saturday 4 August

Britannic County Championship
Southampton: Hants v Warwicks
Canterbury: Kent v Leics
Old Trafford: Lancs v Yorks
Northants v Derbys
Weston-super-Mare: Somerset v Surrey
Eastbourne: Sussex v Essex
Worcester: Worcs v Notts
Tourist Matches
Lord's: *Middx v West Indies
Cheltenham: *Glos v Sri Lanka

Sunday 5 August

John Player Special League
Portsmouth: Hants v Warwickshire
Canterbury: Kent v Leics
Old Trafford: Lancs v Yorks
Northampton: Northants v Derbys
Weston-super-Mare: Somerset v Surrey
Eastbourne: Sussex v Essex
Other Matches
Warwick Under-25 Semi-finals (one day) (or Sunday 12 August)
Cheltenham: Glos v Worcs (Friendly)

Wednesday 8 August

Britannic County Championship
Cheltenham: Glos v Glam
Canterbury: Kent v Surrey
Southport: Lancs v Northants
Leicester: Leics v Yorks
Lord's: Middx v Essex
Trent Bridge: Notts v Derbys

Weston-super-Mare: Somerset v Worcs
Eastbourne: Sussex v Warwicks
Tourist Match
Southampton: Hants v Sri Lanka

Thursday 9 August

CORNHILL INSURANCE TEST SERIES
The Oval: ENGLAND v WEST INDIES (Fifth Test Match)

Saturday 11 August

Britannic County Championship
Derby: Derbys v Sussex
Chelmsford: Essex v Somerset
Cardiff: Glam v Hants
Cheltenham: Glos v Surrey
Leicester: Leics v Lancs
Lord's: Middx v Notts
Wellingborough Sch: Northants v Worcs
Headingley: Yorks v Warwicks
Tourist Match
Canterbury: *Kent v Sri Lanka

Sunday 12 August

John Player Special League
Heanor: Derbys v Sussex
Chelmsford: Essex v Somerset
Cardiff: Glam v Hants
Cheltenham: Glos v Surrey
Leicester: Leics v Lancs
Lord's: Middx v Notts
Wellingborough Sch: Northants v Worcs
Scarborough: Yorks v Warwicks
Other Matches
Warwick Under-25 Semi-finals (one day) (if not played on Sunday 5 August)

Wednesday 15 August

NatWest Bank Trophy Semi-Finals

Saturday 18 August

Britannic County Championship
Colchester: Essex v Hants
Swansea: Glam v Northants
Folkestone: Kent v Notts
Old Trafford: Lancs v Warwicks
Leicester: Leics v Middx
Taunton: Somerset v Derbys
The Oval: Surrey v Yorks
Worcester: Worcs v Glos
Tourist Match
Hove: *Sussex v Sri Lanka

Sunday 19 August

John Player Special League
Colchester: Essex v Hants
Swansea: Glam v Northants
Folkestone: Kent v Notts
Old Trafford: Lancs v Warwicks
Leicester: Leics v Middx
Taunton: Somerset v Derbys
The Oval: Surrey v Yorks
Worcester: Worcs v Glos

Wednesday 22 August

Britannic County Championship
Chesterfield: Derbys v Yorks
Colchester: Essex v Kent
Bournemouth: Hants v Middx
Blackpool: Lancs v Notts
Leicester: Leics v Glos
Northampton: Northants v Sussex
The Oval: Surrey v Somerset
Edgbaston: Warwicks v Glam
Other Match
Glasgow (Titwood): Scotland v Ireland

Thursday 23 August

CORNHILL TEST MATCH
Lord's: ENGLAND v SRI LANKA

Saturday 25 August

Britannic County Championship
Bristol: Glos v Lancs
Bournemouth: Hants v Kent
Northampton: Northants v Leics
Trent Bridge: Notts v Warwicks
The Oval: Surrey v Essex
Hove: Sussex v Middx
Worcester: Worcs v Somerset
Bradford: Yorks v Glam

Sunday 26 August

John Player Special League
Moreton-in-Marsh: Glos v Lancs
Bournemouth: Hants v Kent
Northampton: Northants v Leics
Trent Bridge: Notts v Warwicks
Taunton: Somerset v Worcs

Hove: Sussex v Middx
Headingley: Yorks v Glam
Other Match
Edgbaston: Warwick Under-25 Final (one day)

Wednesday 29 August

Britannic County Championship
Chelmsford: Essex v Middx
Swansea: Glam v Surrey
Trent Bridge: Notts v Northants
Taunton: Somerset v Kent
Hove: Sussex v Glos
Tourist Match
Edgbaston: Warwicks v Sri Lanka
Other Match
Scarborough: Derbys v Yorks
Asda Cricket Challenge (one day)

Thursday 30 August

Scarborough: Hants v Lancs
Asda Cricket Challenge (one day)

Friday 31 August

Scarborough: ASDA Cricket Challenge Final (one day)

Saturday 1 September

Lord's: NATWEST BANK TROPHY FINAL

Sunday 2 September

John Player Special League
Derby: Derbys v Essex
Southampton: Hants v Northants
Trent Bridge: Notts v Surrey
Edgbaston: Warwicks v Glam
Worcester: Worcs v Kent
Tourist Match
Scarborough: Brian Close's XI v Sri Lanka

Wednesday 5 September

Britannic County Championship
Cardiff: Glam v Warwicks
Bristol: Glos v Somerset
Leicester: Leics v Derbys
Lord's: Middx v Kent
Hove: Sussex v Notts
Worcester: Worcs v Northants
Scarborough: Yorks v Hants

Saturday 8 September

Britannic County Championship
Derby: Derbys v Hants
Bristol: Glos v Middx
Canterbury: Kent v Glam
Old Trafford: Lancs v Essex
Taunton: Somerset v Notts
The Oval: Surrey v Worcs
Hove: Sussex v Yorks
Edgbaston: Warwicks v Leics

Sunday 9 September

John Player Special League
Derby: Derbys v Hants
Bristol: Glos v Middx
Canterbury: Kent v Glam
Old Trafford: Lancs v Essex
Taunton: Somerset v Notts
The Oval: Surrey v Worcs
Hove: Sussex v Yorks
Edgbaston: Warwicks v Leics

MINOR COUNTIES FIXTURES 1984
United Friendly Insurance County Championship

(*E*) *Eastern Division* (*W*) *Western Division*

MAY		
Sun 27	(*E*)	Lincolnshire v Staffordshire: Sleaford
	(*E*)	Northumberland v Hertfordshire: Jesmond
Tues 29	(*E*)	Cumberland v Hertfordshire: Carlisle
JUNE		
Wed 6	(*E*)	Cambridgeshire v Hertfordshire: Wisbech
Sun 10	(*W*)	Cheshire v Shropshire: Oxton
	(*E*)	Cumberland v Northumberland: Barrow
	(*E*)	Lincolnshire v Bedfordshire: Cleethorpes
Tues 12	(*E*)	Durham v Bedfordshire: Durham City
Wed 13	(*E*)	Hertfordshire v Staffordshire: Watford
Tues 19	(*E*)	Hertfordshire v Lincolnshire: Hitchin
Sun 24	(*E*)	Bedfordshire v Cambridgeshire: Henlow
	(*W*)	Cornwall v Cheshire: Falmouth
	(*E*)	Durham v Cumberland: Hartlepool
Tues 26	(*W*)	Somerset II v Cheshire: Yeovil
Wed 27	(*E*)	Staffordshire v Bedfordshire: Leek
JULY		
Sun 8	(*W*)	Cheshire v Buckinghamshire: Chester (Boughton Hall)
	(*W*)	Cornwall v Somerset II: Falmouth
	(*E*)	Cumberland v Norfolk: Kendal
	(*E*)	Lincolnshire v Cambridgeshire: Stamford
	(*E*)	Northumberland v Durham: Jesmond
Tues 10	(*W*)	Shropshire v Buckinghamshire: Bridgnorth
	(*E*)	Staffordshire v Norfolk: Bewood
Mon 16	(*W*)	Cheshire v Oxfordshire: Toft
Wed 18	(*E*)	Cambridgeshire v Suffolk: Cambridge (Fenners)
	(*W*)	Devon v Cornwall: Exmouth
	(*W*)	Shropshire v Oxfordshire: Wellington
Sat 21	(*E*)	Bedfordshire v Hertfordshire: Bedford School
Sun 22	(*W*)	Berkshire v Buckinghamshire: Finchampstead
	(*E*)	Durham v Lincolnshire: Stockton-on-Tees
	(*W*)	Oxfordshire v Somerset II: Oxford (Morris Motors)
	(*E*)	Staffordshire v Cumberland: Knypersley
Mon 23	(*E*)	Bedfordshire v Northumberland: Luton (Wardown Park)
	(*W*)	Cornwall v Shropshire: Truro
	(*E*)	Hertfordshire v Suffolk: Bishops Stortford
Tues 24	(*W*)	Dorset v Wiltshire: Weymouth
Wed 25	(*E*)	Cambridgeshire v Northumberland: Peterborough
	(*W*)	Devon v Shropshire: Newton Abbot
Thurs 26	(*W*)	Berkshire v Oxfordshire: Bradfield College
Sun 29	(*W*)	Cheshire v Berkshire: Nantwich
	(*W*)	Cornwall v Dorset: St. Austell
	(*W*)	Somerset II v Wiltshire: Taunton

Tues 31	(*E*)	Norfolk v Lincolnshire: Norwich (Lakenham)
	(*W*)	Shropshire v Berkshire: Shrewsbury
	(*E*)	Suffolk v Durham: Ipswich (GRE)
	(*W*)	Wiltshire v Devon: Salisbury (Bannerton)

AUGUST

Thurs 2	(*W*)	Dorset v Devon: Bournemouth
	(*E*)	Norfolk v Cambridgeshire: Norwich (Lakenham)
Sun 5	(*E*)	Bedfordshire v Cumberland
	(*W*)	Buckinghamshire v Somerset II: Slough
	(*W*)	Dorset v Cheshire: Sherborne
	(*E*)	Lincolnshire v Northumberland: Lincoln (Lindum)
	(*W*)	Oxfordshire v Cornwall: Oxford (St. Edward's Sch.)
Mon 6	(*E*)	Staffordshire v Suffolk: Walsall
Tues 7	(*W*)	Berkshire v Somerset II: Kidmore End
	(*E*)	Norfolk v Northumberland: Norwich (Lakenham)
	(*W*)	Wiltshire v Cornwall: Chippenham
Thurs 9	(*E*)	Norfolk v Durham: Norwich (Lakenham)
Sun 12	(*W*)	Dorset v Berkshire: Bournemouth
	(*W*)	Oxfordshire v Devon: Oxford (Christ Church)
Mon 13	(*E*)	Durham v Cambridgeshire: Chester-le-Street
	(*E*)	Hertfordshire v Norfolk: Hertford
	(*E*)	Northumberland v Staffordshire: Jesmond
	(*W*)	Somerset II v Shropshire: Weston-Super-Mare
	(*E*)	Suffolk v Lincolnshire: Mildenhall
Tues 14	(*W*)	Berkshire v Devon: Reading School
	(*W*)	Wiltshire v Buckinghamshire: Devizes
Wed 15	(*W*)	Dorset v Shropshire: Bournemouth
	(*E*)	Durham v Staffordshire: Gateshead Fell
	(*E*)	Suffolk v Norfolk: Ipswich (Ransomes)
Thurs 16	(*W*)	Buckinghamshire v Devon: Marlow
	(*W*)	Oxforshire v Wiltshire: Banbury (XX Club)
Sun 19	(*E*)	Bedfordshire v Norfolk: Jesmond
	(*W*)	Buckinghamshire v Cornwall: High Wycombe
	(*W*)	Cheshire v Wiltshire: Bowdon
	(*E*)	Cumberland v Lincolnshire: Millom
	(*E*)	Northumberland v Suffolk: Jesmond
	(*W*)	Oxfordshire v Dorset: Oxford (Christ Church)
Mon 20	(*W*)	Devon v Somerset II: Bovey Tracey
	(*E*)	Hertfordshire v Durham: St. Albans
Tues 21	(*W*)	Berkshire v Cornwall: Reading C.C.
	(*W*)	Buckinghamshire v Dorset: Monks Risborough (Molins)
	(*E*)	Cumberland v Suffolk: Netherfield (Kendal)
	(*W*)	Shropshire v Wiltshire: St. George's (Oakengates)
Wed 22	(*E*)	Cambridgeshire v Staffordshire: Cambridge (Fenners)
Sun 26	(*W*)	Buckinghamshire v Oxfordshire: Amersham (Shardeloes)
	(*W*)	Somerset II v Dorset: Street
	(*E*)	Suffolk v Bedfordshire: Bury St. Edmunds
Mon 27	(*W*)	Wiltshire v Berkshire: Trowbridge (County Ground)

SEPTEMBER

Sat 8 (or Sun 9)		One-day match between top County in each Division to decide the Championship: Worcester

English Estates Trophy

MAY

Sun 20	Berkshire v Buckinghamshire: Reading (Courages) Cheshire v Cumberland: Neston Norfolk v Suffolk: Norwich (Pinebanks)

JUNE

Sun 3	Cheshire or Cumberland v Durham: Northwich (Winnington Park) or Penrith Devon v Cornwall: Sidmouth Dorset v Wiltshire: Sherborne Hertfordshire v Cambridgeshire Norfolk or Suffolk v Bedfordshire: Bishops Stortford Oxfordshire v Staffordshire: Oxford (Christ Church) Shropshire v Berkshire or Buckinghamshire: Newport

Quarter-Finals

Sun 17	Devon or Cornwall v Oxfordshire or Staffordshire Cheshire, Cumberland or Durham v Hertfordshire or Cambridgeshire Norfolk, Suffolk or Bedfordshire v Dorset or Wiltshire Berkshire, Buckinghamshire or Shropshire v Lincolnshire or Northumberland

Semi-Finals: July 1; *Final:* July 15 or 16 (Cambridge – Fenners)

MCCA Representative Matches

JUNE

Thurs 21	MCCA v Kenya: Mortlake (Watneys) (3 days)

JULY

Thurs 19	MCCA v West Indies: West Bromwich (Dartmouth) (2 days)

THE 1983 PICK-A-TEAM COMPETITION

(See page 64)

THE WINNING TEAM

(1) Graham Gooch, (2) Wayne Larkins, (3) David Gower (Captain), (4) Allan Lamb, (5) Mike Gatting, (6) Derek Randall, (7) Ian Botham, (8) David Bairstow, (9) Derek Underwood, (10) Bob Willis, (11) Norman Cowans.

There were 1,070 entries.

ISBN 0 356 10237 8

Published in 1984 by Queen Anne Press, Macdonald & Co (Publishers) Ltd,
Maxwell House, 74 Worship Street, London EC2A 2EN. A BPCC plc Company

Filmset, printed and bound in Great Britain by Hazell Watson & Viney Limited,
Member of the BPCC Group, Aylesbury, Bucks